THE RO

CATECHISM OF
THE COUNCIL OF TRENT
FOR PARISH PRIESTS

Issued by order of
POPE ST. PIUS V

Edited by
Paul A. Böer, Sr.

VERITATIS SPLENDOR PUBLICATIONS
et cognoscetis veritatem et veritas liberabit vos (Jn 8:32)
MMXIII

AD MAJOREM DEI GLORIAM

TABLE OF CONTENTS

239

CATECHISM OF THE COUNCIL OF TRENT FOR PARISH PRIESTS

Issued by order of Pope Pius V

INTRODUCTORY

The Necessity Of Religious Instruction

Such is the nature of the human mind and intellect that, although by means of diligent and laborious inquiry it has of itself investigated and discovered many other things pertaining to a knowledge of divine truths; yet guided by its natural lights it never could have known or perceived most of those things by which is attained eternal salvation, the principal end of man's creation and formation to the image and likeness of God.

It is true that the invisible things of God from the creation of the world are, as the Apostle teaches, clearly seen, being understood by the things that are made: his eternal power also, and divinity. But the mystery which hath been hidden from ages and generations so far transcends the reach of man's understanding, that were it not made manifest by God to His Saints, to whom He willed to make known by the gift of faith, the riches of the glory of this mystery among the Gentiles, which is Christ, man could by no effort attain to such wisdom.

But, as faith comes by hearing, it is clear how necessary at all times for the attainment of eternal salvation has been the labour and faithful ministry of an authorised teacher; for it is written, how shall they hear, without a preacher? And how shall they preach unless they be sent?

And, indeed, never, from the very creation of the world, has God, most merciful and benignant, been wanting to His own; but at sundry times and in divers manners spoke to the fathers by the prophets, and pointed out to them in a manner suited to the times and circumstances, a sure and direct path to the happiness of heaven. But, as He had foretold that He would give a teacher of justice to be the light of the Gentiles, that His salvation might reach even to the ends of the earth, in these last days he hath spoken to us by his Son, whom also by a voice from heaven, from the excellent glory, He has commanded all to hear and to obey. Furthermore, the Son gave some to be apostles, and some prophets, and others pastors and teachers, to announce the word of life; that we might not be carried about like children tossed to and fro with every wind of doctrine, but holding fast to the firm foundation of the faith, we might be built together into an habitation of God in the Spirit.

Lest any should receive the Word of God from the ministers of the Church, not as the word of Christ, which it really is, but as the word of man, the same Saviour has ordained that their ministry should be invested with so great authority that He says to them: He that hears you, hears me; and he that despises you despises me. These words He spoke not only of those to whom His words were addressed, but likewise of all who, by legitimate succession, should discharge the ministry of the word, promising to be with them all days even to the consummation of the world.

Need of an Authoritative Catholic Catechism

But while the preaching of the divine Word should never be interrupted in the Church, surely in these, our days, it becomes necessary to labour with more than ordinary zeal and piety to nourish and strengthen the faithful with sound and wholesome doctrine, as with the food of life. For false prophets have gone forth into the world, to corrupt the minds of the faithful with various and strange doctrines, of whom the Lord has said: I did not send prophets, yet they ran; I spoke not to them, yet they prophesied.

In this work, to such extremes has their impiety, practiced in all the arts of Satan, been carried, that it would seem almost impossible to confine it within any bounds; and did we not rely on the splendid promises of the Saviour, who declared that He had built His Church on so solid a foundation that the gates of hell shall not prevail against it, we should have good reason to fear lest, beset on every side by such a host of enemies and assailed and attacked by so many machinations, it would, in these days, fall to the ground.

For - to say nothing of those illustrious States which heretofore professed, in piety and holiness, the true Catholic faith transmitted to them by their ancestors, but are now gone astray wandering from the paths of truth and openly declaring that their best claims to piety are founded on a total abandonment of the faith of their fathers - there is no region, however remote, no place, however securely guarded, no corner of Christendom, into which this pestilence has not sought secretly to insinuate itself.

For those who intended to corrupt the minds of the faithful, knowing that they could not hold immediate personal intercourse with all, and thus pour into their ears their poisoned doctrines, adopted another plan which enabled them to disseminate error and impiety more easily and extensively. Besides those voluminous works by which they sought the subversion of the Catholic faith - to guard against which (volumes) required perhaps little labour or circumspection, since their contents were clearly heretical - they also composed innumerable smaller books, which, veiling their errors under the semblance of piety, deceived with incredible facility the unsuspecting minds of simple folk.

The Nature of this Work

The Fathers, therefore, of the General Council of Trent, anxious to apply some healing remedy to so great and pernicious an evil, were not satisfied with having decided the more important points of Catholic doctrine against the heresies of our times, but deemed it further necessary to issue, for the instruction of the faithful in the very rudiments of faith, a form and method to be followed in all churches by those to whom are lawfully entrusted the duties of pastor and teacher.

To works of this kind many, it is true, had already given their attention, and earned the reputation of great piety and learning. But the Fathers deemed it of the first importance that a work should appear, sanctioned by the authority of the Council, from which pastors and all others on whom the duty of imparting instruction devolves, may be able to seek and find reliable matter for the edification of the faithful; that, as there is one Lord, one faith, there may also be one standard and prescribed form of propounding the dogmas of faith, and instructing Christians in all the duties of piety.

As, therefore, the design of the work embraces a variety of matters, it cannot be supposed that the Council intended that in one volume all the dogmas of Christianity should be explained with that minuteness of detail to be found in the works of those who profess to treat the teaching and doctrines of religion in their entirety. Such a task would be one of almost endless labour, and manifestly ill suited to attain the proposed end. But, having undertaken to instruct pastors and such as have care of souls in those things that belong peculiarly to the pastoral office and are accommodated to the capacity of the faithful, the Council intended that such things only should be treated of as might assist the pious zeal of pastors in discharging the duty of instruction, should they not be very familiar with the more abstruse questions of theology.

The Ends of Religious Instruction

Hence, before we proceed to develop in detail the various parts of this summary of doctrine, our purpose requires that we premise a few observations which the pastor should consider and bear in mind in order to know to what end, as it were, all his plans and labours and efforts are to be directed, and how this desired end may be more easily attained.

Knowledge Of Christ

The first thing is ever to recollect that all Christian knowledge is reduced to one single head, or rather, to use the words of the Apostle, this is eternal life: That they may know thee, the only true God, and Jesus Christ, whom thou hast sent. A teacher in the Church should, therefore, use his best endeavours that the faithful earnestly desire to know Jesus Christ, and him crucified, that they be firmly convinced, and with the most heartfelt piety and devotion believe, that there is no other name under heaven given to men, whereby we must be saved, for he is the propitiation for our sins.

Observance Of The Commandments

But since by this we know that we have known him, if we keep his commandments, the next consideration, and one intimately connected with the preceding, is to press also upon the attention of the faithful that their lives are not to be wasted in ease and indolence, but that we are to walk even as he walked, and pursue with all earnestness, justice, godliness, faith, charity, patience, mildness; for He gave himself for us, that he might redeem us from all iniquity, and might cleanse to himself a people acceptable, a pursuer of good works. These things the Apostle commands pastors to speak and exhort.

Love Of God

But as our Lord and Saviour has not only declared, but has also proved by His own example, that the Law and the Prophets depend on love, and as, according to the Apostle, charity is the end of the commandment, and the fulfilment of the law, it is unquestionably a chief duty of the pastor to use the utmost diligence to excite the faithful to a love of the infinite goodness of God towards us, that, burning with a sort of divine ardour, they may be powerfully attracted to the supreme and all-perfect good, to adhere to which is true and solid happiness, as is fully experienced by him who can say with the Prophet: What have I in heaven? and besides thee what do I desire upon earth?

This, assuredly, is that more excellent way pointed out by the Apostle when he sums up all his doctrines and instructions in charity, which never falleth away. For whatever is proposed by the pastor, whether it be the exercise of faith, of hope, or of some moral virtue, the love of our Lord should at the same time be so strongly insisted upon as to show clearly that all the works of perfect Christian virtue can have no other origin, no other end than divine love.

The Means Required for Religious Instruction

But as in imparting instruction of any sort the manner of communicating it is of highest importance, so in conveying religious instruction to the people, the method should be deemed of the greatest moment.

Instruction Should Be Accommodated To The Capacity Of The Hearer

Age, capacity, manners and condition must be borne in mind, so that he who instructs may become all things to all men, in order that he may be able to gain all to Christ, prove himself a dutiful minister and steward, and, like a good and faithful servant, be found worthy to be placed by his Lord over many things The priest must not imagine that those committed to his care are all on the same level, so that he can follow one fixed and unvarying method of instruction to lead all in the same way to knowledge and true piety; for some are as new-born infants, others are growing up in Christ, while a few are, so to say, of full maturity. Hence the necessity of considering who they are that have occasion for milk, who for more solid food, and of affording to each such nourishment of doctrine as may give spiritual increase, until we all meet in the unity of faith, and of the knowledge of the Son of God, unto a perfect man, unto the measure of the age of the fullness of Christ. This the Apostle inculcates for all by his own example when he says that he is a debtor to the Greeks and to the Barbarians, to the wise and to the unwise, thus giving all who are called to this ministry to understand that in announcing the mysteries of faith and the precepts of life, the instruction is to be so accommodated to the capacity and intelligence of the hearers, that, while the minds of the strong are filled with spiritual food, the little ones be not suffered to perish with hunger, asking for bread, while there is none to break it unto them.

Zeal

Nor should our zeal in communicating Christian knowledge be relaxed because it has sometimes to be exercised in expounding matters apparently humble and unimportant, and whose exposition is usually irksome, especially to minds accustomed to the contemplation of the more sublime truths of religion. If the

Wisdom of the eternal Father descended upon the earth in the meanness of our flesh to teach us the maxims of a heavenly life, who is there whom the love of Christ does not constrain to become little in the midst of his brethren, and, as a nurse fostering her children, so anxiously to wish for the salvation of his neighbours as to be ready, as the Apostle says of himself, to give them not only the gospel of God, but even his own life.

Study Of The Word Of God

Now all the doctrines in which the faithful are to be instructed are contained in the Word of God, which is found in Scripture and tradition. To the study of these, therefore, the pastor should devote his days and his nights, keeping in mind the admonition of St. Paul to Timothy, which all who have the care of souls should consider as addressed to themselves: Attend to reading, to exhortation, and to doctrine, for all Scripture divinely inspired is profitable to teach, to reprove, to correct, to instruct injustice, that the man of God may be perfect, furnished to every good work.

Division of this Catechism

The truths revealed by Almighty God are so many and so various that it is no easy task to acquire a knowledge of them, or, having done so, to remember them so well as to be able to explain them with ease and readiness when occasion requires. Hence our predecessors in the faith have very wisely reduced all the doctrines of salvation to these four heads: The Apostles' Creed, the Sacraments, the Ten Commandments, and the Lord's Prayer.

The part on the Creed contains all that is to be held according to Christian faith, whether it regard the knowledge of God, the creation and government of the world, or the redemption of man, the rewards of the good and the punishments of the wicked. The part devoted to the Seven Sacraments teaches us what are the signs, and, as it were, the instruments of grace. In the part on the Decalogue is described whatever has reference to the law, whose end is charity. Finally, the Lord's Prayer contains whatever can be the object of the Christian's desires, or hopes, or prayers. The exposition, therefore, of these four parts, which are, as it were, the general heads of Sacred Scripture, includes almost everything that a Christian should learn.

How This Work Is To Be Used

We therefore deem it proper to inform pastors that, whenever they have occasion, in the ordinary discharge of their duty, to expound any passage of the Gospel or any other part of Holy Scripture. they will find its subject-matter treated under some one of the four heads already enumerated, to which they recur, as to the source from which their instruction is to be drawn.

Thus, if the Gospel of the first Sunday of Advent is to be explained, There shall be signs in the sun, and in the moon, etc., whatever regards its explanation is contained under the Article of the Creed, He shall come to judge the living and the dead; and by embodying the substance of that Article in his exposition, the pastor will at once instruct his people in the Creed and in the Gospel. Whenever, therefore, he has to communicate instruction and expound the Scriptures, he will observe the same rule of referring all to these four principal heads under which, as we observed, the whole teaching and doctrine of Holy Scripture is contained. As for order, however, he is free to follow that which he deems best suited to the circumstances of persons and time.

PART I : THE CREED

Faith

In preparing and instructing men in the teachings of Christ the Lord, the Fathers began by explaining the meaning of faith. Following their example, we have thought it well to treat first what pertains to that virtue.

Though the word faith has a variety of meanings in the Sacred Scriptures, we here speak only of that faith by which we yield our entire assent to whatever has been divinely revealed.

Necessity Of Faith

That faith thus understood is necessary to salvation no man can reasonably doubt, particularly since it is written: Without faith it is impossible to please God. For as the end proposed to man as his ultimate happiness is far above the reach of human understanding, it was therefore necessary that it should be made known to him by God. This knowledge, however, is nothing else than faith, by which we yield our unhesitating assent to whatever the authority of our Holy Mother the Church teaches us to have been revealed by God; for the faithful cannot doubt those things of which God, who is truth itself, is the author. Hence we see the great difference that exists between this faith which we give to God and that which we yield to the writers of human history.

Unity Of Faith

Faith differs in degree; for we read in Scripture these words: O thou of little faith, why didst thou doubt; and Great is thy faith; and Increase our faith. It also differs in dignity, for we read: Faith without works is dead; and, Faith that worketh by charity. But although faith is so comprehensive, it is yet the same in kind, and the full force of its definition applies equally to all its varieties. How fruitful it is and how great are the advantages we may derive from it we shall point out when explaining the Articles of the Creed.

The Creed

Now the chief truths which Christians ought to hold are those which the holy Apostles, the leaders and teachers of the faith, inspired by the Holy Ghost' have divided into the twelve Articles of the Creed. For having received a command from the Lord to go forth into the whole world, as His ambassadors, and preach the Gospel to every creature, they thought it advisable to draw up a formula of Christian faith, that all might think and speak the same thing, and that among those whom they should have called to the unity of the faith no schisms would exist, but that they should be perfect in the same mind, and in the same judgment.

This profession of Christian faith and hope, drawn up by themselves, the Apostles called a symbol; either because it was made up of various parts, each of which was contributed by an Apostle, or because by it, as by a common sign and watchword, they might easily distinguish deserters from the faith and false brethren unawares brought in, adulterating the word of God, from those who had truly bound themselves by oath to serve under the banner of Christ.

Division Of The Creed

Christianity proposes to the faithful many truths which, either separately or in general, must be held with an assured and firm faith. Among these what must first and necessarily be believed by all is that which God Himself has taught us as the foundation and summary of truth concerning the unity of the Divine Essence, the distinction of Three Persons, and the actions which are peculiarly attributed to each. The pastor should teach that the Apostles, Creed briefly comprehends the doctrine of this mystery.

For, as has been observed by our predecessors in the faith, who have treated this subject with great piety and accuracy, the Creed seems to be divided into three principal parts: one describing the First Person of the Divine Nature, and the stupendous work of the creation; another, the Second Person, and the mystery of man's redemption; a third, the Third Person, the head and source of our sanctification; the whole being expressed in various and most appropriate propositions. These propositions are called Articles, from a comparison frequently used by the Fathers; for as the members of the body are divided by joints (articuli), so in this profession of faith, whatever is to be believed distinctly and separately from anything else is rightly and suitably called an Article.

ARTICLE I : "I BELIEVE IN GOD, THE FATHER ALMIGHTY, CREATOR OF HEAVEN AND EARTH"

Meaning Of This Article

The meaning of the above words is this: I believe with certainty, and without a shadow of doubt profess my belief in God the Father, the First Person of the Trinity, who by His omnipotence created from nothing and preserves and governs the heavens and the earth and all things which they contain; and not only do I believe in Him from my heart and profess this belief with my lips, but with the greatest ardour and piety I tend towards Him, as the supreme and most perfect good.

Let this serve as a brief summary of this first Article. But since great mysteries lie concealed under almost every word, the pastor must now give them a more careful consideration, in order that, as far as God has permitted, the faithful may approach, with fear and trembling, to contemplate the glory of His majesty.

"I Believe"

The word believe does not here mean to think, to suppose, lo be of opinion; but, as the Sacred Scriptures teach, it expresses the deepest conviction, by which the mind gives a firm and unhesitating assent to God revealing His mysterious truths. As far, therefore, as regards use of the word here, he who firmly and without hesitation is convinced of anything is said to believe.

Faith Excludes Doubt

The knowledge derived through faith must not be considered less certain because its objects are not seen; for the divine light by which we know them, although it does not render them evident, yet suffers us not to doubt them. For God, who commanded the light to shine out of darkness, hath himself shone in our hearts, that the gospel be not hidden to us, as to those that perish.

Faith Excludes Curiosity

From what has been said it follows that he who is gifted with this heavenly knowledge of faith is free from an inquisitive curiosity. For when God commands us to believe He does not propose to us to search into His divine judgments, or inquire into their reason and cause, but demands an unchangeable faith, by which the mind rests content in the knowledge of eternal truth. And indeed, since we have the testimony of the Apostle that God is true; and every man a liar, and since it would argue arrogance and presumption to disbelieve the word of a grave and sensible man affirming anything as true, and to demand that he prove his statements by arguments or witnesses, how rash and foolish are those, who, hearing the words of God Himself, demand reasons for His heavenly and saving doctrines? Faith, therefore, must exclude not only all doubt, but all desire for demonstration.

Faith Requires Open Profession

The pastor should also teach that he who says, I believe, besides declaring the inward assent of the mind, which is an internal act of faith, should also openly profess and with alacrity acknowledge and proclaim what he inwardly and in his heart believes. For the faithful should be animated by the same spirit that spoke by the lips of the Prophet when he said: I believe; and therefore did I speak, and should follow the example of the Apostles who replied to the princes of the people: We cannot but speak the things which we have seen and heard. They should be encouraged by these noble words of St. Paul: I am not ashamed of the gospel. For it is the power of God unto salvation to every one that believeth; and likewise by those other words; in which the truth of this doctrine is expressly confirmed: With the heart we believe unto justice; but with the mouth confession is made unto salvation.

"In God"

From these words we may learn how exalted are the dignity and excellence of Christian wisdom, and what a debt of gratitude we owe to the divine goodness. For to us it is given at once to mount as by the steps of faith to the knowledge of what is most sublime and desirable.

Knowledge Of God More Easily Obtained Through Faith Than Through Reason

There is a great difference between Christian philosophy and human wisdom. The latter, guided solely by the light of nature, advances slowly by reasoning on sensible objects and effects, and only after long and laborious investigation is it able at length to contemplate with difficulty the invisible things of God, to discover and understand a First Cause and Author of all things. Christian philosophy, on the contrary, so quickens the human mind that without difficulty it pierces the heavens, and, illumined with divine light, contemplates first, the eternal source of light, and in its radiance all created things: so that we experience with the utmost pleasure of mind that we have been called, as the Prince of the Apostles says, out of darkness into his admirable light, and believing we rejoice with joy unspeakable.

Justly, therefore, do the faithful profess first to believe in God, whose majesty, with the Prophet Jeremias, we declare incomprehensible. For, as the Apostle says, He dwells in light inaccessible, which no man hath seen, nor can see; as God Himself, speaking to Moses, said: No man shall see my face and live. The mind cannot rise to the contemplation of the Deity, whom nothing approaches in sublimity, unless it be entirely disengaged from the senses, and of this in the present life we art naturally incapable.

Knowledge Of God Obtained Through Faith Is Clearer

But while this is so, yet God, as the Apostle says, left not himself without testimony, doing good from heaven, giving rains and fruitful seasons, filling our hearts with food and gladness. Hence it is that the philosophers conceived no mean idea of the Divinity, ascribed to Him nothing corporeal, gross or composite. They considered Him the perfection and fullness of all good, from whom, as from an eternal, inexhaustible fountain of goodness and benignity, flows every perfect gift to all creatures. They called Him the wise, the author and lover of truth, the just, the most beneficent, and gave Him also many other appellations expressive of supreme and absolute perfection. They recognised that His immense and infinite power fills every place and extends to all things

These truths the Sacred Scriptures express far better and much more clearly, as in the following passages: God is a spirit; Be ye perfect, even as also your heavenly Father is perfect; All things are naked and open to his eyes; O the depth of the riches of the wisdom and of the knowledge of God! God is true; I am the way, the truth, and the life; Thy right hand is full of justice; Thou openest thy hand, and fillest with blessing every living creature; and finally: Whither shall go from thy spirit? or whither shall I flee from thy face? If I ascend into heaven, thou art there; if I descend into hell, thou art there. If I take my wings early in the morning, and dwell in the uttermost parts of the sea, etc., and Do I not fill heaven and earth, saith the Lord?

Knowledge Of God Obtained Through Faith Is More Certain

These great and sublime truths regarding the nature of God, which are in full accord with Scripture, the philosophers were able to learn from an investigation of God's works. But even here we see the necessity of divine revelation if we reflect that not only does faith, as we have already observed, make known clearly and at once to the rude and unlettered, those truths which only the learned could discover, and that by long study; but also that the knowledge obtained through faith is much more certain and more secure against error than if it were the result of philosophical inquiry.

Knowledge Of God Obtained Through Faith Is More Ample And Exalted

But how much more exalted must not that knowledge of the Deity be considered, which cannot be acquired in common by all from the contemplation of nature, but is peculiar to those who are illumined by the light of faith ?

This knowledge is contained in the Articles of the Creed, which disclose to us the unity of the Divine Essence and the distinction of Three Persons, and show also that God Himself is the ultimate end of our being, from whom we are to expect the enjoyment of the eternal happiness of heaven, according to the words of St. Paul: God is a rewarder of them that seek Him. How great are these rewards, and whether they are such that human knowledge could aspire to their attainment, we learn from these words of Isaias uttered long before those of the Apostle: From the beginning of the world they have not heard, nor perceived with the ears: the eye hath not seen besides thee, O God, what things thou hast prepared for them that wait for thee.

The Unity Of Nature In God

From what is said it must also be confessed that there is but one God, not many gods. For we attribute to God supreme goodness and infinite perfection, and it is impossible that what? is supreme and most perfect could be common to many. If a being lack anything that constitutes supreme perfection, it is therefore imperfect and cannot have the nature of God.

The unity of God is also proved from many passages of Sacred Scripture. It is written: Hear, O Israel, the Lord our God is one Lord; again the Lord commands: Thou shalt not have strange gods before me; and further He often admonishes us by the Prophet: I am the first, and I am the last, and besides me there is no God. The Apostle also openly declares: One Lord, one faith, one baptism.

It should not, however, excite our surprise if the Sacred Scriptures sometimes give the name of God to creatures. For when they call the Prophets and judges gods, they do not speak according to the manner of the Gentiles, who, in their folly and impiety, formed to themselves many gods; but express, by a manner of speaking then in use, some eminent quality or function conferred on such persons by the gift of God.

The Trinity Of Persons In God

The Christian faith, therefore, believes and professes, as is declared in the Nicene Creed in confirmation of this truth, that God in His Nature, Substance and Essence is one.- But soaring still higher, it so understands Him to be one that it adores unity in trinity and trinity in unity. Of this mystery we now proceed to speak, as it comes next in order in the Creed.

"The Father"

As God is called Father for more reasons than one, we must first determine the more appropriate sense in which the word is used in the present instance.

God Is Called Father Because He Is Creator And Ruler

Even some on whose darkness the light of faith never shone conceived God to be an eternal substance from whom all things have their beginning, and by whose Providence they are governed and preserved in their order and state of existence. Since, therefore, he to whom a family owes its origin and by whose wisdom

derived from human things these persons gave the name Father to God, whom they acknowledge to be the Creator and Governor of the universe. The Sacred Scriptures also, when they wish to show that to God must be ascribed the creation of all things, supreme power and admirable Providence, make use of the same name. Thus we read: Is not he thy Father, that hath possessed thee, and made thee and created thee? And: Have we not all one Father? hath not one God created us?

God Is Called Father Because He Adopts Christians Through Grace

But God, particularly in the New Testament, is much more frequently, and in some sense peculiarly, called the Father of Christians, who have not received the spirit of bondage again in fear; but have received the spirit of adoption of sons (of God), whereby they cry: Abba (Father). For the Father hath bestowed upon us that manner of charity that we should be called, and be the sons of God, and if sons, heirs also; heirs indeed of God, and joint-heirs with Christ, who is the first-born amongst many brethren, and is not ashamed to call us brethren. Whether, therefore, we look to the common title of creation and Providence, or to the special one of spiritual adoption, rightly do the faithful profess their belief that God is their Father.

The Name Father Also Discloses The Plurality Of Persons In God

But the pastor should teach that on hearing the word Father, besides the ideas already unfolded, the mind should rise to more exalted mysteries. Under the name Father, the divine oracles begin to unveil to us a mysterious truth which is more abstruse and more deeply hidden in that inaccessible light in which God dwells, and which human reason and understanding could not attain to, nor even conjecture to exist.

This name implies that in the one Essence of the Godhead is proposed to our belief, not only one Person, but a distinction of persons; for in one Divine Nature there are Three Persons-the Father, begotten of none; the Son, begotten of the Father before all ages; the Holy Ghost, proceeding from the Father and the likewise, from all eternity

The Doctrine Of The Trinity

In the one Substance of the Divinity the Father is the First Person, who with His Only-begotten Son, and the Holy Ghost, is one God and one Lord, not in the singularity of one Person, but in the trinity of one Substance. These Three Persons, since it would be impiety to assert that they are unlike or unequal in any thing, are understood to be distinct only in their respective properties. For the Father is unbegotten, the Son begotten of the Father, and the Holy Ghost proceeds from both. Thus we acknowledge the Essence and the Substance of the Three Persons to be the same in such wise that we believe that in confessing the true and eternal God we are piously and religiously to adore distinction in the Persons, unity in the Essence, and equality in the Trinity.

Hence, when we say that the Father is the First Person, we are not to be understood to mean that in the Trinity there is anything first or last, greater or less. Let none of the faithful be guilty of such impiety, for the Christian religion proclaims the same eternity, the same majesty of glory in the Three Persons. But since the Father is the Beginning without a beginning, we truly and unhesitatingly affirm that He is the First Person, and as He is distinct from the Others by His peculiar relation of paternity, so of Him alone is it true that He begot the Son from eternity. For when in the Creed we pronounce together the words God and Father, it means that He was always both God and Father.

Practical Admonitions Concerning The Mystery Of The Trinity

Since nowhere is a too curious inquiry more dangerous, or error more fatal, than in the knowledge and exposition of this, the most profound and difficult of mysteries, let the pastor teach that the terms nature and person used to express this mystery should be most scrupulously retained; and let the faithful know that unity belongs to essence, and distinction to persons.

But these are truths which should not be made the subject of too subtle investigation, when we recollect that he who is a searcher of majesty shall be overwhelmed by glory. We should be satisfied with the assurance and certitude which faith gives us that we have been taught these truths by God Himself, to doubt whose word is the extreme of folly and misery. He has said: Teach ye all nations, baptising them in the name of the Father, and of the Son, and of the Holy Ghost; and again, there are three who give testimony in heaven, the Father, the Word, and the Holy Ghost; and these three are one.

Let him, however, who by the divine bounty believes these truths, constantly beseech and implore God and the Father, who made all things out of nothing, and ordereth an things sweetly, who gave us power to become the sons of God, and who made known to the human mind the mystery of the Trinity -- let him, I say, pray unceasingly that, admitted one day into the eternal tabernacles, he may be worthy to see how great is the fecundity of the Father, who contemplating and understanding Himself, begot the Son like and equal to Himself, how a love of charity in both, entirely the same and equal, which is the Holy Ghost, proceeding from the Father and the Son, connects the begetter and the begotten by an eternal and indissoluble bond; and that thus the Essence of the Trinity is one and the distinction of the Three Persons perfect.

"Almighty"

The Sacred Scriptures, in order to mark the piety and devotion with which the most holy name of God is to be adored, usually express His supreme power and infinite majesty in a variety of ways; but the pastor should, first of all, teach that almighty power is most frequently attributed to Him. Thus He says of Himself: I am the almighty Lord and again, Jacob when sending his sons to Joseph thus prayed for them: May my almighty God make him favourable to you. In the Apocalypse also it is written: The Lord God, who is, and who was, and who is to come, the almighty; and in another place the last day is called the great day of the almighty God. Sometimes the same attribute is expressed in many words; thus: No word shall be impossible with God; Is the hand of the Lord unable? Thy power is at hand when thou wilt, and so on.

Meaning Of The Term Almighty"

From these various modes of expression it is clearly perceived what is comprehended under this single word almighty. By it we understand that there neither exists nor can be conceived in thought or imagination anything which God cannot do. For not only can He annihilate all created things, and in a moment summon from nothing into existence many other worlds, an exercise of power which, however great, comes in some degree within our comprehension; but He can do many things still greater, of which the human mind can form no conception.

But though God can do all things, yet He cannot lie, or deceive, or be deceived; He cannot sin, or cease to exist, or be ignorant of anything. These defects are compatible with those beings only whose actions are imperfect; but God, whose acts are always most perfect, is said to be incapable of such things, simply because the capability of doing them implies weakness, not the supreme and infinite power over all things which God possesses. Thus we so believe God to be omnipotent that we exclude from Him entirely all that is not intimately connected and consistent with the perfection of His nature.

Why Omnipotence Alone Is Mentioned In The: Creed

The pastor should point out the propriety and wisdom of having omitted all other names of God in the Creed, and of having proposed to us only that of almighty as the object of our belief. For by acknowledging God to be omnipotent, we also of necessity acknowledge Him to be omniscient, and to hold all things in subjection to His supreme authority and dominion. When we do not doubt that He is omnipotent, we must be also convinced of everything else regarding Him, the absence of which would render His omnipotence altogether unintelligible.

Besides, nothing tends more to confirm our faith and animate our hope than a deep conviction that all things are possible to God; for whatever may be afterwards proposed as an object of faith, however great, however wonderful, however raised above the natural order, is easily and without hesitation believed, once the mind has grasped the knowledge of the omnipotence of God. Nay more, the greater the truths which the divine oracles announce, the more willingly does the mind deem them worthy of belief. And should we expect any favour from heaven, we are not discouraged by the greatness of the desired benefit, but are cheered and confirmed by frequently considering that there is nothing which an omnipotent God cannot effect.

Advantages Of Faith In God's Omnipotence

With this faith, then, we should be specially fortified whenever we are required to render any extraordinary service to our neighbour or seek to obtain by prayer any favour from God. Its necessity in the one case we learn from the Lord Himself, who, when rebuking the incredulity of the Apostles, said: If you have faith as a grain of mustard seed, you shall say to this mountain: Remove from hence thither, and it shall remove; and nothing shall be impossible to you; and in the other case, from these words of St. James: Let him ask in faith, nothing wavering. For he that wavereth is like a wave of the sea, which is moved and carried about by the wind. Therefore let not that man think that he shall receive any thing of the Lord.

This faith brings with it also many advantages and helps. It forms us, in the first place, to all humility and lowliness of mind, according to these words of the Prince of the Apostles: Be you humbled therefore under the mighty hand of God. It also teaches us not to fear where there is no cause of fear, but to fear God alone, in whose power we ourselves and all that we have are placed; for our Saviour says: *I will shew you whom you shall fear; fear ye him, who after he hath killed, hath power to cast into hell.* This faith is also useful to enable us to know and exalt the infinite mercies of God towards us. For he who reflects on the omnipotence of God, cannot be so ungrateful as not frequently to exclaim: *He that is mighty, hath done great things to me.*

Not Three Almighties But One Almighty

When, however, in this Article we call the Father almighty, let no one be led into the error of thinking that this attribute is so ascribed to Him as not to belong also to the Son and the Holy Ghost. As we say the Father is God, the Son is God, the Holy Ghost is God, and yet there are not three Gods but one God; so in like manner we confess that the Father is almighty, the Son almighty, and the Holy Ghost almighty, and yet there are not three almighties but one almighty.

The Father, in particular, we call almighty, because He is the Source of all being; as we also attribute wisdom to the Son, because He is the eternal Word of the Father; and goodness to the Holy Ghost, because He is the love of both. These, however, and similar appellations, may be given indiscriminately to the Three Persons, according to the teaching of Catholic faith.

"Creator"

The necessity of having previously imparted to the faithful a knowledge of the omnipotence of God will appear from what we are now about to explain with regard to the creation of the world. The wondrous production of so stupendous a work is more easily believed when all doubt concerning the immense power of the Creator has been removed.

For God formed the world not from materials of any sort, but created it from nothing, and that not by constraint or necessity, but spontaneously, and of His own free will. Nor was He impelled to create by any other cause than a desire to communicate His goodness to creatures. Being essentially happy in Himself He stands not in need of anything, as David expresses it: I have said to the Lord, thou art my God, for thou hast no need of my goods.

As it was His own goodness that influenced Him when He did all things whatsoever He would, so in the work of creation He followed no external form or model; but contemplating, and as it were imitating, the universal model contained in the divine intelligence, the supreme Architect, with infinite wisdom and power-attributes peculiar to the Divinity -- created all things in the be ginning. He spoke and they were made: he commanded and they were created.

"Of Heaven and Earth"

The words heaven and earth include all things which the heaven's and the earth contain; for besides the heavens, which the Prophet has called the works of his fingers, He also gave to the sun its brilliancy, and to the moon and stars their beauty; and that they might be for signs, and for seasons, and for days and years. He so ordered the celestial bodies in a certain and uniform course, that nothing varies more than their continual revolution, while nothing is more fixed than their variety.

Creation Of The World Of Spirits

Moreover, He created out of nothing the spiritual world and Angels innumerable to serve and minister to Him; and these He enriched and adorned with the admirable gifts of His grace and power.

That the devil and the other rebel angels were gifted from the beginning of their creation with grace, clearly follows from these words of the Sacred Scriptures: He (the devil) stood not in the truth. On this subject St. Augustine says: In creating the Angels He endowed them with good will, that is, with pure love that they might adhere to Him, giving them existence and adorning them with grace at one and the same time. Hence we are to believe that the holy Angels were never without good will, that is, the love of God.

As to their knowledge we have this testimony of Holy Scripture: Thou, my Lord, O king, art wise, according to the wisdom of an angel of God, to understand all things upon earth.' Finally, the inspired David ascribes power to them, saying that they are mighty in strength, and execute his word; and on this account they are often called in Scripture the powers and the armies of the Lord.

But although they were all endowed with celestial gifts, very many, having rebelled against God, their Father and Creator, were hurled from those high mansions of bliss, and shut up in the darkest dungeon of earth, there to suffer for eternity the punishment of their pride. Speaking of them the Prince of the Apostles says: God spared not the angels that sinned, but delivered them, drawn by infernal ropes to the lower hell, unto torments, to be reserved unto judgment.

Formation Of The Universe

The earth also God commanded to stand in the midst of the world, rooted in its own foundation, and made the mountains ascend, and the plains descend into the place which he had founded for them. That the waters should not inundate the earth, He set a bound which they shall not pass over; neither shall they return to cover the earth. He next not only clothed and adorned it with trees and every variety of plant and flower, but filled it, as He had already filled the air and water, with innumerable kinds of living creatures.

Production Of Man

Lastly, He formed man from the slime of the earth, so created and constituted in body as to be immortal and impassible, not, however, by the strength of nature, but by the bounty of God. Man's soul He created to His own image and likeness; gifted him with free will, and tempered all his motions and appetites so as to subject them, at all times, to the dictates of reason. He then added the admirable gift of original righteousness, and next gave him dominion over all other animals. By referring to the sacred history of Genesis the pastor will easily make himself familiar with these things for the instruction of the faithful.

"Of all Things Visible and Invisible"

What we have said, then, of the creation of the universe is to be understood as conveyed by the words heaven and earth, and is thus briefly set forth by the Prophet: Thine are the heavens, and thine is the earth: the world and the fullness thereof thou hast founded. Still more briefly the Fathers of the Council of Nice expressed this truth by adding in their Creed these words: of all things visible and invisible. Whatever exists in the universe, whatever we confess to have been created by God, either falls under the senses and is included in the word visible, or is an object of mental perception and intelligence and is expressed by the word invisible.

God Preserves, Rules And Moves All Created Things

We are not, however, to understand that God is in such wise the Creator and Maker of all things that His works, when once created and finished, could thereafter continue to exist unsupported by His omnipotence. For as all things derive existence from the Creator's supreme power, wisdom, and goodness, so unless preserved continually by His Providence, and by the same power which produced them, they would instantly return into their nothingness. This the Scriptures declare when they say: How could anything endure if thou wouldst not? or be preserved, if not called by thee?

Not only does God protect and govern all things by His Providence, but He also by an internal power impels to motion and action whatever moves and acts, and this in such a manner that, although He excludes not, He yet precedes the agency of secondary causes. For His invisible influence extends to all things, and, as the Wise Man says, reaches from end to end mightily, and ordereth all things sweetly. This is the reason why the Apostle, announcing to the Athenians the God whom, not knowing, they adored, said: He is not far from every one of us: for in him we live, and move, and are.

Creation Is The Work Of The Three Persons

Let so much suffice for the explanation of the first Article of the Creed. It may not be superfluous, however, to add that creation is the common work of the Three Persons of the Holy and undivided Trinity, -- of the Father, whom according to the doctrine of the Apostles we here declare to be Creator of heaven and earth; of the Son, of whom the Scripture says, all things were made by him; and of the Holy Ghost, of whom it is written: The spirit of God moved over the waters, and again, By the word of the Lord the heavens were established; and all the power of them by the spirit of his mouth.

ARTICLE II : "AND IN JESUS CHRIST, HIS ONLY SON, OUR LORD"

Advantages Of Faith In This Article

That wonderful and superabundant are the blessings which flow to the human race from the belief and profession of this Article we learn from these words of St. John: Whosoever shall confess that Jesus is the Son of God, God abideth in him, and he in God; and also from the words of Christ the Lord, proclaiming the Prince of the Apostles blessed for the confession of this truth: Blessed art thou, Simon Bar-Jona: for flesh and blood hath not revealed it to thee, but my Father who is in heaven. For this Article is the most firm basis of our salvation and redemption.

But as the fruit of these admirable blessings is best known by considering the ruin brought on man by his fall from that most happy state in which God had placed our first parents, let the pastor be particularly careful to make known to the faithful the cause of this common misery and calamity.

When Adam had departed from the obedience due to God and had violated the prohibition, of every tree of paradise thou shalt eat: But of the tree of knowledge of good and evil, thou shalt not eat, for in what day soever thou shalt eat of it, thou shalt die the death, he fell into the extreme misery of losing the sanctity and righteousness in which he had been placed, and of becoming subject to all those other evils which have been explained more fully by the holy Council of Trent.

Wherefore, the pastor should not omit to remind the faithful that the guilt and punishment of original sin were not confined to Adam, but justly descended from him, as from their source and cause, to all posterity. The human race, having fallen from its elevated dignity, no power of men or Angels could raise it from its fallen condition and replace it in its primitive state. To remedy the evil and repair the loss it became necessary that the Son of God, whose power is infinite, clothed in the weakness of our flesh, should remove the infinite weight of sin and reconcile us to God in His blood.

Necessity Of Faith In This Article

The belief and profession of this our redemption, which God declared from the beginning, are now, and always have been, necessary to salvation. In the sentence of condemnation pronounced against the human race immediately after the sin of Adam the hope of redemption was held out in these words, which announced to the devil the loss he was to sustain by man's redemption: I will put enmities between thee and the woman, and thy seed and her seed: she shall crush thy head, and thou shalt lie in wait f or her heel.

The same promise God again often confirmed and more distinctly manifested to those chiefly whom He desired to make special objects of His favour; among others to the Patriarch Abraham, to whom He often declared this mystery, but more explicitly when, in obedience to His command, Abraham was prepared to sacrifice his only son Isaac. Because, said God, thou hast done this thing, and hast not spared thy only-begotten son f or my sake; I win bless thee, and I will multiply thy seed as the stars of heaven, and as the sand that is by the sea shore. Thy seed shall possess the gates of their enemies, and in thy seed shall all the nations of the earth be blessed, because thou hast obeyed my voice. From these words it was easy to infer that He who was to deliver mankind from the ruthless tyranny of Satan was to be descended from Abraham; and that while He was the Son of God, He was to be born of the seed of Abraham according to the flesh.

Not long after, to preserve the memory of this promise, God renewed the same covenant with Jacob, the grandson of Abraham. When in a vision Jacob saw a ladder standing on earth, and its top reaching to heaven, and the angels of God ascending and descending by it, as the Scriptures testify, he also heard the Lord, who was leaning on the ladder, say to him: I am the Lord God of Abraham thy father, and the God of Isaac; the land, wherein thou sleepest, I will give to thee and to thy seed. And thy seed shall be as the dust of the earth. Thou shalt spread abroad to the west, and to the east, and to the north, and to the south; and in thee and thy seed all the nations of the earth shall be blessed.

Nor did God cease afterwards to excite in the posterity of Abraham and in many others, the expectation of a Saviour, by renewing the recollection of the same promise; for after the establishment of the Jewish State and religion it became better known to His people. Types signified and men foretold what and how great blessings the Saviour and Redeemer, Christ Jesus, was to bring to mankind. And indeed the Prophets, whose minds were illuminated with light from above, foretold the birth of the Son of God, the wondrous works which He wrought while on earth, His doctrine, character, life, death, Resurrection, and the other mysterious circumstances regarding Him, and all these they announced to the people as graphically as if they were passing before their eyes. With the exception that one has reference to the future and the other to the past, we can discover no difference between the predictions of the Prophets and the preaching of the Apostles, between the faith of the ancient Patriarchs and that of Christians.

But we are now to speak of the several parts of this Article.

"Jesus"

Jesus is the proper name of the God-man and signifies Saviour: a name given Him not accidentally, or by the judgment or will of man, but by the counsel and command of God. For the Angel announced to Mary His mother: Behold thou shalt conceive in thy womb, and shalt bring forth a son; and thou shalt call his name Jesus. He afterwards not only commanded Joseph, who was espoused to the Virgin, to call the child by that name, but also declared the reason why He should be so called. Joseph, son of David, said the Angel, fear not to take unto thee Mary thy wife, for that which is conceived in her is of the Holy Ghost. And she shall bring forth a son and thou shalt call his name Jesus. For he shall save his people from their sins.

In the Sacred Scriptures we meet with many who were called by this name. So, for example, was called the son of Nave, who succeeded Moses, and, by special privilege denied to Moses, conducted into the land of promise the people whom Moses had delivered from Egypt; and also the son of Josedech, the priest. But how much more appropriate it is to call by this name our Saviour, who gave light, liberty and salvation, not to one people only, but to all men, of all ages to men oppressed, not by famine, or Egyptian or Babylonian bondage, but sitting in the shadow of death and fettered by the galling chains of sin and of the devil who purchased for them a right to the inheritance of heaven and reconciled them to God the Father! In those men who were designated by the same name we see foreshadowed Christ the Lord, by whom the blessings just enumerated were poured out on the human race.

All other names which according to prophecy were to be given by divine appointment to the Son of God, are comprised in this one name Jesus; for while they partially signified the salvation which He was to bestow upon us, this name included the force and meaning of all human salvation.

"Christ"

To the name Jesus is added that of Christ, which signifies the anointed. This name is expressive of honour and office, and is not peculiar to one thing only, but common to many; for in the Old Law priests and kings, whom God, on account of the dignity of their office, commanded to he anointed, were called christs. For priests commend the people to God by unceasing prayer, offer sacrifice to Him, and turn away His wrath from mankind. Kings are entrusted with the government of the people; and to them principally belong the authority of the law, the protection of innocence and the punishment of guilt. As, therefore, both these functions seem to represent the majesty of God on earth, those who were appointed to the royal or sacerdotal office were anointed with oil. Furthermore, since Prophets, as the interpreters and ambassadors of the immortal God, have unfolded to us the secrets of heaven and by salutary precepts and the prediction of future events have exhorted to amendment of life, it was customary to anoint them also.

When Jesus Christ our Saviour came into the world, He assumed these three characters of Prophet, Priest and King, and was therefore called Christ, having been anointed for the discharge of these functions, not by mortal hand or with earthly ointment, but by the power of His heavenly Father and with a spiritual oil; for the plenitude of the Holy Spirit and a more copious effusion of all gifts than any other created being is capable of receiving were poured into His soul. This the Prophet clearly indicates when he addresses the Redeemer in these words: Thou hast loved justice, and hated iniquity: therefore God, thy God, hath anointed thee with the oil of gladness above thy fellows. The same is also more explicitly declared by the Prophet Isaias: The spirit of the Lord is upon me, because the Lord hath anointed me: he hath sent me to preach to the meek.

Jesus Christ, therefore, was the great Prophet and Teacher, from whom we have learned the will of God and by whom the world has been taught the knowledge of the heavenly Father. The name prophet belongs to Him preeminently, because all others who were dignified with that name were His disciples, sent principally to announce the coming of that Prophet who was to save all men.

Christ was also a Priest, not indeed of the same order as were the priests of the tribe of Levi in the Old Law, but of that of which the Prophet David sang: Thou art a priest for ever according to the order of Melchisedech. This subject the Apostle fully and accurately develops in his Epistle to the Hebrews.

Christ not only as God, but also as man and partaker of our nature, we acknowledge to be a King. Of Him the Angel testified: He shall reign in the house of Jacob for ever. And of his kingdom there shall be no end. This kingdom of Christ is spiritual and eternal, begun on earth but perfected in heaven. He discharges by His admirable Providence the duties of King towards His Church, governing and protecting her against the assaults and snares of her enemies, legislating for her and imparting to her not only holiness and righteousness, but also the power and strength to persevere. But although the good and the bad are found within the limits of this kingdom, and thus all men by right belong to it, yet those who in conformity with His commands lead unsullied and innocent lives, experience beyond all others the sovereign goodness and beneficence of our King. Although descended from the most illustrious race of kings, He obtained this kingdom not by hereditary or other human right, but because God bestowed on Him as man all the power, dignity and majesty of which human nature is capable. To Him, therefore, God delivered the government of the whole world, and to this His sovereignty, which has already commenced, all things shall be made fully and entirely subject on the day of judgment.

"His Only Son"

In these words, mysteries more exalted with regard to Jesus are proposed to the faithful as objects of their belief and contemplation; namely, that He is the Son of God, and true God, like the Father who begot Him from eternity. We also confess that He is the Second Person of the Blessed Trinity, equal in all things to the Father and the Holy Ghost; for in the Divine Persons nothing unequal or unlike should exist, or even be imagined to exist, since we acknowledge the essence, will and power of all to be one. This truth is both clearly revealed in many passages of Holy Scripture and sublimely announced in the testimony of St. John: In the beginning was the Word, and the Word was with God, and the Word was God.

But when we are told that Jesus is the Son of God, we are not to understand anything earthly or mortal in His birth; but are firmly to believe and piously to adore that birth by which, from all eternity, the Father begot the Son, a mystery which reason cannot fully conceive or comprehend, and at the contemplation of which, overwhelmed, as it were, with admiration, we should exclaim with the Prophet: Who shall declare his generation? On this point, then, we are to believe that the Son is of the same nature, of the same power and wisdom, with the Father, as we more fully profess in these words of the Nicene Creed: And in one Lord Jesus Christ, his Only-begotten Son, born of the Father before all ages, God of God, light of light, true God of true God, begotten, not made, consubstantial to the Father, by whom all things were made.

Among the different comparisons employed to elucidate the mode and manner of this eternal generation that which is borrowed from the production of thought in our mind seems to come nearest to its illustration, and hence St. John calls the Son the Word. For as our mind, in some sort understanding itself, forms an image of itself, which theologians express by the term word, so God, as far as we may compare human things to divine, understanding Himself, begets the eternal Word. It is better, however, to contemplate what faith proposes, and in the sincerity of our souls to believe and confess that Jesus Christ is true God and true Man, as God, begotten of the Father before all ages, as Man, born in time of Mary, His Virgin Mother.

While we thus acknowledge His twofold Nativity; we believe Him to be one Son, because His divine and human natures meet in one Person. As to His divine generation He has no brethren or coheirs, being the Only-begotten Son of the Father, while we mortals are the work of His hands. But if we consider His birth as man, He not only calls many by the name of brethren, but treats them as such, since He admits them to share with Him the glory of His paternal inheritance. They are those who by faith have received Christ the Lord, and who really, and by works of charity, show forth the faith which they profess in words. Hence the Apostle calls Christ, the first-born amongst many brethren.

"Our Lord"

Of our Saviour many things are recorded in Sacred Scripture. Some of these, it is evident, apply to Him as God and some as man, because from His two natures He received the different properties which belong to both. Hence we say with truth that Christ is Almighty, Eternal, Infinite, and these attributes He has from His Divine Nature; again, we say of Him that He suffered, died, and rose again, which are properties manifestly that belong to His human nature.

Besides these terms, there are others common to both natures; as when in this Article of the Creed we say our Lord. If, then, this name applies to both natures, rightly is He to be called our Lord. For as He, as well as the Father, is the eternal God, so is He Lord of all things equally with the Father; and as He and the Father are not the one, one God, and the other, another God, but one and the same God, so likewise He and the Father are not the one, one Lord, and the other, another Lord.

As man, He is also for many reasons appropriately called our Lord. First, because He is our Redeemer, who delivered us from sin, He deservedly acquired the power by which He truly is and is called our Lord. This is the doctrine of the Apostle:

> He humbled himself, becoming obedient unto death, even to the death of the cross. For which cause God also hath exalted him, and hath given him a name which is above all names: that at the name of Jesus every knee should bend, of those that are in heaven, on earth, and under the earth: and that every tongue should confess that the Lord Jesus Christ is in the glory of God the Father. And of Himself He said, after His Resurrection: All power is given to me in heaven and in earth.

He is also called Lord because in one Person both natures, the human and the divine, are united; and even though He had not died for us, He would have yet deserved, by this admirable union, to be constituted common Lord of all created things, particularly of the faithful who obey and serve Him with all the fervour of their souls.

Duties Owed To Christ Our Lord

It remains, therefore, that the pastor remind the faithful that: from Christ we take our name and are called Christians; that we cannot be ignorant of the extent of His favours, particularly since by His gift of faith we are enabled to understand all these things. We, above all others, are under the obligation of devoting and consecrating ourselves forever, like faithful servants, to our Redeemer and our Lord.

This indeed, we promised at the doors of the church when about to be baptised; for we then declared that we renounced the devil and the world, and gave ourselves unreservedly to Jesus Christ. But if to be enrolled as soldiers of Christ we consecrated ourselves by so holy and solemn a profession to our Lord, what punishments should we not deserve if after our entrance into the Church, and after having known the will and laws of God and received the grace of the Sacraments, we were to form our lives upon the precepts and maxims of the world and the devil, just as though when cleansed in the waters of Baptism, we had pledged our fidelity to the world and to the devil, and not to Christ the Lord and Saviour!

What heart so cold as not to be inflamed with love by the kindness and good will exercised toward us by so great a Lord, who, though holding us in His power and dominion as slaves ransomed by His blood, yet embraces us with such ardent love as to call us not servants, but friends and brethren? This, assuredly, supplies the most just, and perhaps the strongest, claim to induce us always to acknowledge, venerate, and adore Him as our Lord.

ARTICLE III : "WHO WAS CONCEIVED BY THE HOLY GHOST, BORN OF THE VIRGIN MARY"

Importance Of This Article

From what has been said in the preceding Article, the faithful can understand that in bringing us from the relentless tyranny of Satan into liberty, God has conferred a singular and surpassing blessing on the human race. But if we place before our eyes also the plan and means by which He deigned chiefly to accomplish this, then, indeed, we shall see that there is nothing more glorious or magnificent than this divine goodness and beneficence towards us.

First Part of this Article:

"Who was Conceived,'

The pastor, then, should enter on the exposition of this third Article by developing the grandeur of this mystery, which the Sacred Scriptures very frequently propose for our consideration as the principal source of our eternal salvation. Its meaning he should teach to be that we believe and confess that the same Jesus Christ, our only Lord, the Son of God, when He assumed human flesh for us in the womb of the Virgin, was not conceived like other men, from the seed of man, but in a manner transcending the order of nature, that is, by the power of the Holy Ghost; so that the same Person, remaining God as He was from eternity, became man, what He was not before.

That such is the meaning of the above words is clear from the Creed of the Holy Council of Constantinople, which says: Who for us men, and for our salvation,, came down from heaven, and became incarnate by the Holy Ghost of the Virgin Mary, and was made man. The same truth we also find unfolded by St. John the Evangelist, who imbibed from the bosom of the Lord and Saviour Himself the knowledge of this most profound mystery. For when he had declared the nature of the Divine Word as follows: In the beginning was the Word, and the Word was with God, and the Word was God, he concluded: And the Word was made flesh and dwelt among us.

The Word, which is a Person of the Divine Nature, assumed human nature in such a manner that there should be one and the same Person in both the divine and human natures. Hence this admirable union preserved the actions and properties of both natures; and as Pope St. Leo the Great said: The lowliness of the inferior nature was not consumed in the glory of the superior, nor did the assumption of the inferior lessen the glory of the superior.

"By the Holy Ghost"

As an explanation of the words in which this Article is expressed is not to be omitted, the pastor should teach that when we say that the Son of God was conceived by the power of the Holy Ghost, we do not mean that this Person alone of the Holy Trinity accomplished the mystery of the Incarnation. Although the Son only assumed human nature, yet all the Persons of the Trinity, the Father, the Son, and the Holy Ghost, were authors of this mystery.

It is a principle of Christian faith that whatever God does outside Himself in creation is common to the Three Persons, and that one neither does more than, nor acts without another. But that one emanates from another, this only cannot be common to all; for the Son is begotten of the Father only, and the Holy Ghost proceeds from the Father and the Son. Anything, however, which proceeds from them extrinsically is the work of the Three Persons without difference of any sort, and of this latter description is the Incarnation of the Son of God.

Of those things, nevertheless, that are common to all, the Sacred Scriptures-often attribute some to one person, some to another. Thus, to the Father they attribute power over all things ; to the Son, wisdom; to the Holy Ghost, love. Hence, as the mystery of the Incarnation manifests the singular and boundless love of God towards us, it is therefore in some sort peculiarly attributed to the Holy Ghost.

In The Incarnation Some Things Were Natural, Others Supernatural

In this mystery we perceive that some things were done which transcend the order of nature, some by the power of nature. Thus, in believing that the body of Christ was formed from the most pure blood of His Virgin Mother we acknowledge the operation of human nature, this being a law common to the formation of all human bodies, that they should be formed from the blood of the mother.

But what surpasses the order of nature and human comprehension is, that as soon as the Blessed Virgin assented to the announcement of the Angel in these words, Behold the handmaid of the Lord; be it done unto me according to thy word, the most sacred body of Christ was immediately formed, and to it was united a rational soul enjoying the use of reason; and thus in the same instant of time He was perfect God and perfect man. That this was the astonishing and admirable work of the Holy Ghost cannot be doubted; for according to the order of nature the rational soul is united to the body only after a certain lapse of time.

Again -- and this should overwhelm us with astonishment -- as soon as the soul of Christ was united to His body, the Divinity became united to both; and thus at the same time His body was formed and animated, and the Divinity united to body and soul.

Hence, at the same instant He was perfect God and perfect man, and the most Holy Virgin, having at the same moment conceived God and man, is truly and properly called Mother of God and man. This the Angel signified to her when he said: Behold thou shalt conceive in thy womb, and shalt bring forth a son; and thou shalt call his name Jesus. He shall be great, and shall be called the Son of the Most High. The event verified the prophecy of Isaias: Behold a virgin shall conceive, and bear a son. Elizabeth also declared the same truth when" being filled with the Holy Ghost, she understood the Conception of the Son of God, and said: Whence is this to me, that the mother of my Lord should come to me?

As the body of Christ was formed of the pure blood of the immaculate Virgin without the aid of man, as we have already said, and by the sole operation of the Holy Ghost, so also, at the moment of His Conception, His soul was enriched with an overflowing fullness of the Spirit of God, and a superabundance of all graces. For God gave not to Him, as to others adorned with holiness and grace, His Spirit by measure, as St. John testifies but poured into His soul the plenitude of all graces so abundantly that of his fullness we all have received.

Although possessing that Spirit by which holy men attain the adoption of sons of God, He cannot, however, be called the adopted son of God; for since He is the Son of God by nature, the grace, or name of adoption, can on no account be deemed applicable to Him.

How To Profit By The Mystery Of The Incarnation

These truths comprise the substance of what appears to demand explanation regarding the admirable mystery of the Conception. To reap from them abundant fruit for salvation the faithful should particularly recall, and frequently reflect, that it is God who assumed human flesh; that the manner in which He became man exceeds our comprehension, not to say our powers of expression; and finally, that He vouchsafed to become man in order that we men might be born again as children of God. When to these subjects they shall have given mature consideration, let them, in the humility of faith, believe and adore all the mysteries contained in this Article, and not indulge a curious inquisitiveness by investigating and scrutinising them -- an attempt scarcely ever unattended with danger.

Second Part Of This Article: "Born Of The Virgin Mary"

These words comprise another part of this Article. In its exposition the pastor should exercise considerable diligence, because the faithful are bound to believe that Jesus the Lord was not only conceived by the power of the Holy Ghost, but was also born of the Virgin Mary. The words of the Angel who first announced the happy tidings to the world declare with what joy and delight of soul this mystery of our faith should be meditated upon. Behold, said the Angel, I bring you good tidings of great joy" that shall be to all the people. The same sentiments are clearly conveyed in the song chanted by the heavenly host: Glory to God in the highest; and on earth peace to men of good will. Then began the fulfilment of the splendid promise made by God to Abraham" that in his seed all the nations of the earth should one day be blessed; for Mary" whom we truly proclaim and venerate as Mother of God, because she brought forth Him who is at once God and man, was descended from King David.

The Nativity Of Christ Transcends The Order Of Nature

But as the Conception itself transcends the order of nature, so also the birth of our Lord presents to our contemplation nothing but what is divine.

Besides, what is admirable beyond the power of thoughts or words to express, He is born of His Mother without any diminution of her maternal virginity, just as He afterwards went forth from the sepulchre while it was closed and sealed, and entered the room in which His disciples were assembled, the doors being shut; or, not to depart from every-day examples, just as the rays of the sun penetrate without breaking or injuring in the least the solid substance of glass, so after a like but more exalted manner did Jesus Christ come forth from His mother's womb without injury to her maternal virginity. This immaculate and perpetual virginity forms, therefore, the just theme of our eulogy. Such was the work of the Holy Ghost, who at the Conception and birth of the Son so favoured the Virgin Mother as to impart to her fecundity while preserving inviolate her perpetual virginity.

Christ Compared to Adam" Mary to Eve

The Apostle sometimes calls Jesus Christ the second Adam, and compares Him to the first Adam; for as in the first all men die, so in the second all are made alive: and as in the natural order Adam was the father of the human race, so in the supernatural order Christ is The author of grace and of glory.

The Virgin Mother we may also compare to Eve, making the second Eve, that is, Mary, correspond to the first, as we have already shown that the second Adam, that is, Christ, corresponds to the first Adam. By believing the serpent, Eve brought malediction and death on mankind, and Mary, by believing the Angel, became the instrument of The divine goodness in bringing life and benediction to the human race. From Eve we are born

89

children of wrath; from Mary we have received Jesus Christ, and through Him are regenerated children of grace. To Eve it was said: In sorrow shalt thou bring forth children. Mary was exempt from this law, for preserving her virginal integrity inviolate she brought forth Jesus the Son of God without experiencing, as we have already said, any sense of pain.

Types and Prophecies of the Conception and Nativity

The mysteries of this admirable Conception and Nativity being, therefore, so great and so numerous, it accorded with the plan of divine Providence to signify them by many types and prophecies. Hence the holy Fathers understood many things which we meet in the Sacred Scriptures to refer to these mysteries, particularly that gate of the sanctuary which Ezechiel saw closed; the stone cut out of the mountain without hands, which became a great mountain and filled the universe, of which we read in Daniel; the rod of Aaron, which alone budded of all the rods of the princes of Israel; and the bush which Moses saw burn without being consumed.'

The holy Evangelist describes in detail the history of the birth of Christ; but, as the pastor can easily recur to the Sacred Volume, it is unnecessary for us to say more on the subject.

Lessons which this Article Teaches

The pastor should labor to impress deeply on the minds and hearts of the faithful these mysteries, which were written for our learning; first, that by the commemoration of so great a benefit they may make some return of gratitude to God, its author, and next, in order to place before their eyes, as a model for imitation, this striking and singular example of humility.

Humility And Poverty Of Christ

What can be more useful, what better calculated to subdue the pride and haughtiness of the human heart, than to reflect frequently that God humbles Himself in such a manner as to assume our frailty and weakness, in order to communicate to us His glory; that God becomes man, and that He at whose nod, to use the words of Scripture, the pillars of heaven tremble and are affrighted bows His supreme and infinite majesty to minister to man; that He whom the Angels adore in heaven is born on earth ! When such is the goodness of God towards us, what, I ask, should we not do to testify our obedience to His will? With what willingness and alacrity should we not love, embrace, and perform all the duties of humility ?

The faithful should also consider the salutary lessons which Christ at His birth teaches before He begins to speak. He is born in poverty; He is born a stranger under a roof not His own; He is born in a lonely crib; He is born in the depth of winter ! For St. Luke writes as follows: And it came to pass, that when they were there, her days were accomplished, that she should be delivered. And she brought forth her first-born, and wrapped him up in swaddling clothes, and laid him in a manger; because there was no room for them in the inn. Could the Evangelist have described under more humble terms the majesty and glory that filled the heavens and the earth ? He does not say, there was no room in the inn, but there was no room for him who says, the world is mine, and the fullness thereof. As another Evangelist has expressed it: He came unto his own, and his own received him not.

Elevation And Dignity Of Man

When the faithful have placed these things before their eyes, let them also reflect that God condescended to assume the lowliness and frailty of our flesh in order to exalt man to the highest degree of dignity. This single reflection, that He who is true and perfect God became man, supplies sufficient proof of the exalted dignity conferred on the human race by the divine bounty; since we may now glory that the Son of God is bone of our bone, and flesh of our flesh, a privilege not given to Angels, for nowhere, says the Apostle, doth he take hold of the Angels: but of the seed of Abraham he taketh hold.

Duty Of Spiritual Nativity

We must also take care lest to our great injury it should happen that just as there was no room for Him in the inn at Bethlehem, in which to be born, so likewise now, after He has been born in the flesh, He should find no room in our hearts in which to be born spiritually. For since He is most desirous of our salvation, this spiritual birth is the object of His most earnest solicitude.

As, then, by the power of the Holy Ghost, and in a manner superior to the order of nature, He was made man and was born, was holy and even holiness itself, so does it become our duty to be born, not of blood, nor of the will of the flesh, but of God; to walk as new creatures in newness of spirit, and to preserve that holiness and purity of soul which so much becomes men regenerated by the Spirit of God. Thus shall we reflect some faint image of the holy Conception and Nativity of the Son of God, which are the objects of our firm faith, and believing which we revere and adore the wisdom of God in a mystery which is hidden.

ARTICLE IV : "SUFFERED UNDER PONTIUS PILATE, WAS CRUCIFIED, DEAD, AND BURIED'"

Importance Of This Article

How necessary is a knowledge of this Article, and how assiduous the pastor should be in stirring up in the minds of the faithful the frequent recollection of our Lord's Passion" we learn from the Apostle when he says that he knows nothing but Jesus Christ and him crucified.' The pastor, therefore, should exercise the greatest care and pains in giving a thorough explanation of this subject" in order that the faithful" being moved by the remembrance of so great a benefit" may give themselves entirely to the contemplation of the goodness and love of God towards us.

First Part of this Article: '"Suffered Under Pontius Pilate, was Crucified,,

The first part of this Article (of the second we shall treat hereafter) proposes for our belief that when Pontius Pilate governed the province of Judea" under Tiberius Caesar" Christ the Lord was nailed to a cross. Having been seized" mocked, outraged and tortured in various forms" He was finally crucified.

"Suffered,"

It cannot be a matter of doubt that His soul" as to its inferior part" was sensible of these torments; for as He really assumed human nature" it is a necessary consequence that He really, and in His soul, experienced a most acute sense of pain. Hence these words of the Saviour: My soul is sorrowful even unto death.

Although human nature was united to the Divine Person, He felt the bitterness of His Passion as acutely as if no such union had existed" because in the one Person of Jesus Christ were preserved the properties of both natures" human and divine; and therefore what was passible and mortal remained passible and mortal; while what was impassible and immortal, that is, His Divine Nature, continued impassible and immortal.

"Under Pontius Pilate"

Since we find it here so diligently recorded that Jesus Christ suffered when Pontius Pilate was procurator of Judea, the pastor should explain the reason. By fixing the time, which we find also done by the Apostle Paul, so important and so necessary an event is rendered more easily ascertainable by all. Furthermore those words show that the Saviour's prediction was really verified: They shall deliver him to the Gentiles, to be mocked and scourged and crucified.

"Was Crucified"

The fact that He suffered death precisely on the wood of the cross must also be attributed to a particular counsel of God, which decreed that life should return by the way whence death had arisen The serpent who had triumphed over our first parents by the wood (of a tree) was vanquished by Christ on the wood of the cross.

Many other reasons which the Fathers have discussed in detail might be adduced to show that it was fit that our Redeemer should suffer death on the cross rather than in any other way. But, as the pastor will show" it is enough for the faithful to believe that this kind of death was chosen by the Saviour because it appeared better adapted and more appropriate to the redemption of the human race; for there certainly could be none more ignominious and humiliating. Not only among the Gentiles was the punishment of the cross held accursed and full of shame and infamy, but even in the Law of Moses the man is called accursed that hangeth on a tree.

Importance Of The History Of The Passion

Furthermore, the pastor should not omit the historical part of this Article, which has been so carefully set forth by the holy Evangelists; so that the faithful may be acquainted with at least the principal points of this mystery, that is to say, such as seem more necessary to confirm the truth of our faith. For it is on this Article, as on their foundation, that the Christian faith and religion rest; and if this truth be firmly established, all the rest is secure. Indeed, if one thing more than another presents difficulty to the mind and understanding of man, assuredly it is the mystery of the cross, which, beyond all doubt, must be considered the most difficult of all; so much so that only with great difficulty can we grasp the fact that our salvation depends on the cross, and on Him who for us was nailed thereon. In this, however, as the Apostle teaches, we may well admire the wonderful Providence of God; for, seeing that in the wisdom of God, the world by wisdom knew not God, it pleased God by the foolishness of preaching, to save them that believe. It is no wonder, then, that the Prophets, before the coming of Christ, and the Apostles, after His death and Resurrection, labored so strenuously to convince mankind that He was the Redeemer of the world, and to bring them under the power and obedience of the Crucified.

Figures And Prophecies Of The Passion And Death Of The Saviour

Since, therefore, nothing is so far above the reach of human reason as the mystery of the cross, the Lord immediately after the fall ceased not, both by figures and prophecies, to signify the death by which His Son was to die.

To mention a few of these types. First of all, Abel, who fell a victim of the envy of his brother, Isaac who was commanded to be offered in sacrifice, the lamb immolated by the Jews on their departure from Egypt, and also the brazen serpent lifted up by Moses in the desert, were all figures of the Passion and death of Christ the Lord.

As to the Prophets, how many there were who foretold Christ's Passion and death is too well known to require development here. Not to speak of David, whose Psalms embrace all the principal mysteries of Redemption, the oracles of Isaias in particular are so clear and graphic that he might be said rather to have recorded a past than predicted a future event. a

Second Part Of This Article: "Dead, And Buried"

Christ Really Died

The pastor should explain that these words present for our belief that Jesus Christ, after He was crucified, really died and was buried. It is not without just reason that this is proposed to the faithful as a separate object of belief, since there were some who denied His death upon the cross. The Apostles, therefore, were justly of opinion that to such an error should be opposed the doctrine of faith contained in this Article, the truth of which is placed beyond the possibility of doubt by the united testimony of all the Evangelists, who record that Jesus yielded up the ghost.

Moreover as Christ was true and perfect man, He of course was capable of dying. Now man dies when the soul is separated from the body. When, therefore, we say that Jesus died, we mean that His soul was disunited from His body. We do not admit, however, that the Divinity was separated from His body. On the contrary, we firmly believe and profess that when His soul was dissociated from His body, His Divinity continued always united both to His body in the sepulchre and to His soul in limbo. It became the Son of God to die, that, through death, he might destroy him who had the empire of death that is the devil, and might deliver them, who through the fear of death were all their lifetime subject to servitude.

Christ Died Freely

It was the peculiar privilege of Christ the Lord to have died when He Himself decreed to die, and to have died not so much by external violence as by internal assent. Not only His death, but also its time and place, were ordained by Him. For thus Isaias wrote: He was offered because it was his own will. The Lord before His Passion, declared the same of Himself: I lay down my life, that I may take it again. No man taketh it away from me: but I lay it down of myself, and I have power to lay it down: and I have power to take it again. As to the time and place of His death, He said, when Herod insidiously sought His life: Go and tell that fox: Behold I cast out devils, and do cures to-day and to-morrow, and the third day I am consummated. Nevertheless I must walk today and to-morrow, and the day following, because it cannot be that a prophet perish out of Jerusalem." He therefore offered Himself not involuntarily or by compulsion but of His own free will. Going to meet His enemies He said: I am he; and all the punishments which injustice and cruelty inflicted on Him He endured voluntarily.

The Thought Of Christ's Death Should Excite Our Love And Gratitude

When we meditate on the sufferings and all the torments of the Redeemer, nothing is better calculated to stir our souls than the thought that He endured them thus voluntarily. Were anyone to endure all kinds of suffering for our sake, not because he chose them but simply because he could not escape them, we should not consider this a very great favour; but were he to endure death freely, and for our sake only, having had it in his power to avoid it, this indeed would be a benefit so overwhelming as to deprive even the most grateful heart, not only of the power of returning but even of feeling due thanks. We may hence form an idea of the transcendent and intense love of Jesus Christ towards us, and of His divine and boundless claims to our gratitude.

Christ Was Really Buried

When we confess that He was buried, we do not make this, as it were, a distinct part of the Article, as if it presented any new difficulty which is not implied in what we have said of His death; for if we believe that Christ died, we can also easily believe that He was buried. The word buried was added in the Creed, first, that His death might be rendered more certain, for the strongest argument of a person's death is the proof that his body was buried; and, secondly, to render the miracle of His Resurrection more authentic and illustrious.

It is not, however, our belief that the body of Christ alone was interred. The above words propose, as the principal object of our belief, that God was buried; as according to the rule of Catholic faith we also say with the strictest truth that God died, and that God was born of a virgin. For as the Divinity was never separated from His body which was laid in the sepulchre, we truly confess that God was buried.

Circumstances Of Christ's Burial

As to the manner and place of His burial, what the holy Evangelists record on these subjects will be sufficient for the pastor. There are, however, two things which demand particular attention; the one, that the body of Christ was in no degree corrupted in the sepulchre, according to the prediction of the Prophet: Thou wilt not give thy holy one to see corruption; the other, and it regards the several parts of this Article, that burial, Passion, and also death, apply to Christ Jesus not as God but as man. To suffer and die are incidental to human nature only; yet they are also attributed to God, since, as is clear, they are predicated with propriety of that Person who is at once perfect God and perfect man.

Useful Considerations on the Passion

When the faithful have once attained the knowledge of these things, the pastor should next proceed to explain those particulars of the Passion and death of Christ which may enable them if not to comprehend, at least to contemplate, the immensity of so stupendous a mystery.

The Dignity Of The Sufferer

And first we must consider who it is that suffers all these things. His dignity we cannot express in words or even conceive in mind. Of Him St. John says, that He is the Word which was with God. And the Apostle describes Him in sublime terms, saying that this is He -whom God hath appointed heir of all things, by whom also he made the world, who being the brightness of his glory, and the figure of his substance, and upholding all things by the word of his power, making purgation of sins. sitteth on the right hand of the majesty on high. In a word, Jesus Christ, the God-man, suffers ! The Creator suffers for His creatures, the Master for His servant. He suffers by whom the Angels, men, the heavens, and the elements were made; in whom, by whom, and of whom, are all things.

It cannot, therefore, be a matter of surprise that while He agonised under such an accumulation of torments the whole frame of the universe was convulsed; for as the Scriptures inform us, the earth quaked, and the rocks were rent, there was darkness over all the earth; and the sun was obscured. If, then, even mute and inanimate nature sympathised with the sufferings of her Creator, let the faithful consider with what tears they, the living stones of this edifice, should manifest their sorrow.

Reasons Why Christ Suffered

The reasons why the Saviour suffered are also to be explained, that thus the greatness and intensity of the divine love towards us may the more fully appear. Should anyone inquire why the Son of God underwent His most bitter Passion, he will find that besides the guilt inherited from our first parents the principal causes were the vice's and crimes which have been perpetrated from the beginning of the world to the present day and those which will be committed to the end of time. In His Passion and death the Son of God, our Saviour, intended to atone for and blot out the sins of all ages, to offer for them to his Father a full and abundant satisfaction.

Besides, to increase the dignity of this mystery, Christ not only suffered for sinners, but even for those who were the very authors and ministers of all the torments He endured. Of this the Apostle reminds us in these words addressed to the Hebrews: Think diligently upon him that endured such opposition from sinners against himself; that you be not wearied, fainting in your minds. In this guilt are involved all those who fall frequently into sin; for, as our sins consigned Christ the Lord to the death of the cross, most certainly those who wallow in sin and iniquity crucify to themselves again the Son of God, as far as in them lies, and make a mockery of Him. This guilt seems more enormous in us than in the Jews, since according to the testimony of the same Apostle: If they had known it, they would never have crucified the Lord of glory; while we, on the contrary, professing to know Him, yet denying Him by our actions, seem in some sort to lay violent hands on him.

Christ Was Delivered Over To Death By The Father And By Himself

But that Christ the Lord was also delivered over to death by the Father and by Himself, the Scriptures bear witness. For in Isaias (God the Father) says For the wickedness of my people have I struck him. And a little before the same Prophet filled with the Spirit of God, cried out, as he saw the Lord covered with stripes and wounds: All we like sheep have gone astray, every one hath turned aside into his own way: and the Lord hath laid on him the iniquity of us all. But of the Son it is written: If he shall lay down his life for sin, he shall see a long-lived seed. This the Apostle expresses in language still stronger when, in order to show how confidently we, on our part, should trust in the boundless mercy and goodness of God, he says: He that spared not even his own Son, but delivered him up for us all, how hath he not also, with him, given us all things? a

The: Bitterness Of Christ's Passion

The next subject of the pastor's instruction is the bitterness of the Redeemer's Passion. If we bear m mind that his sweat became as drops of blood, trickling down upon the ground, and this, at the sole anticipation of the torments and agony which He was about to endure, we must at once perceive that His sorrows admitted of no increase. For if the very idea of impending evils was overwhelming, and the sweat of blood shows that it was, what are we to suppose their actual endurance to have been ?

That Christ our Lord suffered the most excruciating torments of mind and body is certain. In the first place, there was no part of His body that did not experience the most agonising torture. His hands and feet were fastened with nails to the cross; His head was pierced with thorns and smitten with a reed; His face was befouled with spittle and buffeted with blows; His whole body was covered with stripes.

Furthermore men of all ranks and conditions were gathered together against the Lord, and against his Christ. Gentiles and Jews were the advisers, the authors, the ministers of His Passion: Judas betrayed Him, Peter denied Him, all the rest deserted Him.

And while He hangs from the cross are we not at a loss which to deplore, His agony, or His ignominy, or both? Surely no death more shameful, none more cruel, could have been devised than this. It was the punishment usually reserved for the most guilty and atrocious malefactors, a death whose slowness aggravated the exquisite pain and torture I

His agony was increased by the very constitution and frame of His body. Formed by the power of the Holy Ghost, it was more perfect and better organised than the bodies of other men can be, and was therefore endowed with a superior susceptibility and a keener sense of all the torments which it endured.

And as to His interior anguish of soul, that too was no doubt extreme; for those among the Saints who had to endure torments and tortures were not without consolation from above, which enabled them not only to bear their sufferings patiently, but in many instances, to feel, in the very midst of them, filled with interior joy. I rejoice, says the Apostle, in my sufferings for you, and fill up those things that are wanting of the sufferings of Christ, in my flesh, for his body, which is the church;' and in another place: I am filled with comfort, I exceedingly abound with joy in all our tribulations. Christ our Lord tempered with no admixture of sweetness the bitter chalice of His Passion but permitted His human nature to feel as acutely every species of torment as if He were only man, and not also God.

Fruits Of Christ's Passion

It only remains now that the pastor carefully explain the blessings and advantages which flow from the Passion of Christ. In the first place, then, the Passion of our Lord was our deliverance from sin; for, as St. John says, He hath loved us, and washed us from our sins in his own blood. He hath quickened you together with him, says the Apostle, forgiving you all offences, blotting out the handwriting of the decree that was against us, which was contrary to us. And he hath taken the same out of the way, fastening it to the cross.

In the next place He has rescued us from the tyranny of the devil, for our Lord Himself says: Now is the judgment of the world; now shall the prance of this world be cast out. And I if I be lifted up from the earth, will draw all things to myself.

Again He discharged the punishment due to our sins. And as no sacrifice more pleasing and acceptable could have been offered to God, He reconciled us to the Father, appeased His wrath, and made Him favourable to us.

Finally, by taking away our sins He opened to us heaven, which was closed by the common sin of mankind. And this the Apostle pointed out when he said: We have confidence in the entering into the holies by the blood of Christ. Nor are we without a type and figure of this mystery in the Old Law. For those who were prohibited to return into their native country before the death of the high-priest typified that no one, however just and holy may have been his life, could gain admission into the celestial country until the eternal High-priest, Christ Jesus, had died, and by His death immediately opened heaven to those who, purified by the Sacraments and gifted with faith, hope, and charity, become partakers of His Passion.

Christ's Passion, -- A Satisfaction, A Sacrifice, A Redemption An Example

The pastor should teach that all these inestimable and divine blessings flow to us from the Passion of Christ. First, indeed, because the satisfaction which Jesus Christ has in an admirable manner made to God the Father for our sins is full and complete. The price which He paid for our ransom was not only adequate and equal to our debts, but far exceeded them.

Again, it (the Passion of Christ) was a sacrifice most acceptable to God, for when offered by His Son on the altar of the cross, it entirely appeased the wrath and indignation of the Father. This word (sacrifice) the Apostle uses when he says: Christ hath loved us, and hath delivered himself for us, an oblation and a sacrifice to God for an odour of sweetness.

Furthermore, it was a redemption, of which the Prince of the Apostles says: You were not redeemed with corruptible things as gold or silver, from your vain conversation of the tradition of your fathers: but with the precious blood of Christ, as of a lamb unspotted and undefiled. While the Apostle teaches: Christ hath redeemed us from the curse of the law, being made a curse for us.

Besides these incomparable blessings, we have also received another of the highest importance; namely, that in the Passion alone we have the most illustrious example of the exercise of every virtue. For He so displayed patience, humility, exalted charity, meekness, obedience and unshaken firmness of soul, not only in suffering for justice, sake, but also in meeting death, that we may truly say on the day of His Passion alone, our Saviour offered, in His own Person, a living exemplification of all the moral precepts inculcated during the entire time of His public ministry.

Admonition

This exposition of the saving Passion and death of Christ the Lord we have given briefly. Would to God that these mysteries were always present to our minds, and that we learned to suffer, die, and be buried together with our Lord; so that from henceforth, having cast aside all stain of sin, and rising with Him to newness of life, we may at length, through His grace and mercy, be found worthy to be made partakers of the celestial kingdom and glory !

ARTICLE V : "HE DESCENDED INTO HELL, THE THIRD DAY HE ROSE AGAIN FROM THE DEAD"

Importance Of This Article

To know the glory of the burial of our Lord Jesus Christ, of which we last treated, is highly important; but of still higher importance is it to the faithful to know the splendid triumphs which He obtained by having subdued the devil and despoiled the abodes of hell. Of these triumphs, and also of His Resurrection, we are now about to speak.

Although the latter presents to us a subject which might with propriety be treated under a separate and distinct head, yet following the example of the holy Fathers, we have deemed it fitting to unite it with His descent into hell.

First Part of this Article: "He Descended into Hell"

In the first part of this Article, then, we profess that immediately after the death of Christ His soul descended into hell, and dwelt there as long as His body remained in the tomb; and also that the one Person of Christ was at the same time in hell and in the sepulchre. Nor should this excite surprise; for, as we have already frequently said, although His soul was separated from His body, His Divinity was never parted from either His soul or His body.

"Hell"

As the pastor, by explaining the meaning of the word hell in this place may throw considerable light on the exposition of this Article, it is to be observed that by the word hell is not here meant the sepulchre, as some have not less impiously than ignorantly imagined; for in the preceding Article we learned that Christ the Lord was buried, and there was no reason why the Apostles, in delivering an Article of faith, should repeat the same thing in other and more obscure terms.

Hell, then, here signifies those secret abodes in which are detained the souls that have not obtained the happiness of heaven. In this sense the word is frequently used in Scripture. Thus the Apostle says: At the name of Jesus every knee shall bow, of those that are in heaven, on earth, and in hell; and in the Acts of the Apostles St. Peter says that Christ the Lord is again risen, having loosed the sorrows of hell.

Different Abodes Called Hell"

These abodes are not all of the same nature, for among them is that most loathsome and dark prison in which the souls of the damned are tormented with the unclean spirits in eternal and inextinguishable fire. This place is called gehenna, the bottomless pit, and is hell strictly so-called.

Among them is also the fire of purgatory, in which the souls of just men are cleansed by a temporary punishment, in order to be admitted into their eternal country, into which nothing defiled entereth. The truth of this doctrine, founded, as holy Councils declare,' on Scripture, and confirmed by Apostolic tradition, demands exposition from the pastor, all the more diligent and frequent, because we live in times when men endure not sound doctrine.

Lastly, the third kind of abode is that into which the souls of the just before the coming of Christ the Lord, were received, and where, without experiencing any sort of pain, but supported by the blessed hope of redemption, they enjoyed peaceful repose. To liberate these holy souls, who, in the bosom of Abraham were expecting the Saviour, Christ the Lord descended into hell.

"He Descended"

We are not to imagine that His power and virtue only, and not also His soul, descended into hell; but we are firmly to believe that His soul itself, really and substantially, descended thither, according to this conclusive testimony of David: Thou wilt not leave my soul in hell.

But although Christ descended into hell, His supreme power was in no degree lessened, nor was the splendour of His sanctity obscured by any blemish. His descent served rather to prove that whatever had been foretold of His sanctity was true; and that, as He had previously demonstrated by so many miracles, He was truly the Son of God.

This we shall easily understand by comparing the causes of the descent of Christ with those of other men. They descended as captives; He as free and victorious among the dead, to subdue those demons by whom, in consequence of guilt, they were held in captivity. Furthermore all others descended, either to endure the most acute torments, or, if exempt from other pain, to be deprived of the vision of God, and to be tortured by the delay of the glory and happiness for which they yearned; Christ the Lord descended, on the contrary, not to suffer, but to liberate the holy and the just from their painful captivity, and to impart to them the fruit of His Passion. His supreme dignity and power, therefore, suffered no diminution by His descent into hell.

Why He Descended into Hell

To Liberate The Just

Having explained these things, the pastor should next proceed to teach that Christ the Lord descended into hell, in order that having despoiled the demons, He might liberate from prison those holy Fathers and the other just souls, and might bring them into heaven with Himself. This He accomplished in an admirable and most glorious manner; for His august presence at once shed a celestial lustre upon the captives and filled them with inconceivable joy and delight. He also imparted to them that supreme happiness which consists in the vision of God, thus verifying His promise to the thief on the cross: This day thou shalt be with me in paradise.

This deliverance of the just was long before predicted by Osee in these words: O death, I will be thy death; O hell, I will be thy bite; ' and also by the Prophet Zachary: Thou also by the blood of thy testament hast sent forth thy prisoners out of the pit, wherein is no water; and lastly, the same is expressed by the Apostle in these words: Despoiling the principalities and powers, he hath exposed them confidently in open show, triumphing over them in himself.

But the better to understand the efficacy of this mystery we should frequently call to mind that not only the just who were born after the coming of our Lord, but also those who preceded Him from the days of Adam, or who shall be born until the end of time, obtain their salvation through the benefit of His Passion. Wherefore before His death and Resurrection heaven was closed against every child of Adam. The souls of the just, on their departure from this life, were either borne to the bosom of Abraham; or, as is still the case with those who have something to be washed away or satisfied for, were purified in the fire of purgatory.

To Proclaim His Power

Another reason why Christ the Lord descended into hell is that there, as well as in heaven and on earth, He might proclaim His power and authority, and that every knee should bow, of those that are in heaven, on earth, and under the earth.

And here, who is not filled with admiration and astonishment when he contemplates the infinite love of God for man! Not satisfied with having undergone for our sake a most cruel death, He penetrates the inmost recesses of the earth to transport into bliss the souls whom He so dearly loved and whose liberation from thence He had achieved.

Second Part of this Article: "The Third Day He arose again from the Dead"

We now come to the second part of the Article, and how indefatigable should be the labours of the pastor in its exposition we learn from these words of the Apostle: Be mindful that the Lord Jesus Christ is risen again from the dead. This command no doubt was addressed not only to Timothy, but to all others who have care of souls.

The meaning of the Article is this: Christ the Lord expired on the cross, on Friday at the ninth hour, and was buried on the evening of the same day by His disciples, who with the permission of the governor, Pilate, laid the body of the Lord, taken down from the cross, in a new tomb, situated in a garden near at hand. Early on the morning of the third day after His death, that is, on Sunday, His soul was reunited to His body, and thus He who was dead during those three days arose, and returned again to life, from which He had departed when dying.

"He arose Again"

By the word Resurrection, however, we are not merely to understand that Christ was raised from the dead, which happened to many others, but that He rose by His own power and virtue, a singular prerogative peculiar to Him alone. For it is incompatible with nature and was never given to man to raise himself by his own power, from death to life. This was reserved for the almighty power of God, as we learn from these words of the Apostle: Although he was crucified through weakness, yet he liveth by the power of God. This divine power, having never been separated, either from His body in the grave, or from His soul in hell, there existed a divine force both within the body, by which it could be again united to the soul, and within the soul, by which it could again return to the body. Thus He was able by His own power to return to life and rise from the dead.

This David, filled with the spirit of God, foretold in these words: His right hand hath wrought for him salvation, and his arm is holy. Our Lord confirmed this by the divine testimony of His own mouth when He said: I lay down my life that I may take it again . . . and I have power to lay it down: and I have power to take it up again. To the Jews He also said, in corroboration of His doctrine: Destroy this temple, and in three days I will raise it up. Although the Jews understood Him to have spoken thus of that magnificent Temple built of stone, yet as the Scripture testifies in the same place, he spoke of the temple of his body. We sometimes, it is true, read in Scripture that He was raised by the Father; but this refers to Him as man, just as those passages on the other hand, which say that He rose by His own power relate to Him as God.

"From the Dead"

It is also the peculiar privilege of Christ to have been the first who enjoyed this divine prerogative of rising from the dead, for He is called in Scripture the first-begotten from the dead, and also the first-born of the dead. The Apostle also says: Christ is risen from the dead, the first-fruits of them that sleep: for by a man came death, and by a man the resurrection of the dead. And as in Adam all die, so also in Christ all shall be made alive. But every one in his own order: the first-fruits Christ, then they that are of Christ.

These words of the Apostle are to be understood of a perfect resurrection, by which we are raised to an immortal life and are no longer subject to the necessity of dying. In this resurrection Christ the Lord holds the first place; for if we speak of resurrection; that is, of a return to life, subject to the necessity of again dying, many were thus raised from the dead before Christ, all of whom, however, were restored to life to die again. But Christ the Lord, having subdued and conquered death, so arose that He could die no morel according to' this most clear testimony: Christ rising again from the dead, dieth now no more, death shall no more have dominion over him.

"The Third Day"

In explanation of the additional words of the Article, the third day, the pastor should inform the people that they must not think our Lord remained in the grave during the whole of these three days. But as He lay in the sepulchre one full day, a part of the preceding and a part of the following day, He is said, with strictest truth, to have lain in the grave for three days, and on the third day to have risen again from the dead.

To prove that He was God He did not delay His Resurrection to the end of the world; while, on the other hand, to convince us that He was truly man and really died, He rose not immediately, but on the third day after His death, a space of time sufficient to prove the reality of His death.

"According to the Scriptures"

Here the Fathers of the first Council of Constantinople added the words, according to the Scriptures, which they took from St. Paul. These words they embodied with the Creed, because the same Apostle teaches the absolute necessity of the mystery of the Resurrection when he says: If Christ be not risen again, then is our preaching vain, and your faith is also vain . . . for you are yet in your sins. Hence,, admiring our belief of this Article St. Augustine says: It is no great thing to believe that Christ died. This the pagans, Jews, and all the wicked believe; in a word, all believe that Christ died. But that He rose from the dead is the belief of the Christians. To believe that He rose again, this we deem of great moment.

Hence it is that our Lord very frequently spoke to His disciples of His Resurrection, and seldom or never of His Passion without adverting to His Resurrection. Thus, when He said: The son of man . . . shall be delivered to the Gentiles, and shall be mocked, and scourged, and spit upon; and after they have scourged him, they will put him to death; He added: and the third day he shall rise again.' Also when the Jews called upon Him to give an attestation of the truth of His doctrine by some miraculous sign He said: A sign shall not be given to them, but the sign of Jonas the prophet. For as Jonas was in the whales belly three days and three nights: so shall the son of man be in the heart of the earth three days and three nights.

Three Useful Considerations on this Article

To understand still better the force and meaning of this Article, there are three things which we must consider and understand: first, why the Resurrection was necessary; secondly, its end and object; thirdly, the blessings and advantages of which it is to us the source.

Necessity Of The Resurrection

With regard to the first, it was necessary that Christ should rise again in order to manifest the justice of God; for it was most congruous that He who through obedience to God was degraded, and loaded with ignominy, should by Him be exalted. This is a reason assigned by the Apostle when he says to the Philippians: He humbled himself, becoming obedient unto death, even to the death of the cross. For which cause God also hath exalted him. He rose also to confirm our faith, which is necessary for justification; for the Resurrection of Christ from the dead by His own power affords an irrefragable proof that He was the Son of God. Again the Resurrection nourishes and sustains our hope. As Christ rose again, we rest on an assured hope that we too shall rise again; the members must necessarily arrive at the condition of their head. This is the conclusion which St. Paul seems to draw when he writes to the Corinthians and to the Thessalonians.' And Peter, the Prince of the Apostles, says: Blessed be the God and Father of our Lord Jesus Christ, who according to his great mercy hath regenerated us unto a lively nope, by the resurrection of Jesus Christ from the dead, unto the inheritance incorruptible.

Finally, the Resurrection of our Lord, as the pastor should inculcate, was necessary to complete the mystery of our salvation and redemption. By His death Christ liberated us from sin; by His Resurrection, He restored to us the most important of those privileges which we had forfeited by sin. Hence these words of the Apostle: He was delivered up for our sins, and rose again for our justification. That nothing, therefore, may be wanting to the work of our salvation, it was necessary that as He died, He should also rise again.'

Ends Of The Resurrection

From what has been said we can perceive what important advantages the Resurrection of Christ the Lord has conferred on the faithful. In the Resurrection we acknowledge God to be immortal, full of glory, the conqueror of death and the devil; and all this we are firmly to believe and openly to profess of Christ Jesus.

Again, the Resurrection of Christ effects for us the resurrection of our bodies not only because it was the efficient cause of this mystery, but also because we all ought to arise after the example of the Lord. For with regard to the resurrection of the body we have this testimony of the Apostle: By a man came death, and by a man the resurrection of the dead. In all that God did to accomplish the mystery of our redemption He made use of the humanity of Christ as an effective instrument, and hence His Resurrection was, as it were, an instrument for the accomplishment of our resurrection.

It may also be called the model of ours, inasmuch as His Resurrection was the most perfect of all. And as His body, rising to immortal glory, was changed, so shall our bodies also, before frail and mortal, be restored and clothed with glory and immortality. In the language of the Apostle: We look for the Saviour, our Lord Jesus Christ, who will reform the body of our lowness, made like to the body of his glory.

The same may be said of a soul dead in sin. How the Resurrection of Christ is proposed to such a soul as the model of her resurrection the same Apostle shows in these words: As Christ is risen from the dead by the glory of the Father, so we also may walk in newness of life. For if we have been planted together in the likeness of his death, we shall be also in the likeness of his resurrection. Again a little further on he says: Knowing that Christ rising again from the dead, dieth now no more, death shall no more have dominion over him. For in that he died to sin, he died once; but in that he liveth, he liveth unto God: so do you also reckon, that you are dead to sin, but alive unto God, in Christ Jesus.

Advantages Of The: Resurrection

From the Resurrection of Christ, therefore, we should draw two lessons: the one, that after we have washed away the stains of sin, we should begin to lead a new life, distinguished by integrity, innocence, holiness, modesty, justice, beneficence and humility; the other, that we should so persevere in that newness of life as never more, with the divine assistance, to stray from the paths of virtue on which we have once entered.

Nor do the words of the Apostle prove only that the Resurrection of Christ is proposed as the model of our resurrection; they also declare that it gives us power to rise again, and imparts to us strength and courage to persevere in holiness and righteousness, and in the observance of the Commandments of God. For as His death not only furnishes us with an example, but also supplies us with strength to die to sin, so also His Resurrection invigorates us to attain righteousness, so that thenceforward serving God in piety and holiness, we may walk in the newness of life to which we have risen. By His Resurrection, our Lord accomplished this especially that we, who before died with Him to sin and to the world, should rise also with Him to a new order and manner of life.

Signs Of Spiritual Resurrection

The principal signs of this resurrection from sin which should be noted are taught us by the Apostle. For when he says: If you be risen with Christ, seek the things that are above, where Christ is sitting at the right hand of God, he distinctly tells us that they who desire to possess life, honour, repose and riches, there chiefly where Christ dwells, have truly risen with Christ.

When he adds: Mind the things that are above, not the things that are upon the earth, he gives, as it were, another sign by which we may ascertain if we have truly risen with Christ. As a relish for food usually indicates a healthy state of the body, so with regard to the soul, if a person relishes whatever things are true, whatever modest, whatever just, whatever holy, and experiences within him the sweetness of heavenly things, this we may consider a very strong proof that such a one has risen with Christ Jesus to a new and spiritual life.

ARTICLE VI : "HE ASCENDED INTO HEAVEN, SITTETH AT THE RIGHT HAND OF GOD THE FATHER ALMIGHTY"

Importance Of This Article

Filled with the Spirit of God, and contemplating the blessed and glorious Ascension of our Lord, the Prophet David exhorts all to celebrate that splendid triumph with the greatest joy and gladness: Clap your hands, all ye nations: shout unto God with he voice of joy.... God is ascended with jubilee.

The pastor will hence learn that this mystery should be explained with the greatest diligence; and that he should take care that the people not only perceive it with faith and understanding, but that they also strive as far as possible, with the Lord's help to reflect it in their lives and actions.

First Part of this Article: "He Ascended into Heaven"

With regard, then, to the exposition of this sixth Article, which has reference principally to this divine mystery, we shall begin with its first part, and point out its force and meaning.

"Into Heaven"

This, then, the faithful must believe without hesitation, that Jesus Christ, having fully accomplished the work of Redemption, ascended as man, body and soul, into heaven; for as God He never forsook heaven, filling as He does all places with His Divinity.

"He Ascended"

The pastor is also to teach that He ascended by His own power, not being taken up by the power of another, as was Elias, who was carried to heaven in a fiery chariot; or, as the Prophet Habacuc, or Philip, the deacon, who were borne through the air by the divine power, and traversed great distances.

Neither did He ascend into heaven solely by the exercise of His supreme power as God, but also by virtue of the power which He possessed as man. Although human power alone was insufficient to accomplish this, yet the virtue with which the blessed soul of Christ was endowed was capable of moving the body as it pleased, and His body, now glorified, readily obeyed the behest of the soul that moved it. Hence, we believe that Christ ascended into heaven as God and man by His own power.

Second Part of this Article: "Sitteth at the Right Hand of God the Father Almighty"

The words He sitteth at the right hand of the Father form the second part of this Article. In these words we observe a figure of speech; that is, a use of words in other than their literal sense, as frequently happens in Scripture, when, accommodating its language to human ideas, it attributes human affections and human members to God, who, spirit as He is, admits of nothing corporeal.

"At the Right Hand"

As among men he who sits at the right hand is considered to occupy the most honourable place, so, transferring the same idea to celestial things, to express the glory which Christ as man has obtained above all others, we confess that He sits at the right hand of the Father.

"Sitteth"

To sit does not imply here position and posture of body, but expresses the firm and permanent possession of royal and supreme power and glory which He received from the Father, and of which the Apostle says: Raising him up from the dead, and setting him on his right hand in the heavenly places, above all principality, and power, and virtue, and domination, and every name that is named, not only in this world, but also in that which is to come; and he hath subjected all things under his feet. These words manifestly imply that this glory belongs to our Lord in so special and exclusive a manner that it cannot apply to any other created being. Hence in another place the Apostle testifies: To which of the angels said he at any time: Sit on my right hand.

Reflections on the Ascension:

Its History

The pastor should explain the sense of the Article more at length by detailing the history of the Ascension, of which the Evangelist St. Luke has left us an orderly description in the Acts of the Apostles.

Greatness Of This Mystery

In this exposition he should observe, in the first place, that all other mysteries refer to the Ascension as to their end and find in it their perfection and completion; for as all the mysteries of religion commence with the Incarnation of our Lord, so His sojourn on earth terminates with His Ascension.

Moreover the other Articles of the Creed which regard Christ the Lord show His great humility and lowliness. Nothing can be conceived more humble, nothing more lowly, than that the Son of God assumed our weak human nature, and suffered and died for us. But nothing more magnificently, nothing more admirably, proclaims His sovereign glory and divine majesty than what is contained in the present and in the preceding Article, in which we declare that He rose from the dead, ascended into heaven, and sits at the right hand of God the Father.

Reasons Of The Ascension

When the pastor has explained these truths, he should next accurately show why Christ the Lord ascended into heaven.

First of all, He ascended because the glorious kingdom of the highest heavens, not the obscure abode of this earth, presented a suitable dwelling place for Him whose body, rising from the tomb, was clothed with the glory of immortality.

He ascended, however, not only to possess the throne of glory and the kingdom which He had merited by His blood, but also to attend to whatever regards our salvation.

Again, He ascended to prove thereby that His kingdom is not of this world. For the kingdoms of this world are earthly and transient, and are based upon wealth and the power of the flesh; but the kingdom of Christ is not, as the Jews expected, earthly, but spiritual and eternal. Its resources and riches, too, are spiritual, as He showed by placing His throne in the heavens, where they are counted richer and wealthier who seek most earnestly the things that are of God, according to these words of St. James: Hath not God chosen the poor in this world, rich in faith, and heirs of the kingdom which God hath promised to them that love him?

He also ascended into heaven in order to teach us to follow Him thither in mind and heart. For as by His death and Resurrection He bequeathed to us an example of dying and rising again in spirit, so by His Ascension He teaches and instructs us that though dwelling on earth, we should raise ourselves in desire to heaven, confessing that we are pilgrims and strangers on the earth, seeking a country and that we are fellow-citizens with the saints, and the domestics of God, for, says the same Apostle, our conversation is in heaven

Results Of The Ascension

The extent and greatness of the unutterable blessings which the bounty of God has showered on us were long before, as the Apostle interprets, sung by the inspired David: Ascending on high, he led captivity captive: He gave gifts to men.' For on the tenth day He sent down the Holy Ghost, with whose power and plenitude He filled the multitude of the faithful then present, and so fulfilled that splendid promise: It is expedient to you that I go: for if I go not, the Paraclete will not come to you; but if I go, I will send him to you.

He also ascended into heaven, according to the Apostle, that he may appear in the presence of God f or us, and discharge for us the office of advocate with the Father. My little children, says St. John, these things I write to you, that you may not sin. But if any man sin, we have an. advocate with the Father, Jesus Christ the just: and

122

he is the propitiation for our sins. There is nothing from which the faithful should derive greater joy and gladness of soul than from the reflection that Jesus Christ is constituted our advocate and the mediator of our salvation with the Eternal Father, with whom His influence and authority are supreme.

Finally, by His Ascension He has prepared for us a place, as He had promised, and has entered, as our head, in the name of us all, into the possession of the glory of heaven." Ascending into heaven, He threw open its gates, which had been closed by the sin of Adam; and, as He foretold to His disciples at His Last Supper, secured to us a way by which we may arrive at eternal happiness. In order to give an open proof of this by its fulfilment, He introduced with Himself into the mansions of eternal bliss the souls of the just whom He had liberated from hell.

Virtues Promoted By The Ascension.

A series of important advantages followed in the train of this admirable profusion of celestial gifts. In the first place, the merit of our faith was considerably augmented; because faith has for its object those things which fall not under the senses, but are far raised above the reach of human reason and intelligence. If, therefore, the Lord had not departed from us, the merit of our faith would not be the same; for Christ the Lord has said: Blessed are they that have not seen, and have believed

In the next place, the Ascension of Christ into heaven contributes much to confirm our hope. Believing that Christ, as man, ascended into heaven, and placed our nature at the right hand of God the Father, we are animated with a strong hope that we, as members, shall also ascend thither, to be there united to our Head, according to these words of our Lord Himself: Father, I will that where I am, they also whom thou hast given me may be with me

Another most important advantage is that He has taken our affections to heaven and inflamed them with the Spirit of God; for most truly has it been said that where our treasure is, there also is our heart. And, indeed, were Christ the Lord still dwelling on earth, the contemplation of His human nature and His company would absorb all our thoughts, and we should view the author of such blessings only as man, and cherish towards Him a sort of earthly affection. But by His Ascension into heaven He has spiritualised our affection and has made us venerate and love as God Him whom, on account of His absence, we see only in thought. This we learn in part from the example of the Apostles, who while our Lord was personally present with them, seemed to judge of Him in some measure in a human light; and in part from these words of our Lord Himself: It is expedient to you that I go. The imperfect affection with which they loved Christ Jesus when present had to be perfected by divine love, and that by the coming of the Holy Ghost; and therefore He immediately subjoins: If I go not, the Paraclete will not come to you.

The Ascension Benefits The Church And The Individual

Besides, He thus enlarged His household on earth, that is, His Church, which was to be governed by the power and guidance of the Holy Spirit. He left Peter, the Prince of the Apostles, as its chief pastor and supreme head upon earth; moreover he gave some apostles, and some prophets, and other some evangelists, and other some pastors and doctors. Thus seated at the right hand of the Father He continually bestows different gifts on different men; for as the Apostle testifies: To every one of us is given grace, according to the measure of the giving of Christ.

Finally, what we have already taught of the mystery of His death and Resurrection the faithful should deem not less true of His Ascension. For although we owe our Redemption and salvation to the Passion of Christ, whose merits opened heaven to the just, yet

His Ascension is not only proposed to us as a model, which teaches us to look on high and ascend in spirit into heaven, but it also imparts to us a divine virtue which enables us to accomplish what it teaches.

ARTICLE VII : "FROM THENCE HE SHALL COME TO JUDGE THE LIVING AND THE DEAD"

Meaning Of This Article

For the glory and adornment of His Church Jesus Christ is invested with three eminent offices and functions: those of Redeemer, Mediator, and Judge. Since in the preceding Articles it was shown that the human race was redeemed by His Passion and death, and since by His Ascension into heaven it is manifest that He has undertaken the perpetual advocacy and patronage of our cause, it remains that in this Article we set forth His character as Judge. The scope and intent of the Article is to declare that on the last day Christ the Lord will judge the whole human race.

"From Thence He Shall Come"

The Sacred Scriptures inform us that there are two comings of the Son of God: the one when He assumed human flesh for our salvation in the womb of a virgin; the other when He shall come at the end of the world to judge all mankind. This latter coming is called in Scripture the day of the Lord. The day of the Lord, says the Apostle, shall come, as a thief in the night; and our Lord Himself says: Of that day and hour no one knoweth.

"To Judge the Living and the Dead"

In proof of the (last) judgment it is enough to adduce the authority of the Apostle: We must all appear before the judgment-seat of Christ, that every one may receive the proper things of the body, according as he hath done, whether it be good or evil. There are numerous passages of Sacred Scripture which the pastor will find in various places and which not only establish the truth of the dogma, but also place it in vivid colours before the eyes of the faithful. And if, from the beginning of the world that day of the Lord, on which He was clothed with our flesh, was sighed for by all as the foundation of their hope of deliverance; so also, after the death and Ascension of the Son of God, we should make that other day of the Lord the object of our most earnest desires, looking for the blessed hope and coming of the glory of the great God.'

Two Judgments

In explaining this subject the pastor should distinguish two different occasions on which everyone must appear in the presence of the Lord to render an account of all his thoughts, words and actions, and to receive immediate sentence from his Judge.

The first takes place when each one of us departs this life; for then he is instantly placed before the judgment-seat of God, where all that he has ever done or spoken or thought during life shall be subjected to the most rigid scrutiny. This is called the particular judgment.

The second occurs when on the same day and in the same place all men shall stand together before the tribunal of their Judge, that in the presence and hearing of all human beings of all times each may know his final doom and sentence. The announcement of this judgment will constitute no small part of the pain and punishment of the wicked; whereas the good and just will derive great reward and consolation from the fact that it will then appear what each one was in life. This is called the general judgment.

Reasons For General Judgment

It is necessary to show why, besides the particular judgment of each individual, a general one should also be passed upon all men.

Those who depart this life sometimes leave behind them children who imitate their conduct, dependents, followers and others who admire and advocate their example, language and actions. Now by all these circumstances the rewards or punishments of the dead must needs be increased, since the good or bad influence of example, affecting as it does the conduct of many, is to terminate only with the end of the world. Justice demands that in order to form a proper estimate of all these good or bad actions and words a thorough investigation should be made. This, however, could not be without a general judgment of all men.

Moreover, as the character of the virtuous frequently suffers from misrepresentation, while that of the wicked obtains the commendation of virtue, the justice of God demands that the former recover, in the public assembly and judgment of all men, the good name of which they had been unjustly deprived before men.

Again, as the just and the wicked performed their good and evil actions in this life not without the cooperation of the body, it necessarily follows that these actions belong also to the body as to their instrument. It was, therefore, altogether suitable that the body should share with the soul the due rewards of eternal glory or punishment. But this can only be accomplished by means of a general resurrection and of a general judgment.

Next, it is important to prove that in prosperity and adversity, which are sometimes the promiscuous lot of the good and of the bad, everything is done and ordered by an all-wise and all-just Providence. It was, therefore, necessary not only that rewards should await the just and punishments the wicked, in the life to come, but that they should be awarded by a public and general judgment. Thus they will become better known and will be rendered more conspicuous to all; and in atonement for the unwarranted murmurings, to which on seeing the wicked abound in wealth and flourish in honours even the Saints themselves, as men, have sometimes given expression, a tribute of praise will be offered by all to the justice and Providence of God. My feet, says the Prophet, were almost moved, my steps had well nigh slipped, because I had a zeal on occasion of the wicked, seeing the prosperity of sinners; and a little after: Behold! these are sinners and yet abounding in the world, they have obtained riches; and I said, Then have I in vain justified my heart, and washed my hands among the innocent; and I have been scourged all the day, and my chastisement hath been in the morning. This has been the frequent complaint of many, and a general judgment is therefore necessary, lest perhaps men may be tempted to say that God walketh about the poles of heaven, and regards not the earth.

This Truth has Rightly been made an Article of the Creed

Wisely, therefore, has this truth been made one of the twelve Articles of the Christian Creed, so that should any begin to waver in mind concerning the Providence and justice of God they might be reassured by this doctrine.

Besides, it was right that the just should be encouraged by the hope, the wicked appalled by the terror, of a future judgment; so that knowing the justice of God the former should not be disheartened, while the latter through fear and expectation of eternal punishment might be recalled from the paths of vice. Hence, speaking of the last day, our Lord and Saviour declares that a general judgment will one day take place, and He describes the signs of its approach, that seeing them, we may know that the end of the world is at hand. At His Ascension also, to console His Apostles, overwhelmed with grief at His departure, He sent Angels, who said to them: This Jesus who is taken up from you into heaven, shall so come, as you have seen him going into heaven

Circumstances of the Judgment:

The Judge

That the judgment of the world has been assigned to Christ the Lord, not only as God, but also as man, is declared in Scripture. Although the power of judging is common to all the Persons of the Blessed Trinity, yet it is specially attributed to the Son, because to Him also in a special manner is ascribed wisdom. But that as man, He will judge the world, is taught by our Lord Himself when He says: As the Father hath life in himself, so he hath given to the Son also, to have life in himself; and he hath given him power to do judgment, because he is the son of man.

There is a peculiar propriety in Christ the Lord sitting in judgment; for sentence is to be pronounced on mankind, and they are thus enabled to see their Judge with their eyes and hear Him with their ears, and so learn their judgment through the medium of the senses.

Most just is it also that He who was most iniquitously condemned by the judgment of men should Himself be afterwards seen by all men sitting in judgment on all. Hence when the Prince of the Apostles had expounded in the house of Cornelius the chief dogmas of Christianity, and had taught that Christ was suspended from a cross and put to death by the Jews and rose the third lay to life, he added: And he commanded us to preach to the people, and to testify that this is he, who was appointed of God, to be the judge of the living and the dead.

Signs Of The General Judgment

The Sacred Scriptures inform us that the general judgment will be preceded by these three principal signs: the preaching of the Gospel throughout the world, a falling away from the faith, and the coming of Antichrist. This gospel of the kingdom, says our Lord, shall be preached in the whole world, for a testimony to all nations, and then shall the consummation come. The Apostle also admonishes us that we be not seduced by anyone, as if the day of the Lord were at hand; for unless there come a revolt first, and the man of sin be revealed, the judgement will not come.

The Sentence Of The Just

The form and procedure of this judgment the pastor will easily learn from the prophecies of Daniel, the writings of the Evangelists and the doctrine of the Apostle. The sentence to be pronounced by the judge is here deserving of more than ordinary attention.

Looking with joyful countenance on the just standing on His right, Christ our Redeemer will pronounce sentence on them with the greatest benignity, in these words: Come ye blessed of my Father, possess the kingdom prepared for you from the beginning of the world. That nothing can be conceived more delightful to the ear than these words, we shall understand if we only compare them with the condemnation of the wicked; and call to mind, that by them the just are invited from labor to rest, from the vale of tears to supreme joy, from misery to eternal happiness, the reward of their works of charity.

The Sentence Of The Wicked

Turning next to those who shall stand on His left, He will pour out His justice upon them in these words: Depart from me, ye cursed, into everlasting fire, prepared f or the devil and his angels.

The first words, depart from me, express the heaviest punishment with which the wicked shall be visited, their eternal banishment from the sight of God, unrelieved by one consolatory hope of ever recovering so great a good. This punishment is called by theologians the pain of loss, because in hell the wicked shall be deprived forever of the light of the vision of God.

The words ye cursed, which follow, increase unutterably their wretched and calamitous condition. If when banished from the divine presence they were deemed worthy to receive some benediction, this would be to them a great source of consolation. But since they can expect nothing of this kind as an alleviation of their misery, the divine justice deservedly pursues them with every species of malediction, once they have been banished.

The next words, into everlasting fire, express another sort of punishment, which is called by theologians the pain of sense, because, like lashes, stripes or other more severe chastisements, among which fire, no doubt, produces the most intense pain, it is felt through the organs of sense. When, moreover, we reflect that this torment is to be eternal, we can see at once that the punishment of the damned includes every kind of suffering.

The concluding words, which was prepared f or the devil and his angels, make this still more clear. For since nature has so provided that we feel miseries less when we have companions and sharers in them who can, at least in some measure, assist us by their advice and kindness, what must be the horrible state of the damned who in such calamities can never separate themselves from the companionship of most wicked demons ? And yet most justly shall this very sentence be pronounced by our Lord and Saviour on those sinners who neglected all the works of true mercy, who gave neither food to the hungry, nor drink to the thirsty, who refused shelter to the stranger and clothing to the naked, and who would not visit the sick and the imprisoned.

Importance of Instruction on this Article

These are thoughts which the pastor should very often bring to the attention of his people; for the truth which is contained in this Article will, if accepted with faithful dispositions, be most powerful in bridling the evil inclinations of the heart and in withdrawing men from sin. Hence we read in Ecclesiasticus: In all thy works remember thy last end, and thou shalt never sin.' And indeed there is scarcely anyone so given over to vice as not to be recalled to virtue by the thought that he must one day render an account before an all-just Judge, not only of all his words and actions, but even of his most secret thoughts, and must suffer punishment according to his deserts.

On the other hand, the just man will be more and more encouraged to lead a good life. Even though his days be passed in poverty, ignominy and suffering, he must be gladdened exceedingly when he looks forward to that day when, the conflicts of this wretched life being over, he shall be declared victorious in the hearing of all men, and shall be admitted into his heavenly country to be crowned with divine honours that shall never fade.

It only remains, then, for the pastor to exhort the faithful to lead holy lives and practice every virtue, that thus they may be enabled to look forward with confidence to the coming of that great day of the Lord -- nay, as becomes children, even to desire it most fervently.

ARTICLE VIII : "I BELIEVE IN THE HOLY GHOST"

Importance Of This Article

Hitherto we have expounded, as far as the nature of the subject seemed to require, what pertains to the First and Second Per sons of the Holy Trinity. It now remains to explain what the Creed contains with regard to the Third Person, the Holy Ghost.

On this subject the pastor should omit nothing that study and industry can effect; for on this Article, no less than on those that preceded, ignorance or error would be unpardonable in a Christian. Hence, the Apostle did not permit some among the Ephesians to remain in ignorance with regard to the Person of the Holy Ghost. Having asked if they had received the Holy Ghost, and having received for answer that they did not so much as know that there was a Holy, Ghost, he at once demanded: In whom, therefore, were you baptised? to signify that a distinct knowledge of this Article is most necessary to the faithful.

From such knowledge they derive special fruit. For, considering attentively that whatever they have, they possess through the bounty and beneficence of the Holy Spirit, they begin to think more modestly and humbly of themselves, and to place all their hopes in the protection of God, which for a Christian is the first step towards consummate wisdom and supreme happiness.

"Holy Ghost"

The exposition of this Article, therefore, should begin with the force and meaning here attached to the words Holy Ghost. This appellation is equally true when applied to the Father and the Son, since both are spirit, both holy, and we confess that God is a Spirit; this name may also be applied to Angels, and the souls of the just. Care must be taken, therefore, that the faithful be not led into error by the ambiguity of the words.

The pastor, then, should teach that by the words Holy Ghost in this Article is understood the Third Person of the Blessed Trinity, a sense in which they are used, sometimes in the Old, and frequently in the New Testament. Thus David prays: Take not thy Holy Spirit from me; and in the Book of Wisdom we read: Who shall know thy thoughts, except thou give wisdom, and send thy Holy Spirit from above? And in another place it is said: He created her in the Holy Ghost.' We are also commanded, in the New Testament to be baptised in the name of the Father, and of the Son, and of the Holy Ghost. We read that the most holy Virgin conceived of the Holy Ghost; and we are sent by St. John to Christ, who baptizeth us in the Holy Ghost.' There are many other passages in which the words Holy Ghost occur.

No one should be surprised that a proper name is not given to the Third, as to the First and Second Persons. The Second Person is designated by a proper name, and called Son, because, as has been explained in the preceding Articles, His eternal birth from the Father is properly called generation. As, therefore, that birth is expressed by the word generation, so the Person, emanating from that generation, is properly called Son, and the Person, from whom he emanates, Father.

But as the production of the Third Person has no proper name, but is called spiration and procession, the Person produced is, consequently, designated by no proper name. His emanation has no proper name simply because we are obliged to borrow from created objects the names given to God and know no other created means of communicating nature and essence than that of generation. Hence we cannot discover a proper name to express the manner in which God communicates Himself entire, by the force of His love. Wherefore we call the Third Person Holy Ghost, a name, however, peculiarly appropriate to Him who infuses into us spiritual life, and without whose holy inspiration we can do nothing meritorious of eternal life.

"I Believe in the Holy Ghost"

The Holy Ghost Is Equal To The Father And The Son

The people, when once acquainted with the meaning of His name, should first of all be taught that the Holy Ghost is equally God with the Father and the Son, equally omnipotent and eternal, infinitely perfect, the supreme good, infinitely wise, and of the same nature as the Father and the Son.

All this is obviously enough implied by the force of the word in, when we say: I believe in the Holy Ghost; for this preposition is prefixed to each Person of the Trinity in order to express the exact nature of our faith.

The Divinity of the Holy Ghost is also clearly established by many passages of Scripture. When, in the Acts of the Apostles, St. Peter says, Ananias, Why hast thou conceived this thing in thy heart? he immediately adds: Thou hast not lied to men, but to God, calling Him God to whom he had just before given the name Holy Ghost.

The Apostle, also, writing to the Corinthians, interprets what he says of God as said of the Holy Ghost. There are, he says, diversities of operations, but the same God, who worketh all in all; but, he continues, all these things one and the same Spirit worketh, dividing to every one according as he will.

In the Acts of the Apostles also what the Prophets attribute to God alone, St. Paul ascribes to the Holy. Ghost. Thus Isaias had said: I heard the voice of the Lord, saying: Whom shall I send? . . . And he said: Go, and thou shalt say to this people: Blind the heart of this people, and make their ears heavy, and shut their eyes, lest they see with their eyes, and hear with their ears. Having cited these words, the Apostle adds: Well did the Holy Ghost speak to our fathers, by Isaias the prophet.

Again, the Sacred Scriptures join the Person of the Holy Ghost to those of the Father and the Son, as, for example, when Baptism is commanded to be administered in the name of the Father, and of the Son, and of the Holy Ghost. There is thus no room left us of doubting the truth of this mystery. For if the Father is God, and the Son God, we must admit that the Holy Ghost, who is united with Them in the same degree of honour, is also God.

Besides, baptism administered in the name of any creature can be of no effect. Were you baptised in the name of Paul? says the Apostle, to show that such baptism could have availed nothing to salvation. Since, therefore, we are baptised in the name of the Holy Ghost, we must acknowledge the Holy Ghost to be God.

This same order of the Three Persons, which proves the Divinity of the Holy Ghost, is also found in the Epistle of St. John: There are three who give testimony in heaven, the Father, the Word, and the Holy Ghost, and these three are one; and also in that noble eulogy of the Holy Trinity, with which the Divine Praises and the Psalms are concluded: Glory be to the Father, and to the Son, and to the Holy Ghost.

Finally, what most strongly confirms this truth is the fact that Holy Scripture assigns to the Holy Ghost whatever attributes we believe proper to God. Wherefore to Him is ascribed the honour of temples, as when the Apostle says: Know you not that your members are the temple of the Holy Ghost? Scripture also attributes to Him the power to sanctify, to vivify, to search the depths of God, to speak by the Prophets, and to be present in all places, all of which can be attributed to God alone.

The Holy Ghost Is Distinct From The Father And The Son

The pastor should also accurately explain to the faithful that the Holy Ghost is not only God, but that we must also confess that He is the Third Person of the Divine Nature, distinct from the Father and the Son, and produced by Their will.

To say nothing of other testimonies of Scripture, the form of Baptism, taught by our Redeemer,' shows most clearly that the Holy Ghost is the Third Person, self-existent in the Divine Nature and distinct from the other Persons. It is a doctrine taught also by the Apostle when he says: The grace of our Lord Jesus Christ, and the charity of God, and the communication of the Holy Ghost, be with you all. Amen.

This same truth is still more explicitly declared in these words added to this Article of the Creed by the Fathers of the First Council of Constantinople to refute the impious folly of Macedonius: And in the Holy Ghost, the Lord and giver of life, who proceedeth from the Father, and the Son; who together with the Father and the Son, is adored and glorified; who spoke by the prophets.

"The Lord"

By confessing the Holy Ghost to be Lord they declare how far He excels the Angels, who are the noblest spirits created by God; for they are all, says the Apostle, ministering spirits, sent to minister for them who shall receive the inheritance of salvation.

"Life-Giver"

They also designate the Holy Ghost the giver of life because the soul lives more by its union with God than the body is nourished and sustained by its union with the soul. Since then, the Sacred Scriptures ascribe to the Holy Ghost this union of the soul with God, it is clear that He is most rightly called the giver of life.

"Who Proceedeth from the Father and the Son"

With regard to the words immediately succeeding: who proceedeth from the Father and the Son, the faithful are to be taught that the Holy Ghost proceeds by an eternal procession from the Father and the Son, as from one principle. This truth is proposed for our belief by the Creed of the Church, from which no Christian may depart, and is confirmed by the authority of the Sacred Scriptures and of Councils.

Christ the Lord, speaking of the Holy Ghost, says: He shall glorify me, because he shall receive of mine. We also find that the Holy Ghost is sometimes called in Scripture the Spirit of Christ, sometimes, the Spirit of the Father; that He is one time said to be sent by the Father, another time, by the Son, -- all of which clearly signifies that He proceeds alike from the Father and the Son. He, says St. Paul, who has not the Spirit of Christ belongs not to him. In his Epistle to the Galatians he also calls the Holy Ghost the Spirit of Christ: God hath sent the Spirit of his Son into your hearts, crying: Abba, Father. In the Gospel of St. Matthew, He is called the Spirit of the Father: It is not you that speak, but the Spirit of your Father that speaketh in you.

Our Lord said, at His Last Supper: When the Paraclete cometh whom I will send you, the Spirit of truth, who proceedeth from the Father, he shall give testimony of me. On another occasion, that the Holy Ghost will be sent by the Father, He declares in these words: whom the Father will send in my name. Understanding these words to denote the procession of the Holy Ghost, we come to the inevitable conclusion that He proceeds from both Father and Son.

The above are the truths that should be taught with regard to the Person of the Holy Ghost.

Certain Divine Works are Appropriated to the Holy Ghost

It is also the duty of the pastor to teach that there are certain admirable effects, certain excellent gifts of the Holy Ghost, which are said to originate and emanate from Him, as from a perennial fountain of goodness. Although the intrinsic works of the most Holy Trinity are common to the Three Persons, yet many of them are attributed specially to the Holy Ghost, to signify that they arise from the boundless charity of God towards us. For as the Holy Ghost proceeds from the divine will, inflamed, as it were, with love, we can perceive that these effects which are referred particularly to the Holy Ghost, are the result of God's supreme love for us.

Hence it is that the Holy Ghost is called a gift; for by the word gift we understand that which is kindly and gratuitously bestowed, without expectation of any return. Whatever gifts and graces, therefore, have been conferred on us by God -- and what have we, says the Apostle, that we have not received from God? -- we should piously and gratefully acknowledge as bestowed by the grace and gift of the Holy Ghost.

Creation, Government, Life

These gifts of the Holy Ghost are numerous. Not to mention the creation of the world, the propagation and government of all created beings, discussed in the first Article, we have just shown that the giving of life is particularly attributed to the Holy Ghost, and this is further confirmed by the testimony of Ezechiel: I will give you spirit and you shall live.

The Seven Gifts

The Prophet (Isaias), however, enumerates the chief effects which are most properly ascribed to the Holy Ghost: The spirit of wisdom and understanding, the spirit of counsel and fortitude, the spirit of knowledge and piety, and the spirit of the fear of the Lord. These effects are called the gifts of the Holy Ghost, and sometimes they are even called the Holy Ghost. Wisely, therefore, does St. Augustine admonish us, whenever we meet the word Holy Ghost in Scripture, to distinguish whether it means the Third Person of the Trinity or His gifts and operations.-' The two are as far apart as the Creator is from the creature.

The diligence of the pastor in expounding these truths should be the greater, since it is from these gifts of the Holy Ghost that we derive rules of Christian life and are enabled to know if the Holy Ghost dwells within us.

Justifying Grace

But the grace of justification, which signs us with the Holy Spirit of promise, who is the pledge of our inheritance,' transcends all His other most ample gifts. It unites us to God in the closest bonds of love, lights up within us the sacred flame of piety, forms us to newness of life, renders us partakers of the divine nature, and enables us to be called and really to be the sons of God.

ARTICLE IX : "I BELIEVE IN THE HOLY CATHOLIC CHURCH; THE COMMUNION OF SAINTS"

The Importance Of This Article

With what great diligence pastors ought to explain to the faithful the truth of this ninth Article will be easily seen, if we attend chiefly to two considerations.

First, as St. Augustine observes, the Prophets spoke more plainly and openly of the Church than of Christ, foreseeing that on this a much greater number may err and be deceived than on the mystery of the Incarnation. For in after ages there would not be wanting wicked men who, like the ape that would fain pass for a man, would claim that they alone were Catholics, and with no less impiety than effrontery assert that with them alone is the Catholic Church.

The second consideration is that he whose mind is strongly impressed with the truth taught in this Article, will easily escape the awful danger of heresy. For a person is not to be called a heretic as soon as he shall have offended in matters of faith; but he is a heretic who, having disregarded the authority of the Church, maintains impious opinions with pertinacity. Since, therefore, it is impossible that anyone be infected with the contagion of heresy, so long as he holds what this Article proposes to be believed, let pastors use every diligence that the faithful, having known this mystery and guarded against the wiles of Satan, may persevere in the true faith.

This Article hinges upon the preceding one; for, it having been already shown that the Holy Ghost is the source and giver of all holiness, we here profess our belief that the Church has been endowed by Him with sanctity.

First Part Of This Article : "I Believe In The Holy Catholic Church

The Latins, having borrowed the word ecclesia (church) from the Greeks, have transferred it, since the preaching of the Gospel, to sacred things. It becomes necessary, therefore, to explain its meaning.

"Church"

The word ecclesia (church) means a calling forth. But writers afterward used it to signify a meeting or assembly, whether the people gathered together were members of a true or of a false religion. Thus in the Acts it is written of the people of Ephesus that when the town-clerk had appeased a tumultuous assemblage he said: And if you inquire after any other matter, it may be decided in a lawful church. The Ephesians, who were worshippers of Diana, are thus called a lawful church (ecclesia). Nor are the Gentiles only, who knew not God, called a church (ecclesia); by the same name at times are also designated the councils of wicked and impious men. I have hated the church (ecclesiam) of the malignant, says the Prophet, and with the wicked I will not sit.

In common Scripture usage, however, the word was subsequently employed to signify the Christian society only, and the assemblies of the faithful; that is, of those who are called by faith to the light of truth and the knowledge of God, that, having forsaken the darkness of ignorance and error, they may worship the living and true God piously and holily, and serve Him from their whole heart. In a word, The Church, says St. Augustine, consists of the faithful dispersed throughout the world.'

Mysteries Which The Word Church Comprises

In this word are contained important mysteries. For, in the calling forth, which it signifies, we recognise at once the benignity and splendour of divine grace, and we understand that the Church is very unlike all other societies. Other bodies rest on human reason and prudence, but the Church reposes on the wisdom and counsels of God who has called us inwardly by the inspiration of the Holy Ghost, who opens the hearts of men; and outwardly, through the labor and ministry of pastors and preachers.

Moreover, the end of this vocation, that is, the knowledge and possession of things eternal will be at once understood if we but remember why the faithful of the Old Law were called a Synagogue, that is, a flock for, as St. Augustine teaches, they were so called, because, like cattle, which are wont to herd together. they looked only to terrestrial and transitory goods. Wherefore, the Christian people are justly called, not a Synagogue, but a Church, because, despising earthly and passing things, they pursue only things heavenly and eternal.

Other Names Given The Church In Scripture

Many names, moreover, which are replete with mysteries, have been used to designate the Christian body. Thus, by the Apostle, it is called the house and edifice of God. If, says he to Timothy, I tarry long, that thou mayest know how thou oughtest to behave thyself in the house of God, which is the church of the living God, the pillar and ground of truth. The Church is called a house, because it is, as it were, one family governed by one father of the family, and enjoying a community of all spiritual goods.

It is also called the flock of the sheep of Christ, of which He is the door and the shepherd. It is called the spouse of Christ. I have espoused you to one husband, says the Apostle to the Corinthians, that I may present you as a chaste virgin to Christ; and to the Ephesians: Husbands love your wives, as Christ also loved the church; and of marriage: This is a great sacrament, but I speak in Christ and in the church.

Finally, the Church is called the body of Christ, as may be seen in the Epistles to the Ephesians and Colossians. Each of these appellations has very great influence in exciting the faithful to prove themselves worthy of the boundless clemency and goodness of God, who chose them to be the people of God.

The Parts of the Church

These things having been explained, it will be necessary to enumerate the several component parts of the Church, and to point out their difference, in order that the faithful may the better comprehend the nature, properties, gifts, and graces of God's beloved Church, and by reason of them unceasingly praise the most holy name of God.

The Church consists principally of two parts, the one called the Church triumphant; the other, the Church militant. The Church triumphant is that most glorious and happy assemblage of blessed spirits, and of those who have triumphed over the world, the flesh, and the iniquity of Satan, and are now exempt and safe from the troubles of this life and enjoy everlasting bliss. The Church militant is the society of all the faithful still dwelling on earth. It is called militant, because it wages eternal war with those implacable enemies, the world, the flesh and the devil.

We are not, however, to infer that there are two Churches. The Church triumphant and the Church militant are two constituent parts of one Church; one part going before, and now in the possession of its heavenly country; the other, following every day, until at length, united with our Saviour, it shall repose in endless felicity.

The Members Of The Church Militant

The Church militant is composed of two classes of persons, the good and the bad, both professing the same faith and partaking of the same Sacraments, yet differing in their manner of life and morality.

The good are those who are linked together not only by the profession of the same faith, and the participation of the same Sacraments, but also by the spirit of grace and the bond of charity. Of these St. Paul says: The Lord knoweth who are his. Who they are that compose this class we also may remotely conjecture, but we can by no means pronounce with certainty. Hence Christ the Saviour does not speak of this portion of His Church when He refers us to the Church and commands us to hear and to obey her. As this part of the Church is unknown, how could we ascertain with certainty whose decision to recur to, whose authority to obey?

The Church, therefore, as the Scriptures and the writings of the Saints testify, includes within her fold the good and the bad; and it was in this sense that St. Paul spoke of one body and one spirit. Thus understood, the Church is known and is compared to a city built on a mountain, and visible from every side. As all must yield obedience to her authority, it is necessary that she may-be known by all.

That the Church is composed of the good and the bad we learn from many parables contained in the Gospel. Thus, the kingdom of heaven, that is, the Church militant, is compared to a net cast into the sea, to a field in which tares were sown with the good grain, to a threshing floor on which the grain is mixed up with the chaff, and also to ten virgins, some of whom were wise, and some foolish.

And long before, we trace a figure and resemblance of this Church in the ark of Noah, which contained not only clean, but also unclean animals.

But although the Catholic faith uniformly and truly teaches that the good and the bad belong to the Church, yet the same faith declares that the condition of both is very different. The wicked are contained in the Church, as the chaff is mingled with the grain on the threshing floor, or as dead members sometimes remain attached to a living body.

Those Who Are Not Members Of The Church

Hence there are but three classes of persons excluded from the Church's pale: infidels, heretics and schismatics, and excommunicated persons. Infidels are outside the Church because they never belonged to, and never knew the Church, and were never made partakers of any of her Sacraments. Heretics and schismatics are excluded from the Church, because they have separated from her and belong to her only as deserters belong to the army from which they have deserted. It is not, however, to be denied that they are still subject to the jurisdiction of the Church, inasmuch as they may be called before her tribunals, punished and anathematised. Finally, excommunicated persons are not members of the Church, because they have been cut off by her sentence from the number of her children and belong not to her communion until they repent.

But with regard to the rest, however wicked and evil they may be, it is certain that they still belong to the Church: Of this the faithful are frequently to be reminded, in order to be convinced that, were even the lives of her ministers debased by crime, they are still within the Church, and therefore lose nothing of their power.

Other Uses of the Word "Church"

Portions of the Universal Church are usually called churches, as when the Apostle mentions the Church at Corinth, at Galatia, of the Laodiceans, of the Thessalonians.

The private families of the faithful he also calls churches. The church in the family of Priscilla and Aquila he commands to be saluted; and in another place, he says: Aquila and Priscilla with the church that is in their house salute you much in the Lord. Writing to Philemon, he makes use of the same word.

Sometimes, also, the word church is used to signify the prelates and pastors of the church. If he will not hear thee, says our Lord, tell the church. Here the word church means the authorities of the-Church.

The place in which the faithful assemble to hear the Word of God, or for other religious purposes, is also called a church. But in this Article, the word church is specially used to signify both the good and the bad, the governed, as well as the governing.

The Marks Of The Church

The distinctive marks of the Church are also to be made known to the faithful, that thus they may be enabled to estimate the extent of the blessing conferred by God on those who have had the happiness to be born and educated within her pale.

"One'

The first mark of the true Church is described in the Nicene Creed, and consists in unity: My dove is one, my beautiful one is one. So vast a multitude, scattered far and wide, is called one for the reasons mentioned by St. Paul in his Epistle to the Ephesians: One Lord, one faith, one baptism.

Unity In Government

The Church has but one ruler and one governor, the invisible one, Christ, whom the eternal Father hath made head over all the Church, which is his body; the visible one, the Pope, who, as legitimate successor of Peter, the Prince of the Apostles, fills the Apostolic chair.

It is the unanimous teaching of the Fathers that this visible head is necessary to establish and preserve unity in the Church. This St. Jerome clearly perceived and as clearly expressed when, in his work against Jovinian, he wrote: One is elected that, by the appointment of a head, all occasion of schism may be removed. In his letter to Pope Damasus the same holy Doctor writes: Away with envy, let the ambition of Roman grandeur cease! I speak to the successor of the fisherman, and to the disciple of the cross. Following no chief but Christ, I am united in communion with your Holiness, that is, with the chair of Peter. I know that on that rock is built the Church. Whoever will eat the lamb outside this house is profane; whoever is not in the ark of Noah shall perish in the .flood.

The same doctrine was long before established by Saints Irenaeus and Cyprian. The latter, speaking of the unity of the Church observes: The Lord said to Peter, I say to thee, Peter! thou art Peter: and upon this rock I will build my Church. He builds His Church on one. And although after His Resurrection He gave equal power to all His Apostles, saying: As the Father hath sent me, I also send you, receive ye the Holy Ghost; yet to make unity more manifest, He decided by His own authority that it should be derived from one alone, etc.

Again, Optatus of Milevi says: You cannot be excused on the score of ignorance, knowing as you do that in the city of Rome the episcopal chair was first conferred on Peter, who occupied it as head of the Apostles; in order that in that one chair the unity of the Church might be preserved by all, and that the other Apostles might not claim each a chair for himself; so that now he who erects another in opposition to this single chair is a schismatic and a prevaricator.

Later on St. Basil wrote: Peter is made the foundation, because he says: Thou art Christ, the Son of the Living God; and hears in reply that he is a rock. But although a rock, he is not such a rock as Christ; for Christ is truly an immovable rock, but Peter, only by virtue of that rock. For Jesus bestows His dignities on others; He is a priest, and He makes priests; a rock, and He makes a rock; what belongs to Himself, He bestows on His servants.

Lastly, St. Ambrose says: Because he alone of all of them professed (Christ) he was placed above all.

Should anyone object that the Church is content with one Head and one Spouse, Jesus Christ, and requires no other, the answer is obvious. For as we deem Christ not only the author of all the Sacraments, but also their invisible minister -- He it is who baptises, He it is who absolves, although men are appointed by Him the external ministers of the Sacraments -- so has He placed over His Church, which He governs by His invisible Spirit, a man to be His vicar and the minister of His power. A visible Church requires a visible head; therefore the Saviour appointed Peter head and pastor of all the faithful, when He committed to his care the feeding of all His sheep, in such ample terms that He willed the very same power of ruling and governing the entire Church to descend to Peter's successors.

Unity In Spirit, Hope And Faith

Moreover, the Apostle, writing to the Corinthians, tells them that there is but one and the same Spirit who imparts grace to the faithful, as the soul communicates life to the members of the body. Exhorting the Ephesians to preserve this unity, he says: Be careful to keep the unity of the Spirit in the bond of peace; one body and one Spirit. As the human body consists of many members, animated by one soul, which gives sight to the eyes, hearing to the ears, and to the other senses the power of discharging their respective functions; so the mystical body of Christ, which is the Church, is composed of many faithful. The hope, to which we are called, is also one, as the Apostle tells us in the same place; for we all hope for the same consummation, eternal and happy life. Finally, the faith which all are bound to believe and to profess is one: Let there be no schisms amongst you, says the Apostle. And Baptism, which is the seal of our Christian faith, is also one.

"Holy"

The second mark of the Church is holiness, as we learn from these words of the Prince of the Apostles: You are a chosen generation, a holy nation.

The Church is called holy because she is consecrated and dedicated to God; for so other things when set apart and dedicated to the worship of God were wont to be called holy, even though they were material. Examples of this in the Old Law were vessels, vestments and altars. In the same sense the first-born who were dedicated to the Most High God were also called holy.

It should not be deemed a matter of surprise that the Church, although numbering among her children many sinners, is called holy. For as those who profess any art, even though they depart from its rules, are still called artists, so in like manner the faithful, although offending in many things and violating the engagements to which they had pledged themselves, are still called holy, because they have been made the people of God and have consecrated themselves to Christ by faith and Baptism. Hence, St. Paul calls the Corinthians sanctified and holy, although it is certain that among them there were some whom he severely rebuked as carnal, and also charged with grosser crimes.

The Church is also to be called holy because she is united to her holy Head, as His body; that is, to Christ the Lord,' the fountain of all holiness, from whom flow the graces of the Holy Spirit and the riches of the divine bounty. St. Augustine, interpreting these words of the Prophet: Preserve my soul, for I am holy," thus admirably expresses himself: Let the body of Christ boldly say, let also that one man, exclaiming from the ends of the earth, boldly say, with his Head, and under his Head, I am holy; for he received the grace of holiness, the grace of Baptism and of remission of sins. And a little further on: If all Christians and all the faithful, having been baptised in Christ, have put Him on, according to these words of the Apostle: "As many of you as have been baptised in Christ, have put on Christ"; if they are made members of his body, and yet say they are not holy, they do an injury to their Head, whose members are holy.

Moreover, the Church alone has the legitimate worship of sacrifice, and the salutary use of the Sacraments, which are the efficacious instruments of divine grace, used by God to produce true holiness. Hence, to possess true holiness, we must belong to this Church. The Church therefore it is clear, is holy, and holy because she is the body of Christ, by whom she is sanctified, and in whose blood she is washed.

"Catholic"

The third mark of the Church is that she is Catholic; that is, universal. And justly is she called Catholic, because, as St. Augustine says, she is diffused by the splendour of one faith from the rising to the setting sun."

Unlike states of human institution, or the sects of heretics, she is not confined to any one country or class of men, but embraces within the amplitude of her love all mankind, whether barbarians or Scythians, slaves or freemen, male or female. Therefore it is written: Thou . . . hast redeemed us to God, in thy blood, out of every tribe, and tongue, and people, and nation, and hast made us to our God a kingdom. Speaking of the Church, David says: Ask of me and I will give thee the Gentiles for thy inheritance, and the utmost parts of the earth for thy possession; and also, I will be mindful of Rahab and of Babylon knowing me; and man is born in her.

Moreover to this Church, built upon the foundation of the apostles and prophets, belong all the faithful who have existed from Adam to the present day, or who shall exist, in the profession of the true faith, to the end of time; all of whom are founded and raised upon the one corner-stone, Christ, who made both one, and announced peace to them that are near and to them that are far.

She is also called universal, because all who desire eternal salvation must cling to and embrace her, like those who entered the ark to escape perishing in the flood.. This (note of catholicity), therefore, is to be taught as a most reliable criterion, by which to distinguish the true from a false Church.

Apostolic

The true Church is also to be recognised from her origin, which can be traced back under the law of grace to the Apostles; for her doctrine is the truth not recently given, nor now first heard of, but delivered of old by the Apostles, and disseminated throughout the entire world. Hence no one can doubt that the impious opinions which heresy invents, opposed as they are to the doctrines taught by the Church from the days of the Apostles to the present time, are very different from the faith of the true Church.

That all, therefore, might know which was the Catholic Church, the Fathers, guided by the Spirit of God, added to the Creed the word Apostolic. For the Holy Ghost, who presides over the Church, governs her by no other ministers than those of Apostolic succession. This Spirit, first imparted to the Apostles, has by the infinite goodness of God always continued in the Church. And just as this one Church cannot err in faith or morals, since it is guided by the Holy Ghost; so, on the contrary, all other societies arrogating to themselves the name of church, must necessarily, because guided by the spirit of the devil, be sunk in the most pernicious errors, both doctrinal and moral.

Figures of the Church

The figures of the Old Testament have great power to stimulate the minds of the faithful and to remind them of these most beautiful truths. It was for this reason chiefly that the Apostles made use of these figures. The pastor, therefore, should not overlook so fruitful a source of instruction.

Among these figures the ark of Noah holds a conspicuous place. It was built by the command of God, in order that there might be no doubt that it was a symbol of the Church, which God has so constituted that all who enter therein through Baptism, may be safe from danger of eternal death, while such as are outside the Church, like those who were not in the ark, are overwhelmed by their own crimes.

Another figure presents itself in the great city of Jerusalem, which, in Scripture, often means the Church. In Jerusalem only was it lawful to offer sacrifice to God, and in the Church of God only are to be found the true worship and true sacrifice which can at all be acceptable to God.

"I Believe the Holy Catholic Church"

Finally, with regard to the Church, the pastor should teach how to believe the Church can constitute an Article of faith. Although reason and the senses are able to ascertain the existence of the Church, that is, of a society of men on earth devoted and consecrated to Jesus Christ, and although faith does not seem necessary in order to understand a truth which even Jews and Turks do not doubt; nevertheless it is from the light of faith only, not from the deductions of reason, that the mind can grasp those mysteries contained in the Church of God which have been partly made known above and will again be treated under the Sacrament of Holy Orders.

Since, therefore, this Article, no less than the others, is placed above the reach, and defies the strength of the human understanding, most justly do we confess that we know not from human reason, but contemplate with the eyes of faith the origin, offices and dignity of the Church.

This Church was founded not by man, but by the immortal God Himself, who built her upon a most solid rock. The Highest himself, says the Prophet, hath founded her. Hence, she is called the inheritance of God, the people of God. The power which she possesses is not from man but from God.

Since this power, therefore, cannot be of human origin, divine faith can alone enable us to understand that the keys of the. kingdom of heaven are deposited with the Church, that to her has been confided the power of remitting sins," of denouncing excommunication, and of consecrating the real body of Christ; and t}tat her children have not here a permanent dwelling, but look for one above.

We are, therefore, bound to believe that there is one Holy Catholic Church. With regard to the Three Persons of the Holy Trinity, the Father, the Son, and the Holy Ghost, we not

only believe them, but also believe in them. But here we make use of a different form of expression, professing to believe the holy, not in the holy Catholic Church. By this difference of expression we distinguish God, the author of all things, from His works, and acknowledge that all the exalted benefits bestowed on the Church are due to God's bounty.

Second Part of this Article: "The Communion of Saints"

The Evangelist St. John, writing to the faithful on the divine mysteries, explains as follows why he undertook to instruct them in these truths: That you may have fellowship with us, and our fellowship may be with the Father, and with his son Jesus Christ. This fellowship consists in the Communion of Saints, the subject of the present Article.

Importance Of This Truth

Would that in its exposition pastors imitated the zeal of Paul and of the other Apostles. For not only is it a development of the preceding Article and a doctrine productive of abundant fruit; it also teaches the use to be made of the mysteries contained in the Creed, because the great end to which we should direct all our study and knowledge of them is that we may be admitted into this most august and blessed society of the Saints, and may steadily persevere therein, giving thanks with joy to God the Father, who hath made us worthy to be partakers of the lot of the saints in light.

Meaning of "The Communion of Saints"

The faithful, therefore, in the first place are to be informed that this part of the Article, is, as it were, a sort of explanation of the preceding part which regards the unity, sanctity and catholicity of the Church. For the unity of the Spirit, by which she is governed, brings it about that whatsoever has been given to the Church is held as a common possession by all her members.

Communion Of Sacraments

The fruit of all the Sacraments is common to all the faithful, and these Sacraments, particularly Baptism, the door, as it were, by which we are admitted into the Church, are so many sacred bonds which bind and unite them to Christ. That this communion of Saints implies a communion of Sacraments, the Fathers declare in these words of the Creed: I confess one Baptism. After Baptism, the Eucharist holds the first place in reference to this communion, and after that the other Sacraments; for although this name (communion) is applicable to all the Sacraments, inasmuch as they unite us to God, and render us partakers of Him whose grace we receive, yet it belongs in a peculiar manner to the Eucharist which actually produces this communion.

Communion Of Good Works

But there is also another communion in the Church which demands attention. Every pious and holy action done by one belongs to and becomes profitable to all through charity, which seeketh not her Own. This is proved by the testimony of St. Ambrose, who, explaining these words of the Psalmist, I am a partaker with all them that f ear thee, observes: As we say that a limb is partaker of the entire body, so are we partakers with all that fear God. Therefore has Christ taught us that form of prayer in which we say our, not my bread; and the other Petitions are equally general, not confined to ourselves alone, but directed also to the common interest and the salvation of all.

This communication of goods is often very aptly illustrated in Scripture by a comparison borrowed from the members of the human body. In the human body there are many members, but though many, they yet constitute but one body, in which each performs its own, not all the same, functions. All do not enjoy equal dignity, or discharge functions alike useful or honourable; nor does one propose to itself its own exclusive advantage, but that Of the entire body. Besides, they are so well organised

and knit together that if one suffers, the rest likewise suffer on account of their affinity and sympathy of nature; and if, on the contrary, one enjoys health, the feeling of pleasure is common to all.

The same may be observed in the Church. She is composed of various members; that is, of different nations, of Jews, Gentiles, freemen and slaves, of rich and poor; when they have been baptised, they constitute one body with Christ, of which He is the Head. To each member of the Church is also assigned his own peculiar office. As some are appointed apostles, some teachers, but all for the common good; so to some it belongs to govern and teach, to others to be subject and to obey.

Those Who Share In This Communion

The advantages of so many and such exalted blessings bestowed by Almighty God are enjoyed by those who lead a Christian life in charity, and are just and beloved of God. As to the dead members; that is, those who are bound in the thraldom of sin and estranged from the grace of God, they are not so deprived of these advantages as to cease to be members of this body; but since they are dead members, they do not share in the spiritual fruit which is communicated to the just and pious. However, as they are in the Church, they are assisted in recovering lost grace and life by those who live by the Spirit; and they also enjoy those benefits which are without doubt denied to those who are entirely cut off from the Church.

Communion In Other Blessings

Not only the gifts which justify and endear us to God are common. Graces gratuitously granted, such as knowledge, prophecy, the gifts of tongues and of miracles, and others of the same sort, are common also, and are granted even to the wicked, not, however, for their own but for the general good, for the edification of the Church. Thus, the gift of healing is given not for the sake of him who heals, but for the sake of him who is healed.

In fine, every true Christian possesses nothing which he should not consider common to all others with himself, and should therefore be prepared promptly to relieve an indigent fellow-creature. For he that is blessed with worldly goods, and sees his brother in want, and will not assist him, is plainly convicted of not having the love of God within him.

Those, therefore, who belong to this holy communion, it is manifest, do now enjoy a certain degree of happiness and can truly say: How lovely are thy tabernacles, O Lord of hosts! my soul longeth and fainteth for the courts of the Lord.... Blessed are they who dwell in thy house, Lord.

ARTICLE X : "THE FORGIVENESS OF SINS"

Importance Of This Article

The enumeration of this among the other Articles of the Creed is alone sufficient to satisfy us that it conveys a truth, which is not only in itself a divine mystery, but also a mystery very necessary to salvation. We have already said that, without a firm belief of all the Articles of the Creed, Christian piety is wholly unattainable. However, should that which ought to be clear in itself seem to require the support of some authority, the declaration of our Lord will suffice. A short time previous to His Ascension into heaven, when opening the understanding of His disciples that they might understand the Scriptures, He bore testimony to this Article of the Creed, in these words: It behooved Christ to suffer, and to rise again from the dead the third day, and that penance and remission of sins should be preached, in his name, unto all nations, beginning at Jerusalem.

Let the pastor but weigh well these words, and he will readily perceive that the Lord has placed him under a most sacred obligation, not only of making known to the faithful whatever regards religion in general, but also of explaining with particular care this Article of the Creed.

The Church Has the Power of Forgiving Sins

On this point of doctrine, then, it is the duty of the pastor to teach that, not only is forgiveness of sins to be found in the Catholic Church, as Isaias had foretold in these words: The people that dwell therein shall have their iniquity taken away from them; but also that in her resides the power of forgiving sins; and furthermore that we are bound to believe that this power, if exercised duly, and according to the laws prescribed by our Lord, is such as truly to pardon and remit sins.

Extent of this Power:

All Sins That Precede Baptism

When we first make a profession of faith and are cleansed in holy Baptism, we receive this pardon entire and unqualified; so that no sin, original or actual, of commission or omission, re- mains to be expiated, no punishment to be endured. The grace of Baptism, however, does not give exemption from all the infirmities of nature. On the contrary, contending, as each of us has to contend, against the motions of concupiscence, which ever tempts us to the commission of sin, there is scarcely one to be found among us, who opposes so vigorous a resistance to its assaults, or who guards his salvation so vigilantly, as to escape all wounds.

All Sins Committed After Baptism

It being necessary, therefore, that a power of forgiving sins, distinct from that of Baptism, should exist in the Church, to her were entrusted the keys of the kingdom of heaven, by which each one, if penitent, may obtain the remission of his sins, even though he were a sinner to the last day of his life. This truth is vouched for by the most unquestionable authority of the Sacred Scriptures. In St. Matthew the Lord says to Peter: I will give to thee the keys of the kingdom of heaven; and whatsoever thou shalt bind upon earth, shall be bound also in heaven; and what- soever thou shalt loose on earth, shall be loosed also in heaven; and again: Whatsoever you shall bind upon earth, shall be bound also in heaven; and whatsoever you shall loose on earth, shall be loosed also in heaven.' Further, the testimony of St. John assures us that the Lord, breathing on the Apostles, said: Receive ye the Holy Ghost, whose sins you shall forgive they are forgiven them; and whose sins you shall retain, they are retained. '

Limitation of this Power:

It Is Not Limited As To Sins, Persons, Or Time

Nor is the exercise of this power restricted to particular sins. No crime, however heinous, can be committed or even conceived which the Church has not power to forgive, just as there is no sinner, however abandoned, however depraved, who should not confidently hope for pardon, provided he sincerely repent of his past transgressions.

Furthermore, the exercise of this power is not restricted to particular times. Whenever the sinner turns from his evil ways he is not to be rejected, as we learn from the reply of our Saviour to the Prince of the Apostles. When St. Peter asked how often we should pardon an offending brother, whether seven times, Not only seven times, said the Redeemer, but till seventy times seven.

It Is Limited As To Its Ministers And Exercise

But if we look to its ministers, or to the manner in which it is to be exercised, the extent of this divine power will not appear so great; for our Lord gave not the power of so sacred a ministry to all, but to Bishops and priests only. The same must be said regarding the manner in which this power is to be exercised; for sins can be forgiven only through the Sacraments, when duly administered. The Church has received no power otherwise to remit sin. Hence it follows that in the forgiveness of sins both priests and Sacraments are, so to speak, the instruments which Christ our Lord, the author and giver of salvation, makes use of, to accomplish in us the pardon of sin and the grace of justification.

Greatness of this Power

To raise the admiration of the faithful for this heavenly gift, bestowed on the Church by God's singular mercy towards us, and to make them approach its use with the more lively sentiments of devotion the pastor should endeavour to point out the dignity and the extent of the grace which it imparts. If there be any one means better calculated than another to accomplish this end, it is carefully to show how great must be the efficacy of that which absolves from sin and restores the unjust to a state of justification.

Sin Can Be Forgiven Only By The Power Of God

This is manifestly an effect of the infinite power of God, of that same power which we believe to have been necessary to raise the dead to life and to summon creation into existence. But if it be true, as the authority of St. Augustine assures us it is, that to recall a sinner from the state of sin to that of righteousness is even a greater work than to create the heavens and the earth from nothing, though their creation can be no other than the effect of infinite power, it follows that we have still stronger reason to consider the remission of sins as an effect proceeding from the exercise of this same infinite power.

With great truth, therefore, have the ancient Fathers declared that God alone can forgive sins, and that to His infinite goodness and power alone is so wonderful a work to be referred. I am he, says the Lord Himself, by the mouth of His Prophet, I am he who blotteth out your iniquities.

The remission of sins seems to bear an exact analogy to the cancelling of a pecuniary debt. None but the creditor can forgive a pecuniary debt. Hence, since by sin we contract a debt to God alone -- wherefore we daily pray: forgive us our debts sin, it is clear, can be forgiven by Him alone, and by none else.

This Power Communicated To None Before Christ

This wonderful and divine power was never communicated to creatures, until God became man. Christ our Saviour, although true God, was the first one who, as man, received this high prerogative from His heavenly Father. That you may know that the son of man hath power on earth to forgive sins (then said he to the man sick of the palsy), rise. take up thy bed, and go into thy house. As, therefore, He became man, in order to bestow on man this forgiveness of sins, He communicated this power to Bishops and priests in the Church, previous to His Ascension into heaven, where He sits forever at the right hand of God. Christ, however, as we have already said, remits sin by virtue of His own authority; all others, by virtue of His authority delegated to them as His ministers.

If, therefore, whatever is the effect of infinite power claims our highest admiration and reverence, we must readily perceive that this gift, bestowed on the Church by the bounteous hand of Christ our Lord, is one of inestimable value.

Sin Remitted Through The Blood Of Christ

The manner too, in which God, in the fullness of His paternal clemency resolved to cancel the sins of the world must powerfully move the faithful to contemplate the greatness of this blessing. It was His will that our offences should be expiated by the blood of His Only-begotten Son; that His Son should voluntarily assume the imputability of our sins, and suffer a most cruel death, the just for the unjust, the innocent for the guilty.

When, therefore, we reflect that we were not redeemed with corruptible things, as gold or silver, but with the precious blood of Christ, as of a lamb unspotted and undefiled, we are naturally led to conclude that we could have received no gift more salutary than this power of forgiving sins, which proclaims the ineffable Providence of God and the excess of His love towards us. This reflection must produce in all the most abundant spiritual fruit.

The Great Evil From Which Forgiveness Delivers Man

For whoever offends God, even by one mortal sin, instantly forfeits whatever merits he may have previously acquired through the sufferings and death of Christ, and is entirely shut out from the gate of heaven which, when already closed, was thrown open to all by the Redeemer's Passion. When we reflect on this, the thought of our misery must fill us with deep anxiety. But if we turn our attention to this admirable power with which God has invested His Church; and, in the firm belief of this Article, feel convinced that to every sinner is offered the means of recovering, with the assistance of divine grace, his former dignity, we must exult with exceeding joy and gladness, and must offer immortal thanks to God.

If, when we are seriously ill, the medicines prepared for us by the art and industry of the physician are wont to be welcome and agreeable to us, how much more welcome and agreeable should those remedies prove which the wisdom of God has established to heal our souls and restore us to the life of grace, especially since they bring with them, not, indeed, uncertain hope of recovery, like the medicines that are applied to the body, but assured health to such as desire to be cured !

Exhortation:

This Remedy To Be Used

The faithful, therefore, having formed a just conception of the dignity of so excellent and exalted a blessing, should be exhorted to profit by it to the best of their ability. For he who makes no use of what is really useful and necessary must be supposed to despise it; particularly since, in communicating to the Church the power of forgiving sin, the Lord did so with the view that all should have recourse to this healing remedy. As without Baptism no one can be cleansed, so in order to recover the grace of Baptism, forfeited by actual mortal guilt, recourse must be had to another means of expiation, -- namely, the Sacrament of Penance.

Abuse To Be Guarded Against

But here the faithful are to be admonished to guard against the danger of becoming more prone to sin, or slow to repentance, from a presumption that they can have recourse to this power of forgiving sins which is so complete and, as we saw, unrestricted as to time. For, as such a propensity to sin would manifestly convict them of acting injuriously and contumaciously to this divine power, and would therefore render them unworthy of the divine mercy; so this slowness to repentance gives great reason to fear that, overtaken by death, they may in vain confess their belief in the remission of sins, which by their tardiness and procrastination they deservedly forfeited.

ARTICLE XI : "THE RESURRECTION OF THE BODY"

Importance Of This Article

That this Article supplies a convincing proof of the truth of our faith appears chiefly from the fact that not only is it proposed in the Sacred Scriptures to the belief of the faithful, but is also confirmed by numerous arguments. This we scarcely find to be the case with regard to the other Articles, which justifies the inference that on this doctrine, as on its most solid basis, rests our hope of salvation; for according to the reasoning of the Apostle, If there be no resurrection of the dead, then Christ is not risen again; and if Christ be not risen again, then is our preaching vain, and your faith is also vain.

The diligence and zeal, therefore, of the pastor in the explanation of this dogma should not be less than the labor which the impiety of many has expended in efforts to overthrow it. That eminently important advantages flow to the faithful from the knowledge of this Article will be shown further on.

"The Resurrection of the Body"

That in this Article the resurrection of mankind is called the resurrection of the body, is a circumstance which deserves special attention. It was not, indeed, so named without a reason for the Apostles intended thus to convey a necessary truth, the immortality of the soul. Lest anyone, despite the fact that many passages of Scripture plainly teach that the soul is immortal, might imagine that it dies with the body, and that both are to be restored to life, the Creed speaks only of the resurrection of the body.

Although in Sacred Scripture the word flesh often signifies the whole man, as in Isaias, All flesh is grass, and in St. John, The Word was made flesh; yet in this place it is used to express the body only, thus giving us to understand that of the two constituent parts of man, soul and body, one only, that is, the body, is corrupted and returns to its original dust, while the soul remains incorrupt and immortal. As then, a man cannot be said to return to life unless he has previously died, so the soul could not with propriety be said to rise again.

The word body is also mentioned, in order to confute the heresy of Hymeneus and Philetus, who, during the lifetime of the Apostle, asserted that whenever the Scriptures speak of the resurrection, they are to be understood to mean not the resurrection of the body, but that of the soul, by which it rises from the death of sin to the life of grace. The words of this Article, therefore, as is clear, exclude that error, and establish a real resurrection of the body.

The Fact of the Resurrection:

Examples And Proofs Derived From Scripture

It will be the duty of the pastor to illustrate this truth by examples taken from the Old and New Testaments, and from all ecclesiastical history. In the Old Testament, some were restored to life by Elias and Eliseus; and, besides those who were raised to life by our Lord, many were raised by the holy Apostles and by many others. These many resurrections confirm the doctrine taught by this Article; for believing that many were recalled from death to life, we are also naturally led to believe the general resurrection of all. In fact the principal fruit which we should derive from these miracles is to yield to this Article our most unhesitating belief.

To pastors ordinarily conversant with the Sacred Volumes many Scripture proofs of this Article will at once present themselves. In the Old Testament the most conspicuous are those afforded by Job, when he says that in his flesh he shall see his God, and by Daniel when, speaking of those who sleep in the dust of the earth, he says, some shall awake to eternal life, others to eternal reproach. In the New Testament (the principal passages are) those of St. Matthew, which record the disputation our Lord held with the Sadducees, and those in which the Evangelists speak concerning the Last Judgment. To these we may also add the accurate reasoning of the Apostle on the subject in his Epistles to the Corinthians and Thessalonians.

Analogies From Nature

But although the resurrection is most certainly established by faith, it will, notwithstanding, be of material advantage to show from analogy and reason that what faith proposes is not at variance with nature or human reason.

To one asking how the dead should rise again, the Apostle answers: Foolish man! that which thou sowest is not quickened, except it die first; and that which thou sowest, thou sowest not the body that shall be, but bare grain, as of wheat, or of some of the rest; but God giveth it a body as he will; and a little after, It is sown in corruption, it shall rise in incorruption.

St. Gregory calls our attention to many other arguments of analogy tending to the same effect. The sun, he says, is every day withdrawn from our eyes, as it were, by dying, and is again recalled, as it were, by rising again; trees lose, and again, as it were, by a resurrection, resume their verdure; seeds die by putrefaction, and rise again by germination.

Arguments Drawn From Reason

The reasons also adduced by ecclesiastical writers seem well calculated to establish this truth. In the first place, as the soul is immortal, and has, as part of man, a natural propensity to be united to the body, its perpetual separation from it must be considered as unnatural. But as that which is contrary to nature and in a state of violence, cannot be permanent, it appears fitting that the soul should be reunited to the body, and consequently that the body should rise again. This argument our Saviour Himself employed, when in His disputation with the Sadducees He deduced the resurrection of the body from the immortality of the soul."

In the next place, as an all-just God holds out punishments to the wicked and rewards to the good, and as very many of the former depart this life unpunished for their crimes and many of the latter unrewarded for their virtues, the soul should be reunited to the body, in order, as the partner of her crimes, or the companion of her virtues, to become a sharer in her punishments or rewards. This argument has been admirably treated by St. Chrysostom in his homily to the people of Antioch.

To this effect also, the Apostle, speaking of the resurrection, says: If in this life only, we have hope in Christ, we are of all men the most miserable.. These words of St. Paul cannot be supposed to refer to the misery of the soul; for since the soul is immortal, it is capable of enjoying happiness in a future life, even though the body did not rise again. His words, then, must refer to the whole man; for, unless the body receive the due rewards of its labours, those who, like the Apostles, endured so many afflictions and calamities in this life, would necessarily be the most miserable of men. On this subject the Apostle is much more explicit in his Epistle to the Thessalonians: We glory in the churches of God, for your patience and faith, in all your persecutions and tribulations which you endure -- for an example of the just judgment of God, that you may be counted worthy of the kingdom of God, for which also you suffer; seeing it is a just thing with God to repay tribulation to them that trouble you; and to you who are troubled, rest with us when the Lord Jesus shall be revealed from heaven with the angels of his power, in a flame of fire, yielding vengeance to them who know not God, and who obey not the gospel of our Lord Jesus Christ.

Again, while the soul is separated from the body, man cannot enjoy that full happiness which is replete with every good. For as a part separated from the whole is imperfect, the soul separated from the body must be imperfect. Therefore, that nothing may be wanting to fill up the measure of its happiness, the resurrection of the body is necessary.

By these, and similar arguments, the pastor will be able to instruct the faithful in this Article.

All Shall Rise

He should also carefully explain from the Apostle who are to be raised to life. Writing to the Corinthians, he (St. Paul) says: As in Adam all die, so also in Christ all shall be made alive.' Good and bad then, without distinction, shall all rise from the dead, although the condition of all will not be the same. Those who have done good, shall rise to the resurrection of life; and those who have done evil to the resurrection of judgment.

When we say all we mean those who will have died before the day of judgment, as well as those who will then die. That the Church acquiesces in the opinion that all, without distinction, shall die, and that this opinion is more consonant with truth, is the teaching of St. Jerome and of St. Augustine.

Nor does the Apostle in his Epistle to the Thessalonians dissent from this doctrine, when he says: The dead who are in Christ shall rise first, then we who are alive, who are left, shall be taken up together with them in the clouds to meet Christ, into the air. St. Ambrose explaining these words says: In that very taking up, death shall take place, as it were, in a deep sleep, and the soul, having gone forth from the body, shall instantly return. For those who are alive shall die when they are taken up that, coming to the Lord, they may receive their souls from His presence; because in His presence they cannot be dead. This opinion is supported by the authority of St. Augustine in his book On the City of God."

The Body Shall Rise Substantially the Same

But as it is of vital importance to be fully convinced that the identical body, which belongs to each one of us during life, shall, though corrupt and dissolved into its original dust, be raised up again to life, this too is a subject which demands accurate explanation on the part of the pastor.

It is a truth conveyed by the Apostle when he says: This corruptible must put on incorruption, evidently designating by the word this, his own body. It is also clearly expressed in the prophecy of Job: In my flesh I shall see my God, whom I myself shall see, and mine eyes behold, and not another.

Further, this same truth is inferred from the very definition of resurrection; for resurrection, as Damascene defines it, is a return to the state from which one has fallen.

Finally, if we bear in mind the arguments by which we have just established a future resurrection, every doubt on the subject must at once disappear.

We have said that the body is to rise again, that every one may receive the proper things of the body, according as he hath done, whether it be good or evil. Man is, therefore, to rise again in the same body with which he served God, or was a slave to the devil;

that in the same body he may experience rewards and a crown of victory, or endure the severest punishments and torments.

Restoration Of All That Pertains To The Nature And Adornment Of The Body

Not only will the body rise, but whatever belongs to the reality of its nature, and adorns and ornaments man will be restored. For this we have the admirable words of St. Augustine: There shall then be no deformity of body; if some have been overburdened with flesh, they shall not resume its entire weight. All that exceeds the proper proportion shall be deemed superfluous. On the other hand, should the body be wasted by disease or old age, or be emaciated from any other cause, it shall be repaired by the divine power of Christ, who will not only restore the body unto us, but will repair whatever it shall have lost through the wretchedness of this life. In another place he says: Man shall not resume his former hair, but shall be adorned with such as will become him, according to the words: "The very hairs of your head are all numbered." God will restore them according to His wisdom.

Restoration Of All That Pertains To The Integrity Of The Body

But the members especially, because they belong to the integrity of human nature, shall all be restored at once. The blind from nature or disease, the lame, the maimed and the paralysed in any of their members shall rise again with entire and perfect bodies. Otherwise the desires of the soul, which so strongly incline it to a union with the body, would be far from satisfied; but we are convinced that in the resurrection these desires will be fully realised.

Besides, the resurrection, like the creation, is clearly to be numbered among the principal works of God. As, therefore, at the creation all things came perfect from the hand of God, we must admit that it will be the same in the resurrection.

These observations are not to be restricted to the bodies of the martyrs, of whom St. Augustine says: As the mutilation which they suffered would prove a deformity, they shall rise with all their members; otherwise those who were beheaded would rise without a head. The scars, however, which they received shall remain, shining like the wounds of Christ, with a brilliance far more resplendent than that of gold and of precious stones.

The wicked, too, shall rise with all their members, even with those lost through their own fault. The greater the number of members which they shall have, the greater will be their torments; and therefore this restoration of members will serve to increase not their happiness but their sorrow and misery; for merit or demerit is ascribed not to the members, but to the person to whose body they are united. To those, therefore, who shall have done penance, they shall be restored as sources of reward; and to those who shall have contemned it, as instruments of punishment.

If the pastor gives attentive consideration to these things, he can never lack words or ideas to move the hearts of the faithful, and enkindle in them the flame of piety; so that having before their minds the troubles and calamities of this life, they may look forward with eager expectations to that blessed glory of the resurrection which awaits the just.

The Condition of the Risen Body Shall be Different

It now remains for the faithful to understand how the body, when raised from the dead, although substantially the same body that had been dead, shall be vastly different and changed in its condition.

Immortality

To omit other points, the chief difference between the state of all bodies when risen from the dead and what they had previously been is that before the resurrection they were subject to dissolution, but when reanimated they shall all, without distinction of good and bad, be invested with immortality.

This admirable restoration of nature, as the Scriptures testify, is the result of the glorious victory of Christ over death. For it is written: He shall cast death down headlong for ever, and, O death! I will be thy death.' Explaining these words the Apostle says: And the enemy death shall be destroyed last; and St. John also says: Death shall be no more.

It was most fitting that the sin of Adam should be far exceeded by the merit of Christ the Lord, who overthrew the empire of death. It was also in keeping with divine justice, that the good should enjoy endless felicity, while the wicked, condemned to everlasting torments, shall seek death, and shall not find it, shall desire to die, and death shall fly from them. Immortality, therefore, will be common to the good and to the bad.

The Qualities Of A Glorified Body

In addition to this, the bodies of the risen Saints will be distinguished by certain transcendent endowments, which will ennoble them far beyond their former condition. Among these endowments four are specially mentioned by the Fathers, which they infer from the doctrine of St. Paul, and which are called gifts.

Impassibility

The first endowment or gift is impassibility, which shall place them beyond the reach of suffering anything disagreeable or of being affected by pain or inconvenience of any sort. Neither the piercing severity of cold, nor the glowing intensity of heat, nor the impetuosity of waters can hurt them. It is sown says the Apostle, in corruption, it shall rise in incorruption This quality the Schoolmen call impassibility, not incorruption, in order to distinguish it as a property peculiar to a glorified body. The bodies of the damned, though incorruptible, will not be impassible; they will be capable of experiencing heat and cold and of suffering various afflictions.

Brightness

The next quality is brightness, by which the bodies of the Saints shall shine like the sun, according to the words of our Lord recorded in the Gospel of St. Matthew: The just shall shine as the sun, in the kingdom of their Father. To remove the possibility of doubt on the subject, He exemplifies this in His Transfiguration. This quality the Apostle sometimes calls glory, sometimes brightness: He will reform the body of our lowness, made like to the body of his glory; " and again, It is sown in dishonour, it shall rise in glory. Of this glory the Israelites beheld some image in the desert, when the face of Moses, after he had enjoyed the presence and conversation of God, shone with such lustre that they could not look on it.

This brightness is a sort of radiance reflected on the body from the supreme happiness of the soul. It is a participation in that bliss which the soul enjoys just as the soul itself is rendered happy by a participation in the happiness of God.

Unlike the gift of impassibility, this quality is not common to all in the same degree. All the bodies of the Saints will be equally impassible; but the brightness of all will not be the same, for, according to the Apostle, One is the glory of the sun, another the glory of the moon, and another the glory of the stars, for star differeth from star in glory: so also is the resurrection of the dead.

Agility

To the preceding quality is united that which is called agility, by which the body will be freed from the heaviness that now presses it down, and will take on a capability of moving with the utmost ease and swiftness, wherever the soul pleases, as St. Augustine teaches in his book On the City of God, and St. Jerome On Isaias. Hence these words of the Apostle: It is sown in weakness, it shall rise in power.

Subtility

Another quality is that of subtility, which subjects the body to the dominion of the soul, so that the body shall be subject to the soul and ever ready to follow her desires. This quality we learn from these words of the Apostle: It is sown a natural body, it shall rise a spiritual body.

These are the principal points which should be dwelt on in the exposition of this Article.

Advantages of Deep Meditation on this Article

But in order that the faithful may appreciate the fruit they derive from a knowledge of so many and such exalted mysteries, it is necessary, first of all, to point out that to God, who has hidden these things from the wise and made them known to little ones, we owe a debt of boundless gratitude. How many men, eminent for wisdom or endowed with singular learning, who ever remained blind to this most certain truth ! The fact, then, that He has made known to us these truths, although we could never have aspired to such knowledge, obliges us to pour forth our gratitude in unceasing praises of His supreme goodness and clemency.

Another important advantage to be derived from reflection on this Article is that in it we shall find consolation both for ourselves and others when we mourn the death of those who were endeared to us by relationship or friendship. Such was the consolation which the Apostle himself gave the Thessalonians when writing to them concerning those who are asleep.

Again, in all our afflictions and calamities the thought of a future resurrection must bring the greatest relief to the troubled heart, as we learn from the example of holy Job, who supported his afflicted and sorrowing soul by this one hope that the day would come when, in the resurrection, he would behold the Lord his God.

The same thought must also prove a powerful incentive to the faithful to use every exertion to lead lives of rectitude and integrity, unsullied by the defilement of sin. For if they reflect that those boundless riches which will follow after the resurrection are now offered to them as rewards, they will be easily attracted to the pursuit of virtue and piety.

On the other hand, nothing will have greater effect in subduing the passions and withdrawing souls from sin, than frequently to remind the sinner of the miseries and torments with which the reprobate will be visited, who on the last day will come forth unto the resurrection of judgment.

ARTICLE XII : "LIFE EVERLASTING"

Importance Of This Article

The holy Apostles, our guides, thought fit to conclude the Creed, which is the summary of our faith, with the Article on eternal life: first, because after the resurrection of the body the only object of the Christian's hope is the reward of everlasting life; and secondly, in order that perfect happiness, embracing as it does the fullness of all good, may be ever present to our minds and absorb all our thoughts and affections.

In his instructions to the faithful the pastor, therefore, should unceasingly endeavour to light up in their souls an ardent desire of the promised rewards of eternal life, so that whatever difficult duties he may inculcate as a part of the Christian's life, the faithful may look upon as light, or even agreeable, and may yield a more willing and cheerful obedience to God.

"Life Everlasting"

As many mysteries lie concealed under the words which are here used to declare the happiness reserved for us, they are to be explained in such a manner as to make them intelligible to all, as far as each one's capacity will allow.

The faithful, therefore, are to be informed that the words, life everlasting, signify not only continuance of existence, which even the demons and the wicked possess, but also that perpetuity of happiness which is to satisfy the desires of the blessed. In this sense they were understood by the lawyer mentioned in the Gospel when he asked the Lord our Saviour: What shall I do to possess everlasting life? as if he had said, What shall I do in order to arrive at the enjoyment of perfect happiness? In this sense these words are understood in the Sacred Scriptures, as is clear from many passages.

"Everlasting"

The supreme happiness of the blessed is called by this name (life everlasting) principally to exclude the notion that it consists in corporeal and transitory things, which cannot be everlasting. The word blessedness is insufficient to express the idea, particularly as there have not been wanting men who, puffed up by the teachings of a vain philosophy, would place the supreme good in sensible things. But these grow old and perish, while supreme happiness is to be terminated by no lapse of time. Nay more, so far is the enjoyment of the goods of this life from conferring real happiness that, on the contrary, he who is captivated by a love of the world is farthest removed from true happiness; for it is written: Love not the world, nor the things which are in the world. If any man love the world, the charity of the Father is not in him, and a little farther on we read: The world passeth away, and the concupiscence thereof.

The pastor, therefore, should be careful to impress these truths on the minds of the faithful, that they may learn to despise earthly things, and to know that in this world, in which we are not citizens but sojourners, happiness is not to be found. Yet even here below we may be said with truth to be happy in hope, if denying ungodliness and worldly desires, we . . . live soberly, and justly, and godly in this world, looking for the blessed hope and coming of the glory of the great God and our Saviour Jesus Christ. Very many who seemed to themselves wise, not understanding these things, and imagining that happiness was to be sought in this life, became fools and the victims of the most deplorable calamities.

These words, life everlasting, also teach us that, contrary to the false notions of some, happiness once attained can never be lost. Happiness is an accumulation of all good without admixture of evil, which, as it fills up the measure of man's desires, must be eternal. He who is blessed with happiness must earnestly desire the continued enjoyment of those goods which he has obtained. Hence, unless its possession be permanent and certain, he is necessarily a prey to the most tormenting apprehension.

Life

The intensity of the happiness which the just enjoy in their celestial country, and its utter incomprehensibility to all but themselves alone, are sufficiently conveyed by the very words blessed life. For when in order to express any idea we make use of a word common to many things, it is clear that we do so because we have no exact term by which to express it fully. Since, therefore, to express happiness, words are adopted which are not more applicable to the blessed than to all who are to live for ever, this proves to us that the idea presents to the mind something too great, too exalted, to be expressed fully by a proper term. True, the happiness of heaven is expressed in Scripture by a variety of other words, such as the kingdom of God, of Christ, of heaven, paradise, the holy city, the new Jerusalem, my Father's house; yet it is clear that none of these appellations is sufficient to convey an adequate idea of its greatness.

The pastor, therefore, should not neglect the opportunity which this Article affords of inviting the faithful to the practice of piety, of justice and of all the other Christian duties, by holding out to them such ample rewards as are announced in the words life everlasting. Among the blessings which we instinctively desire life is certainly esteemed one of the greatest. Now it is chiefly by this blessing that we describe the happiness (of the just) when we say life everlasting. If, then, there is nothing more loved, nothing dearer or sweeter, than this short and calamitous life, which is subject to so many and such various miseries that it should rather be called death; with what ardour of soul, with what earnestness of purpose, should we not seek that eternal life which, without evil of any sort, presents to us the pure and unmixed enjoyment of every good?

Negative and Positive Elements of Eternal Life

The happiness of eternal life is, as defined by the Fathers, an exemption from all evil, and an enjoyment of all good.

The Negative

Concerning (the exemption from all) evil the Scriptures bear witness in the most explicit terms. For it is written in the Apocalypse: They shall no more hunger nor thirst, neither shall the sun fall on them, nor any heat; [10] and again, God shall wipe away all tears from their eyes: and death shall be no more, nor mourning nor crying, nor sorrow shall be any more, for the former things are passed away.

The Positive

As for the glory of the blessed, it shall be without measure, and the kinds of their solid joys and pleasures without number. Since our minds cannot grasp the greatness of this glory, nor can it possibly enter into our souls, it is necessary for us to enter into it, that is, into the joy of the Lord, so that immersed therein we may completely satisfy the longing of our hearts.

Although, as St. Augustine observes, it would seem easier to enumerate the evils from which we shall be exempt than the goods and the pleasures which we shall enjoy; yet we must endeavour to explain, briefly and clearly, these things which are calculated to inflame the faithful with a desire of arriving at the enjoyment of this supreme felicity.

But first of all we should make use of a distinction which has been sanctioned by the most eminent writers on religion; for they teach that there are two sorts of goods, one of which constitutes happiness, the other follows upon it. The former, therefore, for the sake of perspicuity, they have called essential blessings, the latter, accessory.

Essential Happiness

Solid happiness, which we may designate by the common appellation, essential, consists in the vision of God, and the enjoyment of His beauty who is the source and principle of all goodness and perfection. This, says Christ our Lord, is eternal life: that they may know thee, the only true God, and Jesus Christ, whom thou hast sent. These words St. John seems to interpret when he says: Dearly beloved, we are now the sons of God; and it hath not yet appeared what we shall be. We know that when he shall appear, we shall be like to him: because we shawl see him as he is. He shows, then, that beatitude consists of two things: that we shall behold God such as He is in His own nature and substance; and that we ourselves shall become, as it were, gods.

The Light Of Glory

For those who enjoy God while they retain their own nature, assume a certain admirable and almost divine form, so as to seem gods rather than men. Why this transformation takes place becomes at once intelligible if we only reflect that a thing is known either from its essence, or from its image and appearance, consequently, as nothing so resembles God as to afford by its resemblance a perfect knowledge of Him, it follows that no creature can behold His Divine Nature and Essence unless this same Divine Essence has joined itself to us, and this St. Paul means when he says: We now see through a glass in a dark manner; but then face to face.' The words, in a dark manner, St. Augustine understands to mean that we see Him in a resemblance calculated to convey to us some notion of the Deity.

This St. Denis' also clearly shows when he says that the things above cannot be known by comparison with the things below; for the essence and substance of anything incorporeal cannot be known through the image of that which is corporeal, particularly as a resemblance must be less gross and more spiritual than that which it represents, as we easily know from universal experience. Since, therefore, it is impossible that any image drawn from created things should be equally pure and spiritual with God, no resemblance can enable us perfectly to comprehend the Divine Essence. Moreover, all created things are circumscribed within certain limits of perfection, while God is without limits; and therefore nothing created can reflect His immensity.

The only means, then, of arriving at a knowledge of the Divine Essence is that God unite Himself in some sort to us, and after an incomprehensible manner elevate our minds to a higher degree of perfection, and thus render us capable of contemplating the beauty of His Nature. This the light of His glory will accomplish. Illumined by its splendour we shall see God, the true light, in His own light.

The Beatific Vision

For the blessed always see God present and by this greatest and most exalted of gifts, being made partakers of the divine nature, they enjoy true and solid happiness. Our belief in this happiness should be joined with an assured hope that we too shall one day, through the divine goodness, attain it. This the Fathers declared in their Creed, which says: I expect the resurrection of the dead and the life of the world to come.

An Illustration Of This Truth

These are truths, so divine that they cannot be expressed in any words or comprehended by us in thought. We may, however, trace some resemblance of this happiness in sensible objects. Thus, iron when acted on by fire becomes inflamed and while it is substantially the same seems changed into fire, a different substance; so likewise the blessed, who are admitted into the glory of heaven and burn with a love of God, are so affected that, without ceasing to be what they are, they may be said with truth to differ more from those still on earth than red-hot iron differs from itself when cold.

To say all in a few words, supreme and absolute happiness, which we call essential, consists in the possession of God; for what can he lack to consummate his happiness who possesses the God of all goodness and perfection?

Accessory Happiness

To this happiness, however, are added certain gifts which are common to all the blessed, and which, because more within the reach of human comprehension, are generally found more effectual in moving and inflaming the heart. These the Apostle seems to have in view when, in his Epistle to the Romans, he says: Glory and honour, and peace to every one that worketh good.

Glory

For the blessed shall enjoy glory; not only that glory which we have already shown to constitute essential happiness, or to be its inseparable accompaniment, but also that glory which consists in the clear and distinct knowledge which each (of the blessed) shall have of the singular and exalted dignity of his companions (in glory).

Honour

And how distinguished must not that honour be which is conferred by God Himself, who no longer calls them servants, but friends, brethren and sons of God! Hence the Redeemer will address His elect in these most loving and honourable words: Come, ye blessed of my Father, possess you the kingdom prepared for you. Justly, then, may we exclaim: Thy friends, O God, are made exceedingly honourable. They shall also receive the highest praise from Christ the Lord, in presence of His heavenly Father and His Angels.

And if nature has implanted in the heart of every man the common desire of securing the esteem of men eminent for wisdom, because they are deemed the most reliable judges of merit, what an accession of glory to the blessed, to show towards each other the highest veneration !

Peace

To enumerate all the delights with which the souls of the blessed shall be filled would be an endless task. We cannot even conceive them in thought. With this truth, however, the minds of the faithful should be deeply impressed -- that the happiness of the Saints is full to overflowing of all those pleasures which can be enjoyed or even desired in this life, whether they regard the powers of the mind or of the perfection of the body; albeit this must be in a manner more exalted than, to use the Apostle's words, eye hath seen, ear heard, or the heart of man conceived.

Thus the body, which was before gross and material, shall put off in heaven its mortality, and having become refined and spiritualised, will no longer require corporal food; while the soul shall be satiated to its supreme delight with that eternal food of glory which the Master of that great feast passing will minister to all.

Who will desire rich apparel or royal robes, where there shall be no further use for such things, and where all shall be clothed with immortality and splendour, and adorned with a crown of imperishable glory?

And if the possession of a spacious and magnificent mansion contributes to human happiness, what more spacious, what more magnificent, can be conceived than heaven itself, which is illumined throughout with the brightness of God ? Hence the Prophet, contemplating the beauty of this dwelling-place, and burning with the desire of reaching those mansions of bliss, exclaims: How lovely are thy tabernacles, O Lord of hosts! my soul longeth and fainteth for the courts of the Lord. My heart and my flesh have rejoiced in the living God. That the faithful may be all filled with the same sentiments and utter the same language should be the object of the pastor's most earnest desires, as it should also be of his zealous labours. For in my Father's house, says our Lord, there are many mansions," in which shall be distributed rewards of greater and of less value according to each one's deserts. He who soweth sparingly, shall also reap sparingly: and he who soweth in blessings, shall also reap blessings.

How to Arrive at the Enjoyment of this Happiness

The pastor, therefore, should not only encourage the faithful to seek this happiness, but should frequently remind them that the sure way of obtaining it is to possess the virtues of faith and charity, to persevere in prayer and the use of the Sacraments, and to discharge all the duties of kindness towards their neighbour.

Thus, through the mercy of God, who has prepared that blessed glory for those who love Him, shall be one day fulfilled the words of the Prophet: My people shall sit in the beauty of peace, and in the tabernacle of confidence, and in wealthy rest.

PART II : THE SACRAMENTS

Importance Of Instruction On The Sacraments

The exposition of every part of Christian doctrine demands knowledge and industry on the part of the pastor. But instruction on the Sacraments, which, by the ordinance of God, are a necessary means of salvation and a plenteous source of spiritual advantage, demands in a special manner his talents and industry By accurate and frequent instruction (on the Sacraments) the faithful will be enabled to approach worthily and with salutary effect these inestimable and most holy institutions; and the priests will not depart from the rule laid down in the divine prohibition: Give not that which is holy to dogs: neither cast ye your pearls before swine.

The Word "Sacrament"

Since, then, we are about to treat of the Sacraments in general, it is proper to begin in the first place by explaining the force and meaning of the word Sacrament, and showing its various significations, in order the more easily to comprehend the sense in which it is here used. The faithful, therefore, are to be informed that the word Sacrament, in so far as it concerns our present purpose, is differently understood by sacred and profane writers.

By some it has been used to express the obligation which arises from an oath, pledging to the performance of some service; and hence the oath by which soldiers promise military service to the State has been called a military sacrament. Among profane writers this seems to have been the most ordinary meaning of the word.

But by the Latin Fathers who have written on theological subjects, the word sacrament is used to signify a sacred thing which lies concealed. The Greeks, to express the same idea, made use of the word mystery. This we understand to be the meaning of the word, when, in the Epistle to the Ephesians, it is said: That he might make known to us the mystery (sacramentum) of his will; and to Timothy: great is the mystery (sacramentum) of godliness; and in the Book of Wisdom: They knew not the secrets (sacramenta) of God. In these and many other passages the word sacrament,- it will be perceived, signifies nothing more than a holy thing that lies concealed and hidden.

The Latin Doctors, therefore, deemed the word a very appropriate term to express certain sensible signs which at once communicate grace, declare it, and, as it were, place it before the eyes. St. Gregory, however, is of the opinion that such a sign is called a Sacrament, because the divine power secretly operates our salvation under the veil of sensible things.

Let it not, however, be supposed that the word sacrament is of recent ecclesiastical usage. Whoever peruses the works of Saints Jerome and Augustine will at once perceive that ancient ecclesiastical writers made use of the word sacrament, and some times also of the word symbol, or mystical sign or sacred sign, to designate that of which we here speak.

So much will suffice in explanation of the word sacrament. What we have said applies equally to the Sacraments of the Old Law; but since they have been superseded by the Gospel Law and grace, it is not necessary that pastors give instruction concerning them.

Definition of a Sacrament

Besides the meaning of the word, which has hitherto engaged our attention, the nature and efficacy of the thing which the word signifies must be diligently considered, and the faithful must be taught what constitutes a Sacrament. No one can doubt that the Sacraments are among the means of attaining righteousness and salvation. But of the many definitions, each of them sufficiently appropriate, which may serve to explain the nature of a Sacrament, there is none more comprehensive, none more perspicuous, than the definition given by St. Augustine and adopted by all scholastic writers. A Sacrament, he says, is a sign of a sacred thing; or, as it has been expressed in other words of the same import: A Sacrament is a visible sign of an invisible grace, instituted for our justification.

"A Sacrament is a Sign"

The more fully to develop this definition, the pastor should ex plain it in all its parts. He should first observe that sensible objects are of two sorts: some have been invented precisely to serve as signs; others have been established not for the sake of signifying something else, but for their own sakes alone. To the latter class almost every object in nature may be said to belong; to the former, spoken and written languages, military standards, images, trumpets, signals a and a multiplicity of other things of the same sort. Thus with regard to words; take away their power of expressing ideas, and you seem to take away the only reason for their invention. Such things are, therefore, properly called signs. For, according to St. Augustine, a sign, besides what it presents to the senses, is a medium through which we arrive at the knowledge of something else. From a footstep, for instance, which we see traced on the ground, we instantly infer that some one whose trace appears has passed.

Proof From Reason

A Sacrament, therefore, is clearly to be numbered among those things which have been instituted as signs. It makes known to us by a certain appearance and resemblance that which God, by His invisible power, accomplishes in our souls. Let us illustrate what we have said by an example. Baptism, for instance, which is administered by external ablution, accompanied with certain solemn words, signifies that by the power of the Holy Ghost all stain and defilement of sin is inwardly washed away, and that the soul is enriched and adorned with the admirable gift of heavenly justification; while, at the same time, the bodily washing, as we shall hereafter explain in its proper place, accomplishes in the soul that which it signifies.

Proof From Scripture

That a Sacrament is to be numbered among signs is dearly inferred also from Scripture. Speaking of circumcision, a Sacrament of the Old Law which was given to Abraham, the father of all believers," the Apostle in his Epistle to the Romans, says: And he received the sign of circumcision, a seal of the justice of the faith. In another place he says: All we who are baptised in Christ Jesus, are baptised in his death, words which justify the inference that Baptism signifies, to use the words of the same Apostle, that we are buried together with him by baptism into death.

Nor is it unimportant that the faithful should know that the Sacraments are signs. This knowledge will lead them more readily to believe that what the Sacraments signify, contain and effect is holy and august; and recognising their sanctity they will be more disposed to venerate and adore the beneficence of God displayed towards us.

"Sign of a Sacred Thing" : Kind of Sign Meant Here

We now come to explain the words, sacred thing, which constitute the second part of the definition. To render this explanation satisfactory we must enter somewhat more minutely into the accurate and acute remarks of St. Augustine on the variety of signs.

Natural Signs

Some signs are called natural. These, besides making themselves known to us, also convey a knowledge of something else, an effect, as we have already said, common to all signs. Smoke, for instance, is a natural sign from which we immediately infer the existence of fire. It is called a natural sign, because it implies the existence of fire, not by arbitrary institution, but from experience. If we see smoke, we are at once convinced of the presence of fire, even though it is hidden.

Signs Invented By Man,

Other signs are not natural, but conventional, and are invented by men to enable them to converse one with another, to convey their thoughts to others, and in turn to learn the opinions and receive the advice of other men. The variety and multiplicity of such signs may be inferred from the fact that some belong to the eyes, many to the ears, and the rest to the other senses. Thus when we intimate any thing to another by such a sensible sign as the raising of a flag, it is obvious that such intimation is conveyed only through the medium of the eyes; and it is equally obvious that the sound of the trumpet, of the lute and of the lyre,-instruments which are not only sources of pleasure, but frequently signs of ideas -- is addressed to the ear. Through the latter sense especially are also conveyed words, which are the best medium of communicating our inmost thoughts.

Signs Instituted By God

Besides the signs instituted by the will and agreement of men, of which we have been speaking so far, there are certain other signs appointed by God. These latter, as all admit, are not all of the same kind. Some were instituted by God to indicate something or to bring back its recollection. Such were the purifications of the Law, the unleavened bread, and many other things which belonged to the ceremonies of the Mosaic worship. But God has appointed other signs with power not only to signify, but also to accomplish (what they signify).

Among these are manifestly to be numbered the Sacraments of the New Law. They are signs instituted not by man but by God, which we firmly believe have in themselves the power of producing the sacred effects of which they are the signs.

Kind of Sacred Thing Meant Here

We have seen that there are many kinds of signs. The sacred thing referred to is also of more than one kind. As regards the definition already given of a Sacrament, theologians prove that by the words sacred thing is to be understood the grace of God, which sanctifies the soul and adorns it with the habit of all the divine virtues; and of this grace they rightly consider the words sacred thing, an appropriate appellation, because by its salutary influence the soul is consecrated and united to God.

In order, therefore, to explain more fully the nature of a Sacrament, it should be taught that it is a sensible object which possesses, by divine institution, the power not only of signifying, but also of accomplishing holiness and righteousness. Hence it follows, as everyone can easily see, that the images of the Saints, crosses and the like, although signs of sacred things, cannot be called Sacraments. That such is the nature of a Sacrament is easily proved by the example of all the Sacraments, if we apply to the others what has been already said of Baptism; namely, that the solemn ablution of the body not only signifies, but has power to effect a sacred thing which is wrought interiorly by the operation of the Holy Ghost.

Other Sacred Things Signified By The Sacraments

Now it is especially appropriate that these mystical signs, instituted by God, should signify by the appointment of the Lord not only one thing, but several things at once.

All The Sacraments Signify Something Present, Something Past, Something Future:

This applies to all the Sacraments; for all of them declare not only our sanctity and justification, but also two other things most intimately connected with sanctification, namely, the Passion of Christ our Redeemer, which is the source of our sanctification, and also eternal life and heavenly bliss, which are the end of sanctification. Such, then, being the nature of all the Sacraments, holy Doctors justly hold that each of them has a threefold significance: they remind us of something past; they indicate and point out something present; they foretell something future.

Nor should it be supposed that this teaching of the Doctors is unsupported by the testimony of Holy Scripture. When the Apostle says: All we who are baptised in Christ Jesus, are baptised in his

199

death, he gives us clearly to understand that Baptism is called a sign, because it reminds us of the death and Passion of our Lord. When he says, We are buried together with him by baptism into death; that as Christ is risen from the dead by the glory of the Father, so, we also may walk in newness of life, he also clearly shows that Baptism is a sign which indicates the infusion of divine grace into our souls, which enables us to lead a new life and to perform all the duties of true piety with ease and cheerfulness. Finally, when he adds: If we have been planted together in the likeness of his death, we shall be also in the likeness of his resurrection, he teaches that Baptism clearly foreshadows eternal life also, which we are to reach through its efficacy.

A Sacrament Sometimes Signifies The Presence Of More Than One Thing

Besides the different significations already mentioned, a Sacrament also not infrequently indicates and marks the presence of more than one thing. This we readily perceive when we reflect that the Holy Eucharist at once signifies the presence of the real body and blood of Christ and the grace which it imparts to the worthy receiver of the sacred mysteries.

What has been said, therefore, cannot fail to supply the pastor with arguments to prove how much the power of God is displayed, how many hidden miracles are contained in the Sacraments of the New Law; that thus all may understand that they are to be venerated and received with utmost devotion.'

Why the Sacraments were Instituted

Of all the means employed to teach the proper use of the Sacraments, there is none more effectual than a careful exposition of the reasons of their institution. Many such reasons are commonly assigned.

The first of these reasons is the feebleness of the human mind. We are so constituted by nature that no one can aspire to mental and intellectual knowledge unless through the medium of sensible objects. In order, therefore, that we might more easily understand what is accomplished by the hidden power of God, the same sovereign Creator of the universe has most wisely, and out of His tender kindness towards us, ordained that His power should be manifested to us through the intervention of certain sensible signs. As St. Chrysostom happily expresses it: If man were not clothed with a material body, these good things would have been presented to him naked and without any covering; but as the soul is joined to the body, it was absolutely necessary to employ sensible things in order to assist in making them understood.

Another reason is because the mind yields a reluctant assent to promises. Hence, from the beginning of the world, God was accustomed to indicate, and usually in words, that which He had resolved to do; but sometimes, when designing to execute something, the magnitude of which might weaken a belief in its accomplishment, He added to words other signs, which sometimes appeared miraculous. When, for instance, God sent Moses to deliver the people of Israel, and Moses, distrusting the help even of God who had commissioned him, feared that the burden imposed was heavier than he could bear, or that the people would not heed his message, the Lord confirmed His promise by a great variety of signs. As, then, in the Old Law, God ordained that every important promise should be confirmed by certain signs, so in the New Law, Christ our Saviour, when He promised pardon of sin, divine grace, the communication of the Holy Spirit, instituted certain visible and sensible signs by which He might oblige Himself, as it were, by pledges, and make it impossible to doubt that He would be true to His promises.

A third reason is that the Sacraments, to use the words of St. Ambrose, may be at hand, as the remedies and medicines of the Samaritan in the Gospel, to preserve or recover the health of the soul. For, through the Sacraments, as through a channel, must flow into the soul the efficacy of the Passion of Christ, that is, the grace which He merited for us on the altar of the cross, and without which we cannot hope for salvation. Hence, our most merciful Lord has bequeathed to His Church, Sacraments stamped with the sanction of His word and promise, through which, provided we make pious and devout use of these remedies, we firmly believe that the fruit of His Passion is really communicated to us.

A fourth reason why the institution of the Sacraments seems necessary is that there may be certain marks and symbols to distinguish the faithful; particularly since, as St. Augustine observes, no society of men, professing a true or a false religion, can be, so to speak, consolidated into one body, unless united and held together by some bond of sensible signs. Both these objects the Sacraments of the New Law accomplish, distinguishing the Christian from the infidel, and uniting the faithful by a sort of sacred bond.

Another very just cause for the institution of the Sacraments may be shown from the words of the Apostle: With the heart we believe unto justice; but with the mouth confession is made unto salvation. By approaching them we make a public profession of our faith in the sight of men. Thus, when we approach Baptism, we openly profess our belief that, by virtue of its salutary waters in which we are washed, the soul is spiritually cleansed.

The Sacraments have also great influence, not only in exciting and exercising our faith, but also in inflaming that charity with which we should love one another, when we recollect that, by partaking of these mysteries in common, we are knit together in the closest bonds and are made members of one body.

A final consideration, which is of greatest importance for the life of a Christian, is that the Sacraments repress and subdue the pride of the human heart, and exercise us in the practice of humility; for they oblige us to subject ourselves to sensible elements in obedience to God, from whom we had before impiously revolted in order to serve the elements of the world.

These are the chief points that appeared to us necessary for the instruction of the faithful on the name, nature, and institution of a Sacrament. When they shall have been accurately expounded by the pastor, his next duty will be to explain the constituents of each Sacrament, its parts, and the rites and ceremonies which have been added to its administration.

Constituent Parts of the Sacraments

In the first place, then, it should be explained that the sensible thing which enters into the definition of a Sacrament as already given, although constituting but one sign, is twofold. Every Sacrament consists of two things, matter, which is called the element, and form, which is commonly called the word.

This is the doctrine of the Fathers of the Church; and the testimony of St. Augustine on the subject is familiar to all. The word, he says, is joined to the element and it becomes a Sacrament. By the words sensible thing, therefore, the Fathers understand not only the matter or element, such as water in Baptism, chrism in confirmation, and oil in Extreme Unction, all of which fall under the eye; but also the words which constitute the form, and which are addressed to the ear.

Both are clearly pointed out by the Apostle, when he says: Christ loved the Church, and delivered himself up for it, that he might sanctify it, cleansing it by the laver of water in the word of life. Here both the matter and form of the Sacrament are expressly mentioned.

In order to make the meaning of the rite that is being performed easier and clearer, words had to be added to the matter. For of all signs words are evidently the most significant, and without them, what the matter for the Sacraments designates and declares would be utterly obscure. Water, for instance, has the quality of cooling as well as cleansing, and may be symbolic of either. In Baptism, therefore, unless the words were added, it would not be certain, but only conjectural, which signification was intended; but when the words are added, we immediately understand that the Sacrament possesses and signifies the power of cleansing.

In this the Sacraments of the New Law excel those of the Old that, as far as we know, there was no definite form of administering the latter, and hence they were very uncertain and obscure. In our Sacraments, on the contrary, the form is so definite that any, even a casual deviation from it renders the Sacrament null. Hence the form is expressed in the clearest terms, such as exclude the possibility of doubt.

These, then, are the parts which belong to the nature and substance of the Sacraments, and of which every Sacrament is necessarily composed.

Ceremonies Used in the Administration of the Sacraments

To (the matter and form) are added certain ceremonies. These cannot be omitted without sin, unless in case of necessity; yet, if at any time they be omitted, the Sacrament is not thereby invalidated, since the ceremonies do not pertain to its essence. It is not without good reason that the administration of the Sacraments has been at all times, from the earliest ages of the Church, accompanied with certain solemn rites.

There is, in the first place, the greatest propriety in manifesting such a religious reverence to the sacred mysteries as to make it appear that holy things are handled by holy men.

Secondly, these ceremonies serve to display more fully the effects of the Sacraments, placing them, as it were, before our eyes, and to impress more deeply on the minds of the faithful the sanctity of these sacred institutions.

Thirdly, they elevate to sublime contemplation the minds of those who behold and observe them with attention, and excite within them faith and charity.

To enable the faithful, therefore, to know and understand clearly the meaning of the ceremonies made use of in the administration of each Sacrament should be an object of special care and attention.

The Number Of The Sacraments

We now come to explain the number of the Sacraments. A knowledge of this point is very advantageous to the faithful; for the greater the number of aids to salvation and the life of bliss which they understand to have been provided by God, the more ardent will be the piety with which they will direct all the powers of their souls to praise and proclaim His singular goodness towards us.

The Sacraments of the Catholic Church are seven in number, as is proved from Scripture, from the tradition handed down to us from the Fathers, and from the authority of Councils. Why they are neither more nor less in number may be shown, at least

with some probability, from the analogy that exists between the natural and the spiritual life. In order to exist, to preserve existence, and to contribute to his own and to the public good, seven things seem necessary to man: to be born, to grow, to be nurtured, to be cured when sick, when weak to be strengthened; as far as regards the public welfare, to have magistrates invested with authority to govern, and to perpetuate himself and his species by legitimate offspring. Now, since it is quite clear that all these things are sufficiently analogous to that life by which the soul lives to God, we discover in them a reason to account for the number of the Sacraments.

First comes Baptism, which is the gate, as it were, to all the other Sacraments, and by which we are born again unto Christ. The next is Confirmation, by which we grow up and are strengthened in the grace of God; for, as St. Augustine observes, to the Apostles who had already received Baptism, the Redeemer said: "Stay you in the city till you be endued with power from on high.„ The third is the Eucharist, that true bread from heaven which nourishes and sustains our souls to eternal life, according to these words of the Saviour: My flesh is meat indeed, and my blood is drink indeed. The fourth is Penance, through which lost health is recovered after we have been wounded by sin. Next is Extreme Unction, which obliterates the remains of sin and invigorates the powers of the soul; for speaking of this Sacrament St. James says: If he be in sins, they shall be forgiven him. Then follows Holy Orders, by which power is given to exercise perpetually in the Church the public administration of the Sacraments and to perform all the sacred functions. The last is Matrimony, instituted to the end that, by means of the legitimate and holy union of man and woman, children may be procreated and religiously educated for the service of God, and for the preservation of the human race.

Comparisons among the Sacraments

Though all the Sacraments possess a divine and admirable efficacy, it is well worthy of special remark that all are not of equal necessity or of equal dignity, nor is the signification of all the same.

Among them three are said to be necessary beyond the rest, although in all three this necessity is not of the same kind. The universal and absolute necessity of Baptism our Saviour has declared in these words: Unless a man be born again of water and the Holy Ghost, he cannot enter into the kingdom of God. Penance, on the other hand, is necessary for those only who have stained themselves after Baptism by any mortal guilt. Without sincere repentance, their eternal ruin is inevitable. Orders, too, although not necessary to each of the faithful, are of absolute necessity to the Church as a whole.

But if we consider the dignity of the Sacraments, the Eucharist, for holiness and for the number and greatness of its mysteries, is far superior to all the rest. These, however, are matters which will be more easily understood, when we come to explain, in its proper place, what regards each of the Sacraments.

The Author of the Sacraments

It now remains to inquire from whom we have received these sacred and divine mysteries. Any gift, however excellent in itself, undoubtedly receives an increased value from the dignity and excellence of him by whom it is bestowed.

The present question, however, is not hard to answer. For since human justification comes from God, and since the Sacraments are the wonderful instruments of justification, it is evident that one and the same God in Christ, must be acknowledged to be the author of justification and of the Sacraments.

Furthermore, the Sacraments contain a power and efficacy which reach the inmost soul; and as God alone has power to enter into the hearts and minds of men, He alone, through Christ, is manifestly the author of the Sacraments.

That they are also interiorly dispensed by Him we must hold with a firm and certain faith, according to these words of St. John, in which he declares that he learned this truth concerning Christ: He who sent me to baptise with water, said to me: He, upon whom thou shalt see the Spirit descending, and remaining upon him, he it is that baptizeth with the Holy Ghost.

The Ministers of the Sacraments

But although God is the author and dispenser of the Sacraments, He nevertheless willed that they should be administered in His Church by men, not by Angels. To constitute a Sacrament, as the unbroken tradition of the Fathers testifies, matter and form are not more necessary than is the ministry of men.

Unworthiness Of The Minister And Validity

Since the ministers of the Sacraments represent in the discharge of their sacred functions, not their own, but the person of Christ, be they good or bad, they validly perform and confer the Sacraments, provided they make use of the matter and form always observed in the Catholic Church according to the institution of Christ, and provided they intend to do what the Church does in their administration. Hence, unless the recipients wish to deprive themselves of so great a good and resist the Holy Ghost, nothing can prevent them from receiving (through the Sacraments) the fruit of grace.

That this was, at all times, a fixed and well ascertained doctrine of the Church, is established beyond all doubt by St. Augustine, in his disputations against the Donatists. And should we desire Scriptural proof also, let us listen to these words of the Apostle: I have planted; Apollo watered; but God gave the increase Therefore neither he that planteth nor he that watereth is any

thing, but God who giveth the increase. From these words it is clear that as trees are not injured by the wickedness of those who planted them, so those who were planted in Christ by the ministry of bad men sustain no injury from the guilt of those others.

Judas Iscariot, as the holy Fathers infer from the Gospel of St. John, conferred Baptism on many; and yet none of those whom he baptised are recorded to have been baptised again. To use the memorable words of St. Augustine: Judas baptised, and yet after him none were rebaptised; John baptised, and after John they were rebaptised . For the Baptism administered by Judas was the Baptism of Christ, but that administered by John was the baptism of John. Not that we prefer Judas to John, but that we justly prefer the Baptism of Christ, although administered by Judas, to that of John although administered by the hands of John.

Lawfulness Of Administration

But let not pastors, or other ministers of the Sacraments, hence infer that they fully acquit themselves of their duty, if, disregarding integrity of life and purity of morals, they attend only to the administration of the Sacraments in the manner prescribed. True, the manner of administering them demands particular diligence; yet this alone does not constitute all that pertains to that duty. It should never be forgotten that the Sacraments, although they cannot lose the divine efficacy inherent in them, bring eternal death and perdition to him who dares administer them unworthily.

Holy things, it cannot be too often repeated, should be treated holily and with due reverence. To the sinner, says the Prophet, God has said: Why dost thou declare my justices, and take my covenant in thy mouth, seeing that thou hast hated discipline? If then, for him who is defiled by sin it is unlawful to speak on divine things, how enormous the guilt of that man, who, conscious of many crimes, dreads not to accomplish with polluted lips the holy mysteries, to take them into his befouled hands, to touch

them, and to present and administer them to others? All the more since St. Denis says that the wicked may not even touch the symbols, as he calls the Sacraments.

It therefore becomes the first duty of the minister of holy things to follow holiness of life, to approach with purity the administration of the Sacraments, and so to exercise himself in piety, that, from their frequent administration and use, he may every day receive, with the divine assistance, more abundant grace.

Effects of the Sacraments

When these matters have been explained, the effects of the Sacraments are the next subject of instruction. This subject should throw considerable light on the definition of a Sacrament as already given.

First Effect: Justifying Grace

The principal effects of the Sacraments are two. The first place is rightly held by that grace which we, following the usage of the holy Doctors, call sanctifying. For so the Apostle most clearly taught when he said: Christ loved the church, and delivered himself up for it; that he might sanctify it, cleansing it by the laver of water in the word of life. But how so great and so admirable an effect is produced by the Sacrament that, to use the well-known saying of St. Augustine, water cleanses the body and reaches the heart, -- this, indeed, cannot be comprehended by human reason and intelligence. It may be taken for granted that no sensible thing is of its own nature able to reach the soul; but we know by the light of faith that in the Sacraments there exists the power of almighty God by which they effect that which the natural elements cannot of themselves accomplish.

Lest on this subject any doubt should exist in the minds of the faithful, God, in the abundance of His mercy, was pleased,

from the moment when the Sacraments began to be administered, to manifest by the evidence of miracles the effects which they operate interiorly in the soul. (This He did) in order that we may most firmly believe that the same effects, although far removed from the senses, are always inwardly produced. To say nothing of the fact that at the Baptism of the Redeemer in the Jordan the heavens were opened and the Holy Ghost appeared in the form of a dove, to teach us that when we are washed in the sacred font His grace is infused into our souls -- to omit this, which has reference rather to the signification of Baptism than to the administration of the Sacrament -- do we not read that on the day of Pentecost, when the Apostles received the Holy Ghost, by whom they were thenceforward inspired with greater alacrity and resolution to preach the faith and brave dangers for the glory of Christ, there came suddenly a sound from heaven, as of a mighty wind coming, and it filled the whole house where they were sitting, and there appeared to them parted tongues, as it were, of fire? By this it was understood that in the Sacrament of Confirmation the same Spirit is given us, and such strength is imparted as enables us resolutely to encounter and resist our incessant enemies, the world, the flesh and the devil. For some time in the beginning of the Church, whenever these Sacraments were administered by the Apostles, the same miraculous effects were witnessed, and they ceased only when the faith had acquired maturity and strength.

From what has been said of sanctifying grace, the first effect of the Sacraments, it clearly follows that there resides in the Sacraments of the New Law, a virtue more exalted and efficacious than that of the sacraments of the Old Law. Those ancient sacraments, being weak and needy elements, sanctified such as were defiled to the cleansing of the flesh, but not of the spirit. They were, therefore, instituted only as signs of those things, which were to be accomplished by our mysteries. The Sacraments of the New Law, on the contrary, flowing from the side of Christ, who, by the Holy Ghost, offered himself unspotted unto God, cleanse our consciences from dead works, to

serve the living God, and thus work in us, through the blood of Christ, the grace which they signify. Comparing our Sacraments, therefore, with those of the Old Law we find that they are not only more efficacious, but also more fruitful in spiritual advantages, and more august in holiness.

Second Effect: Sacramental Character

The second effect of the Sacraments -- which, however, is not common to all, but peculiar to three, Baptism, Confirmation, and Holy Orders -- is the character which they impress on the soul. When the Apostle says: God hath anointed us, who also hath sealed us, and given the pledge of the Spirit in our hearts, he not obscurely describes by the word sealed a character, the property of which is to impress a seal and mark.

This character is, as it were, a distinctive impression stamped on the soul which perpetually inheres and cannot be blotted out. Of this St. Augustine says: Shall the Christian Sacraments accomplish less than the bodily mark impressed on the soldier? That mark is not stamped on his person anew as often as he resumes the military service which he had relinquished, but the old is recognised and approved.

This character has a twofold effect: it qualifies us to receive or perform something sacred, and distinguishes us by some mark one from another. In the character impressed by Baptism, both effects are exemplified. By it we are qualified to receive the other Sacraments, and the Christian is distinguished from those who do not profess the faith. The same illustration is afforded by the characters impressed by Confirmation and Holy Orders. By Confirmation we are armed and arrayed as soldiers of Christ, publicly to profess and defend His name, to fight against our internal enemy and against the spiritual powers of wickedness in the high places; and at the same time we are distinguished from those who, being recently baptised, are, as it were, new-born infants. Holy Orders confers the power of consecrating and administering the Sacraments, and also distinguishes those who are invested

with this power from the rest of the faithful. The rule of the Catholic Church is, therefore, to be observed, which teaches that these three Sacraments impress a character and are never to be repeated.

How to Make Instruction on the Sacraments Profitable

On the subject of the Sacraments in general, the above are the matters on which instruction should be given. In explaining them, pastors should keep in view principally two things, which they should zealously strive to accomplish. The first is that the faithful understand the high honour, respect and veneration due to these divine and celestial gifts. The second is that, since the Sacraments have been established by the God of infinite mercy for the common salvation of all, the people should make pious and religious use of them, and be so inflamed with the desire of Christian perfection as to deem it a very great loss to be for any time deprived of the salutary use, particularly of Penance and the Holy Eucharist.

These objects pastors will find little difficulty in accomplishing, if they call frequently to the attention of the faithful what we have already said on the divine character and fruit of the Sacraments: first, that they were instituted by our Lord and Saviour from whom can proceed nothing but what is most perfect; further that when administered, the most powerful influence of the Holy Ghost is present, pervading the inmost sanctuary of the soul; next that they possess an admirable and unfailing virtue to cure our spiritual maladies, and communicate to us the inexhaustible riches of the Passion of our Lord.

Finally, let them point out, that although the whole edifice of Christian piety rests on the most firm foundation of the cornerstone; yet, unless it be supported on every side by the preaching of the divine Word and by the use of the Sacraments, it is greatly to be feared that it may to a great extent totter and fall to the ground. For as we are ushered into spiritual life by means of the Sacraments, so by the same means are we nourished and preserved, and grow to spiritual increase.

THE SACRAMENT OF BAPTISM

Importance Of Instruction On Baptism

From what has been hitherto said on the Sacraments in general, we may judge how necessary it is, to a proper understanding of the doctrines of the Christian faith and to the practice of Christian piety, to know what the Catholic Church proposes for our belief on each Sacrament in particular.

Whoever reads the Apostle carefully will unhesitatingly conclude that a perfect knowledge of Baptism is particularly necessary to the faithful. For not only frequently, but also in language the most energetic, in language full of the Spirit of God, he renews the recollection of this mystery, declares its divine character, and in it places before us the death, burial and Resurrection of. our Lord as objects both of our contemplation and imitation.

Pastors, therefore, can never think that they have bestowed sufficient labor and attention on the exposition of this Sacrament. Besides the Vigils of Easter and Pentecost, days on which the Church used to celebrate this Sacrament with the greatest devotion and special solemnity, and on which particularly, according to ancient practice, its divine mysteries were to be explained, pastors should also take occasion at other times to make it the subject of their instructions.

For this purpose a most convenient opportunity would seem to present itself whenever a pastor, being about to administer this Sacrament, finds himself surrounded by a considerable number of the faithful. On such occasions, it is true, his exposition cannot embrace everything that regards Baptism; but it will then be much easier to develop one or two points when the faithful can contemplate with a pious and attentive mind the meaning of those things which they hear and at the same time see it illustrated by the sacred ceremonies of Baptism. Each person, reading a lesson of admonition in the person of him who is receiving Baptism, will call to mind the promises by which he bound himself to God when he was baptised, and will reflect whether his life and conduct have been such as are promised by the profession of Christianity.

Names of this Sacrament

In order that the treatment of the subject. may be clear, we must explain the nature and substance of Baptism, premising, however, an explanation of the word itself.

The word baptism, as is well known, is of Greek derivation. Although used in Sacred Scripture to express not only that ablution which forms part of the Sacrament, but also every species of ablution, and sometimes, figuratively, to express sufferings; yet it is employed by ecclesiastical writers to designate not every sort of bodily ablution, but that which forms part of the Sacrament and is administered with the prescribed form of words. In this sense the Apostles very frequently make use of the word in accordance with the institution of Christ the Lord.

This Sacrament the holy Fathers designate also by other names. St. Augustine informs us that it was sometimes called the Sacrament of Faith, because by receiving it we profess our faith in all the doctrines of Christianity.

By others it was termed Illumination, because by the faith which we profess in Baptism the heart is illumined; for as the Apostle also says, alluding to the time of Baptism, Call to mind the former days, wherein, being illumined, you endured a great fight of afflictions Chrysostom, in his sermon to the baptised, calls it a purgation, because through it we purge away the old leaven, that we may become a new paste. He also calls it a burial, a planting, and the cross of Christ, the reasons for all which appellations may be gathered from the Epistle to the Romans.

St. Denis calls it the beginning of the most holy Commandments, for this obvious reason, that Baptism is, as it were, the gate through which we enter into the fellowship of the Christian life, and begin thenceforward to obey the Commandments. So much should be briefly explained concerning the name (of this Sacrament) .

Definition Of Baptism

With regard to the definition of Baptism although many can be given from sacred writers, nevertheless that which may be gathered from the words of our Lord recorded in John, and of the Apostle to the Ephesians, appears the most appropriate and suitable. Unless, says our Lord, a man be born again of water and the Holy Ghost, he cannot enter into the kingdom of God; and, speaking of the Church, the Apostle says, cleansing it by the laver of water in the word of life. Thus it follows that Baptism may be rightly and accurately defined: The Sacrament of regeneration by water in the word. By nature we are born from Adam children of wrath, but by Baptism we are regenerated in Christ, children of mercy. For He gave power to men to be made the sons of God, to them that believe in his name, who are born, not of blood, nor of the will of the flesh, nor of the will of man, but of God.

Constituent Elements Of Baptism

But define Baptism as we may, the faithful are to be informed that this Sacrament consists of ablution, accompanied necessarily, according to the institution of our Lord, by certain solemn words. This is the uniform doctrine of the holy Fathers, as is proved by the following most explicit testimony of St. Augustine: The word is joined to the element, and it becomes a Sacrament.

It is all the more necessary to impress this on the minds of the faithful lest they fall into the common error of thinking that the baptismal water, preserved in the sacred font, constitutes the Sacrament. The Sacrament of Baptism can be said to exist only when we actually apply the water to someone by way of ablution, while using the words appointed by our Lord.

Matter of Baptism

Now since we said above, when treating of the Sacraments in general, that every Sacrament consists of matter and form, it is therefore necessary that pastors point out what constitutes each of these in Baptism. The matter, then, or element of this Sacrament, is any sort of natural water, which is simply and without qualification commonly called water, be it sea water, river water, water from a pond, well or fountain.

Testimony Of Scripture Concerning The Matter Of Baptism

For the Saviour taught that unless a man be born again of water and the Holy Ghost, he cannot enter into the kingdom of God. The Apostle also says that the Church was cleansed by the laver of water; and in the Epistle of St. John we read these words: There are three that give testimony on earth: the spirit, and the water, and the blood. Scripture affords other proofs which establish the same truth.

When, however, John the Baptist says that the Lord will come who will baptise in the Holy Ghost, and in fire, that is by no means to be understood of the matter of Baptism; but should be applied either to the interior operation of the Holy Ghost, or at least to the miracle performed on the day of Pentecost, when the Holy Ghost descended on the Apostles in the form of fire, as was foretold by Christ our Lord in these words: John indeed baptised with water, but you shall be baptised with the Holy Ghost, not many days hence.

Figures

The same was also signified by the Lord both by figures and by prophecies, as we know from Holy Scripture. According to the Prince of the Apostles in his first Epistle, the deluge which cleansed the world because the wickedness of men was great on the earth, and all the thought of their heart was bent upon evil, was a figure and image of this water. To omit the cleansing of Naaman the Syrian, and the admirable virtue of the pool of Bethsaida, and many similar types, manifestly symbolic of this mystery, the passage through the Red Sea, according to St. Paul in his Epistle to the Corinthians, was typical of this same water.

Prophecies

With regard to the predictions, the waters to which the Prophet Isaias so freely invites all that thirst, and those which Ezechiel in spirit saw issuing from the Temple, and also the fountain which Zachary foresaw, open to the house of David, and to the inhabitants of Jerusalem: for the washing of the sinner, and of the unclean woman, were, no doubt, intended to indicate and express the salutary waters of Baptism.

Fitness

The propriety of constituting water the matter of Baptism, of the nature and efficacy of which it is at once expressive, St. Jerome, in his Epistle to Oceanus, proves by many arguments.

Upon this subject pastors can teach in the first place that water, which is always at hand and within the reach of all, was the fittest matter of a Sacrament which is necessary to all for salvation. In the next place water is best adapted to signify the effect of Baptism. It washes away uncleanness, and is, therefore, strikingly illustrative of the virtue and efficacy of Baptism, which washes away the stains of sin. We may also add that, like water which cools the body, Baptism in a great measure extinguishes the fire of concupiscence.

Chrism Added To Water For Solemn Baptism

But it should be noted that while in case of necessity simple water unmixed with any other ingredient is sufficient for the matter of this Sacrament, yet when Baptism is administered in public with solemn ceremonies the Catholic Church, guided by Apostolic tradition, has uniformly observed the practice of adding holy chrism which, as is clear, more fully signifies the effect of Baptism. The people should also be taught that although it may sometimes be doubtful whether this or that water be genuine, such as the perfection of the Sacrament requires, it can never be a subject of doubt that the only matter from which the Sacrament of Baptism can be formed is natural water.

Form of Baptism

Having carefully explained the matter, which is one of the two parts of which Baptism consists, pastors must show equal diligence in explaining the form, which is the other essential part. In the explanation of this Sacrament a necessity of increased care and study arises, as pastors will perceive, from the circumstance that the knowledge of so holy a mystery is not only in itself a source of pleasure to the faithful, as is generally the case with regard to religious knowledge, but also very desirable for almost daily practical use. As we shall explain in its proper place, circumstances often arise where Baptism requires to be administered by the laity, and most frequently by women; and it therefore becomes necessary to make all the faithful, indiscriminately, well acquainted with whatever regards the substance of this Sacrament.

Words Of The Form

Pastors, therefore, should teach, in clear, unambiguous language, intelligible to every capacity, that the true and essential form of Baptism is: I baptise thee in the name of the Father, and of the Son, and of the Holy Ghost. For so it was delivered by our Lord and Saviour when, as we read in St. Matthew He gave to His Apostles the command: Going, . . . teach ye all nations: baptising them in the name of the Father, and of the Son, and of the Holy Ghost.

By the word baptising, the Catholic Church, instructed from above, most justly understood that the form of the Sacrament should express the action of the minister; and this takes place when he pronounces the words, I baptise thee.

Besides the minister of the Sacrament, the person to be baptised and the principal efficient cause of Baptism should be mentioned.

The pronoun thee, and the distinctive names of the Divine Persons are therefore added. Thus the complete form of the Sacrament is expressed in the words already mentioned: I baptise thee in the name of the Father, and of the Son, and of the Holy Ghost.

Baptism is the work not of the Son alone, of whom St. John says, He it is that baptizeth, but of the Three Persons of the Blessed Trinity together. By saying, however, in the name, not in the names, we distinctly declare that in the Trinity there is but one Nature and Godhead. The word name is here referred not to the Persons, but to the Divine Essence, virtue and power, which are one and the same in Three Persons.

Essential And Non-Essential Words Of The Form

It is, however, to be observed that of the words contained in this form, which we have shown to be the complete and perfect one, some are absolutely necessary, so that the omission of them renders the valid administration of the Sacrament impossible; while others on the contrary, are not so essential as to affect its validity.

Of the latter kind is the word ego (I), the force of which is included in the word baptizo (I baptise). Nay more, the Greek Church, adopting a different manner of expressing the form, and being of opinion that it is unnecessary to make mention of the minister, omits the pronoun altogether. The form universally used in the Greek Church is: Let this servant of Christ be baptised in the name of the Father, and of the Son, and of the Holy Ghost. It appears, however, from the decision and definition of the Council of Florence, that those who use this form administer the Sacraments validly, because the words sufficiently express what is essential to the validity of Baptism, that is, the ablution which then takes place.

Baptism In The Name Of Christ

If at any time the Apostles baptised in the name of the Lord Jesus Christ only, we can be sure they did so by the inspiration of the Holy Ghost, in order, in the infancy of the Church, to render their preaching more illustrious by the name of Jesus Christ, and to proclaim more effectually His divine and infinite power. If, however, we examine the matter more closely, we shall find that such a form omits nothing which the Saviour Himself commands to be observed; for he who mentions Jesus Christ implies the Person of the Father, by whom, and that of the Holy Ghost, in whom, He was anointed.

And yet, the use of this form by the Apostles seems rather doubtful if we accept the opinions of Ambrose and Basil, holy Fathers eminent for sanctity and authority, who interpret baptism in the name of Jesus Christ to mean the Baptism instituted by Christ our Lord, as distinguished from that of John, and who say that the Apostles did not depart from the ordinary and usual form which comprises the distinct names of the Three Persons. Paul also, in his Epistle to the Galatians, seems to have expressed himself in a similar manner, when he says: As many of you as have been baptised in Christ, have put on Christ, meaning that they were baptised in the faith of Christ, but with no other form than that which the same Saviour our Lord had commanded to be observed.

Administration of Baptism

What has been said on the matter and form, which are required for the essence of the Sacrament, will be found sufficient for the instruction of the faithful; but as in the administration of the Sacrament the legitimate manner of ablution should also be observed, pastors should teach the doctrine of this-point also.

They should briefly explain that, according to the common custom and practice of the Church, Baptism may be administered in three ways, -- by immersion, infusion or aspersion.

Whichever of these rites be observed, we must believe that Baptism is rightly administered. For in Baptism water is used to signify the spiritual ablution which it accomplishes, and on this account Baptism is called by the Apostle a laver. Now this ablution is not more really accomplished by immersion, which was for a considerable time the practice in the early ages of the Church, than by infusion, which we now see in general use, or by aspersion, which there is reason to believe was the manner in which Peter baptised, when on one day he converted and gave Baptism to about three thousand souls.

It is a matter of indifference whether the ablution be performed once or thrice. For it is evident from the Epistle of St. Gregory the Great to Leander that Baptism was formerly and may still be validly administered in the Church in either way. The faithful, however, should follow the practice of the particular Church to which they belong.

Pastors should be particularly careful to observe that the baptismal ablution is not to be applied indifferently to any part of the body, but principally to the head, which is the seat of all the internal and external senses; and also that he who baptises is to pronounce the sacramental words which constitute the form, not before or after, but when performing the ablution.

Institution Of Baptism

When these things have been explained, it will also be expedient to teach and remind the faithful that, in common with the other Sacraments, Baptism was instituted by Christ the Lord. On this subject the pastor should frequently teach and point out that there are two different periods of time which relate to Baptism, -- one the period of its institution by the Redeemer; the other, the establishment of the law regarding its reception.

Baptism Instituted At Christ's Baptism

With regard to the former, it is clear that this Sacrament was instituted by our Lord when, having been baptised by John, He gave to water the power of sanctifying. St. Gregory Nazianzen and St. Augustine · testify that to water was then. imparted the power of regenerating to spiritual life. In another place St. Augustine says: From the moment that Christ is immersed in water, water washes away all sins. And again: The Lord is baptised, not because He had need to be cleansed, but in order that, by the contact of His pure flesh, He might purify the waters and impart to them the power of cleansing.

A very strong argument to prove that Baptism was then instituted by our Lord might be afforded by the fact the most Holy Trinity, in whose name Baptism is conferred, manifested Its divine presence on that occasion. The voice of the Father was heard, the Person of the Son was present, the Holy Ghost descended in the form of a dove; and the heavens, into which we are enabled to enter by Baptism, were thrown open.

Should anyone desire to know how our Lord has endowed water with a virtue so great, so divine, this indeed transcends the power of the human understanding. Yet this we can know, that when our Lord was baptised, water, by contact with His most holy and pure body, was consecrated to the salutary use of Baptism, in such a way, however, that, although instituted before the Passion, we must believe that this Sacrament derives all its virtue and efficacy from the Passion, which is the consummation, as it were, of all the actions of Christ.

Baptism Made Obligatory After Christ's Resurrection

The second period to be distinguished, that is, the time when the law of Baptism was made, also admits of no doubt. Holy writers are unanimous in saying that after the Resurrection of our Lord, when He gave to His Apostles the command to go and teach all nations: baptising them in the name of the Father, and of the Son, and of the Holy Ghost, the law of Baptism became obligatory on all who were to be saved.

This is inferred from the authority of the Prince of the Apostles when he says: Who hath regenerated us into a lively hope, by the resurrection of Jesus Christ from the dead;' and also from what Paul says of the Church: He delivered himself up for it: that he might sanctify it, cleansing it by the laver of water in the word of life. By both Apostles the obligation of Baptism seems to be referred to the time which followed the death of our Lord. Hence we can have no doubt that the words of the Saviour: Unless a man be born again of water and the Holy Ghost, he cannot enter into the kingdom of God, refer also to the same time which was to follow after His Passion.

Reflection

If, then, pastors explain these truths accurately, there can be no doubt that the faithful will recognise the high dignity of this Sacrament and venerate it with the most profound piety, particularly when they reflect that each of them receives in Baptism by the interior operation of the Holy Ghost the same glorious and most ample gifts which were so strikingly manifested by miracles at the Baptism of Christ the Lord.

Were our eyes, like those of the servant of Eliseus, opened to see heavenly things, who can be supposed so senseless as not to be lost in rapturous admiration of the divine mysteries of Baptism ! When, therefore, the riches of this Sacrament are unfolded to the faithful by the pastor, so as to enable them to behold them, if not with the eyes of the body, yet with those of the soul illumined by the light of faith, may we not anticipate similar results ?

The Ministers of Baptism

In the next place, it appears not only expedient, but necessary to say who are ministers of this Sacrament; both in order that those to whom this office is specially confided may study to perform its functions religiously and holily; and that no one, outstepping, as it were, his proper limits, may unseasonably take possession of, or arrogantly assume, what belongs to another; for, as the Apostle teaches, order is to be observed in all things.

Bishops And Priests The Ordinary Ministers

The faithful, therefore, are to be informed that of those (who administer Baptism) there are three gradations. Bishops and priests hold the first place. To them belongs the administration of this Sacrament, not by any extraordinary concession of power, but by right of office; for to them, in the persons of the Apostles, was addressed the command of our Lord: Go, baptise. Bishops, it is true, in order not to neglect the more weighty charge of instructing the faithful, have generally left its administration to priests. But the authority of the Fathers and the usage of the Church prove that priests exercise this function by their own right, so much so that they may baptise even in the presence of the Bishop. Ordained to consecrate the Holy Eucharist, the Sacrament of peace and unity, it was fitting that they be invested with power to administer all those things which are required to enable others to participate in that peace and unity. If, therefore, the Fathers have at any time said that without the leave of the Bishop the priest has not the right to baptise, they are to be understood to speak of that Baptism only which was administered on certain days of the year with solemn ceremonies.

Deacons Extraordinary Ministers Of Baptism

Next among the ministers are deacons, for whom, as numerous decrees of the holy Fathers attest it is not lawful without the permission of the Bishop or priest to administer this Sacrament.

Ministers In Case Of Necessity

Those who may administer Baptism in case of necessity, but without its solemn ceremonies, hold the last place; and in this class are included all, even the laity, men and women, to whatever sect they may belong. This office extends in case of necessity, even to Jews, infidels and heretics, provided, however, they intend to do what the Catholic Church does in that act of her ministry. These things were established by many decrees of the ancient Fathers and Councils; and the holy Council of Trent denounces anathema against those who dare to say, that Baptism, even when administered by heretics, in the name of the Father, and of the Son, and of the Holy Ghost, with the intention of doing what the Church does, is not true Baptism.

And here indeed let us admire the supreme goodness and wisdom of our Lord. Seeing the necessity of this Sacrament for all, He not only instituted water, than which nothing can be more common, as its matter, but also placed its administration within the power of all. In its administration, however, as we have already observed, all are not allowed to use the solemn ceremonies; not that rites and ceremonies are of higher dignity, but because they are less necessary than the Sacrament.

Let not the faithful, however, imagine that this office is given promiscuously to all, so as to do away with the propriety of observing a certain precedence among those who are its ministers. When a man is present a woman should not baptise; an ecclesiastic takes precedence over a layman, and a priest over a simple ecclesiastic. Midwives, however, when accustomed to its administration, are not to be found fault with if sometimes, when a man is present who is unacquainted with the manner of its administration, they perform what may otherwise appear to belong more properly to men.

The Sponsors at Baptism

Besides the ministers who, as just explained, confer Baptism, another class of persons, according to the most ancient practice of the Church, is admitted to assist at the baptismal font. In former times these were commonly called by sacred writers receivers, sponsors or sureties, and are now called godfathers and godmothers. As this is an office pertaining almost to all the laity, pastors should explain it with care, so that the faithful may understand what is chiefly necessary for its proper performance.

Why Sponsors Are Required At Baptism

In the first instance it should be explained why at Baptism, besides those who administer the Sacrament, godparents and sponsors are also required. The propriety of the practice will at once appear to all if they recollect that Baptism is a spiritual regeneration by which we are born children of God; for of it St. Peter says: As newborn infants, desire the rational milk without guile. As, therefore, every one, after his birth, requires a nurse and instructor by whose assistance and attention he is brought up and formed to learning and useful knowledge, so those, who, by the waters of Baptism, begin to live a spiritual life should be entrusted to the fidelity and prudence of some one from whom they may imbibe the precepts of the Christian religion and may be brought up in all holiness, and thus grow gradually in Christ, until, with the Lord's help, they at length arrive at perfect manhood.

This necessity must appear still more imperative, if we recollect that pastors, who are charged with the public care of parishes have not sufficient time to undertake the private instruction of children in the rudiments of faith.

Antiquity Of This Law

Concerning this very ancient practice we have this noteworthy testimony of St. Denis: It occurred to our divine leaders (so he called the Apostles), and they in their wisdom ordained that infants should be introduced (into the Church) in this holy manner that their natural parents should deliver them to the care of some one well skilled in divine things, as to a master under whom, as a spiritual father and guardian of his salvation in holiness, the child should lead the remainder of his life. The same doctrine is confirmed by the authority of Hyginus.

Affinity Contracted By Sponsors

The Church, therefore, in her wisdom has ordained that not only the person who baptises contracts a spiritual affinity with the person baptised, but also the sponsor with the godchild and its natural parents, so that between all these marriage cannot be lawfully contracted, and if contracted, it is null and void.

Duties Of Sponsors

The faithful are also to be taught the duty of sponsors; for such is the negligence with which this office is treated in the Church that only the bare name of the function remains, while none seem to have the least idea of its sanctity. Let all sponsors, then, at all times recollect that they are strictly bound by this law to exercise a constant vigilance over their spiritual children, and carefully to instruct them in the maxims of a Christian life; so that these may show themselves throughout life to be what their sponsors promised in the solemn ceremony.

On this subject let us hear the words of St. Denis. Speaking in the person of the sponsor he says: I promise, by my constant exhortations to induce this child, when he comes to a knowledge of religion, to renounce every thing opposed (to his Christian calling) and to profess and perform the sacred promises which he now makes.

St. Augustine also says: I most especially admonish you, men and women, who have acquired godchildren through Baptism, to consider that you stood as sureties before God, for those whom you received at the sacred font. Indeed it preeminently becomes every man, who undertakes any office, to be indefatigable in the discharge of its duties; and he who promised to be the teacher and guardian of another should never allow to be deserted him whom he once received under his care and protection as long as he knows the latter to stand in need of either.

Speaking of this same duty of sponsors, St. Augustine sums up in a few words the lessons of instruction which they are bound to impart to their spiritual children. They ought, he says, to admonish them to observe chastity, love justice, cling to charity; and above all they should teach them the Creed, the Lord's Prayer, the Ten Commandments, and the rudiments of the Christian religion.

Who May Not Be Sponsors

It is easy, therefore, to decide who are inadmissible to this holy guardianship, that is, those who are unwilling to discharge its duties with fidelity, or who cannot do so with care and accuracy.

Wherefore, besides the natural parents, who, to mark the great difference that exists between this spiritual and the carnal bringing up of youth, are not permitted to undertake this charge, heretics, Jews and infidels are on no account to be admitted to this office, since their thoughts and efforts are continually employed in darkening by falsehood the true faith and in subverting all Christian piety.

Number Of Sponsors

The number of sponsors is limited by the Council of Trent to one godfather or one godmother, or at most, to a godfather and a godmother; because a number of teachers may confuse the order of discipline and instruction, and also because it was necessary to prevent the multiplication of affinities which would impede a wider diffusion of society by means of lawful marriage.

Necessity of Baptism

If the knowledge of what has been hitherto explained be, as it is, of highest importance to the faithful, it is no less important to them to learn that the law of Baptism, as established by our Lord, extends to all, so that unless they are regenerated to God through the grace of Baptism, be their parents Christians or infidels, they are born to eternal misery and destruction. Pastors, therefore, should often explain these words of the Gospel: Unless a man be born again of water and the Holy Ghost, he cannot enter into the kingdom of God.

Infant Baptism: It's Necessity

That this law extends not only to adults but also to infants and children, and that the Church has received this from Apostolic tradition, is confirmed by the unanimous teaching and authority of the Fathers.

Besides, it is not to be supposed that Christ the Lord would have withheld the Sacrament and grace of Baptism from children, of whom He said: Suffer the little children, and forbid them not to come to me; for the kingdom of heaven is for such; ° whom also He embraced, upon whom He imposed hands, to whom He gave His blessing.

Moreover, when we read that an entire family was baptised by Paul, it is sufficiently obvious that the children of the family must also have been cleansed in the saving font.

Circumcision, too, which was a figure of Baptism, affords strong argument in proof of this practice. That children were circumcised on the eighth day is universally known. If then circumcision, made by hand, in despoiling of the body of the flesh, was profitable to children, it is clear that Baptism, which is the circumcision of Christ, not made by hand, is also profitable to them.

Finally, as the Apostle teaches, if by one man's offence death reigned through one, much more they who receive abundance of grace, and of the gift, and of justice, shall reign in life through one,

Jesus Christ. If, then, through the transgression of Adam, children inherit original sin, with still stronger reason can they attain through Christ our Lord grace and justice that they may reign in life. This, however, cannot be effected otherwise than by Baptism.

Pastors, therefore, should inculcate the absolute necessity of administering Baptism to infants, and of gradually forming their tender minds to piety by education in the Christian religion. For according to these admirable words of the wise man: A young man according to his way, even when he is old, he will not depart from it.

Infants Receive The Graces Of Baptism

It may not be doubted that in Baptism infants receive the mysterious gifts of faith. Not that they believe with the assent of the mind, but they are established in the faith of their parents, if the parents profess the true faith; if not--to use the words of St. Augustine,--then in that of the universal society of the saints; for they are rightly said to be presented for Baptism by all those to whom their initiation in that sacred rite is a source of joy, and by whose charity they are united to the communion of the Holy Ghost.

Baptism Of Infants Should Not Be Delayed

The faithful are earnestly to be exhorted to take care that their children be brought to the church, as soon as it can be done with safety, to receive solemn Baptism. Since infant children have no other means of salvation except Baptism, we may easily understand how grievously those persons sin who permit them to remain without the grace of the Sacrament longer than necessity may require, particularly at an age so tender as to be exposed to numberless dangers of death.

Baptism Of Adults

With regard to those of adult age who enjoy the perfect use of reason, persons, namely, born of infidel parents, the practice of the primitive Church points out that a different manner of proceeding should be followed. To them the Christian faith is to be proposed; and they are earnestly to be exhorted, persuaded and invited to embrace it.

They Should Not Delay Their Baptism Unduly

If converted to the Lord God, they are then to be admonished not to defer the Sacrament of Baptism beyond the time prescribed by the Church. For since it is written, delay not to be converted to the Lord, and defer it not from day to day, they are to be taught that in their regard perfect conversion consists in regeneration by Baptism. Besides, the longer they defer Baptism, the longer are they deprived of the use and graces of the other Sacraments, by which the Christian religion is practised, since the other Sacraments are accessible through Baptism only.

They are also deprived of the abundant fruits of Baptism, the waters of which not only wash away all the stains and defilements of past sins, but also enrich us with divine grace which enables us to avoid sin for the future and preserve righteousness and innocence, which constitute the sum of a Christian life, as all can easily understand.

Ordinarily They Are Not Baptised At Once

On adults, however, the Church has not been accustomed to confer the Sacrament of Baptism at once, but has ordained that it be deferred for a certain time. The delay is not attended with the same danger as in the case of infants, which we have already mentioned; should any unforeseen accident make it impossible for adults to be washed in the salutary waters, their intention and determination to receive Baptism and their repentance for past sins, will avail them to grace and righteousness.

Nay, this delay seems to be attended with some advantages. And first, since the Church must take particular care that none approach this Sacrament through hypocrisy and dissimulation, the intentions of such as seek Baptism, are better examined and ascertained. Hence it is that we read in the decrees of ancient Councils that Jewish converts to the Catholic faith, before admission to Baptism, should spend some months in the ranks of the catechumens.

Furthermore, the candidate for Baptism is thus better instructed in the doctrine of the faith which he is to profess, and in the practices of the Christian life. Finally, when Baptism is administered to adults with solemn ceremonies on the appointed days of Easter and Pentecost only greater religious reverence is shown to the Sacrament.

In Case Of Necessity Adults May Be: Baptised At Once

Sometimes, however, when there exists a just and necessary cause, as in the case of imminent danger of death, Baptism is not to be deferred, particularly if the person to be baptised is well instructed in the mysteries of faith. This we find to have been done by Philip, and by the Prince of the Apostles, when without any delay, the one baptised the eunuch of Queen Candace; the other, Cornelius, as soon as they expressed a wish to embrace the faith.

Dispositions for Baptism

Intention

The faithful are also to be instructed in the necessary dispositions for Baptism. In the first place they must desire and intend to receive it; for as in Baptism we all die to sin and resolve to live a new life, it is fit that it be administered to those only who receive it of their own free will and accord; it is to be forced upon none. Hence we learn from holy tradition that it has been the invariable practice to administer Baptism to no individual without previously asking him if he be willing to receive it. This disposition even infants are presumed to have, since the will of the Church, which promises for them, cannot be mistaken.

Insane, delirious persons who were once of sound mind and afterwards became deranged, having in their present state no wish to be baptised, are not to be admitted to Baptism, unless in danger of death. In such cases, if previous to insanity they give intimation of a wish to be baptised, the Sacrament is to be administered; without such indication previously given it is not to be administered. The same rule is to be followed with regard to persons who are unconscious.

But if they (the insane) never enjoyed the use of reason, the authority and practice of the Church decide that they are to be baptised in the faith of the Church, just as children are baptised before they come to the use of reason.

Faith

Besides a wish to be baptised, in order to obtain the grace of the Sacrament, faith is also necessary. Our Lord and Saviour has said: He that believes and is baptised shall be saved.

Repentance

Another necessary condition is repentance for past sins, and a fixed determination to avoid all sin in the future. Should anyone desire Baptism and be unwilling to correct the habit of sinning, he should be altogether rejected. For nothing is so opposed to the grace and power of Baptism as the intention and purpose of those who resolve never to abandon sin.

Seeing that Baptism should be sought with a view to put on Christ and to be united to Him, it is manifest that he who purposes to continue in sin should justly be repelled from the sacred font, particularly since none of those things which belong to Christ and His Church are to be received in vain, and since we well understand that, as far as regards sanctifying and saving grace, Baptism is received in vain by him who purposes to live according to the flesh, and not according to the spirit. As far, however, as the Sacrament is concerned, if the person who is rightly baptised intends to receive what the Church administers, he without doubt validly receives the Sacrament.

Hence, to the vast multitude who, in compunction of heart, as the Scripture says, asked him and the other Apostles what they should do, the Prince of the Apostles answered: Do penance and be baptised every one of you; and in another place he said: Be penitent, therefore, and be converted, that your sins may be blotted out. Writing to the Romans, St. Paul also clearly shows that he who is baptised should entirely die to sin; and he therefore admonishes us not to yield our members as instruments of iniquity unto sin, but present ourselves to God, as those who are alive from the dead.

Advantages To Be Derived From These Reflections

Frequent reflection upon these truths cannot fail, in the first place, to fill the minds of the faithful with admiration for the infinite goodness of God, who, uninfluenced by any other consideration than that of His mercy, gratuitously bestowed upon us, undeserving as we are, a blessing so extraordinary and divine as that of Baptism.

If in the next place they consider how spotless should be the lives of those who have been made the objects of such munificence, they cannot fail to be convinced of the special obligation imposed on every Christian to spend each day of his life in such sanctity and fervour, as if on that very day he had received the Sacrament and grace of Baptism.

Effects of Baptism

To inflame the minds of the faithful, however, with a zeal for true piety, pastors will find no means more efficacious than an accurate exposition of the effects of Baptism.

The effects of Baptism should be frequently explained, in order that the faithful may be rendered more sensible of the high dignity to which they have been raised, and may never suffer themselves to be cast down therefrom by the snares or assaults of Satan.

First Effect Of Baptism: Remission Of Sin

They are to be taught, in the first place, that such is the admirable efficacy of this Sacrament that it remits original sin and actual guilt, however unthinkable its enormity may seem.

This was foretold long before by Ezechiel, through whom God said: I will pour upon you clean water, and you shall be cleansed from all your filthiness. The Apostle also, writing to the Corinthians, after having enumerated a long catalogue of sins, adds: such you were, but you are washed, but you are sanctified.

That such was at all times the doctrine handed down by holy Church is clear. By the generation of the flesh, says St. Augustine in his book On the Baptism of Infants, we contract original sin only; by the regeneration of the Spirit, we obtain forgiveness not only of original, but also of actual sins. St. Jerome also, writing to Oceanus, says: all sins are forgiven in Baptism.

To remove all further doubt on the subject, the Council of Trent, after other Councils had defined this, declared it anew, pronouncing anathema against those who should presume to think otherwise, or should dare to assert that although sin is forgiven in Baptism, it is not entirely removed or totally eradicated, but is cut away in such a manner as to leave its roots still fixed in the soul. To use the words of the same holy Council, God hates nothing in those who are regenerated; for there remains nothing deserving of condemnation in those who are truly buried with Christ by Baptism unto death, "who walk not according to the flesh" but putting off the old man, and putting on the new, who is created according to God, become innocent, spotless, pure, upright, and beloved of God.

Concupiscence Which Remains After Baptism Is No Sin

We must confess, however, that concupiscence, or the fuel of sin, still remains, as the Council declares in the same place. But concupiscence does not constitute sin, for, as St. Augustine observes, in children who have been baptised the guilt of concupiscence is removed, (the concupiscence itself) remains for probation; and in another place he says: the guilt of concupiscence is pardoned in Baptism, but its infirmity remains. For concupiscence which is the effect of sin is nothing more than an appetite of the soul in itself repugnant to reason. But if it is not accompanied by the consent of the will or by negligence, it is very far from being sin.

When St. Paul says, I did not know concupiscence, if the law did not say: Thou shalt not covet, he speaks not of concupiscence itself, but of the fault of the will.

The same doctrine is taught by St. Gregory when he says: If there are any who assert that in Baptism sin is but superficially effaced, what could be more untrue than their statement? By the Sacrament of faith the soul, entirely freed from sin, adheres to God alone. In proof of this doctrine he has recourse to the testimony of our Saviour who says in St. John: He that is -washed, needeth not but to wash his feet, but is clean wholly.

Further Proof Of The First Effect Of Baptism

Should anyone desire a striking figure and image (of the efficacy of Baptism) let him consider the history of Naaman the Syrian leper, of whom the Scriptures inform us that when he had washed seven times in the waters of the Jordan he was so cleansed from his leprosy that his flesh became like the flesh of a child.

The remission of all sin, original and actual, is therefore the peculiar effect of Baptism. That this was the object of its institution by our Lord and Saviour is clearly stated by the Prince of the Apostles, to say nothing of other testimonies, when he says: Do penance and be baptised every one of you, in the name of Jesus Christ, for the remission of sins.

The Second Effect Of Baptism: Remission Of All Punishment Due To Sin

In Baptism not only is sin forgiven, but with it all the punishment due to sin is mercifully remitted by God. To communicate the efficacy of the Passion of Christ our Lord is an effect common to all the Sacraments; but of Baptism alone does the Apostle say, that by it we die and are buried together with Christ.

Hence holy Church has always understood that to impose those works of piety, usually called by the holy Fathers works of satisfaction, on one who is to be cleansed in Baptism, would be injurious to this Sacrament in the highest degree.

Nor is there any discrepancy between the doctrine here taught and the practice of the primitive Church, which of old commanded the Jews, when preparing for Baptism, to observe a fast of forty successive days. (The fast thus imposed) was not enjoined as a work of satisfaction; but those who had received Baptism were thus admonished to devote some time to the uninterrupted exercise of fasting and prayer in honour of so great a Sacrament.

Baptism Does Not Exempt From Penalties Of The Civil Law

Although the remission by Baptism of the punishments due to sin cannot be questioned, we are not to infer that it exempts an offender from the punishments decreed by civil tribunals for some grave crime. Thus a person sentenced to death is not rescued by Baptism from the penalty ordained by the law.

We cannot, however, too highly commend the religion and piety of those rulers who remit the sentence of the law, that the glory of God may be the more strikingly displayed in His Sacraments.

Baptism Remits The Punishment Due To Original Sin After Death

Baptism also remits all the punishment due to original sin after this life, for through the merit of the death of our Lord we are able to attain this blessing. By Baptism, as we have already said, we die with Christ. For if, says the Apostle, we have been planted together in the likeness of his death, we shall be also in the likeness of his resurrection.

Baptism Does Not Free Us From The Miseries Of Life

Should it be asked why immediately after Baptism we are not exempt in this mortal life from misfortunes and restored by the influence of this sacred ablution to that state of perfection in which Adam, the father of the human race, was placed before his fall, the answer will be that there are two chief reasons for this.

In the first place we who by Baptism are united to, and become members of Christ's body, should not be more honoured than our Head. Now Christ our Lord, although clothed from His birth with the plenitude of grace and truth, was not divested of human infirmity which He assumed, until, having suffered and died, He rose to the glory of immortality. It cannot appear extraordinary, therefore, if the faithful, even after they have received the grace of justification by Baptism, are clothed with frail and perishable bodies until, having undergone many labours for the sake of Christ, and having closed their earthly career, they are recalled to life and found worthy to enjoy with Him an eternity of bliss.

The second reason why bodily infirmity, disease, sense of pain and motions of concupiscence remain after Baptism is that in them we may have the seed and material of virtue from which we shall hereafter receive a more abundant harvest of glory and more ample rewards. When, with patient resignation, we bear all the trials of life, and, aided by the divine assistance, subject to the dominion of reason the rebellious desires of the heart, we ought to cherish an assured hope that if, with the Apostle we shall have fought a good fight, finished the course, and kept the faith, the Lord, the just judge, will render to us on that day a crown of justice which is laid up for us.

Such seems to have been the divine plan with regard to the children of Israel. God delivered them from the bondage of Egypt, having drowned Pharaoh and his hosts in the sea; yet He did not conduct them immediately into the happy land of promise; He first tried them by a variety and multiplicity of sufferings. And when He afterwards placed them in possession of the promised land and expelled the previous inhabitants from their native territories, yet He left a few other nations whom the Israelites could not exterminate, in order that His people might always have occasion to exercise fortitude and warlike courage.

We may add that if, to the heavenly gifts with which the soul is adorned in Baptism, were joined temporal advantages, there would be good reason to doubt whether many might not approach Baptism with a view to obtain such advantages in this life, rather than the glory to be hoped for in the next; whereas the Christian should always propose to himself, not these delusive and uncertain goods which are seen, but the solid and eternal ones which are not seen.

Baptism A Source Of Happiness To The Christian Even In This Life

This life, however, although full of misery, does not lack its pleasures and joys. To us, who by Baptism are engrafted as branches on Christ's what could be more pleasing or desirable than, taking up the cross upon our shoulders, to follow Him as our leader, fatigued by no labor, retarded by no danger, in ardent pursuit of the rewards of our high vocation; some to receive the laurel of virginity, others the crown of teaching and preaching, some the palm of martyrdom, others the honours appropriate to their respective virtues? These splendid titles of exalted dignity none of us should receive, had we not contended in the race of this calamitous life and stood unconquered in the conflict.

Third Effect Of Baptism: Grace Of Regeneration

But to return to the effects of Baptism, it should be taught that by virtue of this Sacrament we are not only delivered from what are justly deemed the greatest of all evils, but are also enriched with invaluable goods and blessings. Our souls are replenished with divine grace, by which we are rendered just and children of God and are made heirs to eternal salvation. For it is written: He that believeth and is baptised, shall be saved, and the Apostle testifies that the Church is cleansed by the laver of water in the word of life. Now according to the definition of the Council of Trent, which under pain of anathema we are bound to believe, grace not only remits sin, but is also a divine quality inherent in the soul, and, as it were, a brilliant light that effaces all those stains which obscure the lustre of the soul, investing it with increased brightness and beauty. This is also a clear inference from the words of Scripture when it says that grace is poured forth, and also when it usually calls grace, the pledge of the Holy Ghost.

Fourth Effect Of Baptism: Infused Virtues And Incorporation With Christ

This grace is accompanied by a most splendid train of all virtues, which are divinely infused into the soul along with grace. Hence, when writing to Titus, the Apostle says: He saved us by the laver of regeneration and renovation of the Holy Ghost, whom he hath poured forth upon us abundantly, through Jesus Christ our Saviour. St. Augustine, in explanation of the words, poured forth abundantly, says: that is, for the remission of sins and for abundance of virtues.

By Baptism we are also united to Christ, as members to their Head. As therefore from the head proceeds the power by which the different members of the body are moved to the proper performance of their respective functions, so from the fullness of Christ the Lord are diffused divine grace and virtue through all those who are justified, qualifying them for the performance of all the duties of Christian piety.

Why The Practice Of Virtue Is Difficult Even After Baptism

Though we are thus supported by a powerful array of virtues, it should not excite our surprise if we cannot, without much labor and difficulty, undertake, or at least, perform acts of piety and of moral virtue. If this is so, it is not because the goodness of God has not bestowed on us the virtues from which these good works proceed; but because there still remains after Baptism a severe conflict of the flesh against the spirit, in which, however, it would not become a Christian to be dispirited or grow faint.

Relying on the divine goodness we should confidently hope that by a constant habit of leading a holy life the time will come when whatever things are modest, whatever just, whatever holy, will also prove easy and agreeable. Let these be the subjects of our willing consideration, the objects of our cheerful practice, that the God of peace may be with us.

Fifth Effect Of Baptism: Character Of Christian

By Baptism, moreover, we are sealed with a character that can never be effaced from the soul. On this point, however, we need not speak at length, for what we have already sufficiently said on the subject, when treating of the Sacraments in general, may be applied here.

Baptism Not To Be Repeated

Since on account of the nature and efficacy of this character it has been defined by the Church that this Sacrament is on no account to be reiterated, pastors should frequently and diligently admonish the faithful on this subject, lest at any time they may be led into error.

This doctrine is taught by the Apostle when he says: One Lord, one faith, one baptism. Again, when exhorting the Romans, that being dead in Christ by Baptism they should take care not to lose the life which they had received from Him, he says: In that Christ died unto sin, he died once. These words seem clearly to signify that as Christ cannot die again, neither can we die again by Baptism. Hence the holy Church also openly professes that she believes one Baptism. That this agrees with the nature of the thing and with reason is understood from the very idea of Baptism, which is a spiritual regeneration. As then, by virtue of the laws of nature, we are generated and born but once, and, as St. Augustine observes, there is no returning to the womb; so, in like manner, there is but one spiritual generation, and Baptism is never at any time to be repeated.

In Conditional Baptism The Sacrament Is Not Repeated

Nor let anyone suppose that it is repeated by the Church when she baptises anyone whose previous Baptism was doubtful, making use of this formula: If thou art baptised, I baptise thee not again but if thou art not yet baptised, I baptise thee in the name of the Father, and of the Son, and of the Holy Ghost. In such cases Baptism is not to be considered as impiously repeated, but as holily, yet conditionally, administered.

In this connection, however, there are some matters, in which, to the very great injury of the Sacrament, abuses are of almost daily occurrence, and which therefore demand the diligent attention of pastors. For there are not wanting those who think that no sin is committed if they indiscriminately administer conditional Baptism. Hence if an infant be brought to them, they think that no inquiry need be made as to whether it was previously baptised, but proceed immediately to baptise the child. Nay more, although they be well aware that the Sacrament was administered at home, they do not hesitate to repeat its administration in the Church conditionally, making use of the solemn ceremonies of the Church.

This certainly they cannot do without sacrilege and without incurring what theologians call an irregularity. According to the authority of Pope Alexander the conditional form of Baptism is to be used only when after due inquiry doubts are entertained as to the validity of the previous Baptism. In no other case is it ever lawful to administer Baptism a second time, even conditionally.

Sixth Effect Of Baptism: Opening The Gates Of Heaven

Besides the other advantages which accrue to us from Baptism, the last, to which all the others seem to be referred, is that it opens to us the portals of heaven which sin had closed against us.

Effects Of Baptism Foreshadowed In The Baptism Of Christ

These effects which are wrought in us by virtue of Baptism are distinctly marked by the circumstances which, as the Gospel relates, accompanied the Baptism of our Saviour. The heavens were opened and the Holy Ghost appeared descending upon Christ our Lord in the form of a dove. By this we are given to understand that to those who are baptised are imparted the gifts of the Holy Spirit, that to them are opened the gates of heaven. The baptised, it is true, do not enter heaven immediately after Baptism, but in due season. When they shall have been freed from all misery which is incompatible with a state of bliss, they shall exchange a mortal for an immortal life.

Measure In Which Those Effects Are Obtained

These are the fruits of Baptism, which, if we consider the efficacy of the Sacrament, are, no doubt, equally common to all; but if we consider the dispositions with which it is received, it is no less certain that all do not share to the same extent in these heavenly gifts and graces.

Ceremonies of Baptism

Their Importance

It now remains to explain, clearly and concisely, what is to be taught concerning the prayers, rites, and ceremonies of this

Sacrament. To rites and ceremonies may, in some measure, be applied what the Apostle says of the gift of tongues, that it is unprofitable to speak, unless the faithful understand. They present an image, and convey the signification of the things that are done in the Sacrament; but if the people do not understand the force and meaning of these signs, there is but little advantage derived from ceremonies. Pastors should take care, therefore, to make them understood and to impress the minds of the faithful with a conviction that, although ceremonies are not of absolute necessity, they are of very great importance and deserve great veneration.

This the authority of those by whom they were instituted, who were, no doubt, the Apostles, and also the object of their institution, sufficiently prove. It is manifest that ceremonies contribute to the more religious and holy administration of the Sacraments, serve to place, as it were, before the eyes the exalted and inestimable gifts which they contain, and impress on the minds of the faithful a deeper sense of the boundless beneficence of God.

Three Classes Of Ceremonies In Baptism

In order that the pastor's instructions may follow a certain plan and that the people may find it: easier to remember his words, all the ceremonies and prayers which the Church uses in the administration of Baptism are to be reduced to three heads. The first comprehends such as are observed before coming to the baptismal font; the second, such as are used at the font; the third, those that usually follow the administration of the Sacrament.

Ceremonies That Are Observed Before Coming To The Font: Consecration Of Baptismal Water

In the first place, then, the water to be used in Baptism should be prepared. The baptismal font is consecrated with the oil of mystic unction; not, however, at all times, but, according to ancient usage, only on certain feasts, which are justly deemed the greatest and the most holy solemnities in the year. The water of Baptism was consecrated on the vigils of those feasts; and on those days alone, except in cases of necessity, it was also the practice of the ancient Church to administer Baptism. But although the Church, on account of the dangers to which life is continually exposed, has deemed it expedient to change her discipline in this respect, she still observes with the greatest solemnity the festivals of Easter and Pentecost on which the baptismal water is to be consecrated.

The Person To Be Baptised Stands At The Church Door

After the consecration of the water the other ceremonies that precede Baptism are next to be explained. The persons to be baptised are brought or conducted a to the door of the church and are strictly forbidden to enter, as unworthy to be admitted into the house of God, until they have cast off the yoke of the most degrading servitude and devoted themselves unreservedly to Christ the Lord and His most just authority.

Catechetical Instruction

The priest then asks what they demand of the Church; and having received the answer, he first instructs them in the doctrines of the Christian faith, of which a profession is to be made in Baptism.

This the priest does in a brief catechetical instruction, a practice which originated, no doubt, in the precept of our Lord addressed to His Apostles: Go ye into the whole world, and teach all nations, baptising them in the name of the Father, and of the Son, and of the Holy Ghost, teaching them to observe all things whatsoever I have commanded you. From this command we may learn that Baptism is not to be administered until, at least, the principal truths of our religion are explained.

But as the catechetical form consists of many interrogations, if the person to be instructed be an adult, he himself answers; if an infant, the sponsor answers for him according to the prescribed form and makes the solemn promise.

The Exorcism

The exorcism comes next in order. It consists of words of sacred and religious import and of prayers, and is used to expel the devil, to weaken and crush his power.

The Salt

To the exorcism are added other ceremonies, each of which, being mystical, has its own clear signification. When, for instance, salt is put into the mouth of the person to be baptised, this evidently means that, by the doctrines of faith and by the gift of grace, he shall be delivered from the corruption of sin, shall experience a relish for good works, and shall be delighted with the food of divine wisdom.

The Sign Of The Cross

Next his forehead, eyes, breast, shoulders and ears are signed with the sign of the cross, to declare, that by the mystery of Baptism, the senses of the person baptised are opened and strengthened, to enable him to receive God, and to understand and observe His Commandments.

The Saliva

His nostrils and ears are next touched with spittle, and he is then immediately admitted to the baptismal font. By this ceremony we understand that, as sight was given to the blind man mentioned in the Gospel, whom the Lord after He had spread clay on his eyes commanded to wash them in the waters of Siloe, so through the efficacy of holy Baptism a light is let in on the mind, which enables it to discern heavenly truth.

The Ceremonies Observed After Coming To The Font

After the performance of these ceremonies the persons to be baptised approach the baptismal font, at which are performed other rites and ceremonies which present a summary of the Christian religion.

The Renunciation Of Satan

Three distinct times the person to be baptised is asked by the priest: Dost thou renounce Satan, and all his works, and all his pomps? To each of which he, or the sponsor in his name, replies, I renounce. Whoever, then, purposes to enlist, under the standard of Christ, must first of all, enter into a sacred and solemn engagement to renounce the devil and the world, and always to hold them in utter detestation as his worst enemies.

The Profession Of Faith

Next, standing at the baptismal font, he is interrogated by the priest in these words: Dost thou believe in God, the Father Almighty? To which he answers: I believe. Being similarly questioned on the remaining Articles of the Creed, he solemnly professes his faith. These two promises contain, it is clear, the sum and substance of the law of Christ.

The Wish To Be Baptised

When the Sacrament is now about to be administered, the priest asks the candidate if he wishes to be baptised. After an answer in the affirmative has been given by him, or, if he is an infant, by the sponsor, the priest immediately performs the salutary ablution, in the name of the Father, and of the Son, and of the Holy Ghost.

As man, by yielding the assent of his will to the wicked suggestions of Satan, fell under a just sentence of condemnation; so God will have none enrolled in the number of His soldiers but those whose service is voluntary, that by a willing obedience to His commands they may obtain eternal salvation.

The Ceremonies That Follow Baptism: Chrism

After the person has been baptised, the priest anoints the crown of his head with chrism, thus giving him to understand, that from that day he is united as a member to Christ, His Head, and ingrafted on His body; and that he is, therefore, called a Christian from Christ, as Christ is so called from chrism. What the chrism signifies, the prayers then offered by the priest, as St. Ambrose observes, sufficiently explain.

The White Garment

On the person baptised the priest then puts a white garment saying: Receive this white garment, which mayest thou carry unstained before the judgment-seat of our Lord Jesus Christ; that thou mayest have eternal life. Instead of a white garment, infants, because not formally dressed, receive a white cloth, accompanied by the same words.

According to the teaching of the Fathers this symbol signifies the glory of the resurrection to which we are born by Baptism, the brightness and beauty with which the soul, when purified from the stains of sin, is invested in Baptism, and the innocence and integrity which the person who has received Baptism should preserve throughout life.

The Lighted Candle

A lighted taper is then put into the hand of the baptised to signify that faith, inflamed by charity, which is received in Baptism, is to be fed and augmented by the exercise of good works.

The Name Given In Baptism

Finally, a name is given the person baptised. It should be taken from some person whose eminent sanctity has given him a place in the catalogue of the Saints. The similarity of name will stimulate each one to imitate the virtues and holiness of the Saint, and, moreover, to hope and pray that he who is the model for his imitation will also be his advocate and watch over the safety of his body and soul.

Wherefore those are to be reproved who search for the names of heathens, especially of those who were the greatest monsters of iniquity, to bestow upon their children. By such conduct they practically prove how little they regard Christian piety when they so fondly cherish the memory of impious men, as to wish to have their profane names continually echo in the ears of the faithful.

Recapitulation

This exposition of the Sacrament of Baptism, if given by pastors, will be found to embrace almost everything which should be known regarding this Sacrament. We have explained the meaning of the word Baptism, the nature and substance of the Sacrament, and also the parts of which it is composed. We have said by whom it was instituted; who are the ministers necessary to its administration; who should be, as it were, the tutors whose instructions should sustain the weakness of the person baptised; to whom Baptism should be administered; and how they should be disposed; what are the virtue and efficacy of the Sacrament; finally, we have developed, at sufficient length for our purpose, the rites and ceremonies that should accompany its administration.

Pastors should recollect that the chief purpose of all these instructions is to induce the faithful to direct their constant attention and solicitude to the fulfilment of the promises so sacredly made at Baptism, and to lead lives not unworthy of the sanctity that should accompany the name and profession of Christian.

THE SACRAMENT OF CONFIRMATION

Importance Of Instruction On Confirmation

If ever there was a time demanding the diligence of pastors in explaining the Sacrament of Confirmation, in these days certainly it requires special attention, when there are found in the holy Church of God many by whom this Sacrament is altogether omitted; while very few seek to obtain from it the fruit of divine grace which they should derive from its participation.

Lest, therefore, this divine blessing may seem, through their fault, and to their most serious injury, to have been conferred on them in vain, the faithful are to be instructed both on Whitsunday, on which day it is principally administered, and also on such other days as pastors shall deem convenient. Their instructions should so treat the nature, power, and dignity of this Sacrament, that the faithful may understand not only that it is not to be neglected, hut that it is to be received with the greatest piety and devotion.

Name of this Sacrament

To begin with the name, it should be taught that this Sacrament is called by the Church Confirmation because, if there is no obstacle to the efficacy of the Sacrament, a baptised person, when anointed with the sacred chrism by the Bishop, with the accompanying solemn words: I sign thee with the sign of the cross, and confirm thee with the chrism of salvation, in the name of the Father, and of the Son, and of the Holy Ghost, becomes stronger with the strength of a new power, and thus begins to be a perfect soldier of Christ.

Confirmation is a Sacrament

That in Confirmation is contained the true and proper nature of a Sacrament has always been acknowledged by the Catholic Church, as Pope Melchiades and many other very holy and very ancient Pontiffs expressly declare. The truth of this doctrine St. Clement could not confirm in stronger terms than when he says: All should hasten without delay to be born again unto God, and afterwards to be signed by the Bishop, that is, to receive the sevenfold grace of the Holy Ghost; for, as has been handed down to us from St. Peter, and as the other Apostles taught in obedience to the command and of our Lord, he who culpably and voluntarily, and not from necessity, neglects to receive this Sacrament, cannot possibly be a perfect Christian. This same faith has been confirmed, as may be seen in their decrees, by Popes Urban, Fabian and Eusebius, who, filled with the same spirit, shed their blood for the name of Christ.

The unanimous authority of the Fathers must be added. Among them Denis the Areopagite, Bishop of Athens, when teaching how to consecrate and make use of this holy ointment, says: The priests clothe the person Baptised with a garment emblematic of purity, in order to conduct him to the Bishop; and the Bishop, signing him with the sacred and truly divine ointment, makes him partaker of the most holy communion. Of such importance does Eusebius of Caesarea also deem this Sacrament as not to hesitate to say that the heretic Novatus could not deserve to receive the Holy Ghost, because, having been baptised in a state of severe illness, he was not anointed with the sign of chrism. But on this subject we have the most distinct testimonies from St. Ambrose in his book On the Initiated, and from St. Augustine in his books Against the Epistles of Petilian the Donatist.

Both of them were so persuaded that no doubt could exist as to the reality of this Sacrament that they even taught and confirmed the doctrine by passages of Scripture, the one testifying that to the Sacrament of Confirmation apply these words of the Apostle:

Grieve not the Holy Spirit of God, whereby you are sealed; the other, these words of the Psalmist: Like the precious ointment on the head, that ran down upon the beard, the beard of Aaron, and also these words of the same Apostle: The charity of God is poured forth in our hearts by the Holy Ghost, who is given to us.

Confirmation is Distinct from Baptism

Although said by Melchiades to have a most intimate connection with Baptism, Confirmation is still not to be regarded as the same, but as a very different Sacrament; for the variety of the grace which each of the Sacraments confers, and of the sensible sign employed to signify that grace, evidently render them distinct and different Sacraments.

Since, then, by the grace of Baptism we are begotten unto newness of life, whereas by that of Confirmation we grow to full maturity, having put away the things of a child, we can sufficiently understand that the same difference that exists in the natural life between birth and growth exists also between Baptism, which regenerates, and Confirmation, by virtue of which growth and perfect spiritual strength are imparted to the faithful.

Besides, as there should be a new and distinct kind of Sacrament when the soul has to encounter any new difficulty, it may easily be perceived that as we require the grace of Baptism to form the mind unto faith, so is it also of the utmost advantage that the souls of the faithful be strengthened by a different grace, to the end that they be deterred by no danger, or fear of pains, tortures or death, from the confession of the true faith. This, then, being accomplished by the sacred chrism of Confirmation, it is hence clearly inferred, that the nature of this Sacrament is different from Baptism.

Hence Pope Melchiades accurately evolves the difference between them, writing as follows: In Baptism man is enlisted into the service, in Confirmation he is equipped for battle; at the baptismal font the Holy Ghost imparts fullness to accomplish innocence, but in Confirmation he ministers perfection to grace; in Baptism we are regenerated unto life, after Baptism we are fortified for the combat; in Baptism we are cleansed, after Baptism we are strengthened; regeneration of itself saves those who receive Baptism in time of peace, Confirmation arms and makes ready for conflicts.

These are truths not only already recorded by other Councils, but specially defined by the holy Council of Trent; so that we are therefore no longer at liberty not only to think otherwise, but even to entertain the least doubt concerning them.

Institution of Confirmation

It was shown above how necessary it is to teach concerning all the Sacraments in common from whom they had their origin. Wherefore the same is also to be taught as regards Confirmation, in order that the faithful may be impressed with a deeper sense of the sanctity of this Sacrament. Accordingly, pastors must explain that not only was it instituted by Christ the Lord, but that by Him were also ordained, as Pope St. Fabian testifies, the rite of chrism and the words which the Catholic Church uses in its administration. This is a fact easy to prove to those who acknowledge Confirmation to be a Sacrament, because all the sacred mysteries exceed the powers of human nature and could be instituted by no other than God alone.

Component Parts of Confirmation

The Matter

We now come to treat of the component parts of the Sacrament, and first of its matter. This is called chrism, a word borrowed from the Greek language, and which, although used by profane writers to designate any sort of ointment, is appropriated by common usage among ecclesiastical writers to signify that ointment only which is composed of oil and balsam with the solemn consecration of the Bishop. A mixture of two material things, therefore, furnishes the matter of Confirmation; and this mixture of different things not only declares the manifold grace of the Holy Ghost given to those who are confirmed but also sufficiently shows the excellence of the Sacrament itself.

The Remote Matter Of Confirmation Is Chrism

That such is the matter of this Sacrament the holy Church and her Councils have always taught; and the same doctrine has been handed-down to us by St. Denis and by many other Fathers of the gravest authority, particularly by Pope Fabian,' who testifies that the Apostles received the composition of chrism from our Lord and transmitted it to us.

The Appropriateness Of Chrism

Nor indeed could any other matter than that of chrism seem more appropriate to declare the effects of this Sacrament. Oil, by its nature rich, unctuous and fluid, expresses the fullness of grace, which, through the Holy Ghost, overflows and is poured into others from Christ the head, like the ointment that ran down upon the beard of Aaron, to the skirt of his garment; for God anointed him with the oil of gladness, above his fellows, and of his fullness we all have received.

Balsam, the door of which is most pleasant, can signify nought save that the faithful, when made perfect by the grace of Confirmation, diffuse around them such a sweet door of all virtues, that they may say with the Apostle: We are unto God the good odour of Christ. Balsam has also the power of preserving from corruption whatever it is used to anoint. This property seems admirably suited to express the virtue of the Sacrament, since it is quite evident that the souls of the faithful, prepared by the heavenly grace of Confirmation, are easily protected from the contagion of sins.

Chrism To Be Consecrated By The Bishop

The chrism is consecrated by the Bishop with solemn ceremonies; for that our Saviour gave this instruction at His last supper, when He committed to His Apostles the manner of making chrism, we learn from Fabian, a pontiff eminently distinguished by his sanctity and by the glory of martyrdom.

The necessity of this consecration may, however, be shown from reason also. In most of the other Sacraments Christ so instituted their matter as to impart holiness also to it. For not only did He designate water as the element of Baptism, saying: Except a man be born again of water and the Holy Ghost, he cannot enter the kingdom of God; but He also, at His own Baptism, imparted to it the power of sanctifying thereafter. Hence these words of St. Chrysostom: The water of Baptism, had it not been sanctified by contact with the body of our Lord, could not purge away the sins of believers. As, then, our Lord did not consecrate this matter of Confirmation by actually using and handling it, it is necessary that it be consecrated by holy and religious prayers; and this consecration can appertain to none save the Bishop, who has been appointed the ordinary minister of this Sacrament.

The Form Of Confirmation

The other component part of Confirmation, that is, its form and the words used at the sacred unction, must also be explained. The faithful are to be admonished that in receiving this Sacrament they are, in particular on hearing the words pronounced, to excite their minds to piety, faith and religion, that no obstacle may be placed to heavenly grace.

The form of Confirmation, then, is comprised in these words: I sign thee with the sign of the cross, and I confirm thee with the chrism of salvation, in the name of the Father, and of the Son, and of the Holy Ghost. If we call upon reason regarding this truth, we may also easily prove the same thing; for the form of a Sacrament should comprise all those things that explain the nature and substance of the Sacrament itself. But in Confirmation these three things are chiefly to be noted: the divine power which, as a principal cause, operates in the Sacrament; the strength of mind and soul which is imparted by the sacred unction to the faithful unto salvation; and finally, the sign impressed on him who is to enter upon the warfare of Christ. Now of these the first is sufficiently declared by the concluding words of the form: In the name of the Father, and of the Son, and of the Holy Ghost; the second, by the words immediately preceding them: I confirm thee with the chrism of salvation; and the third, by the words with which the form opens: I sign thee with the sign of the cross.

But were we even unable to prove by reason that this is the true and perfect form of this Sacrament, the authority of the Catholic Church, under whose guidance we have always been thus taught, suffers us not to entertain the least doubt on the subject.

Minister of Confirmation

Pastors should also teach to whom especially has been committed the administration of this Sacrament; for as, according to the Prophet, there are many who run without being sent, it is necessary to teach who are its true and legitimate ministers, in order that the faithful may be enabled to receive the Sacrament and grace of Confirmation.

Now the Holy Scriptures show that the Bishop alone is the ordinary minister of this Sacrament, because we read in the Acts of the Apostles that when Samaria had received the Word of God, Peter and John were sent to them, who prayed for them that they might receive the Holy Ghost: for he was not as yet come upon any of them, but they were only baptised. Here we may see that he who had baptised, having been only a deacon, had no power to confirm; but that its administration was reserved to a more perfect order of ministers, that is, to the Apostles. The same may be observed whenever the Sacred Scriptures make mention of this Sacrament.

Nor are there wanting in proof of this matter the clearest testimonies of the holy Fathers and of Popes Urban, Eusebius, Damasus, Innocent and Leo, as is evident from their decrees. St. Augustine, also, seriously complains of the corrupt practice of the Egyptians and Alexandrians, whose priests dared to administer the Sacrament of Confirmation.

The thorough propriety of reserving this function to Bishops the pastor may illustrate by the following comparison. As in the construction of buildings the artisans, who are inferior agents, prepare and dispose cement, lime, timbers and the other material, while to the architect belongs the completion of the work; so in like manner this Sacrament, which is, at it were, the completion of the spiritual edifice, should be performed by no other than the chief priest.

Sponsors at Confirmation

A sponsor is also required, as we have already shown to be the case in Baptism. For if they who enter the fencing lists have need for some one whose skill and counsel may teach them the thrusts and passes by which to overcome their adversaries, while remaining safe themselves; how much more will the faithful require a leader and monitor, when, sheathed, as it were, in the stoutest armour by this Sacrament of Confirmation, they engage in the spiritual conflict, in which eternal salvation is the proposed reward. With good reason, therefore, are sponsors employed in the administration of this Sacrament also; and the same spiritual affinity is contracted in Confirmation, which, as we have already shown, is contracted by sponsors in Baptism, so as to impede the lawful marriage of the parties.

The Subject of Confirmation

It often happens that, in receiving this Sacrament, the faithful are guilty of either precipitate haste or a gross neglect and delay; concerning those who have become so impious as to have the hardihood to contemn and despise it, we have nothing to say. Pastors, therefore, should also explain who may receive Confirmation, and what should be their age and dispositions.

All Should Be Confirmed

First, it is necessary to teach that this Sacrament is not so necessary as to be utterly essential to salvation. Although not essential, however, it ought to be omitted by no one, but rather, on the contrary, in a matter so full of holiness through which the divine gifts are so liberally bestowed, the greater care should be taken to avoid all neglect. What God has proposed in common unto all for their sanctification, all should 'likewise most earnestly desire.

St. Luke, indeed, describing this admirable effusion of the Holy Spirit, says: And suddenly there came a sound from heaven, as of a mighty wind coming, and it filled the whole house, where they were sitting; and a little after: And they were all filled with the Holy Ghost. From these words we may understand that, as that house was a type and figure of the Church, the Sacrament of Confirmation, which took its beginning from that day, appertains to all the faithful.

This may also be easily inferred from the nature of the Sacrament itself. For they ought to be confirmed with the sacred chrism who have need of spiritual increase, and who are to be led to the perfection of the Christian religion. But this is, without exception, suited to all; because as nature intends that all her children should grow up and attain full maturity, although she does not always realise her wishes; so the Catholic Church, the common mother of all, earnestly desires that, in those whom she has regenerated by Baptism, the perfection of Christian manhood be completed. Now as this is accomplished through the Sacrament of mystic Unction, it is clear that Confirmation belongs alike to all the faithful.

The Proper Age For Confirmation

Here it is to be observed, that, after Baptism, the Sacrament of Confirmation may indeed be administered to all; but that, until children shall have attained the use of reason, its administration is inexpedient. If it does not seem well to defer (Confirmation) to the age of twelve, it is most proper to postpone this Sacrament at least to that of seven years.

Confirmation has not been instituted as necessary to salvation, but that by virtue thereof we may be found very well armed and prepared when called upon to fight for the faith of Christ; and for this conflict no one assuredly will consider children who as yet lack the use of reason to be qualified.

Dispositions For Receiving Confirmation

From this, therefore, it follows that persons of mature age, who are to be confirmed, must, if they desire to obtain the grace and gifts of this Sacrament, not only bring with them faith and piety, but also grieve from their hearts for the serious sins which they have committed.

The pastor should take care that they have previous recourse to confession of their sins; should exhort them to fasting and other works of piety; and admonish them of the propriety of reviving that laudable practice of the ancient Church, of receiving this Sacrament fasting. It is to be presumed that to this the faithful may be easily persuaded, if they but understand the gifts and admirable effects of this Sacrament.

The Effects of Confirmation

Pastors, therefore, should teach that, in common with the other Sacraments, Confirmation, unless some obstacle be present on the part of the receiver, imparts new grace. For we have shown that these sacred and mystical signs are of such a character as to indicate and produce grace.

The Grace Of Strength

But besides these things, which are common to this and the other (Sacraments), it is peculiar to Confirmation first to perfect the grace of Baptism. For those who have been made Christians by Baptism, still have in some sort the tenderness and softness, as it were, of new-born infants, and afterwards become, by means of the Sacrament of chrism, stronger to resist all the assaults of the world, the flesh and the devil, while their minds are fully confirmed in faith to confess and glorify the name of our Lord Jesus Christ. Hence; also, originated the very name (Confirmation), as no one will doubt. For the word Confirmation is not derived, as some not less ignorantly than impiously have pretended, from the circumstance that persons baptised in infancy, when arrived at mature years, were of old brought to the Bishop, in order to confirm their faith in Christ, which they had embraced ill Baptism, so that Confirmation would seem not to differ from catechetical instruction. Of such a practice no reliable testimony can be adduced. On the contrary, the name has been derived from the fact that by virtue of this Sacrament God confirms in us the work He commenced in Baptism, leading us to the perfection of solid Christian virtue.

Increase In Grace

But not only does it confirm, it also increases (divine grace), as says Melchiades: The Holy Ghost, whose salutary descent upon the waters of Baptism, imparts in the font fullness to the accomplishment of innocence, in Confirmation gives an increase of grace; and not only an increase, but an increase after a wonderful manner. This the Scriptures beautifully express by a metaphor taken from clothing: Stay you in the city, said our Lord and Saviour, speaking of this Sacrament, until you be clothed with power from on high.

If pastors wish to show the divine efficacy of this Sacrament -- and this, no doubt, will have great influence in affecting the minds of the faithful -- it will be sufficient if they explain what occurred to the Apostles themselves. So weak and timid were they before, and even at the very time of the Passion, that no sooner was our Lord apprehended, than they instantly fled ; and Peter, who had been designated the rock and foundation of the Church, and who had displayed unshaken constancy and exalted magnanimity, terrified at the voice of one weak woman, denied, not once nor twice only, but a third time, that he was a disciple of Jesus Christ; and after the Resurrection they all remained shut up at home for fear of the Jews. But, on the day of Pentecost, so great was the power of the Holy Ghost with which they were all filled that, while they boldly and freely disseminated the Gospel confided to them, not only through Judea, but throughout the world, they thought no greater happiness could await them than that of being accounted worthy to suffer contumely, chains, torments and crucifixion, for the name of Christ.

Character Of Soldier Of Christ

Confirmation has also the effect of impressing a character. Hence, as we before said of Baptism, and as will be more fully explained in its proper place with regard to the Sacrament of Orders also, it can on no account ever be repeated.

If, then, these things be frequently and accurately explained by pastors, it will be almost impossible that the faithful, having known the utility and dignity of this Sacrament, should not use every exertion to receive it with purity and devotion.

Ceremonies Of Confirmation

It remains now briefly to glance at the rites and ceremonies used by the Catholic Church in the administration of this Sacrament; and pastors will understand the great advantages of this explanation, if they revert to what we already said on this subject under its proper head.

The Anointing Of The Forehead

The forehead, then, of the persons to be confirmed is anointed with sacred chrism; for by this Sacrament the Holy Spirit infuses Himself into the souls of the faithful, and increases in them strength and fortitude to enable them, in the spiritual contest, to fight manfully and to resist their most wicked foes. Wherefore it is indicated that they are to be deterred by no fear or shame, the signs of which appear chiefly on the forehead, from the open confession of the name of Christ.

The Sign Of The Cross

Besides, that mark by which the Christian is distinguished from all others, as the soldier is by certain badges, should be impressed on the more conspicuous part of the body.

Time When Confirmation Should Be Conferred

It has also been a matter of solemn religious observance in the Church of God that this Sacrament should be administered principally at Pentecost, because on that day especially were the Apostles strengthened and confirmed by the power of the Holy Ghost. By the recollection of this supernatural event the faithful should be admonished of the nature and magnitude of the mysteries contained in the sacred unction.

The Slap On The Cheek

The person when anointed and confirmed next receives a gentle slap on the cheek from the hand of the Bishop to make him recollect that, as a valiant combatant, he should be prepared to endure with unconquered spirit all adversities for the name of Christ.

The Pax

Lastly, the peace is given him, that he may understand that he has attained the fullness of divine grace and that peace which passeth all understanding.

Admonition

Let this, then, serve as a summary of those things which pastors are to expound touching the Sacrament of chrism. The exposition, however, should not be given so much in empty words and cold language, as in the burning accents of pious and glowing zeal, so as to seem to imprint them on the souls and inmost thoughts of the faithful.

THE SACRAMENT OF THE EUCHARIST

Importance Of Instruction On The Eucharist

As of all the sacred mysteries bequeathed to us by our Lord and Saviour as most infallible instruments of divine grace, there is none comparable to the most holy Sacrament of the Eucharist; so, for no crime is there a heavier punishment to be feared from God than for the unholy or irreligious use by the faithful of that which is full of holiness, or rather which contains the very author and source of holiness. This the Apostle wisely saw, and has openly admonished us of it. For when he had declared the enormity of their guilt who discerned not the body of the Lord, he immediately subjoined: Therefore are there many infirm and weak among you, and many sleep.

In order that the faithful, therefore, aware of the divine honours due to this heavenly Sacrament, may derive therefrom abundant fruit of grace and escape the most just anger of God, pastors should explain with the greatest diligence all those things which may seem calculated more fully to display its majesty.

Institution of the Eucharist

In this matter it will be necessary that pastors, following the example of the Apostle Paul, who professes to have delivered to the Corinthians what he had received from the Lord, first of all explain to the faithful the institution of this Sacrament.

That its institution was as follows, is clearly inferred from the Evangelist. Our Lord, having loved his own, loved them to the end. As a divine and admirable pledge of this love, knowing that the hour had now come that He should pass from the world to the Father, that He-might not ever at any period be absent from His own, He accomplished with inexplicable wisdom that which surpasses all the order and condition of nature. For having kept the supper of the Paschal lamb with His disciples, that the figure might yield to the reality, the shadow to the substance, He took bread, and giving thanks unto God, He blessed, and brake, and gave to the disciples, and said: "Take ye and eat, this is my body which shall be delivered for you; this do for a commemoration of me." In like manner also, He took the chalice after he had supped, saying: "This chalice is the new testament in my blood; this do, as often as you shall drink it, in commemoration of me".

Meaning of the Word "Eucharist"

Wherefore sacred writers, seeing that it was not at all possible that they should manifest by one term the dignity and excellence of this admirable Sacrament, endeavoured to express it by many words.

For sometimes they call it Eucharist, which word we may render either by good grace, or by thanksgiving. And rightly, indeed, is it to be called good grace, as well because it first signifies eternal life, concerning which it has been written: The grace of God is eternal life; and also because it contains Christ the Lord, who is true grace and the fountain of all favours.

No less aptly do we interpret it thanksgiving; inasmuch as when we immolate this purest victim, we give daily unbounded thanks to God for all His kindnesses towards us, and above all for so excellent a gift of His grace, which He grants to us in this Sacrament. This same name, also, is fully in keeping with those things which we read were done by Christ the Lord at the institution of this mystery. For taking bread he brake it, and gave thanks. David also, when contemplating the greatness of this mystery, before he pronounced that song: He hath made a remembrance of his wonderful works, being a merciful and gracious Lord, he hath given food to them that fear him, thought that he should first make this act of thanksgiving: His work is praise and magnificence.

Other Names Of This Sacrament

Frequently, also, it is called Sacrifice. Concerning this mystery there will be occasion to speak more at length presently.

It is called, moreover, communion, the term being evidently borrowed from that passage of the Apostle where we read: The chalice of benediction which we bless, is it not the communion of the blood of Christ? And the bread which we break, is it not the partaking of the body of the Lord? For, as Damascene has explained, this Sacrament unites us to Christ, renders us partakers of His flesh and Divinity, reconciles and unites us to one another in the same Christ, and forms us, as it were, into one body.

Whence it came to pass, that i. was called also the Sacrament of peace and love. We can understand then how unworthy they are of the name of Christian who cherish enmities, and how hatred, dissensions and discord should be entirely put away, as the most destructive bane of the faithful, especially since by the daily Sacrifice of our religion, we profess to preserve nothing with more anxious care, than peace and love.

It is also frequently called the Viaticum by sacred writers, both because it is spiritual food by which we are sustained in our pilgrimage through this life, and also because it paves our way to eternal glory and happiness. Wherefore, according to an ancient usage of the Catholic Church, we see that none of the faithful are permitted to die without this Sacrament.

The most ancient Fathers, following the authority of the Apostle, have sometimes also called the Holy Eucharist by the name of Supper, because it was instituted by Christ the Lord at the salutary mystery of the Last Supper.

It is not, however, lawful to consecrate or partake of the Eucharist after eating or drinking, because, according to a custom wisely introduced by the Apostles, as ancient writers have recorded, and which has ever been retained and preserved, Communion is received only by persons who are fasting.

The Eucharist Is a Sacrament Properly So Called

The meaning of the name having been explained, it will be necessary to show that this is a true Sacrament, and one of those seven which the holy Church has ever revered and venerated religiously. For when the consecration of the chalice is effected, it is called a mystery of faith.

Besides, to omit the almost endless testimonies of sacred writers, who have invariably thought that this was to be numbered among the real Sacraments, the same thing is proved from the very principle and nature of a Sacrament. For there are in it signs that are external and subject to the senses. In the next place it signifies and produces grace. Moreover, neither the Evangelists nor the Apostle leave room for doubt regarding its institution by Christ. Since all these things concur to establish the fact of the Sacrament, there is obviously no need of any other argument.

In What Respect The Eucharist Is A Sacrament

But pastors should carefully observe that in this mystery there are many things to which sacred writers have from time to time attributed the name of Sacrament. For, sometimes, both the consecration and the Communion; nay, frequently also the body and blood itself of our Lord, which is contained in the Eucharist, used to be called a Sacrament. Thus St. Augustine says that this Sacrament consists of two things, -- the visible species of the elements, and the invisible flesh and blood of our Lord Jesus Christ Himself. And it is in the same sense that we say that this Sacrament is to be adored, meaning the body and blood of our Lord.

Now it is plain that all these are less properly called Sacraments. The species of bread and wine themselves are truly and strictly designated by this name.

How The Eucharist Differs From All The Other Sacraments

How much this Sacrament differs from all the others is easily inferred. For all the other Sacraments are completed by the use of the material, that is, while they are being administered to some one. Thus Baptism. attains the nature of a Sacrament when the individual is actually being washed in the water. For the perfecting of the Eucharist on the other hand, the consecration of the material itself suffices, since neither (species) ceases to be a Sacrament, though kept in the pyx.

Again in perfecting the other Sacraments there is no change of the matter and element into another nature. The water of Baptism, or the oil of Confirmation, when those Sacraments are being administered, do not lose their former nature of water and oil; but in the Eucharist, that which was bread and wine before consecration, after consecration is truly the substance of the body and blood of the Lord.

The Eucharist Is But One Sacrament

But although there are two elements, as bread and wine, of which the entire Sacrament of the Eucharist is constituted, yet guided by the authority of the Church, we confess that this is not many Sacraments, but only one.

Otherwise, there cannot be the exact number of seven Sacraments, as has ever been handed down, and as was decreed by the Councils of Lateran, Florence and Trent.

Moreover, by virtue of the Sacrament, one mystical body is effected; hence, that the Sacrament itself may correspond to the thing which it effects, it must be one.

It is one not because it is indivisible, but because it signifies a single thing. For as food and drink, which are two different things, are employed only for one purpose, namely, that the vigour of the body may be recruited; so also it was but natural that there should be an analogy to them in the two different species of the Sacrament, which should signify the spiritual food by which souls are supported and refreshed. Wherefore we have been assured by our Lord the Saviour: My flesh is meat indeed, and my blood is drink indeed.

The Eucharist Signifies Three Things

It must, therefore, be diligently explained what the Sacrament of the Eucharist signifies, that the faithful, beholding the sacred mysteries with their eyes, may also at the same time feed their souls with the contemplation of divine things. Three things, then, are signified by this Sacrament. The first is the Passion of Christ our Lord, a thing past; for He Himself said: Do this for a commemoration of me, and the Apostle says: As often as you shall eat this bread, and drink the chalice, you shall show the death of the Lord, until he come.

It is also significant of divine and heavenly grace, which is imparted at the present time by this Sacrament to nurture and preserve the soul. Just as in Baptism we are begotten unto newness of life and by Confirmation are strengthened to resist Satan and openly to profess the name of Christ, so by the Sacrament of the Eucharist are we nurtured and supported.

It is, thirdly, a foreshadowing of future eternal joy and glory, which, according to God's promises, we shall receive in our heavenly country.

These three things, then, which are clearly distinguished by their reference to past, present and future times, are so well represented by the Eucharistic mysteries that the whole Sacrament, though consisting of different species, signifies the three as if it referred to one thing only.

Constituent Parts of the Eucharist

The Matter

It is particularly incumbent on pastors to know the matter of this Sacrament, in order that they themselves may rightly consecrate it, and also that they may be able to instruct the faithful as to its significance, inflaming them with an earnest desire of that which it signifies.

The First Element Of The Eucharist Is Bread

The matter of this Sacrament is twofold. The first element is wheaten bread, of which we shall now speak. Of the second we shall treat hereafter. As the Evangelists, Matthew, Mark and Luke testify, Christ the Lord took bread into His hands, blessed, and brake, saying: This is my body; and, according to John, the same Saviour called Himself bread in these words: I am the living bread, that came down from heaven.

The Sacramental Bread Must Be Wheaten

There are, however, various sorts of bread, either because they consist of different materials, -- such as wheat, barley, pulse and other products of the earth; or because they possess different qualities, -- some being leavened, others altogether without leaven. It is to be observed that, with regard to the former kinds, the words of the Saviour show that the bread should be wheaten; for, according to common usage, when we simply say bread, we are sufficiently understood to mean wheaten bread. This is also declared by a figure in the Old Testament, because the Lord commanded that the loaves of proposition, which signified this Sacrament, should be made of fine flour.

The Sacramental Bread Should Be Unleavened

But as wheaten bread alone is to be considered the proper matter for this Sacrament -- a doctrine which has been handed down by Apostolic tradition and confirmed by the authority of the Catholic Church -- so it may be easily inferred from the doings of Christ the Lord that this bread should be unleavened. It was consecrated and instituted by Him on the first day of unleavened bread, on which it was not lawful for the Jews to have anything leavened in their house.

Should the authority of John the Evangelist, who says that all this was done before the feast of the Passover, be objected to, the argument is one of easy solution. For by the day before the pasch John understands the same day which the other Evangelists designate as the first day of unleavened bread. He wished particularly to mark the natural day, which commences at sunrise; whereas they wanted to point out that our Lord celebrated the Pasch on Thursday evening just when the days of the unleavened bread were beginning. Hence St. Chrysostom also understands the first day of unleavened bread to be the day on the evening of which unleavened bread was to be eaten.

The peculiar suitableness of the consecration of unleavened bread to express that integrity and purity of mind which the faithful should bring to this Sacrament we learn from these words of the Apostle: Purge out the old leaven, that you may be a new paste, as you are unleavened. For Christ our Passover is sacrificed. Therefore, let us feast, not with the old leaven, nor with the leaven of malice and wickedness, but with the unleavened bread of sincerity and truth.

Unleavened Bread Not Essential

This quality of the bread, however, is not to be deemed so essential that, if it be wanting, the Sacrament cannot exist; for both kinds are called by the one name and have the true and proper nature of bread. No one, however, is at liberty on his own private authority, or rather presumption, to transgress the laudable rite of his Church. And such departure is the less warrantable in priests of the Latin Church, expressly obliged as they are by the supreme Pontiffs, to consecrate the sacred mysteries with unleavened bread only.

Quantity Of The Bread

With regard to the first matter of this Sacrament, let this exposition suffice. It is, however, to be observed, that the quantity of the matter to be consecrated is not defined, since we cannot define the exact number of those who can or ought to receive the sacred mysteries.'

The Second Element Of The Eucharist Is Wine

It remains for us to treat of the other matter and element of this Sacrament, which is wine pressed from the fruit of the vine, with which is mingled a little water.

That in the institution of this Sacrament our Lord and Saviour made use of wine has beep at all times the doctrine of the Catholic Church, for He Himself said: I will not drink from henceforth of this fruit of the vine until that day. On this passage Chrysostom observes: He says, "Of the fruit of the vine," which certainly produced wine not water; as if he had it in view, even at so early a period, to uproot the heresy which asserted that in these mysteries water alone is to be used.

Water Should Be Mixed With The Wine

With the wine, however, the Church of God has always mingled water. First, because Christ the Lord did so, as is proved by the authority of Councils and the testimony of St. Cyprian; next, because by this mixture is renewed the recollection of the blood and water that issued from His side. Waters, also, as we read in the Apocalypse, signify the people; and hence, water mixed with the wine signifies the union of the faithful with Christ their Head. This rite, derived as it is from Apostolic tradition, the Catholic Church has always observed.

But although there are reasons so grave for mingling water with the wine that it cannot be omitted without incurring the guilt of mortal sin, yet its omission does not render the Sacrament null.

Again as in the sacred mysteries priests must be mindful to mingle water with wine, so, also, must they take care to mingle it in small quantity, for, in the opinion and judgment of ecclesiastical writers, that water is changed into wine. Hence these words of Pope Honorius on the subject: A pernicious abuse has prevailed in your district of using in the sacrifice a greater quantity of water than of wine; whereas, according to the rational practice of the universal Church, the wine should be used in much greater quantity than the water.

No Other Elements Pertain To This Sacrament

These, then, are the only two elements of this Sacrament; and with reason has it been enacted by many decrees that, although there have been those who were not afraid to do so, it is unlawful to offer anything but bread and wine.

Peculiar Fitness Of Bread And Wine

We have now to consider the aptitude of these two symbols of bread and wine to represent those things of which we believe and confess they are the sensible signs.

In the first place, then, they signify to us Christ, as the true life of men; for our Lord Himself says: My flesh is meat indeed, and my blood is drink indeed. As, then, the body of Christ the Lord furnishes nourishment unto eternal life to those who receive this Sacrament with purity and holiness, rightly is the matter composed chiefly of those elements by which our present life is sustained, in order that the faithful may easily understand that the mind and soul are satiated by the Communion of the precious body and blood of Christ.

These very elements serve also somewhat to suggest to men the truth of the Real Presence of the body and blood of the Lord in the Sacrament. Observing, as we do, that bread and wine are every day changed by the power of nature into human flesh and blood, we are led the more easily by this analogy to believe that the substance of the bread and wine is changed, by the heavenly benediction, into the real flesh and real blood of Christ.

This admirable change of the elements also helps to shadow forth what takes place in the soul. Although no change of the bread and wine appears externally, yet their substance is truly changed into the flesh and blood of Christ; so, in like manner, although in us nothing appears changed, yet we are renewed inwardly unto life, when we receive in the Sacrament of the Eucharist the true life.

Moreover, the body of the Church, which is one, consists of many members, and of this union nothing is more strikingly illustrative than the elements of bread and wine; for bread is made from many grains and wine is pressed from many clusters of grapes. Thus they signify that we, though many, are most closely bound together by the bond of this divine mystery and made, as it were, one body.

Form Of The Eucharist

The form to be used in the consecration of the bread is next to be treated of, not, however, in order that the faithful should be taught these mysteries, unless necessity require it; for this knowledge is not needful for those who have not received Holy Orders. The purpose (of this section) is to guard against most shameful mistakes on the part of priests, at the time of the consecration, due to ignorance of the form.

Form To Be Used In The Consecration Of The Bread

We are then taught by the holy Evangelists, Matthew and Luke, and also by the Apostle, that the form consists of these words: This is my body; for it is written: Whilst they were at supper, Jesus took bread, and blessed it, and brake, and gave to his disciples, and said: Take and eat, This is my body.

This form of consecration having been observed by Christ the Lord has been always used by the Catholic Church. The testimonies of the Fathers, the enumeration of which would be endless, and also the decree of the Council of Florence, which is well known and accessible to all, must here be omitted, especially as the knowledge which they convey may be obtained from these words of the Saviour: Do this for a commemoration of me. For what the Lord enjoined was not only what He had done, but also what he had said; and especially is this true, since the words were uttered not only to signify, but also to accomplish.

That these words constitute the form is easily proved from reason also. The form is that which signifies what is accomplished in this Sacrament; but as the preceding words signify and declare what takes place in the Eucharist, that is, the conversion of the bread into the true body of our Lord, it therefore follows that these very words constitute the form. In this sense may be understood the words of the Evangelist: He blessed; for they seem equivalent to this: Taking bread, he blessed it, saying: "This is my body".

Not All The Words Used Are Essential

Although in the Evangelist the words, Take and eat, precede the words (This is my body), they evidently express the use only, not the consecration, of the matter. Wherefore, while they are not necessary to the consecration of the Sacrament, they are by all means to be pronounced by the priest, as is also the conjunction for in the consecration of the body and blood. But they are not necessary to the validity of the Sacrament, otherwise it would follow that, if this Sacrament were not to be administered to anyone, it should not, or indeed could not, be consecrated; whereas, no one can lawfully doubt that the priest, by pronouncing the words of our Lord according to the institution and practice of the Church, truly consecrates the proper matter of the bread, even though it should afterwards never be administered.

Form To Be Used In The Consecration Of The Wine

With regard lo the consecration of the wine, which is the other element of this Sacrament, the priest, for the reason we have already assigned, ought of necessity to be well acquainted with, and well understand its form. We are then firmly to believe that it consists in the following words: This is the chalice of my blood, of the new and eternal testament, the mystery of faith, which shall be shed for you and for many, to the remission of sins. Of these words the greater part are taken from Scripture; but some have been preserved in the Church from Apostolic tradition.

Thus the words, this is the chalice, are found in St. Luke and in the Apostle; but the words that immediately follow, of my blood, or my blood of the new testament, which shall be shed for you and for many to the remission of sins, are found partly in St. Luke and partly in St. Matthew. But the words, eternal, and the mystery of faith, have been taught us by holy tradition, the interpreter and keeper of Catholic truth.

Concerning this form no one can doubt, if he here also attend to what has been already said about the form used in the consecration of the bread. The form to be used (in the consecration) of this element, evidently consists of those words which signify that the substance of the wine is changed into the blood of our Lord. since, therefore, the words already cited clearly declare this, it is plain that no other words constitute the form.

They moreover express certain admirable fruits of the blood shed in the Passion of our Lord, fruits which pertain in a most special manner to this Sacrament. Of these, one is access to the eternal inheritance, which has come to us by right of the new and everlasting testament. Another is access to righteousness by the mystery of faith; for God hath set forth Jesus to be a propitiator through faith in his blood, that he himself may be just, and the justifier of him, who is of the faith of Jesus. Christ. A third effect is the remission of sins.

Explanation Of The Form Used In The Consecration Of The Wine

Since these very words of consecration are replete with mysteries and most appropriately suitable to the subject, they demand a more minute consideration.

The words: This is the chalice of my blood, are to be understood to mean: This is my blood, which is contained in this chalice. The mention of the chalice made at the consecration of the blood is right and appropriate, inasmuch as the blood is the drink of the faithful, and this would not be sufficiently signified if it were not contained in some drinking vessel.

Next follow the words: Of the new testament. These have been added that we might understand the blood of Christ the Lord to be given not under a figure, as was done in the Old Law, of which we read in the Epistle to the Hebrews that without blood a testament is not dedicated; but to be given to men in truth and in reality, as becomes the New Testament. Hence the Apostle says: Christ therefore is the mediator of the new testament, that by means of his death, they who are called may receive the promise of eternal inheritance.

The word eternal refers to the eternal inheritance, the right to which we acquire by the death of Christ the Lord, the eternal testator.

The words mystery of faith, which are subjoined, do not exclude the reality, but signify that what lies hidden and concealed and far removed from the perception of the eye, is to be believed with firm faith. In this passage, however, these words bear a meaning different from that which they have when applied also to Baptism. Here the mystery of faith consists in seeing by faith the blood of Christ veiled under the species of wine; but Baptism is justly called by us the Sacrament of faith, by the Greeks, the mystery of faith, because it embraces the entire profession of the Christian faith.

Another reason why we call the blood of the Lord the mystery of faith is that human reason is particularly beset with difficulty and embarrassment when faith proposes to our belief that Christ the Lord, the true Son of God, at once God and man, suffered death for us, and this death is designated by the Sacrament of His blood.

Here, therefore, rather than at the consecration of His body, is appropriately commemorated the Passion of our Lord, by the words. which shall be shed for the remission of sins. For the blood, separately consecrated, serves to place before the eyes of all, in a more forcible manner, the Passion of our Lord, His death, and the nature of His sufferings.

The additional words for you and for many, are taken, some from Matthew, some from Luke, but were joined together by the Catholic Church under the guidance of the Spirit of God. They serve to declare the fruit and advantage of His Passion. For if we look to its value, we must confess that the Redeemer shed His blood for the salvation of all; but if we look to the fruit which mankind have received from it, we shall easily find that it pertains not unto all, but to many of the human race. When therefore ('our Lord) said: For you, He meant either those who were present, or those chosen from among the Jewish people, such as were, with the exception of Judas, the disciples with whom He was speaking. When He added, And for many, He wished to be understood to mean the remainder of the elect from among the Jews or Gentiles.

With reason, therefore, were the words for all not used, as in this place the fruits of the Passion are alone spoken of, and to the elect only did His Passion bring the fruit of salvation. And this is the purport of the Apostle when he says: Christ was offered once to exhaust the sins of many; and also of the words of our Lord in John: I pray for them; I pray not for the world, but for them whom thou hast given me, because they are thine.

Beneath the words of this consecration lie hid many other mysteries, which by frequent meditation and study of sacred things, pastors will find it easy, with the divine assistance, to discover for themselves.

Three Mysteries Of The Eucharist

We must now return to an explanation of those truths concerning the Eucharist about which the faithful are on no account to be left in ignorance. Pastors, aware of the warning of the Apostle that those who discern not the body of the Lord are guilty of a most grave crime, should first of all impress on the minds of the faithful the necessity of detaching, as much as possible, their mind and understanding from the dominion of the senses; for if they believe that this Sacrament contains only what the senses disclose, they will of necessity fall into enormous impiety. Consulting the sight, the touch, the smell, the taste and finding nothing but the appearances of bread and wine, they will naturally judge that this Sacrament contains nothing more than bread and wine. Their minds, therefore, are as much as possible to be withdrawn from subjection to the senses and excited to the contemplation of the stupendous might and power of God.

The Catholic Church firmly believes and professes that in this Sacrament the words of consecration accomplish three wondrous and admirable effects.

The first is that the true body of Christ the Lord, the same that was born of the Virgin, and is now seated at the right hand of the Father in heaven, is contained in this Sacrament.

The second, however repugnant it may appear to the senses, is that none of the substance of the elements remains in the Sacrament.

The third, which may be deduced from the two preceding. although the words of consecration themselves clearly express it, is that the accidents which present themselves to the eyes or other senses exist in a wonderful and ineffable manner without a subject. All the accidents of bread and wine we can see, but they inhere in no substance, and exist independently of any; for the substance of the bread and wine is so changed into the body and blood of our Lord that they altogether cease to be the substance of bread and wine.

The Mystery of the Real Presence

To begin with the first (of these mysteries), pastors should give their best attention to show how clear and explicit are the words of our Saviour which establish the Real Presence of His body in this Sacrament.

Proof From Scripture

When our Lord says: This is my body, this is my blood, no person of sound mind can mistake His meaning, particularly since there is reference to Christ's human nature, the reality of which the Catholic faith permits no one to doubt. The admirable words of St. Hilary, a man not less eminent for piety than learning, are apt here: When our Lord himself declares, as our faith teaches us, that His flesh is food indeed, what room can remain for doubt concerning the real presence of His body and blood?

Pastors should also adduce another passage from which it can be clearly seen that the true body and blood of our Lord are contained in the Eucharist. The Apostle, after having recorded the consecration of bread and wine by our Lord, and also the administration of Communion to the Apostles, adds: But let a man prove himself, and so eat of that bread and drink of the chalice; for he that eateth and drinketh unworthily, eateth and drinketh judgment to himself, not discerning the body of the Lord. If, as heretics continually repeat, the Sacrament presents nothing to our veneration but a memorial and sign of the Passion of Christ, why was there need to exhort the faithful, in language so energetic, to prove themselves? By the terrible word judgment, the Apostle shows how enormous is the guilt of those who receive unworthily and do not distinguish from common food the body of the Lord concealed in the Eucharist. In the same Epistle St. Paul had already developed this doctrine more fully, when he said: The chalice of benediction which we bless, is it not the communion of the blood of Christ? and the bread which we break, is it not the participation of the body of the Lord ? Now these words signify the real substance of the body and blood of Christ the Lord.

Proof From The Teaching Of The Church

These passages of Scripture are therefore to be expounded by pastors; and they should especially teach that there is nothing doubtful or uncertain about them. All the more certain are they since the infallible teaching of God's Church has interpreted them, as may be ascertained in a twofold manner.

Testimony Of The Fathers

The first is by consulting the Fathers who flourished in the early ages of the Church and in each succeeding century, who are the most unexceptionable witnesses of her doctrine. All of these teach in the clearest terms and with the most entire unanimity the truth of this dogma. To adduce the individual testimony of each Father would prove an endless task. It is enough, therefore, that we cite, or rather point out a few, whose testimony will afford an easy criterion by which to judge of the rest.

Let St. Ambrose first declare his faith. In his book On Those Who are Initiated Into the Mysteries he says that the true body of Christ is received in this Sacrament, just as the true body of Christ was derived from the Virgin, and that this truth is to be believed with the firm certainty of faith. In another place he teaches that before consecration there is only bread, but after consecration there is the flesh of Christ.

St. Chrysostom, another witness of equal authority and gravity, professes and proclaims this mysterious truth in many passages, but particularly in his sixtieth homily, On Those Who Receive The Sacred Mysteries Unworthily; and also in his forty-fourth and forty-fifth homilies on St. John. Let us, he says, obey, not contradict God, although what He says may seem contrary to our reason and our sight. His words cannot deceive, our senses are easily deceived.

With this doctrine fully agrees the uniform teaching of St. Augustine, that most zealous defender of Catholic faith, particularly when in his explanation of the thirty-third Psalm he says: To carry himself in his own hands is impossible to man, and peculiar to Christ alone; He was carried in His own hands when, giving His body to be eaten, He said, This is my body.

To pass by Justin and Irenaeus, St. Cyril, in his fourth book on St. John, declares in such express terms that the true body of our Lord is contained in this Sacrament, that no sophistry, no captious interpretations can obscure his meaning.

Should pastors wish for additional testimonies of the Fathers, they will find it easy to add St. Denis,- St. Hilary, St. Jerome, St. Damascene and a host of others, whose weighty teaching on this most important subject has been collected by the labor and industry of learned and pious men.

Teaching Of The Councils

Another means of ascertaining the belief of the holy Church on matters of faith is the condemnation of the contrary doctrine and opinion. It is manifest that belief in the Real Presence of the body of Christ in the holy Sacrament of the Eucharist was so spread and taught throughout the universal Church and unanimously professed by all the faithful, that when, five centuries ago, Berengarius presumed to deny this dogma, asserting that the Eucharist was only a sign, he was unanimously condemned in the Council of Vercelli, which Leo IX had immediately convoked, whereupon he himself anathematised his error.

Relapsing, however, into the same wicked folly, he was condemned by three different Councils, convened, one at Tours, the other two at Rome; of the two latter, one was summoned by Pope Nicholas II, the other by Pope Gregory VIII.' The General Council of Lateran, held under Innocent III, further ratified the sentence. Finally this truth was more clearly defined and established in the Councils of Florence and Trent.

Two Great Benefits Of Proving The Real Presence

If, then, pastors will carefully explain these particulars, they will be able, while ignoring those who are blinded by error and hate nothing more than the light of truth, to strengthen the weak and administer joy and consolation to the pious, all the more as the faithful cannot doubt that this dogma is numbered among the Articles of faith.

Faith Is Strengthened

Believing and confessing, as they do, that the power of God is supreme over all things, they must also believe that His omnipotence can accomplish the great work which we admire and adore in the Sacrament of the Eucharist. And again since they believe the Holy Catholic Church, they must necessarily believe that the true doctrine of this Sacrament is that which we have set forth.

The Soul Is Gladdened

Nothing contributes more to the spiritual joy and advantage of pious persons than the contemplation of the exalted dignity of this most august Sacrament. In the first place they learn how great is the perfection of the Gospel Dispensation, under which we enjoy the reality of that which under the Mosaic Law was only shadowed forth by types and figures. Hence St. Denis divinely says that our Church is midway between the Synagogue and the heavenly Jerusalem, and consequently participates of the nature of both. Certainly, then, the faithful can never sufficiently admire the perfection of holy Church and her exalted glory which seems to be removed only by one degree from the bliss of heaven. In common with the inhabitants of heaven, we too possess Christ, God and man, present with us. They are raised a degree above us, inasmuch as they are present with Christ and enjoy the Beatific Vision; while we, with a firm and unwavering faith, adore the Divine Majesty present with us, not, it is true, in a manner visible to mortal eye, but hidden by a miracle of power under the veil of the sacred mysteries.

Furthermore the faithful experience in this Sacrament the most perfect love of Christ our Saviour. It became the goodness of the Saviour not to withdraw from us that nature which He assumed from us, but to desire, as far as possible, to remain among us so that at all times He might be seen to verify the words: My delight is to be with the children of men.

Meaning of the Real Presence

Christ Whole And Entire Is Present In The Eucharist

Here the pastor should explain that in this Sacrament are contained not only the true body of. Christ and all the constituents of a true body, such as bones and sinews, but also Christ whole and entire. He should point out that the word Christ designates the God-man, that is to say, one Person in whom are united the divine and human natures; that the Holy Eucharist, therefore, contains both, and whatever is included in the idea of both, the Divinity and humanity whole and entire, consisting of the soul, all the parts of the body and the blood,- all of which must be believed to be in this Sacrament. In heaven the whole humanity is united to the Divinity in one hypostasis, or Person; hence it would be impious, to suppose that the body of Christ, which contained in the Sacrament, is separated from His Divinity.

Presence In Virtue Of The Sacrament And In Virtue Of Concomitance

Pastors, however, should not fail to observe that in this Sacrament not all these things are contained after the same manner, or by the same power. Some things, we say, are present in virtue of the consecration; for as the words of consecration effect what they signify, sacred writers usually say that whatever the form expresses, is contained in the Sacrament by virtue of the Sacrament. Hence, could we suppose any one thing to be entirely separated from the rest, the Sacrament, they teach, would be found to contain solely what the form expresses and nothing more.

On the other hand, some things are contained in the Sacrament because they are united to those which are expressed in the form. For instance, the words This is my body, which comprise the form used to consecrate the bread, signify the body of the Lord, and hence the body itself of Christ the Lord is contained in the Eucharist by virtue of the Sacrament. Since, however, to Christ's body are united His blood, His soul, and His Divinity, all of these also must be found to coexist in the Sacrament; not, however, by virtue of the consecration, but by virtue of the union that subsists between them and His body. All these are said to be in the Eucharist by virtue of concomitance. Hence it is clear that Christ, whole and entire, is contained in the Sacrament; for when two things are actually united, where one is, the other must also be.

Christ Whole And Entire Present Under Each Species

Hence it also follows that Christ is so contained, whole and entire, under either species, that, as under the species of bread are contained not only the body, but also the blood and Christ entire; so in like manner, under the species of wine are truly contained not only the blood, but also the body and Christ entire.

But although these are matters on which the faithful cannot entertain a doubt, it was nevertheless wisely ordained that two distinct consecrations should take place. First, because they represent in a more lively manner the Passion of our Lord, in -which His blood was separated from His body; and hence in the form of consecration we commemorate the shedding of His blood. Secondly, since the Sacrament is to be used by us as the food and nourishment of our souls, it was most appropriate that it should be instituted as food and drink, two things which obviously constitute the complete sustenance of the (human) body.

Christ Whole And Entire Present In Every Part Of Each Species

Nor should it be forgotten that Christ, whole and entire, is contained not only under either species, but also in each particle of either species. Each, says St. Augustine, receives Christ the Lord, and He is entire in each portion. He is not diminished by being given to many, but gives Himself whole and entire to each.

This is also an obvious inference from the narrative of the Evangelists. It is not to be supposed that our Lord consecrated the bread used at the Last Supper in separate parts, applying the form particularly to each, but that all the bread then used for the sacred mysteries was consecrated at the same time and with the same form, and in a quantity sufficient for all the Apostles. That the consecration of the chalice was performed in this manner, is clear from these words of the Saviour: Take and divide it among you.

What has hitherto been said is intended to enable pastors to show that the true body and blood of Christ are contained in the Sacrament of the Eucharist.

The Mystery of Transubstantiation

The next point to be explained is that the substance of the bread and wine does not continue to exist in the Sacrament after consecration. This truth, although well calculated to excite our profound admiration, is yet a necessary consequence from what has been already established.

Proof From The Dogma Of The Real Presence

If, after consecration, the true body of Christ is present under the species of bread and wine, since it was not there before, it must have become present either by change of place, or by creation, or by the change of some other thing into it. It cannot be rendered present by change of place, because it would then cease to be in heaven; for whatever is moved must necessarily cease to occupy the place from which it is moved. Still less can we suppose the body of Christ to be rendered present by creation; nay, the very idea is inconceivable. In order that the body of our Lord be present in the Sacrament, it remains, therefore, that it be rendered present by the change of the bread into it. Wherefore it is necessary that none of the substance of the bread remain.

Proof From The Councils

Hence our predecessors in the faith, the Fathers of the General Councils of Lateran and of Florence, confirmed by solemn decrees the truth of this dogma. In the Council of Trent it was still more fully defined in these words: If any one shall say that in the most Holy Sacrament of the Eucharist the substance of the bread and wine remains, together with the body and blood of our Lord Jesus Christ, let hint be anathema.

Proof From Scripture

The doctrine thus defined is a natural inference from the words of Scripture. When instituting this Sacrament, our Lord Himself said: This is my body. The word this expresses the entire substance of the thing present; and therefore if the substance of the bread remained, our Lord could not have truly said: This is my body.

In St. John Christ the Lord also says: The bread that I will give is my flesh, for the life of the world. The bread which He promises to give, He here declares to be His flesh. A little after He adds: Unless you eat the flesh of the son of man, and drink his blood, you shall not have life in you. And again: My flesh is meat indeed, and my blood is drink indeed. Since, therefore, in terms so clear and so explicit, He calls His flesh bread and meat indeed, and His blood drink indeed, He gives us sufficiently to understand that none of the substance of the bread and wine remains in the Sacrament.

Proof From The Fathers

Whoever turns over the pages of the holy Fathers will easily perceive that on this doctrine (of transubstantiation) they have been at all times unanimous. St. Ambrose says: You say, perhaps, "this bread is no other than what is used for common food." True, before consecration it is bread; but no sooner are the words of consecration pronounced than from bread it becomes the flesh of Christ. To prove this position more clearly, he elucidates it by a variety of comparisons and examples. In another place, when explaining these words of the Psalmist, Whatsoever the Lord pleased he hath done in heaven and on earth, St. Ambrose says: Although the species of bread and wine are visible, yet we must believe that after consecration, the body and blood of Christ are alone there. Explaining the same doctrine almost in the same words, St. Hilary says that although externally it appear bread and wine, yet in reality it is the body and blood of the Lord.

Why The Eucharist Is Called Bread After Consecration

Here pastors should observe that we should not at all be surprised, if, even after consecration, the Eucharist is sometimes called bread. It is so called, first because it retains the appearance of bread, and secondly because it keeps the natural quality of bread, which is to support and nourish the body.

Moreover, such phraseology is in perfect accordance with the usage of the Holy Scriptures, which call things by what they appear to be, as may be seen from the words of Genesis which say that Abraham saw three men, when in reality he saw three Angels. In like manner the two Angels who appeared to the Apostles after the Ascension of Christ the Lord into heaven, are called not Angels, but men.

The Meaning of Transubstantiation

To explain this mystery is extremely difficult. The pastor, however, should endeavour to instruct those who are more advanced in the knowledge of divine things on the manner of this admirable change. As for those who are yet weak in faith, they might possibly be overwhelmed by its greatness.

Transubstantiation A Total Conversion

This conversion, then, is so effected that the whole substance of the bread is changed by the power of God into the whole substance of the body of Christ, and the whole substance of the wine into the whole substance of His blood, and this, without any change in our Lord Himself. He is neither begotten, nor changed, not increased, but remains entire in His substance.

This sublime mystery St. Ambrose thus declares: You see how efficacious are the words of Christ. If the word of the Lord Jesus is so powerful as to summon into existence that which did not exist, namely the world, how much more powerful is His word to change into something else that which already has existence ?

Many other ancient and most authoritative Fathers have written to the same effect. We faithfully confess, says St. Augustine, that before consecration it is bread and wine, the product of nature; but after consecration it is the body and blood of Christ, consecrated by the blessing. The body, says Damascene, is truly united to the Divinity, that body which was derived from the virgin; not that the body thus derived descends from heaven, but that the bread and wine are changed into the body and blood of Christ.

This admirable change, as the Council of Trent teaches, the Holy Catholic Church most appropriately expresses by the word transubstantiation. Since natural changes are rightly called transformations, because they involve a change of form; so likewise our predecessors in the faith wisely and appropriately introduced the term transubstantiation, in order to signify that in the Sacrament of the Eucharist the whole substance of one thing passes into the whole substance of another.

According to the admonition so frequently repeated by the holy Fathers, the faithful are to be admonished against curious searching into the manner in which this change is effected. It defies the powers of conception; nor can we find any example of it in natural transmutations, or even in the very work of creation. That such a change takes place must be recognised by faith; how it takes place we must not curiously inquire.

No less of caution should be observed by pastors in explaining the mysterious manner in which the body of our Lord is contained whole and entire under the least particle of the bread. Indeed, discussions of this kind should scarcely ever be entered upon. Should Christian charity, however, require a departure from this rule, the pastor should remember first of all to prepare and fortify his hearers by reminding them that no word shall be impossible with God.

A Consequence Of Transubstantiation

The pastor should next teach that our Lord is not in the Sacrament as in a place. Place regards things only inasmuch as they have magnitude. Now we do not say that Christ is in the Sacrament inasmuch as He is great or small, terms which belong to quantity, but inasmuch as He is a substance. The substance of the bread is changed into the substance of Christ, not into magnitude or quantity; and substance, it will be acknowledged by all, is contained in a small as well as in a large space. The substance of air, for instance, and its entire nature must be present under a small as well as a large quantity, and likewise the entire nature of water must be present no less in a glass than in a river. Since, then, the body of our Lord succeeds to the substance of the bread, we must confess it to be in the Sacrament after the same manner as the substance of the bread was before consecration; whether the substance of the bread was present in greater or less quantity is a matter of entire indifference.

The Mystery of the Accidents without a Subject

We now come to the third great and wondrous effect of this Sacrament, namely, the existence of the species of bread and wine without a subject.

Proof From The Preceding Dogmas

What has been said in explanation of the two preceding points must facilitate for pastors the exposition of this truth. For, since we have already proved that the body and blood of our Lord are really and truly contained in the Sacrament, to the entire exclusion of the substance of the bread and wine, and since the accidents of bread and wine cannot inhere in the body and blood of Christ, it remains that, contrary to physical laws, they must subsist of themselves, inhering in no subject.

Proof From The Teaching Of The Church

This has been at all times the uniform doctrine of the Catholic Church; and it can be easily established by the same authorities which, as we have already proved, make it plain that the substance of the bread and wine ceases to exist in the Eucharist.

Advantages Of This Mystery

Nothing more becomes the piety of the faithful than, omitting all curious questionings, to revere and adore the majesty of this august Sacrament, and to recognise the wisdom of God in commanding that these holy mysteries should be administered under the species of bread and wine. For since it is most revolting to human nature to eat human flesh or drink human blood, therefore God in His infinite wisdom has established the administration of the body and blood of Christ under the forms of bread and wine, which are the ordinary and agreeable food of man.

There are two further advantages: first, it prevents the calumnious reproaches of the unbeliever, from which the eating of our Lord under His visible form could not easily be defended; secondly, the receiving Him under a form in which He is impervious to the senses avails much for increasing our faith. For faith, as the well known saying of St. Gregory declares, has no merit in those things which fall under the proof of reason.

The doctrines treated above should be explained with great caution, according to the capacity of the hearers and the necessities of the times.

The Effects of the Eucharist

But with regard to the admirable virtue and fruits of this Sacrament, there is no class of the faithful to whom a knowledge of them is not most necessary. For all that has been said at such length on this Sacrament has principally for its object, to make the faithful sensible of the advantages of the Eucharist. As, however, no language can convey an adequate idea of its utility and fruits, pastors must be content to treat of one or two points, in order to show what an abundance and profusion of all goods are contained in those sacred mysteries.

The Eucharist Contains Christ And Is The Food Of The Soul

This they will in some degree accomplish, if, having explained the efficacy and nature of all the Sacraments, they compare the Eucharist to a fountain, the other Sacraments to rivulets. For the Holy Eucharist is truly and necessarily to be called the fountain of all graces, containing, as it does, after an admirable manner, the fountain itself of celestial gifts and graces, and the author of all the Sacrament, Christ our Lord, from whom, as from its source, is derived whatever of goodness and perfection the other Sacraments possess. From this (comparison), therefore, we may easily infer what most ample gifts of divine grace are bestowed on us by this Sacrament.

It will also be useful to consider attentively the nature of bread and wine, which are the symbols of this Sacrament. For what bread and wine are to the body, the Eucharist is to the health and delight of the soul, but in a higher and better way. This Sacrament is not, like bread and wine, changed into our substance; but we are, in some wise, changed into its nature, so that we may well apply here the words of St. Augustine: I am the food of the frown. Grow and thou shalt eat Me; nor shalt thou change Me into thee, as thy bodily food, but thou shalt be changed into Me.

The Eucharist Gives Grace

If, then, grace and truth came by Jesus Christ, they must surely be poured into the soul which receives with purity and holiness Him who said of Himself: He that eateth my flesh and drinketh my blood abideth in me and I in him. Those who receive this

Sacrament piously and fervently must, beyond all doubt, so receive the Son of God into their souls as to be ingrafted as living members on His body. For it is written: He that eateth me, the same also shall live by me; also: The bread which I will give is my flesh for the life of the world. Explaining this passage, St. Cyril says: The Word of God, uniting Himself to His own flesh, imparted to it a vivifying power: it became Him, therefore, to unite Himself to our bodies in a wonderful manner, through His sacred flesh and precious blood, which we receive in the bread and wine, consecrated by His vivifying benediction.

The Grace Of The Eucharist Sustains

When it is said that the Eucharist imparts grace, pastors must admonish that this does not mean that the state of grace is not required for a profitable reception of this Sacrament. For as natural food can be of no use to the dead, so in like manner the sacred mysteries can evidently be of no avail to a soul which lives not by the spirit. Hence this Sacrament has been instituted under the forms of bread and wine to signify that the object of its institution is not to recall the soul to life, but to preserve its life.

The reason, then, for saying that this Sacrament imparts grace, is that even the first grace, with which all should be clothed before they presume to approach the Holy Eucharist, lest they eat and drink judgment to themselves,' is given to none unless they receive in wish and desire this very Sacrament. For the Eucharist is the end of all the Sacraments, and the symbol of unity and brotherhood in the Church, outside which none can attain grace.

The Grace Of The Eucharist Invigorates And Delights

Again, just as the body is not only supported but also increased by natural food, from which the taste every day derives new relish and pleasure; so also is the soul not only sustained but invigorated by feasting on the food of the Eucharist, which gives to the spirit an increasing zest for heavenly things. Most truly and fitly therefore do we say that grace is imparted by this Sacrament, for it may be justly compared to the manna having in it the sweetness of every taste.

The Eucharist Remits Venial Sins

It cannot be doubted that by the Eucharist are remitted and pardoned lighter sins, commonly called venial. Whatever the soul has lost through the fire of passion, by falling into some slight offence, all this the Eucharist, cancelling those lesser faults, repairs, in the same way -- not to depart from the illustration already adduced -- as natural food gradually restores and repairs the daily waste caused by the force of the vital heat within us. Justly, therefore, has St. Ambrose said of this heavenly Sacrament: That daily bread is taken as a remedy for daily infirmity. But these things are to be understood of those sins for which no actual affection is retained.

The Eucharist Strengthens Against Temptation

There is, furthermore, such a power in the sacred mysteries as to preserve us pure and unsullied from sin, keep us safe from the assaults of temptation, and, as by some heavenly medicine, prepare the soul against the easy approach and infection of virulent and deadly disease. Hence, as St. Cyprian records, when the faithful were formerly hurried in multitudes by tyrants to torments and death, because they confessed the name of Christ, it was an ancient usage in the Catholic Church to give them, by the hands of the Bishop, the Sacrament of the body and blood of our Lord, lest perhaps overcome by the severity of their sufferings, they should fail in the fight for salvation.

It also restrains and represses the lusts of the flesh, for while it inflames the soul more ardently with the fire of charity, it of necessity extinguishes the ardour of concupiscence.

The Eucharist Facilitates The Attainment Of Eternal Life

Finally, to comprise all the advantages and blessings of this Sacrament in one word, it must be taught that the Holy Eucharist is most efficacious towards the attainment of eternal glory. For it is written: He that eateth my flesh, and drinketh my blood, hath everlasting life, and I will raise him up on the last day. That is to say, by the grace of this Sacrament men enjoy the greatest peace and tranquillity of conscience during the present life; and, when the hour of departing from this world shall have arrived, like Elias, who in the strength of the bread baked on the hearth, walked to Horeb, the mount of God, they, too, invigorated by the strengthening influence of this (heavenly food), will ascend to unfading glory and bliss.

How The Effects Of The Eucharist May Be Developed And Illustrated

All these matters will be most fully expounded by pastors, if they but dwell or. the sixth chapter of St. John, in which are developed the manifold effects of this Sacrament. Or again, glancing at the admirable actions of Christ our Lord, they may show that if those who received Him beneath their roof during His mortal life, or were restored to health by touching His vesture or the hem of His garment, were justly and deservedly deemed most blessed, how much more fortunate and happy we, into whose soul, resplendent as He is with unfading glory, He disdains not to enter, to heal all its wounds, to adorn it with His choicest gifts, and unite it to Himself.

Recipient of the Eucharist

Threefold Manner Of Communicating

That the faithful may learn to be zealous for the better gifts, they must be shown who can obtain these abundant fruits from the Holy Eucharist, must be reminded that there is not only one way of communicating. Wisely and rightly, then, did our predecessors in the faith, as we read in the Council of Trent, distinguish three ways of receiving this Sacrament.

Some receive it sacramentally only. Such are those sinners who do not fear to approach the holy mysteries with polluted lips and heart, who, as the Apostle says, eat and drink the Lord's body unworthily. Of this class of communicants St. Augustine says: He who dwells not in Christ, and in whom Christ dwells not, most certainly does not eat spiritually His flesh, although carnally and visibly he press with his teeth the Sacrament of His flesh and blood. Those, therefore, who receive the sacred mysteries with such a disposition, not only obtain no fruit therefrom, but, as the Apostle himself testifies, eat and drink judgment to themselves.

Others are said to receive the Eucharist in spirit only. They are those who, inflamed with a lively faith which worketh by charity,' partake in wish and desire of that celestial bread offered to them, from which they receive, if not the entire, at least very great fruits.

Lastly, there are some who receive the Holy Eucharist both sacramentally and spiritually, those who, according to the teaching of the Apostle, having first proved themselves and having approached this divine banquet adorned with the nuptial garment, derive from the Eucharist those most abundant fruits which we have already described. Hence it is clear that those who, having it in their power to receive with fitting preparation the Sacrament of the body of the Lord, are yet satisfied with a spiritual Communion only, deprive themselves of the greatest and most heavenly advantages.

Necessity Of Previous Preparation For Communion

We now come to point out the manner in which the faithful should be previously prepared for sacramental Communion. To demonstrate the great necessity of this previous preparation, the example of the Saviour should be adduced. Before He gave to His Apostles the Sacrament of His precious body and blood, although they were already clean, He washed their feet to show that we must use extreme diligence before Holy Communion in order to approach it with the greatest purity and innocence of soul.

In the next place, the faithful are to understand that as he who approaches thus prepared and disposed is adorned with the most ample gifts of heavenly grace; so, on the contrary, he who approaches without this preparation not only derives from it no advantage, but even incurs the greatest misfortune and loss. It is characteristic of the best and most salutary things that, if seasonably made use of, they are productive of the greatest benefit; but if employed out of time, they prove most pernicious and destructive. It cannot, therefore, excite out surprise that the great and exalted gifts of God; when received into a soul properly disposed, are of the greatest assistance towards the attainment of salvation; while to those who receive them unworthily, they bring with them eternal death.

Of this the Ark of the Lord affords a convincing illustration. The people of Israel possessed nothing more precious and it was to them the source of innumerable blessings from God; but when the Philistines carried it away, it brought on them a most destructive plague and the heaviest calamities, together with eternal disgrace. Thus also food when received from the mouth into a healthy stomach nourishes and supports the body; but when received into an indisposed stomach, causes grave disorders.

Preparation Of Soul

The first preparation, then, which the faithful should make, is to distinguish table from table, this sacred table from profane tables, this celestial bread from common bread. This we do when we firmly believe that there is truly present the body and blood of the Lord, of Him whom the Angels adore in heaven, at whose nod the pillars of heaven fear and tremble, of whose glory the heavens and the earth are full. This is to discern the body of the Lord in accordance with the admonition of the Apostle. We should venerate the greatness of the mystery rather than too curiously investigate its truth by idle inquiry.

Another very necessary preparation is to ask ourselves if we are at peace with and sincerely love our neigh r. If, therefore, thou offerest thy gift at the altar, and there rememberest that thy brother hath anything against thee, leave there thy offering before the altar, and go first to be reconciled to thy brother, and then coming thou shalt offer thy gift.

We should, in the next place, carefully examine whether our consciences be defiled by mortal sin, which has to be repented of, in order that it may be blotted out before Communion by the remedy of contrition and confession. The Council of Trent has defined that no one conscious of mortal sin and having an opportunity of going to confession, however contrite he may deem himself, is to approach the Holy Eucharist until he has been purified by sacramental confession.

We should also reflect in the silence of our own hearts how unworthy we are that the Lord should bestow on us this divine gift, and with the centurion of whom our Lord declared that he found not so great faith in Israel, we should exclaim from our hearts: Lord, I am not worthy that thou shouldst enter under my roof.

We should also put the question to ourselves whether we can truly say with Peter: Lord, thou knowest that I love thee, and should recollect that he who sat down at the banquet of the Lord without a wedding garment was cast into a dark dungeon and condemned to eternal torments.

Preparation Of Body

Our preparation should not, however, be confined to the soul; it should also extend to the body. We are to approach the Holy Table fasting, having neither eaten nor drunk anything at least from the preceding midnight until the moment of Communion.

The dignity of so great a Sacrament also demands that married persons abstain from the marriage debt for some days previous to Communion. This observance is recommended by the example of David, who, when about to receive the show-bread from the hands of the priest, declared that he and his servants had been clean from women for three days.

The above are the principal things to be done by the faithful preparatory to receiving the sacred mysteries with profit; and to these heads may be reduced whatever other things may seem desirable by way of preparation.

The Obligation of Communion

How Often Must Communion Be Received?

Lest any be kept away from Communion by the fear that the requisite preparation is too hard and laborious, the faithful are frequently to be reminded that they are all bound to receive the Holy Eucharist. Furthermore, the Church has decreed that whoever neglects to approach Holy Communion once a year, at Easter, is liable to sentence of excommunication.

The Church Desires The Faithful To Communicate Daily

However, let not the faithful imagine that it is enough to receive the body of the Lord once a year only, in obedience to the decree of the Church. They should approach oftener; but whether monthly, weekly, or daily, cannot be decided by any fixed universal rule. St. Augustine, however, lays down a most certain norm: Live in such a manner as to be able to receive every day.

It will therefore be the duty of the pastor frequently to admonish the faithful that, as they deem it necessary to afford daily nutriment to the body, they should also feel solicitous to feed and nourish the soul every day with this heavenly food. It is clear that the soul stands not less in need of spiritual, than the body of corporal food. Here it will be found most useful to recall the inestimable and divine advantages which, as we have already shown, flow from sacramental Communion. It will be well also to refer to the manna, which was a figure (of this Sacrament), and which refreshed the bodily powers every day. The Fathers who earnestly recommended the frequent reception of this Sacrament may also be cited. The words of St. Augustine, Thou sinnest daily, receive daily, express not his opinion only, but that of all the Fathers who have written on the subject, as anyone may easily discover who will carefully read them.

That there was a time when the faithful approached Holy Communion every day we learn from the Acts of the Apostles. All who then professed the faith of Christ burned with such true and sincere charity that, devoting themselves to prayer and other works of piety, they were found prepared to communicate daily. This devout practice, which seems to have been interrupted for a time, was again partially revived by the holy Pope and martyr Anacletus, who commanded that all the ministers who assisted at the Sacrifice of the Mass should communicate-an ordinance, as the Pontiff declares, of Apostolic institution. It was also for a long time the practice of the Church that, as soon as the Sacrifice was complete, and when the priest himself had communicated, he turned to the congregation and invited the faithful to the Holy Table in these words: Come, brethren, and receive Communion; and thereupon those who were prepared, advanced to receive the holy mysteries with the most fervent devotion.

The Church Commands; The Faithful To Communicate Once A Year

But subsequently, when charity and devotion had grown so cold that the faithful very seldom approached Communion, it was decreed by Pope Fabian, that all should communicate thrice every year, at Christmas, at Easter and at Pentecost. This decree was afterwards confirmed by many Councils, particularly by the first of Agde.

Such at length was the decay of piety that not only was this holy and salutary law unobserved, but Communion was deferred for years. The Council of Lateran, therefore, decreed that all the faithful should receive the sacred body of the Lord, at least once a year, at Easter, and that neglect of this duty should be chastised by exclusion from the society of the faithful.

Who Are Obliged By The Law Of Communion

But although this law, sanctioned by the authority of God and of His Church, concerns all the faithful, it should be taught that it does not extend to those who on account of their tender age have not attained the use of reason. For these are not able to distinguish the Holy Eucharist from common and ordinary bread and cannot bring with them to this Sacrament piety and devotion. Furthermore (to extend the precept to them) would appear inconsistent with the ordinance of our Lord, for He said: Take and eat - words which cannot apply to infants, who are evidently incapable of taking and eating.

In some places, it is true, an ancient practice prevailed of giving the Holy Eucharist even to infants; but, for the reasons already assigned, and for other reasons in keeping with Christian piety, this practice has been long discontinued by authority of the Church.

With regard to the age at which children should be given the holy mysteries, this the parents and confessor can best determine. To them it belongs to inquire and to ascertain from the children themselves whether they have some knowledge of this admirable Sacrament and whether they desire to receive it.

Communion must not be given to persons who are insane and incapable of devotion. However, according to the decree of the Council of Carthage, it may be administered to them at the close of life, provided they have shown, before losing their minds, a pious and religious disposition, and no danger, arising from the state of the stomach or other inconvenience or disrespect, is likely.

The Rite of Administering Communion

As to the rite to be observed in communicating, pastors should teach that the law of the holy Church forbids Communion under both kinds to anyone but the officiating priests, without the authority of the Church itself.

Christ the Lord, it is true, as has been explained by the Council of Trent, instituted and delivered to His Apostles at His Last Supper this most sublime Sacrament under the species of bread and wine; but it does not follow that by doing so our Lord and Saviour established a law ordering its administration to all the faithful under both species. For speaking of this Sacrament, He Himself frequently mentions it under one kind only, as, for instance, when He says: If any man eat of this bread, he shall live for ever, and: The bread that I will give is my flesh for the life of the world, and: He that eateth this bread shall live for ever.

Why The Celebrant Alone Receives Under Both Species

It is clear that the Church was influenced by numerous and most cogent reasons, not only to approve, but also to confirm by authority of its decree, the general practice of communicating under one species. In the first place, the greatest caution was necessary to avoid spilling the blood of the Lord on the ground, a thing that seemed not easily to be avoided, if the chalice were administered in a large assemblage of the people.

In the next place, whereas the Holy Eucharist ought to be in readiness for the sick, it was very much to be apprehended, were the species of wine to remain long unconsumed, that it might turn acid.

Besides, there are many who cannot at all bear the taste or even the smell of wine. Lest, therefore, what is intended for the spiritual health should prove hurtful to the health of the body, it has been most prudently provided by the Church that it should be administered to the people under the species of bread only.

We may also further observe that in many countries wine is extremely scarce; nor can it, moreover, be brought from elsewhere without incurring very heavy expenses and encountering very tedious and difficult journeys.

Finally, a most important reason was the necessity of opposing the heresy of those who denied that Christ, whole and entire, is contained under either species, and asserted that the body is contained under the species of bread without the blood, and the blood under the species of wine without the body. In order, therefore, to place more clearly before the eyes of all the truth of the Catholic faith, Communion under one kind, that is, under the species of bread, was most wisely introduced.

There are also other reasons, collected by those who have treated on this subject, and which, if it shall appear necessary, can be brought forward by pastors.

The Minister of the Eucharist

To omit nothing doctrinal on this Sacrament, we now come to speak of its minister, a point, however. on which scarcely anyone can be ignorant.

Only Priests Have Power To Consecrate And Administer The Eucharist

It must be taught, then, that to priests alone has been given power to consecrate and administer to the faithful, the Holy Eucharist. That this has been the unvarying practice of the Church, that the faithful should receive the Sacrament from the priests, and that the officiating priests should communicate themselves, has been explained by the holy Council of Trent, which has also shown that this practice, as having proceeded from Apostolic tradition, is to be religiously retained, particularly as Christ the Lord has left us an illustrious example thereof, having consecrated His own most sacred body, and given it to the Apostles with His own hands.

The Laity Prohibited To Touch The Sacred Vessels

To safeguard in every possible way the dignity of so august a Sacrament, not only is the power of its administration entrusted exclusively to priests, but the Church has also prohibited by law any but consecrated persons, unless some case of great necessity intervene, to dare handle or touch the sacred vessels, the linen, or other instruments necessary to its completion.

Priests themselves and the rest of the faithful may hence understand how great should be the piety and holiness of those who approach to consecrate, administer or receive the Eucharist.

The Unworthiness Of The Minister Does Not Invalidate The Sacrament

What, however, has been already said of the other Sacraments, holds good also with regard to the Sacrament of the Eucharist; namely, that a Sacrament is validly administered even by the wicked, provided all the essentials have been duly observed. For we are to believe that all these depend not on the merit of the minister, but are operated by the virtue and power of Christ our Lord.

These are the things necessary to be explained regarding the Eucharist as a Sacrament.

The Eucharist as a Sacrifice

We must now proceed to explain its nature as a Sacrifice, that pastors may understand what are the principal instructions which they ought to impart to the faithful on Sundays and holy days, regarding this mystery in conformity with the decree of the holy Council (of Trent).

Importance Of Instruction On The Mass

This Sacrament is not only a treasure of heavenly riches, which if turned to good account will obtain for us the grace and love of God; but it also possesses a peculiar character, by which we are enabled to make some return to God for the immense benefits bestowed upon us.

How grateful and acceptable to God is this victim, if duly and legitimately immolated, is inferred from the following consideration. Of the sacrifices of the Old Law it is written: Sacrifice and oblation thou wouldst not; and again: If thou hadst desired sacrifice, I would indeed have given it: with burnt-offerings thou wilt not be delighted. Now if these were so pleasing in the Lord's sight that, as the Scripture testifies, from them God smelled a sweet savour, that is to say, they were grateful and acceptable to Him; what have we not to hope from that Sacrifice in which is immolated and offered He Himself of whom a voice from heaven twice proclaimed: This is my beloved Son, in whom I am well pleased.

This mystery, therefore, pastors should carefully explain, so that when the faithful are assembled at the celebration of divine service, they may learn to meditate with attention and devotion on the sacred things at which they are present.

Distinction of Sacrament and Sacrifice

They should teach, then, in the first place, that the Eucharist was instituted by Christ for two purposes: one, that it might be the heavenly food of our souls, enabling us to support and preserve spiritual life; and the other, that the Church might have a perpetual Sacrifice, by which our sins might be expiated, and our heavenly Father, oftentimes grievously offended by our crimes, might be turned away from wrath to mercy, from the severity of just chastisement to clemency. Of this thing we may observe a type and resemblance in the Paschal lamb, which was wont to be offered and eaten by the children of Israel as a sacrament and a sacrifice.

Nor could our Saviour, when about to offer Himself to God the Father on the altar of the cross, have given any more illustrious indication of His unbounded love towards us than by bequeathing to us a visible Sacrifice, by which that bloody Sacrifice, which was soon after to be offered once on the cross, would be renewed, and its memory daily celebrated with the greatest utility, unto the consummation of ages by the Church diffused throughout the world.

But (between the Eucharist as a Sacrament and a Sacrifice) the difference is very great; for as a Sacrament it is perfected by consecration; as a Sacrifice, all its force consists in its oblation. When, therefore, kept in a pyx, or borne to the sick, it is a Sacrament, not a Sacrifice. As a Sacrament also, it is to them that receive it a source of merit, and brings with it all those advantages which have been already mentioned; but as a Sacrifice, it is not only a source of merit, but also of satisfaction. For as, in His Passion, Christ the Lord merited and satisfied for us; so also those who offer this Sacrifice, by which they communicate with us, merit the fruit of His Passion, and satisfy.

The Mass Is a True Sacrifice

Proof From The Council Of Trent

With regard to the institution of this Sacrifice, the holy Council of Trent has left no room for doubt, by declaring that it was instituted by our Lord at His Last Supper; while it condemns under anathema all those who assert that in it is not offered to God a true and proper Sacrifice; or that to offer means nothing else than that Christ is given as our spiritual food.

Nor did (the Council) omit carefully to explain that to God alone is offered this Sacrifice. For although the Church sometimes offers Masses in honour and in memory of the Saints, yet she teaches that the Sacrifice is offered, not to them, but to God alone, who has crowned the Saints with immortal glory. Hence the priest never says: I offer Sacrifice to thee Peter, or to thee Paul; but, while he offers Sacrifice to God alone, he renders Him thanks for the signal victory won by the blessed martyrs, and thus implores their patronage, that they, whose memory we celebrate on earth, may vouchsafe to intercede for us in heaven."

Proof From Scripture

This doctrine, handed down by the Catholic Church, concerning the truth of this Sacrifice, she received from the words of our Lord, when, on that last night, committing to His Apostles these same sacred mysteries, He said: Do this for a commemoration of me; for then, as was defined by the holy Council, He ordained them priests, and commanded that they and their successors in the priestly office, should immolate and offer His body.

Of this the words of the Apostle to the Corinthians also afford a sufficient proof: You cannot drink the chalice of the Lord, and the chalice of devils: you cannot be partakers of the table of the Lord and of the? table of devils. As then by the table of devils must be understood the altar on which sacrifice was offered to them; so also - if the conclusion proposed to himself by the Apostle is to be legitimately drawn -- by the table of the Lord can be understood nothing else than the altar on which Sacrifice was offered to the Lord.

Should we look for figures and prophecies of this Sacrifice in the Old Testament, in the first place Malachy most clearly prophesied thereof in these words: From the rising of the sun even to the going down, my name is great among the Gentiles, and in every place there is sacrifice, and there is offered to my name a clean oblation: for my name is great among the Gentiles, saith the Lord of hosts.

Moreover, this victim was foretold, as well before as after the promulgation of the Law, by various kinds of sacrifices; for this victim alone, as the perfection and completion of all, comprises all the blessings which were signified by the other sacrifices. In nothing, however, do we behold a more lively image of the Eucharistic Sacrifice than in that of Melchisedech; for the Saviour Himself offered to God the Father, at His Last Supper, His body and blood, under the appearances of bread and wine, declaring that

He was constituted a priest for ever, after the order of Melchisedech.

Excellence of the Mass

The Mass Is The Same Sacrifice As That Of The Cross

We therefore confess that the Sacrifice of the Mass is and ought to be considered one and the same Sacrifice as that of the cross, for the victim is one and the same, namely, Christ our Lord, who offered Himself, once only, a bloody Sacrifice on the altar of the cross. The bloody and unbloody victim are not two, but one victim only, whose Sacrifice is daily renewed in the Eucharist, in obedience to the command of our Lord: Do this for a commemoration of me.

The priest is also one and the same, Christ the Lord; for the ministers who offer Sacrifice, consecrate the holy mysteries, not in their own person, but in that of Christ, as the words of consecration itself show, for the priest does not say: This is the body of Christ, but, This is my body; and thus, acting in the Person of Christ the Lord, he changes the substance of the bread and wine into the true substance of His body and blood.

The Mass A Sacrifice Of Praise, Thanksgiving And Propitiation

This being the case, it must be taught without any hesitation that, as the holy Council (of Trent) has also) explained, the sacred and holy Sacrifice of the Mass is not a Sacrifice of praise and thanksgiving only, or a mere commemoration of the Sacrifice performed on the cross, but also truly a propitiatory Sacrifice, by which God is appeased and rendered propitious to us. If, therefore, with a pure heart, a lively faith, and affected with an inward sorrow for our transgressions, we immolate and offer this most holy victim, we shall, without doubt, obtain mercy from the Lord, and grace in time of need; for SO delighted is the Lord with the door of this victim that, bestowing on us the gift of grace and repentance, He pardons our sins. Hence this usual prayer of the Church: As often as the commemoration of this victim is celebrated, so often is the work of our salvation being done; that is to say, through this unbloody Sacrifice flow to us the most plenteous fruits of that bloody victim.

The Mass Profits Both The Living And The Dead

Pastors should next teach that such is the efficacy of this Sacrifice that its benefits extend not only to the celebrant and communicant, but to all the faithful, whether living with us on earth, or already numbered with those who are dead in the Lord, but whose sins have not yet been fully expiated. For, according to the most authentic Apostolic tradition, it is not less available when offered for them, than when offered for the sins of the living, their punishments, satisfactions, calamities and difficulties of every sort.

It is hence easy to perceive, that all Masses, as being conducive to the common interest and salvation of all the faithful, are to be considered common to all.

The Rites and ceremonies of the Mass

The Sacrifice (of the Mass) is celebrated with many solemn rites and ceremonies, none of which should be deemed useless or superfluous. On the contrary, all of them tend to display the majesty of this august Sacrifice, and to excite the faithful when beholding these saving mysteries, to contemplate the divine things which lie concealed in the Eucharistic Sacrifice. On these rites and ceremonies we shall not dwell, since they require a more lengthy exposition than is compatible with the nature of the present work; moreover priests can easily consult on the subject some of the many booklets and works that have been written by pious and learned men.

What has been said so far will, with the divine assistance, be found sufficient to explain the principal things which regard the Holy Eucharist both as a Sacrament and Sacrifice.

THE SACRAMENT OF PENANCE

Importance Of Instruction On This Sacrament

As the frailty and weakness of human nature are universally known and felt by each one in himself, no one can be ignorant of the great necessity of the Sacrament of Penance. If, there- fore, the diligence of pastors should be proportioned to the weight and importance of the subject, we must admit that in ex pounding this Sacrament they can never be sufficiently diligent. Nay, it should be explained with more care than Baptism. Baptism is administered but once, and cannot be repeated; Penance may be administered and becomes necessary, as often as we may have sinned after Baptism. Hence the- Council of Trent declares: For those who fall into sin after Baptism the Sacrament of Penance is as necessary to salvation as is Baptism for those who have not been already baptised. The saying of St. Jerome that Penance is a second plank, is universally known and highly commended by all subsequent writers on sacred things. As he who suffers shipwreck has no hope of safety, unless, perchance, he seize on some plank from the wreck, so he that suffers the shipwreck of baptismal innocence, unless he cling to the saving plank of Penance, has doubtless lost all hope of salvation.

These instructions are intended not only for the benefit of pastors, but also for that of the faithful at large, to awaken attention, lest they be found culpably negligent in a matter so very important. Impressed with a just sense of the frailty of human nature, their first and most earnest desire should be to advance with the divine assistance in the ways of God, without sin or failing. But should they at any time prove so unfortunate as to fall, then, looking at the infinite goodness of God, who like the good shepherd binds up and heals the wounds of His sheep, they should not postpone recourse to the most saving remedy of Penance.

Different Meanings of the Word "Penance"

To enter at once on the subject, and to avoid all error to which the ambiguity of the word may give rise, its different meanings are first to be explained. By penance some understand satisfaction; while others, who wander far from the doctrine of the Catholic faith, supposing penance to have no reference to the past, define it to be nothing more than newness of life. It must, therefore, be shown that the word has a variety of meanings.

In the first place, it is said of those to whom that which was before pleasing is now displeasing, whether the object itself was good or bad. In this sense all those repent whose sorrow is according to the world, not according to God; and therefore, worketh not salvation, but death.

In the second place, it is used to express that sorrow which the sinner conceives, not, however, for the sake of God, but for his own sake, concerning some sin of his in which he once took pleasure.

A third kind of penance is that by which we experience interior sorrow of heart, or give exterior indication of such sorrow for the sake of God alone. To all these kinds of sorrow the word repentance properly applies.

When the Sacred Scriptures say that God repented, the expression is evidently figurative. When we repent of any thing, we are most anxious to change it; and hence when God has resolved to change any thing, the Scriptures, accommodating their language to our manner of speaking, say that He repents. Thus we read that it repented him that he had made man, and also that He was sorry that He had made Saul king.

But an important distinction is to be made between these different significations of the word. The first kind of penance must be considered faulty; the second is only the agitation of a disturbed mind; the third we call both a virtue and a Sacrament. In this last sense penance is taken here.

The Virtue of Penance

We shall first treat of penance as a virtue, not only because it is the duty of the pastor to lead the faithful to the practice of every virtue; but also, because the acts which proceed from penance as a virtue, constitute the matter, as it were, of Penance as a Sacrament, and unless the virtue be rightly understood, the force of the Sacrament cannot be appreciated.

The faithful, therefore, are first to be admonished and exhorted to labor strenuously to attain this interior penance of the heart which we call a virtue, and without which exterior penance can avail them very little.

Meaning Of Penance

Interior penance consists in turning to God sincerely and from heart, and in hating and detesting our past transgressions, with a firm resolution of amendment of life, hoping to obtain pardon through the mercy. Accompanying this penance, like inseparable companion of detestation for sin, is a sorrow and sadness, which is a certain agitation and disturbance of the soul, and is called by many a passion. Hence many of the Fathers define penance as an anguish of soul.

Penance, however, in those who repent, must be preceded by faith, for without faith no man can turn to God. Faith, therefore, cannot on any account be called a part of penance.

Penance Proved To Be A Virtue

That this inward penance is, as we have already said, a virtue, the various commands which have been given regarding it clearly show; for the law commands only those actions that are virtuous.

Furthermore, no one can deny that it is a virtue to be sorrowful at the time, in the manner, and to the extent which are required. To regulate sorrow in this manner belongs to the virtue of penance. Some conceive a sorrow which bears no proportion to their crimes. Nay, there are some, says Solomon, who are glad when they have done evil. Others, on the contrary, give themselves to such melancholy and grief, as utterly to abandon all hope of salvation. Such, perhaps, was the condition of Cain when he exclaimed: My iniquity is greater than that I may deserve pardon. Such certainly was the condition of Judas, who, repenting, hanged himself, and thus lost soul and body. Penance, therefore, considered as a virtue, assists us in restraining within the bounds of moderation our sense of sorrow.

That penance is a virtue may also be inferred from the ends which the true penitent proposes to himself. The first is to destroy sin and efface from the soul its every spot and stain. The second is to make satisfaction to God for the sins which he has committed, which is clearly an act of justice. Between God and man, it is true, no relation of strict justice can exist, so great is the distance that separates them; yet between them there is evidently a sort of justice, such as exists between a father and his children, between a master and his servants. The third (end of the penitent) is to reinstate himself in the favour and friendship of God whom he has offended and whose hatred he has earned by the turpitude of sin. The foregoing considerations sufficiently prove that penance is a virtue.

The Steps Which Lead Up To This Virtue

We must also point out the steps by which we may ascend to this divine virtue. I The mercy of God first goes before us and converts our hearts to Him. This was the object of the Prophet's prayer: Convert us, O Lord, to thee, and we shall be converted.

Illumined by this light the soul next tends to God by faith. He that cometh to God, says the Apostle, must believe that he is, and is a rewarder of them that seek him.

A salutary fear of God's judgments follows, and the soul, contemplating the punishments that await sin, is recalled from the paths of vice. To this (state of soul) seem to refer these words of Isaias: As a woman with child, when she draweth near the time of her delivery, is in pain and crieth out in her pangs, so are we become.

Then follows a hope of obtaining mercy from God, encouraged by which we resolve on improvement of life.

Lastly, our hearts are inflamed by charity, whence springs that filial fear which good and dutiful children experience; and thus dreading only to offend the majesty of God in anything, we entirely abandon the ways of sin.

Fruits Of This Virtue

Such are, as it were, the steps by which we ascend to this most exalted virtue, a virtue altogether heavenly and divine, to which the Sacred Scriptures promise the kingdom of heaven; for it is written in St. Matthew: Do penance, for the kingdom of heaven is at hand. If, says Ezechiel, the wicked do penance for all his sins which he hath committed, and keep all my commandments, and do judgment and justice, living he shall live. In another place: I desire not the death of the wicked, but that the wicked turn from his way and live, words which are evidently understood of eternal life.

Penance as a Sacrament

Regarding external penance it will be necessary to show that in it the Sacrament properly consists, and that it possesses certain outward and sensible signs which denote the effect that takes place interiorly in the soul.

Why Christ Instituted This Sacrament

In the first place, however, it will be well to explain why it is that Christ our Lord was pleased to number Penance among the Sacraments. One of His reasons certainly was to leave us no room for doubt regarding the remission of sin which was promised by God when He said: If the wicked do penance, etc. For each one has good reason to distrust the accuracy of his own judgment on his own actions, and hence we could not but be very much in doubt regarding the truth of our internal penance. It was to destroy this, our uneasiness, that our Lord instituted the Sacrament of Penance, by means of which we are assured that our sins are pardoned by the absolution of the priest; and also to tranquilize our conscience by means of the trust we rightly repose in the virtue of the Sacraments. The words of the priest sacramentally and lawfully absolving us from our sins are to be accepted in the same sense as the words of Christ our Lord when He said to the paralytic: Son, be of good heart: thy sins are forgiven thee.

In the second place, no one can obtain salvation unless through Christ and the merits of His Passion. Hence it was becoming in itself, and highly advantageous to us, that a Sacrament should be instituted through the force and efficacy of which the blood of Christ flows into our souls, washes- away-all the sins committed after Baptism, and thus leads us to recognise that it is to our Saviour alone we owe the blessing of reconciliation.

Penance Is a Sacrament

That Penance is a Sacrament pastors can easily show from what follows. As Baptism is a Sacrament because it blots out all sins, and especially original sin, so for the same reason Penance, which takes away all the sins of thought and deed committed after Baptism, must be regarded as a true Sacrament in the proper sense of the word.

Moreover -- and this is the principal reason -- since what is exteriorly done, both by priest and penitent, signifies the inward effects that take place in the soul, who will venture to deny that Penance is invested with the nature of a proper and true Sacrament ? For a Sacrament is a sign of a sacred thing. Now the sinner who repents plainly expresses by his words and actions that he has turned his heart from sin; while from the words and actions of the priest we easily recognise the mercy of God exercised in the remission of sins.

In any event, the words of our Saviour furnish a clear proof: I will give to thee the keys of the kingdom of heaven whatsoever thou shalt loose upon earth, shall be loosed also in heaven. The absolution announced in the words of the priest expresses the remission of sins which it accomplishes in the soul.

This Sacrament May Be Repeated

The faithful should be instructed not only that Penance is to be numbered among the Sacraments, but that it is one of the Sacraments which may be repeated. To Peter, who had asked whether pardon could be given to sin seven times, our Lord replied: I say not to thee, till seven times; but till seventy times seven.

If, then, (the pastor) happens to encounter those who seem to distrust the infinite goodness and clemency of God, let him endeavour to inspire their minds with confidence, and raise them up to the hope of obtaining the grace of God. He will easily accomplish this object by explaining the above and other passages which are frequently met with in Holy Writ; as well as by using the arguments and reasons which may be found in St. Chrysostom's book On the Lapsed, and St. Ambrose's books On Penance.

The Constituent Parts of Penance

The Matter

There is nothing that should be better known to the faithful than the matter of this Sacrament; hence they should be taught that Penance differs from the other Sacraments in this that while the matter of the other Sacraments is some thing, whether natural or artificial, the matter, as it were, of the Sacrament of Penance is the acts of the penitent, -- namely, contrition, confession and satisfaction, -- as has been declared by the council of Trent. Now, inasmuch as these acts are by divine institution required on the part of the penitent for the integrity of the Sacrament, and for the full and perfect remission of sin, they are called parts of Penance. It is not because they are not the real matter that they are called by the Council the matter as it were, but because they are not of that sort of matter which is applied externally, such, for instance, as water in Baptism and chrism in Confirmation.

As regards the opinion of some who hold that sins themselves are the matter of this Sacrament, it will be found, when carefully examined, that it does not really differ from the explanation already given. Thus we say that wood which is consumed by fire is the matter of fire. In the same way, sins which are destroyed by Penance may properly be called the matter of Penance.

The Form Of Penance

Pastors should not neglect to explain the form of the Sacrament of Penance. A knowledge of it will excite the faithful to receive the grace of this Sacrament with the greatest possible devotion. Now the form is: I absolve thee, as may be inferred not only from the words, whatsoever you shall bind upon earth shall be bound also in heaven, but also from the teaching of Christ our Lord, handed down to us by the Apostles.

Moreover, since the Sacraments signify what they effect, the words, I absolve thee, signify that remission of sin is effected by the administration of this Sacrament; and hence it is plain that such is the perfect form of the Sacrament. For sins are, so to say, the chains by which the soul is bound, and from which it is freed by the Sacrament of Penance. And none the less truly does the priest pronounce the form over the penitent who, through perfect contrition, accompanied by the desire of confession, has already obtained remission of his sins from God.

Several prayers are added, not that they are necessary to the form, but in order to remove every obstacle that can impede the force and efficacy of the Sacrament owing to the fault of him to whom it is administered.

How thankful, then, should not sinners be to God for having bestowed such ample power on the priests of His Church ! Unlike the priests of the Old Law who merely declared the leper cleansed from his leprosy, the power now given to the priests of the New Law is not limited to declaring the sinner absolved from his sins, but, as a minister of God, he truly absolves from sin. This is an effect of which God Himself, the author and source of grace and justice, is the principal cause.

The Rites Observed in the Sacrament of Penance

The faithful should take great care to observe the rites which accompany the administration o f this Sacrament. In this way they will have a higher idea of what they obtain from this Sacrament, that is, that they have been reconciled as slaves to their kind master, or rather, as children to their best of fathers; and at the same time they will also better understand what is the duty of those who desire, as everyone should, to show their gratitude and remembrance of so great a benefit.

The sinner, then, who repents, casts himself humbly and sorrowfully at the feet of the priest, in order that by there humbling himself he may the more easily be led to see that he must tear up the roots of pride whence spring and flourish all the sins he now deplores. In the priest, who is his legitimate judge, he venerates the person and the power of Christ our Lord; for in the administration of the Sacrament of Penance, as in that of the other Sacraments, the priest holds the place of Christ. Next the penitent enumerates his sins, acknowledging, at the same time, that he deserves the greatest and severest chastisements; and finally, suppliantly asks pardon for his faults.

All these rites have a sure guarantee for their antiquity in the authority of St. Denis.

Effects of the Sacrament of Penance

Nothing will prove of greater advantage to the faithful, nothing will be found to conduce more to a willing reception of the Sacrament of Penance, than for pastors to explain frequently the great advantage to be derived therefrom. They will then see that of Penance it is truly said that its roots ale bitter, but its fruit sweet indeed.

First of all, then, the great efficacy o Penance consists in this, that it restores us to the grace of God, and unites us to Him in the closest friendship.

In pious souls who approach this Sacrament with devotion, profound peace and tranquillity of conscience, together with ineffable joy of soul, accompany this reconciliation. For there is no sin, however great or horrible, which cannot be effaced by the Sacrament of Penance, and that not merely once, but over and over again. On this point God Himself thus speaks through the Prophet: If the wicked do penance for all his sins which he hath committed, and keep all my commandments, and do judgment, and justice, living he shall live, and shall not die, and I will not remember all his iniquities that he hath done. And St. John says: If we confess our sins; he is faithful and just, to forgive us our sins; and a little later, he adds: If any man sin, -- he excepts no sin whatever, -- we have an advocate with the Father, Jesus Christ, the just; for he is the propitiation for our sins; and not for ours only, but for the sins of the whole world.

When we read in Scripture that certain persons did not obtain pardon from God, even though they earnestly implored it, we know that this was due to the fact that they had not a true and heartfelt sorrow for their sins. Thus when we find in Sacred Scripture and in the writings of the Fathers passages which seem to assert that certain sins are irremissible, we must understand the meaning to be that it is very difficult to obtain pardon for them. A disease is sometimes called incurable, because the patient is so disposed as to loathe the medicines that could afford him relief. Ill the same way certain sins are not remitted or pardoned because the sinner rejects the grace of God, the only medicine for salvation. It is in this sense that St. Augustine wrote: When a man who, through the grace of Jesus Christ, has once arrived at a knowledge of God, wounds fraternal charity, and, driven by the fury of envy, lifts up his head against grace, the enormity of his sin is so great that, though compelled by a guilty conscience to acknowledge and confess his fault, he finds himself unable to submit to the humiliation of imploring pardon.

The Necessity of the Sacrament of Penance

Returning now to the Sacrament, it is so much the special province of Penance to remit sins that it is impossible to obtain or even to hope for remission of sins by any other means; for it is written: Unless you do penance, you shall all likewise perish. These words were said by our Lord in reference to grievous and mortal sins, although at the same time lighter sins, which are called venial, also require some sort of penance. St. Augustine observes that the kind of penance which is daily performed in the Church for venial sins, would be absolutely useless, if venial sin could be remitted without penance.

The Three Integral Parts of Penance

But as it is not enough to speak in general terms when treating of practical matters, the pastors should take care to explain, one by one, those things from which the faithful can understand the meaning of true and salutary Penance.

Their Existence

Now it is peculiar to this Sacrament that besides matter and form, which it has in common with all the other Sacraments, it has also, as we have said, those parts which constitute Penance, so to say, whole and entire; namely, contrition, confession and satisfaction. On these St. Chrysostom thus speaks: Penance enables the sinner to bear all willingly in his heart is contrition; on his lips confession; in his actions entire humility or salutary satisfaction.

Their Nature

These three parts belong to that class of parts which are necessary to constitute a whole. The human body is composed of many members, -- -hands, feet, eyes and the various other parts; the want of any one of which makes the body be justly considered imperfect, while if none of them is missing, the body is regarded as perfect. In the same way, Penance is composed of these three parts in such a way that though contrition and confession, which justify man, are alone required to constitute its essence, yet, unless accompanied by its third part, satisfaction, it necessarily remains short of its absolute perfection.

These three parts, then, are so intimately connected with one another, that contrition includes the intention and resolution of confessing and making satisfaction; contrition and the resolution of making satisfaction imply confession; while the other two precede satisfaction.

Necessity Of These Integral Parts

The reason why these are the integral parts may be thus explained. Sins against God are committed by thought, by word and by deed. It is, then, but reasonable, that in recurring to the power of the keys we should endeavour to appease God's wrath, and obtain pardon for our sins by means of the very same things which we employed to offend His sovereignty.

A further reason by way of confirmation can also be assigned. Penance is a sort of compensation for sin, springing from the free will of the delinquent, and is appointed by God, against whom the offence has been committed. Hence, on the one hand, there is required the willingness to make compensation, in which willingness contrition chiefly consists; while, on the other hand, the penitent must submit himself to the judgment of the priest, who holds God's place, in order to enable him to award a punishment proportioned to the gravity of the sin committed. Hence the reason for and the necessity of confession and satisfaction are easily inferred.

The First Part of Penance

Contrition

As the faithful require instruction on the nature and efficacy of the parts of Penance, we must begin with contrition. This subject demands careful explanation; for as often as we call to mind our past transgressions, or offend God anew, so often should our hearts be pierced with contrition.

The Meaning Of Contrition

By the Fathers of the Council of Trent, contrition is defined: A sorrow and detestation for sin committed, with a purpose of sinning no more. and a little further on the Council, speaking of the motion of the will to contrition, adds: If joined with a confidence in the mercy of God and an earnest desire of per forming whatever is necessary to the proper reception of the Sacrament, it thus prepares us for the remission of sin.

Contrition Is A Detestation Of Sin

From this definition, therefore, the faithful will perceive that the efficacy of contrition does not simply consist in ceasing to sin, or in resolving to begin, or having actually begun a new life; it supposes first of all a hatred of one's ill-spent life and a desire of atoning for past transgressions.

This is especially confirmed by those cries of the holy Fathers,. which we so frequently meet with in Holy Scripture. I have laboured in my groaning, says David; every night I will wash my bed; and again, The Lord hath heard the voice of my weeping. I will recount to thee all my years, says another, in the bitterness of my soul. These and many like expressions were called forth by an intense hatred and a lively detestation of past transgressions.

Contrition Produces Sorrow

But although contrition is defined as sorrow, the faithful are not thence to conclude that this sorrow consists in sensible feeling; for contrition is an act of the will, and, as St. Augustine observes, grief is not penance but the accompaniment of penance. By sorrow the

Fathers understood a hatred and detestation of sin; in the first place, because the Sacred Scriptures frequently use the word in this sense. How long, says David, shall I take counsels in my soul, sorrow in my heart all the day. And secondly, because from contrition arises sorrow in the inferior part of the soul which is called the seat of concupiscence.

With propriety, therefore, is contrition defined a sorrow, because it produces sorrow; hence penitents, in order to express it, used to change their garments. Our Lord alludes to this custom when He says: Woe to thee, Corozain, woe to thee, Bethsaida: for if in Tyre and Sidon had been wrought the miracles that have been wrought in you, they had long ago done penance in sack-cloth and ashes.

Names Of Sorrow For Sin

To signify the intensity of this sorrow the name contrition has rightly been given to the detestation of sin of which we speak. The word means the breaking of an object into small parts by means of a stone or some harder substance; and here it is used metaphorically, to signify that our hearts, hardened by pride, are beaten and broken by penance. Hence no-other sorrow, not even that which is felt for the death of parents, or children, or for any other calamity, is called contrition. The word is exclusively employed to express the sorrow with which we are overwhelmed by the forfeiture of the grace of God and of our own innocence.

Contrition, however, is often designated by other names. Sometimes it is called contrition of heart, because the word heart is frequently used in Scripture to express the will. As the movement of the body originates in the heart, so the will is the faculty which governs and controls the other powers of the soul.

By the holy Fathers it is also called compunction of heart, and hence they preferred to entitle their works on contrition treatises

On Compunction of Heart; for as ulcers are lanced with a knife in order to allow the escape of the poisonous matter accumulated within, so the heart, as it were, is pierced with the lance of contrition, to enable it to emit the deadly poison of sin.

Hence, contrition is called by the Prophet Joel, a rending of the heart. Be converted to me, he says, with all your hearts in fasting, in weeping, in mourning, and rend your hearts.

Qualities of Sorrow for Sin

It Should Be Supreme

That sorrow for sins committed should be so profound and supreme that no greater sorrow could be thought of will easily appear from the considerations that follow.

Perfect contrition is an act of charity, emanating from what is called filial fear; hence it is clear that the measure of contrition and of charity should be the same. Since, therefore, the charity which we cherish towards God, is the most perfect love, it follows that contrition should be the keenest sorrow of the soul. God is to be loved above all things, and whatever separates us from God is therefore to be hated above all things. It is also worthy of note that to charity and contrition the language of Scripture assigns the same extent. Of charity it is said: Thou shalt love the Lord thy God with thy whole heart.' Of contrition the Lord says through the Prophet: Be converted with your whole heart.

Secondly, it is true that of all objects which deserve our love, God is the supreme good, and it is not less true that of all objects which deserve our execration sin is the supreme evil. The same reason, then, which prompts us to confess that God is to be loved above all things, obliges us also of necessity to acknowledge that sin is to be hated above all things. That God is to be loved above all things, so that we should be prepared to sacrifice our lives rather than offend Him, these words of the Lord clearly declare: He that loveth father or mother more than me, is not worthy of me; He that will save his life shall lose it.

Further, it should be noted that since, as St. Bernard says, there is no limit or measure to charity, or to use his own words, as the measure of loving God is to love Him without measure, there should be no limit to the hatred of sin.

Sorrow For Sin Should Be Intense

Besides, our contrition should be not only the greatest, but also the most intense, and so perfect that it excludes all apathy and indifference; for it is written in Deuteronomy: When thou shalt seek the Lord thy God, thou shalt find him: yet so if thou seek him with all thy heart, and all the affliction of thy soul, and in Jeremias.: Thou shalt seek me and shalt find me, when thou shalt seek me unto all thy heart; and I will be found by thee, saith the Lord.

If, however, our contrition be not perfect, it may nevertheless be true and efficacious. For as things which fall under the senses frequently touch the heart more sensibly than things purely spiritual, it sometimes happens that persons feel more intense sorrow for the death of their children than for the grievousness of their sins.

Our contrition may also be true and efficacious, although unaccompanied by tears. Penitential tears, however, are much to be desired and commended. On this subject St. Augustine has well said: The spirit of Christian charity lives not within you, if you lament the body from which the soul has departed, but lament not the soul from which God has departed. To the same effect are the words of the Redeemer above cited: Woe to thee, Corozain, woe to thee, Bethsaida: for if in Tyre and Sidon had been wrought the miracles that have been wrought in you, they had long since done penance, in sack-cloth and ashes. To establish this truth it will suffice to recall the well-known examples of the Ninivites, of David, of the woman who was a sinner, and of the Prince of the Apostles, all. of whom obtained the pardon of their sins when they implored the mercy of God with abundant tears.

Sorrow For Sin Should Be Universal

The faithful should be earnestly exhorted and admonished to strive to extend their contrition to each mortal sin. For it is thus that Ezechias describes contrition: I will recount to thee all my years in the bitterness of my soul. To recount all our years is to examine our sins one by one in order to have sorrow for them from our hearts. In Ezechiel also we read: If the wicked do penance for all his sins, he shall live. In this sense St. Augustine says: Let the sinner consider the quality of his sins, as to time, place, variety and person.

In this matter, however, the faithful should not despair of the infinite goodness and mercy of God. For since God is most desirous of our salvation, He will not delay to pardon us. With a father's fondness, He embraces the sinner the moment he enters into himself, turns to the Lord, and, having detested all his sins, resolves that later on, as far as he is able, he will call them singly to mind and detest them. The Almighty Himself, by the mouth of His Prophet, commands us to hope, when He says: The wickedness of the wicked shall not hurt him, in what day soever he shall turn from his wickedness.

Conditions Required for Contrition

From what has been said we may gather the chief requisites of true contrition. In these the faithful are to be accurately instructed, that each may know the means of attaining, and may have a fixed standard by which to determine, how far he may be removed from the perfection of this virtue.

Detestation Of Sin

We must, then, in the first place, detest and deplore all out sins. If our sorrow and detestation extend only to some sins, our repentance is not salutary, but feigned and false. Whosoever shall keep the whole law, says St. James, but offend in one point, is become guilty of all.

Intention Of Confession And Satisfaction

In the next place, our contrition must be accompanied with a desire of confessing and satisfying for our sins. Concerning these dispositions we shall treat in their proper place.

Purpose Of Amendment

Thirdly, the penitent must form a fixed and firm purpose of amendment of life. This the Prophet clearly teaches in the following words: If the wicked do penance for all his sins which he hath committed, and keep all my commandments, and do judgment, and justice, living Ice shall live, and shall not die: I will not remember all his iniquities which he hath done. And a little after: When the wicked turneth himself away from his wickedness which he hath wrought, and doth judgment and justice, he shall save his soul alive. Still further on he adds: Be converted and do penance for all your iniquities, and iniquity shall not be your ruin. Cast away from you all your transgressions, by which you have transgressed, and make yourselves a new heart and a new spirit. To the woman taken in adultery Christ our Lord commanded the same thing: Go thy way, and sin no more; and also to the lame man whom He cured at the pool of Bethsaida: Behold, thou art made whole, sin no more.

Reasons For These Conditions

That a sorrow for sin and a firm purpose of avoiding sin for the future are two conditions indispensable to contrition nature and reason clearly show. He who would be reconciled to a friend whom he has wronged must regret to have injured and offended him, and his future conduct must be such as to avoid offending in anything against friendship.

Furthermore, these are conditions to which man is bound to yield obedience; for the law to which man is subject, be it natural, divine, or human, he is bound to obey. If, therefore, by force or fraud, the penitent has taken anything from his neighbour, he is bound to restitution. Likewise if, by word or deed he has injured his neighbour's honour or reputation, he is under an obligation of repairing the injury by procuring him some advantage or rendering him some service. Well known to all is the maxim of St. Augustine: The sin is not forgiven unless what has been taken away is restored.

Forgiveness Of Injuries

Again, not less necessary for contrition than the other chief conditions is a care that it be accompanied by entire forgiveness of the injuries which we may have received from others. This our Lord and Saviour admonishes when He declares: If you will forgive men their offences, your heavenly Father will forgive you also your offences, but if you will not forgive men, neither will your Father forgive you your offences.

These are the conditions which the faithful should observe as regards contrition. There are other dispositions which, although not essential to true and salutary penance, contribute to render contrition more perfect and complete in its kind, and which pastors will readily discover.

The Effects of Contrition

Simply to make known those things which pertain to salvation should not be deemed a full discharge of the duty of pastors; their zeal and industry should be exerted to persuade the people to adopt these truths as their rule of conduct and as the governing principle of their actions. Hence it will be highly useful often to explain the power and utility of contrition.

For whereas most other pious practices, such as alms, fasting, prayer and similar holy and commendable works, are sometimes rejected by God on account of the faults of those who perform them, contrition can never be other than pleasing and acceptable to Him. A contrite and humble heart, O God, exclaims the Prophet, thou wilt not despise.

Nay more, the same Prophet declares elsewhere that, as soon as we have conceived this contrition in our hearts, our sins are forgiven by God: I said, I will confess my injustice to the Lord, and thou hast forgiven the wickedness of my sin. Of this truth we have a figure in the ten lepers, who, when sent by our Lord to the priests, were cured of their leprosy before they had reached them; which gives us to understand that such is the efficacy of true contrition, of which we have spoken above, that through it we obtain from the Lord the immediate pardon of all sins.

Means of Arousing True Contrition

To move the faithful to contrition, it will be very useful if pastors point out some method by which each one may excite himself to contrition.

They should all be admonished frequently to examine their consciences, in order to ascertain if they have been faithful in the observance of those things which God and His Church require. Should anyone be conscious of sin, he should immediately accuse himself, humbly solicit pardon from God, and implore time to confess and satisfy for his sins. Above all, let him supplicate the aid of divine grace, in order that he may not relapse into those sins which he now penitently deplores.

Pastors should also take care that the faithful be excited to a supreme hatred of sin, both because its turpitude and baseness are very great and because it brings us the gravest losses and misfortunes. For sin deprives us of the friendship of God, to whom we are indebted for so many invaluable blessings, and from whom we might have expected and received gifts of still higher value; and along with this it consigns us to eternal death and to torments unending and most severe.

The Second Part of Penance

Confession

Having said so much on contrition, we now come to confession, which is another part of Penance. The care and exactness which its exposition demands of pastors must be at once obvious, if we only reflect that most holy persons are firmly persuaded that whatever of piety, of holiness, of religion, has been preserved to our times in the Church, through God's goodness, must be ascribed in great measure to confession. It cannot, therefore, be a matter of surprise that the enemy of the human race, in his efforts to destroy utterly the Catholic Church, should, through the agency of the ministers of his wicked designs, have assailed with all his might this bulwark, as it were, of Christian virtue. It should be shown, therefore, in the first place that the institution of confession is most useful and even necessary to us.

Necessity Of Confession

Contrition, it is true, blots out sin; but who does not know that to effect this it must be so intense, so ardent, so vehement, as to bear a proportion to the magnitude of the crimes which it effaces? This is a degree of contrition which few reach; and hence, in this way, very few indeed could hope to obtain the pardon of their sins. It, therefore, became necessary that the most merciful Lord should provide by some easier means for the common salvation of men; and this He has done in His admirable wisdom, by giving to His Church the keys of the kingdom of heaven.

According to the doctrine of the Catholic Church, a doctrine firmly to be believed and constantly professed by all, if the sinner have a sincere sorrow for his sins and a firm resolution of avoiding them in future, although he bring not with him that contrition which may be sufficient of itself to obtain pardon, all his sins are forgiven and remitted through the power of the keys, when he confesses them properly to the priest. Justly, then, do those most holy men, our Fathers, proclaim that by the keys of the Church the gate of heaven is thrown open, a truth which no one can doubt since the Council of Florence has decreed that the effect of Penance is absolution from sin.

Advantages Of Confession

To appreciate further the great advantages of confession we may turn to a fact taught by experience. To those who have led immoral lives nothing is found so useful towards a reformation of morals as sometimes to disclose their secret thoughts, all their words and actions, to a prudent and faithful friend, who can assist them by his advice and cooperation. For the same reason it must prove most salutary to those whose minds are agitated by the consciousness of guilt to make known the diseases and wounds of their souls to the priest, as the vicegerent of Christ our Lord, bound to eternal secrecy by the strictest of laws. (In the Sacrament of Penance) they will find immediate remedies, the healing qualities of which will not only remove the present malady, but will also have such a heavenly efficacy in preparing the soul against an easy relapse into the same kind of disease and infirmity.

Another advantage of confession, which should not be overlooked, is that it contributes powerfully to the preservation of social order. Abolish sacramental confession, and that moment you deluge society with all sorts of secret and heinous crimes -- crimes too, and others of still greater enormity, which men, once that they have been depraved by vicious habits, will not dread to commit in open day. The salutary shame that attends confession restrains licentiousness, bridles desire and checks wickedness.

Definition Of Confession

Having explained the advantages of confession, pastors should next unfold its nature and efficacy. Confession, then, is defined: A sacramental accusation of one's sins, made to obtain pardon by virtue of the keys.

It is rightly called an accusation, because sins are not to be told as if the sinner boasted of his crimes, as they do who are glad when they have done evil; nor are they to be related as stories told for the sake of amusing idle listeners. They are to be confessed as matters of self-accusation, with a desire, as it were, to avenge them on ourselves.

We confess our sins with a view to obtain pardon. In this respect the tribunal of penance differs from other tribunals, which take cognisance of capital offences, and before which a confession of guilt does not secure acquittal and pardon, but penalty and punishment.

The definition of confession by the holy Fathers, although different in words, is substantially the same. Confession, says St. Augustine, is the disclosure of a secret disease, with the hope of obtaining pardon; and St. Gregory: Confession is a detestation of sins. Both of these definitions accord with, and are contained in the preceding definition.

Confession Instituted By Christ

In the next place, it is a duty of greatest moment that pastors should unhesitatingly teach that this Sacrament owes its institution to the singular goodness and mercy of our Lord Jesus Christ, who has ordered all things well, and solely with a view to our salvation.

After His Resurrection He breathed on the Apostles, assembled together, saying: Receive ye the Holy Ghost, whose sins you shall forgive, they are forgiven; and whose sins you shall retain, they are retained. Now in giving to priests the power to retain and forgive sins, it is evident that our Lord made them also judges in this matter.

Our Lord seems to have signified the same thing when, having raised Lazarus from the dead, He commanded His Apostles to loose him from the bands in which he was bound. This is the interpretation of St. Augustine. The priests, he says, can now do more: they can exercise greater clemency towards those who confess and whose sins they forgive. The Lord, in giving over Lazarus, whom He had already raised from the dead, to be loosed by the hands of His disciples, wished us to understand that to priests was given the power of loosing.

To this also refers the command given by our Lord to the lepers cured on the way, that they show themselves to the priests, and subject themselves to their judgment.

Invested, then, as they are, by our Lord with power to remit and retain sins, priests are evidently appointed judges of the matter on which they are to pronounce; and since, according to the wise remark of the Council of Trent, we cannot form an accurate judgment on any matter, or award to crime a just proportion of punishment without having previously examined and made ourselves well acquainted with the case, it follows that the penitent is obliged to make known to the priests, through the medium of confession, each and every sin.

This doctrine the pastors should teach as defined by the holy Council of Trent, and handed down by the uniform doctrine of the Catholic Church. An attentive perusal of the Fathers will present passages throughout their works, proving in the clearest terms that this Sacrament was instituted by our Lord, and that the law of sacramental confession, which, from the Greek, they call exomologesis, and exagoreusis, is to be received as true Gospel teaching.

If we seek figures in the Old Testament, the different kinds of sacrifices which were offered by the priests for the expiation of different sorts of sins, seem, beyond all doubt, to have reference to confession of sins.

Rites Added By The Church

Not only are the faithful to be taught that confession was instituted by our Lord. They are also to be reminded that, by authority of the Church, certain rites and solemn ceremonies have been added which, although not essential to the Sacrament, serve to place its dignity more fully before the eyes of the penitent, and to prepare his soul, so that, kindled with devotion, he may more easily receive the grace of God. When, with uncovered head and bended knees, with eyes fixed on the earth and hands raised in supplication, and with other indications of Christian humility not essential to the Sacrament, we confess our sins, our minds are thus deeply impressed with a clear conviction of the heavenly virtue of the Sacrament, and also of the necessity of most earnestly beseeching and imploring the mercy of God.

The Law of Confession

Nor let it be supposed that, although confession was instituted by our Lord, He did not declare its use to be necessary. The faithful must be impressed with the conviction that he who is dead in sin is to be recalled to spiritual life by means of sacramental confession.

Proof Of The Obligation

This truth is clearly conveyed by our Lord Himself, when, by a most beautiful metaphor, He calls the power of administering this Sacrament, the key of the kingdom of heaven. Just as no one can enter any place without the help of him who has the keys, so no one is admitted to heaven unless its gates be unlocked by the priests to whose custody the Lord gave the keys. This power would otherwise be of no use in the Church. If heaven can be entered without the power of the keys, in vain would they to whom the keys were given seek to prevent entrance within its portals.

This thought was familiar to the mind of St. Augustine. Let no man, he says, say within himself: "I repent in secret to the Lord. God, who has power to pardon me, knows the inmost sentiments of my heart.,, Was there, then, no reason for saying "whatsoever you loose on earth, shall be loosed in heaven," no reason why the keys were given to the Church of God? The same doctrine is taught by St. Ambrose in his treatise On Penance, when refuting the heresy of the Novatians who asserted that the power of forgiving sins belonged solely to God.' Who, says he, yields greater reverence to God, he who obeys or he who resists His commands? God commands us to obey His ministers; and by obeying them, we honour God alone.

The Age At Which The Law Of Confession Obliges

As the law of confession was no doubt enacted and established by our Lord Himself, it is our duty to ascertain, on whom, at what age, and at what period of the year, it becomes obligatory. According to the canon of the Council of Lateran, which begins: Omnis utriusque sexus, no person is bound by the law of Confession until he has arrived at the use of reason, -- a time determinable by no fixed number of years. It may, however, be laid down as a general principle, that children are bound to go to confession as soon as they are able to discern good from evil, and are capable of malice; for, when a person has arrived at an age when he must begin to attend to the work of his salvation, he is bound to confess his sins to a priest, since there is no other salvation for one whose conscience is burdened with sin.

At What Time The Law Of Confession Obliges

In the same canon holy Church has defined the period within which we are especially bound to discharge the duty of confession. It commands all the faithful to confess their sins at least once a year. If, however, we consult our eternal interests, we will certainly not neglect to have recourse to confession as often, at least, as we are in danger of death, or undertake to perform any act incompatible with the state of sin, such as to administer or receive the Sacraments. The same rule should be strictly followed when we are apprehensive of forgetting some sin, into which we may have fallen; for we cannot confess sins unless we remember them, neither do we obtain pardon unless our sins are blotted out through sacramental confession.

The Qualities of Confession

But since in confession many things are to be observed, some of which are essential, some not essential to the Sacrament, all these matters should be carefully treated. Access can easily be had to works and treatises from which an explanation of all these things can be drawn.

Confession Should Be Entire

Pastors should teach, first of all, that care must be exercised that confession be complete and entire. All mortal sins must be revealed to the priest. Venial sins, which do not separate us from the grace of God, and into which we frequently fall, although they may be usefully confessed, as the experience of the pious proves, may be omitted without sin, and expiated by a variety of other means. Mortal sins, as we have already said, are all to be confessed, even though they be most secret, or be opposed only to the last two Commandments of the Decalogue. Such secret sins often inflict deeper wounds on the soul than those which are committed openly and publicly.

So the Council of Trent has defined, and such has been the constant teaching of the Church, as the Fathers declare. St. Ambrose speaks thus: Without the confession of his sin, no man can be justified from his sin. In confirmation of the same doctrine, St. Jerome, on Ecclesiastes, says: If the serpent, the devil, has secretly and without the knowledge of a third person, bitten anyone, and has infused into him the poison of sin; if unwilling to disclose his wound to his brother or master, he is silent and will not do penance, his master, who has a tongue ready to cure him, can render him no service. The same doctrine we find in St. Cyprian, in his sermon On the Fallen. Although guiltless, he says, of the heinous crime of sacrificing to idols, or of having purchased certificates to that effect; yet, as they entertained the thought of doing so, they should confess it with grief to the priests of God. In fine, such is the unanimous voice and teaching of all the Doctors of the Church.

In confession we should employ all that care and exactness which we usually bestow upon worldly concerns of great moment, and all our efforts should be directed to the cure of our soul's wounds and to the destruction of the roots of sin. We should not be satisfied with the bare enumeration of our mortal sins, but should mention such circumstances as considerably aggravate or extenuate their malice. Some circumstances are so serious as of themselves to constitute mortal guilt. On no account whatever, therefore, are such circumstances to be omitted. Thus if one man has killed another, he must state whether his victim was a layman or an ecclesiastic. Or, if he has had sinful relations with a woman, he must state whether the female was unmarried or married, a relative or a person consecrated to God by vow. These circumstances change the nature of the sins; so that the first kind of unlawful intercourse is called by theologians simple fornication, the second adultery, the third incest, and the fourth sacrilege. Again, theft is numbered in the catalogue of sins. But if a person has stolen one golden coin, his sin is less grievous than if he had stolen a hundred or two hundred, or an immense sum; and if the stolen money belonged to the Church, the sin would be still more grievous. The same rule applies to the circumstances of time and place, but' the examples are too well known from many books to require mention here. Circumstances such as these are, therefore, to be mentioned; but those which do not considerably aggravate the malice of the sin may be lawfully omitted.

Sins Concealed

So important is it that confession be entire that if the penitent confesses only some of his sins and wilfully neglects to accuse himself of others which should be confessed, he not only does not profit by his confession, but involves himself in new guilt. Such an enumeration of sins cannot be called sacramental confession; on the contrary, the penitent must repeat his confession, not omitting to accuse himself of having, under the semblance of confession, profaned the sanctity of the Sacrament.

Sins Forgotten

But should the confession seem defective, either because the penitent forgot some grievous sins, or because, although intent on confessing all his sins, he did not examine the recesses of his conscience with sufficient accuracy, he is not bound to repeat his confession. It will be sufficient, when he recollects the sins which he had forgotten, to confess them to a priest on a future occasion.

It should be noted, however, that we are not to examine our consciences with careless indifference, or to be so negligent in recalling our sins as to seem as if unwilling to remember them. Should this have been the case, the confession must by all means be made over again.

Confession Should Be Plain, Simple, Sincere

In the second place our confession should be plain, simple and undisguised; not artfully made, as is the case with some who seem more intent on defending themselves than on confessing their sins. Our confession should be such as to disclose to the priest a true image of our lives, such as we ourselves know them to be, exhibiting as doubtful that which is doubtful, and as certain that which is certain. If, then, we neglect to enumerate our sins, or introduce extraneous matter, our confession, it is clear, lacks this quality.

Confession Should Be Prudent, Modest, Brief

Prudence and modesty in explaining matters of confession are also much to be commended, and a superfluity of words is to be carefully avoided. Whatever is necessary to make known the nature of every sin is to be explained briefly and modestly.

Confession Should Be Made Privately And Often

Secrecy as regards confession should be strictly observed, as well by the penitent as by the priest. Hence, no one can, on any account, confess by messenger or letter, because in those cases secrecy would not be possible.

The faithful should be careful above all to cleanse their consciences from sin by frequent confession. When a person is in mortal sin nothing can be more salutary, so precarious is human life, than to have immediate recourse to confession. But even if we could promise ourselves a long life, yet it would be truly disgraceful that we who are so particular in whatever relates to cleanliness of dress or person, were not at least equally careful in preserving the lustre of the soul unsullied from the foul stains of sin.

The Minister of the Sacrament of Penance

The Usual Minister

We now come to treat of the minister of this Sacrament. That the minister of the Sacrament of Penance must be a priest possessing ordinary or delegated jurisdiction the laws of the Church sufficiently declare. Whoever discharges this sacred function must be invested not only with the power of orders, but also with that of jurisdiction. Of this ministry we have an illustrious proof in these words of our Lord, recorded by St. John: Whose sins you shall forgive, they are forgiven them; and whose sins you shall retain, they are retained, words addressed not to all, but to the Apostles only, to whom, in this function of the ministry, priests succeed.

This is also most fitting, for as all the grace imparted by this Sacrament is communicated from Christ the Head to His members, they who alone have power to consecrate His true body should alone have power to administer this Sacrament to His mystical body, the faithful, particularly as these are qualified and disposed by means of the Sacrament of Penance to receive the Holy Eucharist.

The scrupulous care which in the primitive ages of the Church guarded the right of the ordinary priest is easily seen from the ancient decrees of the Fathers, which provided that no Bishop or priest, except in case of great necessity, presume to exercise any function in the parish of another without the authority of him who governed there. This law derives its sanction from the Apostle when he commanded Titus to ordain priests in every city, to administer to the faithful the heavenly food of doctrine and of the Sacraments.

The Minister In Danger Of Death

In order that none may perish, if there is imminent danger of death, and recourse cannot be had to the proper priest, the Council of Trent teaches that according to the ancient practice of the Church of God it is then lawful for any priest, not only to remit all kinds of Sill, whatever faculties they might otherwise require, but also to absolve from excommunication.

Qualifications Of The Minister

Besides the powers of orders and of jurisdiction, which are of absolute necessity, the minister of this Sacrament, holding as he does the place at once of judge and physician, should be gifted not only with knowledge and erudition, but also with prudence.

As judge, his knowledge, it is evident, should be more than ordinary, for by it he is to examine into the nature of sins, and among the various kinds of sins to judge which are grievous and which are not, keeping in view the rank and condition of the person.

As physician he has also occasion for consummate prudence, for to him it belongs to administer to the diseased soul those healing medicines which will not only effect the cure, but prove suitable preservatives against its future contagion.

The faithful, therefore, will see the great care that each one should take in selecting (as confessor) a priest, who is recommended by integrity of life, by learning and prudence, who is deeply impressed with the awful weight and responsibility of the station which he holds, who understands well the punishment due to every sin, and can also discern who are to be loosed and who to be bound.

The Confessor Must Observe The Seal Of Confession

Since each one is most anxious that his sins and defilements should be buried in oblivion, the faithful are to be admonished that there is no reason whatever to apprehend that what is made known in confession will ever be revealed by the priest to anyone, or that by it the penitent can at any time be brought into danger of any sort. The laws of the Church threaten the severest penalties against any priests who would fail to observe a perpetual and religious silence concerning all the sins confessed to them. Let the priest, says the great Council of Lateran, take special care, neither by word or sign, nor by any other means whatever, to betray in the least degree the sinner.

Duties of the Confessor towards Various Classes of Penitents

Having treated of the minister of this Sacrament, the order of our matter requires that we next proceed to explain some general heads which are of considerable importance with regard to the use and practice of confession.

Many of the faithful, to whom, as a rule, no time seems to pass so slowly as that which is appointed by the laws of the Church for the duty of confession, are so removed from Christian perfection that, far from bestowing attention on those other matters which are obviously most efficacious in conciliating the favour and friendship of God, they do not even try to remember the sins that are to be confessed to the priest.

Since, therefore, nothing is to be omitted which can assist the faithful in the important work of salvation, the priest should be careful to observe if the penitent be truly contrite for his sins, and deliberately and firmly resolved to avoid sin for the future.

The Well Disposed Should Be Exhorted To Thanksgiving And Perseverance

If the sinner is found to be thus disposed, he is to be admonished and earnestly exhorted to pour out his heart in gratitude to God for so great and so singular a blessing, and to supplicate unceasingly the aid of divine grace, shielded by which he may securely combat his evil propensities.

He should also be taught not to suffer a day to pass without devoting a portion of it to meditation on some mystery of the Passion of our Lord, and to exciting and inflaming himself to the imitation and most ardent love of his Redeemer. The fruit of such meditation will be to fortify him more and more every day against all the assaults of the devil. For what other reason is there why our courage sinks and our strength fails the moment the enemy makes even the slightest attack on us, but that we neglect by pious meditation to kindle within us the fire of divine love, which animates and invigorates the soul?

The Indisposed Should Be Helped

But should the priest perceive that the penitent is not truly contrite, he will endeavour to inspire him with an anxious desire for contrition, inflamed by which he may resolve to ask and implore this heavenly gift from the mercy of God.

Those Who Seek To Excuse Their Sins Should Be Corrected

The pride of some who seek by vain excuses to justify or extenuate their offences is carefully to be repressed. If, for instance, a penitent confesses that he was wrought up to anger, and immediately transfers the blame of the excitement to another, who, he complains, was the aggressor, he is to be reminded that such apologies are indications of a proud spirit, and of a man who either thinks lightly of, or is unacquainted with the enormity of his sin, while they serve rather to aggravate than to extenuate his guilt. He who thus labours to justify his conduct seems to say that then only will he exercise patience, when no one injures him -- a disposition than which nothing can be more unworthy of a Christian. Instead of lamenting the state of him who inflicted the injury he disregards the grievousness of the sin, and is angry with his brother. Having had an opportunity of honouring God by his exemplary patience, and of correcting a brother by his meekness, he turns the very means of salvation to his own destruction.

Those Who Are Ashamed To Confess Their Sins Should Be Instructed

Still more pernicious is the fault of those who, yielding to a foolish bashfulness, cannot induce themselves to confess their sins. Such persons are to be encouraged by exhortation, and are to be reminded that there is no reason whatever why they should fear to disclose their sins, that to no one can it appear surprising if persons fall into sin, the common malady of the human race and the natural consequence of human infirmity.

The Careless Should Be Rebuked

There are others who, either because they seldom confess their sins, or because they have bestowed no care or attention on the examination of their consciences, do not know well how to begin or end their confession. Such persons deserve to be severely rebuked, and are to be taught that before anyone approaches the tribunal of Penance he should employ every diligence to excite himself to contrition for his sins, and that this he cannot do without endeavouring to know and recollect them severally.

The Unprepared Should Be Dismissed Or Led To Good Disposition

Should the confessor meet persons of this class entirely unprepared, he should dismiss them without harshness, exhorting them in the kindest terms to take some time to reflect on their sins, and then return; but should they declare that they have already done everything in their power to prepare, and there is reason to apprehend that if sent away they may not return, their confession is to be heard, particularly if they manifest some disposition to amend their lives and can be induced to accuse their own negligence and promise to atone for it at another time by a diligent and accurate scrutiny of conscience. In such cases, however, the confessor should proceed with caution. If, after having heard the confession, he is of the opinion that the penitent did not entirely lack diligence in examining his conscience or sorrow in detesting his sins, he may absolve him; but if he has found him deficient in both, he should, as we have already said, admonish him to use greater care in his examination of conscience, and dismiss him as kindly as he can.

The Pastor Should Show The Wrong Of Human Respect

But as it sometimes happens that females, who may have forgotten some sin in a former confession, cannot bring themselves to return to the confessor, dreading to expose themselves before the people to the suspicion of having been guilty of something grievous or of looking for the praise of extraordinary piety, the pastor should frequently remind the faithful, both publicly and privately, that no one is gifted with so tenacious a memory as to be able to recollect all his thoughts, words and actions; that the faithful, therefore, should they call to mind some sin which they had previously forgotten, should not be deterred from returning to the priest. These and many other matters of the same nature demand the attention of priests in confession.

The Third Part of Penance

Satisfaction

Let us now come to the third part of Penance, which is called satisfaction. We shall begin by explaining its nature and efficacy, because the enemies of the Catholic Church have on these subjects taken ample occasion to sow discord and division, to the serious detriment of Christians.

General Meaning Of The Word "Satisfaction,"

Satisfaction is the full payment of a debt; for that is sufficient or satisfactory to which nothing is wanting. Hence, when we speak of reconciliation to favour, to satisfy means to do what is sufficient to atone to the angered mind for an injury offered; and in this sense satisfaction is nothing more than compensation for an injury done to another. But, to come to the object that now engages us, theologians make use of the word satisfaction to signify the compensation man makes, by offering to God some reparation for the sins he has committed.

Various Kinds Of Satisfaction To God

This sort of satisfaction, since it has several degrees, can be understood in various senses.

The first and highest degree of satisfaction is that by which whatever we owe to God on account of our sins is paid abundantly, even though He should deal with us according to the strictest rigour of His justice. This degree of satisfaction appeases God and renders Him propitious to us; and it is a satisfaction for which we are indebted to Christ our Lord alone, who paid the price of our sins on the cross, and offered to God a superabundant satisfaction. No created being could have been of such worth as to deliver us from so heavy a debt. He is the propitiation for our sins, says St. John, and not for ours only but also for those of the whole world. This satisfaction, therefore, is full and superabundant, perfectly adequate to the debt of all sins committed in this world. It gives to man's actions great worth before God, and without it they would be deserving of no esteem whatever. This David seems to have had in view when, having asked himself, what shall I render to the -Lord, for all the things that he hath rendered to me? and finding nothing besides this satisfaction, which he expressed by the word chalice, a worthy return for so many and such great favours, he replied: I will take the chalice of salvation, and I will call upon the name of the Lord.

There is another kind of satisfaction, which is called canonical, and is performed within a certain fixed period of time. Hence, according to the most ancient practice of the Church, when penitents are absolved from their sins, some penance is imposed, the performance of which is commonly called satisfaction.

By the same name is called any sort of punishment endured for sin, although not imposed by the priest, but spontaneously undertaken and performed by ourselves.

Elements Of Sacramental Satisfaction

This, however, does not belong to Penance as a Sacrament. Only that satisfaction constitutes part of the Sacrament which, as we have already said, is offered to God for sins at the command of the priest. Furthermore, it must be accompanied by a deliberate and firm purpose carefully to avoid sin for the future.

For to satisfy, as some define it, is to pay due honour to God: and this, it is evident, no person can do, who is not entirely resolved to avoid sin. Again, to satisfy is to cut off all occasions of sin, and to close every avenue against its suggestions. In accordance with this idea of satisfaction some have defined it as a cleansing, which effaces whatever defilement may remain in the soul from the stains of sin, and which exempts us from the temporal chastisements due to sin.

Necessity Of Satisfaction

Such being the nature of satisfaction, it will not be difficult to convince the faithful of the necessity imposed on the penitent of performing works of satisfaction. They are to be taught that sin carries in its train two evils, the stain and the punishment. Whenever the stain is effaced, the punishment of eternal death is forgiven with the guilt to which it was due; yet, as the Council of Trent declares, the remains of sin and the temporal punishment are not always remitted.

Of this the Scriptures afford many conspicuous examples, such as are found in the third chapter of Genesis, in the twelfth and twenty-second of Numbers, and in many other places. That of David, however, is the best known and most striking. Although the Prophet Nathan had announced to him: The Lord also hath taken a-way thy sin, thou shalt not , yet David voluntarily subjected himself to the most severe penance, imploring night and day the mercy of God in these words: Wash me yet more from my iniquity, and cleanse me from my sin; for I know my iniquity, and my sin is always before me. Thus did he beseech the Lord to pardon not only the crime, but also the punishment due to it, and to restore him, cleansed from the remains of sin, to his former state of purity and integrity. This he besought with most earnest supplications, and yet the Lord punished his transgression with the loss of his adulterous offspring, the rebellion and death of his beloved son Absalom, and with the other chastisements and calamities with which he had previously threatened him.

In Exodus, too, we read that though the Lord yielded to the prayers of Moses and spared the idolatrous Israelites, yet He threatened the enormity of their crime with heavy chastisement, and Moses himself declared that the Lord would take severest vengeance on it, even to the third and fourth generations.

That such was at all times the doctrine of the holy Fathers in the Catholic Church, their own testimony most clearly proves.

Advantages of Satisfaction

It Is Required By God's Justice And Mercy

Why in the Sacrament of Penance, as in that of Baptism, the punishment due to sin is not entirely remitted is admirably explained in these words of the Council of Trent: Divine justice seems to require that they who through ignorance sinned before Baptism, should recover the friendship of God in a different manner from those who, after they have been freed from the thraldom, of sin and the devil and have received the gifts of the Holy Ghost, dread not knowingly to violate the temple of God and grieve the Holy Spirit. It is also in keeping with the divine mercy not to remit our sins without any satisfaction, lest, taking occasion hence, and imagining our sins less grievous than they are, we should become injurious, as it were, and contumelious to the Holy Ghost, and should fall into greater enormities, treasuring up to ourselves wrath against the day of wrath. These satisfactory penances have, no doubt, great influence in recalling from and, as it were, bridling against sin, and in rendering the sinner more vigilant and cautious for the future.

Satisfaction Atones To The Church

Furthermore (these satisfactions) serve as testimonies of our sorrow for sin committed, and thus atone to the Church which is grievously insulted by our crimes. God, says St. Augustine, despises not a contrite and humble heart; but, as heartfelt grief is generally concealed from others, and is not manifested by words or other signs, wisely, therefore, are penitential times appointed by those who preside over the Church, in order to atone to the Church, in which sins are forgiven.

Satisfaction Deters Others From Sin

Besides, the example presented by our penitential practices serves as a lesson to others, how to regulate their lives and practice piety. Seeing the punishments inflicted on sin, they must feel the necessity of using the greatest circumspection through life, and of correcting their former habits.

The Church, therefore, with great wisdom ordained that when anyone had committed a public crime, a public penance should be imposed on him, in order that others, being deterred by fear, might more carefully avoid sin in future. This has sometimes been observed even with regard to secret sins of more than usual gravity.

But with regard to public sinners, as we have already said, they were never absolved until they had performed public penance. During the performance of this penance, the pastors poured out prayers to God for their salvation, and ceased not to exhort the penitents to do the same. In this respect, great was the care and solicitude of St. Ambrose, of whom it is related that many who came to the tribunal of Penance with hardened hearts were so softened by his tears as to conceive the sorrow of true contrition. But in process of time the severity of ancient discipline was so relaxed and charity grew so cold, that in our days many of the faithful think inward sorrow of soul and grief of heart unnecessary for obtaining pardon, imagining that a mere appearance of sorrow is sufficient.

By Satisfaction We Are Made Like Unto Christ

Again, by undergoing these penances we are made like unto Jesus Christ our Head, inasmuch as He Himself suffered and was tempted. As St. Bernard observes, nothing can appear so unseemly as a delicate member under a head crowned with thorns. To use the words of the Apostle: We are joint-heirs with Christ, yet so if we suffer with him; and again, If we be dead with him, we shall live also with him; if we suffer, we shall also reign with him.

Satisfaction Heals The Wounds Of Sin

St. Bernard also observes that sin produces two effects: a stain on the soul and a wound; that the stain is removed through the mercy of God, while to heal the wound inflicted by sin the remedy of penance is most necessary. When a wound has been healed, some scars remain which demand attention; likewise, with regard to the soul, after the guilt of sin is forgiven, some of its effects remain, from which the soul requires to be cleansed.

St. Chrysostom fully confirms the same doctrine when he says: It is not enough that the arrow has been extracted from the body; the wound which it inflicted must also be healed. So with regard to the soul, it is not enough that sin has been pardoned; the wound which it has left must also be healed by penance.

St. Augustine also frequently teaches that penance exhibits at once the mercy and the justice of God, -- His mercy by which He pardons sin and the eternal punishment due to sin; His justice by which He exacts temporary punishment from the sinner.

Satisfaction Disarms The Divine Vengeance

Finally, the punishment which the sinner endures disarms the vengeance of God and averts the punishments decreed against us. Thus the Apostle says: If we would judge ourselves, we should not be judged; but whilst we are judged, we are chastised by the Lord, that we be not condemned with this world. If all this is explained to the faithful, it must have great influence in exciting them to perform works of penance.

Source of the Efficacy of Satisfactory Works

Of the great efficacy of penance we may form some idea, if we reflect that it arises entirely from the merits of the Passion of Christ our Lord. It is His Passion that imparts to our good actions two greatest advantages: the first, that we may merit the rewards of eternal glory, so that a cup of cold water given in His name shall not be without its reward; the second, that we may be able to satisfy for our sins.

Nor does this lessen the most perfect and superabundant satisfaction of Christ our Lord, but, on the contrary, renders it still more conspicuous and illustrious. For the grace of Christ is seen to abound more, inasmuch as it communicates to us not only what He merited and paid of Himself alone, but also what, as Head, He merited and paid in His members, that is, in holy and just men. Hence it can be seen how such great weight and dignity belong to the good actions of the pious. For Christ our Lord continually infuses His grace into the devout soul united to Him by charity, as the head to the members, or as the vine through the branches. This grace always precedes, accompanies and follows our good works, and without it we can have no merit, nor can we at all satisfy God.

Hence it is that nothing seems wanting to the just. Through their works done by the power of God, they are able, on the one hand, to satisfy God's law, as far as their human and mortal condition will allow; and, on the other hand, they can merit eternal life, to the fruition of which they will be admitted if they die in the state of God's grace. Well known are the words of the Saviour: He that shall drink of the water that I will give him shall not thirst for ever; but the water that I will give him shall become in him a fountain of water, springing up into life everlasting.

Conditions for Satisfaction

In satisfaction two things are particularly required: the one, that he who satisfies be in a state of grace, the friend of God, since works done without faith and charity cannot be acceptable to God; the other, that the works performed be such as are of their own nature painful or laborious. They are a compensation for past sins, and, to use the words of the holy martyr Cyprian, the redeemers, as it were, of past sins, and must, therefore, in some way be disagreeable.

It does not, however, always follow that they are painful or laborious to those who undergo them. The influence of habit, or the intensity of divine love, frequently renders the soul insensible to things the most difficult. Such works, however, do not therefore cease to be satisfactory. It is the privilege of the children of God to be so inflamed with His love, that while undergoing the most cruel tortures, they are either almost insensible to them, or bear them all with the greatest joy.

Works Of Satisfaction Are Of Three Kinds

Pastors should teach that all kinds of satisfaction are reducible to three heads: prayer, fasting and almsdeeds, which correspond to three kinds of goods which we have received from God, those of the soul, those of the body and what are called external goods.

Nothing can be more effectual in uprooting all sin from the soul than these three kinds of satisfaction. For since whatever is in the world is the concupiscence of the flesh, the concupiscence of the eyes, and the pride of life, everyone can see that to these three causes of disease are opposed also three remedies. To the first is opposed fasting; to the second, almsdeeds; to the third, prayer.

Moreover, if we consider those whom our sins injure, we shall easily perceive why all kinds of satisfaction are reduced especially to these three. For those (we offend by our sins) are: God, our neighbour and ourselves. God we appease by prayer, our neighbour we satisfy by alms, and ourselves we chastise by fasting.

As this life is chequered by many and various afflictions, the faithful are to be particularly reminded that those who patiently bear all the trials and afflictions coming from the hand of God acquire abundant satisfaction and merit; whereas those who suffer with reluctance and impatience deprive themselves of all the fruits of satisfaction, merely enduring the punishment which the just judgment of God inflicts upon their sins.

One Can Satisfy For Another

In this the supreme mercy and goodness of God deserve our grateful acknowledgment and praise, that He has granted to our frailty the privilege that one may satisfy for another. This, however, is a privilege which is confined to the satisfactory part of Penance alone. As regards contrition and confession, no one is able to be contrite for another; but those who are in the state of grace may pay for others what is due to God, and thus we may be said in some measure to bear each other's burdens.

This is a doctrine on which the faithful cannot for a moment entertain a doubt, since we profess in the Apostle's Creed our belief in the Communion of Saints. For since we are all reborn to Christ in the same cleansing waters of Baptism and are partakers of the same Sacraments, and, above all, are nourished with the same body and blood of Christ our Lord, as our food and drink, we are all, it is manifest, members of the same body. As then the foot does not perform its functions solely for itself, but also for the sake of the eyes, and as the eyes see not only for their own sake, but for the general good of all the members, so also works of satisfaction must be considered common to us all.

This, however, is not true in reference to all the advantages to be derived from satisfaction. For works of satisfaction are also medicinal, and are so many remedies prescribed to the penitent to heal the depraved affections of the soul. It is clear that those who do not satisfy for themselves can have no share in this fruit of penance.

These three parts of Penance, contrition, confession and satisfaction, should be fully and clearly explained.

Duties of the Confessor as Regards Satisfaction

Restitution Must Be Insisted On

Above all, priests should be very careful not to give absolution to any penitent, whose confession they have heard, without obliging him to make full satisfaction for any injury to his neighbour's goods or character for which he seems responsible. No person is to be absolved until he has first faithfully promised to restore all that belongs to others.

But as there are many who readily promise to comply with their duty in this respect, yet are deliberately determined never to fulfil their promises, these persons should be obliged to make restitution, and the words of the Apostle are to be frequently pressed upon their minds: He that stole, let him now steal no more; but rather let him labour, working with his hands the thing which is good, that he may have something to give to him that suffereth need.

Quantity And Quality Of Penances Should Be Reasonable

In imposing penance priests should do nothing arbitrarily, but should be guided solely by justice, prudence and piety. In order to show that they follow this rule, and also to impress more deeply on the mind of the penitent the enormity of his sin, it will be useful sometimes to remind him of the severe punishments inflicted by the ancient penitential canons, as they are called, for certain sins. The nature of the sin, therefore, will regulate the extent of the satisfaction.

No satisfaction can be more salutary than to require of the penitent to devote, for a certain number of days, some time to prayer, not omitting to pray to God in behalf of all mankind, and particularly for those who have departed this life in the Lord.

Voluntary Works Of Penance Should Be Recommended

Penitents should also be exhorted to undertake of their own accord the frequent performance of the penances imposed by the confessor, and thus so to conduct their lives that, having faithfully complied with everything which the Sacrament of Penance demands, they may never cease earnestly to practice the virtue of penance.

PUBLIC PENANCES SHOULD SOMETIMES BE GIVEN

Should it be deemed proper sometimes to visit public crimes with public penance, and should the penitent express great reluctance of seek to escape from its performance, he should not be listened to too readily, but should be persuaded to embrace with cheerfulness and readiness that which will be salutary to himself and to others.

Admonition

These things concerning the Sacrament of Penance and its several parts should be taught in such a manner as to enable the faithful not only to understand them perfectly, but also, with the Lord's help, to resolve to put them in practice piously and religiously.

THE SACRAMENT OF EXTREME UNCTION

Importance Of Instruction On Extreme Unction

In all thy works, the Scriptures teach, remember thy last end, and thou shalt never sin, words which convey to the pastor a silent admonition to omit no opportunity of exhorting the faithful to constant meditation on death. The Sacrament of Extreme Unction, because inseparably associated with recollection of the day of death, should, it is obvious, form a subject of frequent instruction, not only because it is right to explain the mysteries of salvation, but also because death, the inevitable doom of all men, when recalled to the minds of the faithful, represses depraved passion. Thus shall they be less disturbed by the approach of death, and will pour forth their gratitude in endless praises to God, who has not only opened to us the way to true life in the Sacrament of Baptism, but has also instituted that of Extreme Unction, to afford us, when departing this mortal life, an easier way to heaven.

Names of this Sacrament

In explaining what is more necessary on this subject we shall follow almost the same order observed in the exposition of the other Sacraments. Hence we shall first show that this Sacrament is called Extreme Unction, because among all the unctions prescribed by our Lord to His Church, this is the last to be administered.

For this reason it was also called by our predecessors in the faith, the Sacrament of the anointing of the sick, and also the Sacrament of the dying, names which easily turn the minds of the faithful to the remembrance of that last hour.

Extreme Unction Is a True Sacrament

That Extreme Unction is strictly speaking a Sacrament, is first to be explained; and this the words of St. James the Apostle, promulgating the law of this Sacrament, clearly establish. Is any man, he says, sick amongst you ? Let him bring in the priests of the church, and let them pray over him, anointing him with oil in the name of the Lord: and the prayer of faith shall save the sick man; and the Lord shall raise him up; and if he be in sins, they shall be forgiven him. When the Apostle says that sins are forgiven, he ascribes to Extreme Unction the nature and efficacy of a Sacrament.

That such has been at all times the doctrine of the Catholic Church on Extreme Unction, many Councils testify, and the Council of Trent denounces anathema against all who presume to teach or think otherwise. Innocent I also recommends this Sacrament with great earnestness to the attention of the faithful.

Extreme Unction Is But One Sacrament

Pastors, therefore, should teach that Extreme Unction is a true Sacrament, and that, although administered with many anointings, each given with a peculiar prayer, and under a peculiar form, it constitutes not many, but one Sacrament. It is one, however, not in the sense that it is composed of inseparable parts, but because each of the parts contributes to its perfection, as is the case with every object composed of many parts. As a house which consists of a great variety of parts derives its perfection from unity of plan, so is this Sacrament, although composed of many and different things and words, but one sign, and it effects only that one thing of which it is the sign.

Essential Parts of Extreme Unction

Pastors should also teach what are the component parts of this Sacrament, its matter and form. These St. James does not omit, and each is replete with its own peculiar mysteries.

The Matter Of Extreme Unction

Its element, then, or matter, as defined by Councils, particularly by the Council of Trent, consists of oil consecrated by the Bishop. Not any kind of oil extracted from fatty or greasy substances, but olive oil alone (can be the matter of this Sacrament).

Thus its matter is most significant of what is inwardly effected in the soul by the Sacrament. Oil is very efficacious in soothing bodily pain, and the power of this Sacrament lessens the pain and anguish of the soul. Oil also restores health, brings joy, feeds light, and is very efficacious in refreshing bodily fatigue. All these effects signify what the divine power accomplishes in the sick man through the administration of this Sacrament. So much will suffice in explanation of the matter.

The Form Of Extreme Unction

The form of the Sacrament is the word and solemn prayer which the priest uses at each anointing: By this Holy Unction may God pardon thee whatever sins thou hast committed by the evil use of sight, smell or touch.

That this is the true form of this Sacrament we learn from these words of St. James: Let them pray over him . . . and the prayer of faith shall save the sick man. Hence we can see that the form is to be applied by way of prayer. The Apostle does not say of what particular words that prayer is to consist; but this form has been handed down to us by the faithful tradition of the Fathers, so that all the Churches retain the form observed by the Church of Rome, the mother and mistress of all Churches. Some, it is true, alter a few words, as when for God pardon thee, they say (God) remit, or (God) spare, and sometimes, May (God) remedy all the evil thou hast committed. But as there is no change of meaning, it is clear that all religiously observe the same form.

It should not excite surprise that, while the form of each of the other Sacraments either absolutely signifies what it expresses, such as I baptise thee, or I Sign thee with the sign of the cross, or is pronounced, as it were, by way of command, as in administering Holy Orders, Receive power, the form of Extreme Unction alone is expressed by way of prayer. Wisely has it been so appointed. For since this Sacrament is administered not only for the spiritual grace which it bestows, but also for the recovery of health, which, however, is not always obtained, therefore use a deprecative form, in order to implore of God's mercy what the virtue of the Sacrament does not always and uniformly effect.

The Ceremonies Of Extreme Unction

In the administration of this Sacrament special rites are also used, consisting principally of prayers offered by the priest for the recovery of the sick person. There is no Sacrament, the administration of which is accompanied with more numerous prayers; and with good reason, for at that moment more than ever the faithful require the assistance of pious prayers. All who may be present, and especially the pastor, should pour out their fervent aspirations to God, and earnestly commend to His mercy the life and salvation of the sufferer.

Institution of Extreme Unction

Having thus proved that Extreme Unction is truly and properly to be numbered among the Sacraments, we rightly infer that it owes its institution to Christ our Lord. It was subsequently made known and promulgated to the faithful by the Apostle St. James.

Our Saviour Himself, however, seems to have given some indication of it, when He sent His disciples two and two before Him; for the Evangelist informs us that going forth, they preached that all should do penance; and they cast out many devils, and anointed with oil many who were sick, and healed them.

This anointing cannot be supposed to have been invented by the Apostles, but was commanded by our Lord. Nor did its power arise from any natural virtue. Its efficacy, we must believe, was mystical, having been instituted to heal the maladies of the soul, rather than to cure the diseases of the body. This is the doctrine taught by St. Denis, St. Ambrose, St. Chrysostom and St. Gregory the Great; so that it cannot be at all doubted that Extreme Unction is to be recognised and venerated as one of the seven Sacraments of the Catholic Church.

The Subject of Extreme Unction

But although instituted for the use of all, Extreme Unction is not lo be administered indiscriminately to all.

The Subject Must Be In Danger Of Death

In the first place, it is not to be administered to persons in sound health, according to these words of St. James: Is anyone sick amongst you? This is also proved by the fact that Extreme Unction was instituted as a remedy not only for the diseases of the soul, but also for those of the body. Now only the sick need a remedy, and therefore this Sacrament is to be administered to those only whose malady is such as to excite apprehensions of approaching death.

It is, however, a very grievous sin to defer the Holy Unction until, all hope of recovery being lost, life begins to ebb, and the sick person is fast verging into a state of insensibility. It is obvious that if the Sacrament is administered while consciousness and reason are yet unimpaired, and the mind is capable of eliciting acts of faith and of directing the will to sentiments of piety, a more abundant participation of its graces must be received. Though this heavenly medicine is in itself always salutary, pastors should be careful to apply it when its efficacy can be aided by the piety and devotion of the sick person.

The Danger Must Arise From Sickness

Extreme Unction, then, can be administered to no one who is not dangerously sick; not even to those who are in danger of death, as when they undertake a perilous voyage, or enter into battle with the sure prospect of death, or have been condemned to death and are on the way to execution.

The Person Anointed Must Have Attained The Use Of Reason

Furthermore, all those who have not the use of reason are not fit subjects for this Sacrament; and likewise children who, having committed no sins, do not need the Sacrament as a remedy against the remains of sin. The same is true of idiots and insane persons, unless they give indications in their lucid intervals of a disposition to piety, and express a desire to be anointed. To persons who from their birth never enjoyed the use of reason this Sacrament is not to be administered; but if a sick person, while in the possession of his faculties, expresses a wish to receive Extreme Unction and afterwards becomes delirious he is to be anointed.

Administration of Extreme Unction

The Sacred Unction is to be applied not to the entire body, but to the organs of sense only, -- to the eyes, on account of sight; to the ears, on account of hearing; to the nostrils, on account of smell; to the mouth, on account of taste and speech; to the hands, on account of touch. The sense of touch, it is true, is diffused throughout the entire body, yet it is more developed in the hands.

This manner of administering Extreme Unction is observed throughout the universal Church, and is in keeping with the medicinal nature of the Sacrament. As in corporal disease, although the malady affects the entire body, yet the cure is applied to that part only which is the seat and origin of the disease; so likewise this Sacrament is applied not to the entire body, but to those members in which the power of sensation is most conspicuous, and also to the loins, which are, as it were, the seat of concupiscence, and to the feet, by which we move from one place to another.

Here it is to be observed that, during the same illness, and while the danger of dying continues the same, the sick person is to be anointed but once. Should he, however, recover after he has been anointed, he may receive the aid of this Sacrament as often as he shall have relapsed into the same danger of death. This Sacrament, therefore, is evidently to be numbered among those which may be repeated.

Dispositions for the Reception of Extreme Unction

As all care should be taken that nothing impede the. grace of the Sacrament, and as nothing is more opposed to it than the consciousness of mortal guilt, the constant practice of the Catholic Church must be observed of administering the Sacrament of Penance and the Eucharist before Extreme Unction.

And next, let parish priests strive to persuade the sick person to receive this Sacrament from the priest with the same faith with which those of old who were to be healed by the Apostles used to present themselves. But the salvation of his soul is to be the first object of the sick man's wishes, and after that the health of the body, with this qualification, if it be for the good of his soul.

Nor should the faithful doubt that those holy and solemn prayers which are used by the priest, not in his own person, but in that of the Church and of our Lord Jesus Christ, are heard by God; and they are most particularly to be exhorted on this one point, to take care that the Sacrament of this most salutary oil be administered to them holily and religiously, when the sharper conflict seems at hand, and the energies of the mind as well as of the body appear to be failing.

The Minister of Extreme Unction

Who the minister of Extreme Unction is we learn from the same Apostle that promulgated the law of the Lord; for he says: Let him bring in the priests (presbyters). By which name, as the Council of Trent has well explained, he does not mean persons advanced in years, or of chief authority among the people, but priests who have been duly ordained by Bishops with the imposition of hands.

To the priest, therefore, has been committed the administration of this Sacrament; not, however, to every priest, as holy Church has decreed, but to the proper pastor who has jurisdiction, or to another authorised by him to discharge this office.

In this, however, as also in the administration of the other Sacraments, it is to be most distinctly remembered that the priest is the representative of Christ our Lord, and of His spouse, holy Church.

The Effects of Extreme Unction

The advantages we receive from this Sacrament are also to be accurately explained, so that if nothing else can allure the faithful to its reception, they may be induced at least by its utility; for we are naturally disposed to measure almost all things by our interests.

Pastors, therefore, should teach that by this Sacrament is imparted grace that remits sins, and especially lighter, or as they are commonly called, venial sins; for mortal sins are removed by the Sacrament of Penance. Extreme Unction was not instituted primarily for the remission of grave offences; only Baptism and Penance accomplish this directly.

Another advantage of the Sacred Unction is that it liberates the soul from the languor and infirmity which it contracted from sins, and from all the other remains of sin. The time most opportune for this cure is when we are afflicted with severe illness and danger to life impends, for it has been implanted in man by nature to dread no human visitation so much as death. This dread is greatly augmented by the recollection of our past sins, especially if our conscience accuses us of grave offences; for it is written: They shall come with fear at the thought of their sins, and their iniquities shall stand against them to convict them. Another source of vehement anguish is the anxious thought that we must soon afterwards stand before the judgment seat of God, who will pass on us a sentence of strictest justice according to our deserts. It often happens that, struck with this terror, the faithful feel themselves deeply agitated; and nothing conduces more to a tranquil death than to banish sadness, await with a joyous mind the coming of our Lord, and be ready willingly to surrender the deposit entrusted whenever it shall be His will to demand it back. To free the minds of the faithful from this solicitude, and fill the soul with pious and holy joy is, then, an effect of the Sacrament of Extreme Unction.

From it, moreover, we derive another advantage, which may justly be deemed the greatest of all. For although the enemy of the human race never ceases, while we live, to meditate our ruin and destruction, yet at no time does he more violently use every effort utterly to destroy us, and, if possible, deprive us of all hope of the divine mercy, than when he sees the last day of life approach. Therefore arms and strength are supplied to the faithful in this Sacrament to enable them to break the violence and impetuosity of the adversary, and to fight bravely against him; for the soul of the sick is relieved and encouraged by the hope of the divine goodness, strengthened by which it bears more lightly ail the burdens of sickness, and eludes with greater ease the artifice and cunning of the devil who lies in wait for it.

Finally, the recovery of health, if indeed advantageous, is another effect of this Sacrament. And if in our days the sick obtain this effect less frequently, this is to be attributed, not to any defect of the Sacrament, but rather to the weaker faith of a great part of those who are anointed with the sacred oil, or by whom it is administered; for the Evangelist bears witness that the Lord wrought not many miracles among His own, because of their unbelief.

It may also be truly said at the Christian religion, since it has struck its roots more deeply in the minds of men, stands now less in need of the aids of such miracles than it did formerly, at the commencement of the rising Church. Nevertheless, faith should be strongly excited in this respect, and whatever it may please God in His wisdom to do with regard to the health of the body, the faithful ought to rely on a sure hope of attaining, by virtue of this sacred oil, health of the soul, and of experiencing, should the hour of their departure from life be at hand, the fruit of that glorious assurance: Blessed are the dead who die in the Lord.

Admonition

We have thus explained briefly the Sacrament of Extreme Unction. But if these points are developed by the pastor at greater length and with the care the subject demands, it is not to be doubted that the faithful will derive very great fruit of piety from his instruction.

THE SACRAMENT OF HOLY ORDERS

Importance Of Instruction On This Sacrament

If one attentively considers the nature and essence of the other Sacraments, it will readily be seen that they all depend on the Sacrament of Orders to such an extent that without it some of them could not be constituted or administered at all; while others would be deprived of all their solemn ceremonies, as well as of a certain part of the religious respect and exterior honour accorded to them. Wherefore in continuing the exposition of the doctrine of the Sacraments, it will be necessary for pastors to bear in mind that it is their duty to explain with even special care the Sacrament of Orders.

This explanation will be highly advantageous. First of all to the pastor himself, then to all those who have entered on the ecclesiastical state, and finally to the people in general. To the pastor himself, because by treating of this subject he himself will be more deeply moved to stir up within him the grace he has received in this Sacrament; to those who have been called to the portion of the Lord, partly by animating them with a like spirit of piety, and partly by affording them an opportunity of acquiring a knowledge of such things as will enable them all the more easily to advance to higher orders; to the rest of the faithful, first, because it enables them to understand the respect due to the Church's ministers, and secondly, because as it often happens that many may be present who have destined their children, while yet young, for the Church's service, or who desire to embrace that life themselves, it is far from right that such persons should be unacquainted with the principal truths regarding this particular state.

Dignity of this Sacrament

In the first place, then, the faithful should be shown how great is the dignity and excellence of this Sacrament considered in its highest degree, the priesthood.

Bishops and priests being, as they are, God's interpreters and ambassadors, empowered in His name to teach mankind the divine law and the rules of conduct, and holding, as they do, His place on earth, it is evident that no nobler function than theirs can be imagined. Justly, therefore, are they called not only Angels, but even gods, because of the fact that they exercise in our midst the power and prerogatives of the immortal God.

In all ages, priests have been held in the highest honour; yet the priests of the New Testament far exceed all others. For the power of consecrating and offering the body and blood of our Lord and of forgiving sins, which has been conferred on them, not only has nothing equal or like to it on earth, but even surpasses human reason and understanding.

And as our Saviour was sent by His Father, and as the Apostles and disciples were sent into the whole world by Christ our Lord, so priests are daily sent with the same powers, for the perfecting of the saints, for the work of the ministry, and the edifying of the body of Christ.

Requirements in Candidates for Orders

Holiness, Knowledge, Prudence

The burden of this great office, therefore, should not be rashly imposed on anyone, but is to be conferred on those only who by their holiness of life, their knowledge, faith and prudence, are able to bear it.

Divine Call

Let no one take the honour to himself, but he that is called by God as Aaron was; and they are called by God who are

called by the lawful ministers of His Church. It is to those who arrogantly intrude themselves into this ministry that the Lord must be understood to refer when He says: I did not send prophets, yet they ran. Nothing can be more unhappy and wretched than such a class of men as this, and nothing more calamitous to the Church of God.

Right Intention

In every action we undertake it is of the highest importance to have a good motive in view, for if the motive is good, the rest proceeds harmoniously. The candidate for Holy Orders, therefore, should first of all be admonished to entertain no purpose unworthy of so exalted an office.

This subject demands all the greater attention, since in these days the faithful often sin gravely in this respect. Some there are who embrace this state to secure the necessaries of life, and who, consequently, seek in the priesthood, just as other men do in the lowest walks of life, nothing more or less than gain. Though both the natural and divine law lay down, as the Apostle remarks, that he who serves the altar should live by the altar; yet to approach the altar for the sake of gain and money is one of the very gravest of sacrileges.

Some are attracted to the priesthood by ambition and love of honours; while there are others who desire to be ordained simply in order that they may abound in riches, as is proved by the fact that unless some wealthy benefice were conferred on them, they would not dream of receiving Holy Orders. It is such as these that our Saviour describes as hirelings, who, in the words of Ezechiel, feed themselves and not the sheep, and whose baseness and dishonesty have not only brought great disgrace on the ecclesiastical state, so much so that hardly anything is now more vile and contemptible in the eyes of the faithful, but also end in this, that they derive no other fruit from their priesthood than was derived by Judas from the Apostleship, which only brought him everlasting destruction.

But they, on the other hand, who are lawfully called by God, and who undertake the ecclesiastical state with the single motive of promoting the honour of God, are truly said to enter the Church by the door.

This, however, must not be understood as if the same law did not bind all men equally. Men have been created to honour God, and this the faithful in particular, who have obtained the grace of Baptism, should do with their whole heart, their whole soul, and with all their strength.

But those who desire to receive the Sacrament of Orders, should aim not only at seeking the glory of God in all things-an obligation admittedly common to all men, and particularly to the faithful --

but also to serve Him in holiness and justice in whatever sphere of His ministry they may be placed. Just as in the army all the soldiers obey the general's orders, though they all have not the same functions to discharge, one being a centurion, another a prefect, so in like manner, though all the faithful should diligently practice piety and innocence, which are the chief means of honouring God, yet they who are in Holy Otters have certain special duties and functions to discharge in the Church. Thus they offer Sacrifice for themselves and for all the people; they explain God's law and exhort and form the faithful to observe it promptly and cheerfully; they administer the Sacraments of Christ our Lord by means of which all grace is conferred and increased; and, in a word, they are separated from the rest of the people to fill by far the greatest and noblest of all ministries.

The Twofold Power Conferred by this Sacrament

Having explained all this, the pastor should now turn his attention to the special properties of this Sacrament, so that the faithful who desire to enter into the ecclesiastical state may understand the nature of the office to which they are called and the extent of the power bestowed by God on the Church and her ministers.

This power is twofold: the powers of orders and the power of jurisdiction. The power of orders has for its object the real body of Christ our Lord in the Blessed Eucharist. The power of jurisdiction refers altogether to the mystical body of (Christ. The scope of this power is to govern and rule the Christian people, and lead them to the unending bliss of heaven.

The Power Of Orders

The power of orders not only embraces the power of consecrating the Eucharist, but also fits and prepares the souls of men for its reception. It also embraces all else that can have any reference to the Eucharist. Regarding this power numerous passages of Sacred Scripture may be adduced; but the weightiest and most striking are those which are read in St. John and St. Matthew: As the Father, says our Lord, hath sent me I also send you. .... Receive ye the Holy Ghost; whose sins you shall forgive they are forgiven them, and whose sins you shall retain they are retained; and: Amen, I say to you, whatsoever you shall bind upon earth shall be bound also in heaven; and whatsoever you shall loose upon earth shall be loosed a also in heaven. These texts, when expounded by pastors, in accordance with the teaching and authority of the Fathers, will throw great light on this truth.

Greatness Of This Power

This power far excels that given under the law of nature to certain ones who had charge of sacred things. The period previous to the written law must have had its priesthood and its spiritual power, since it is certain that it had its law; for these two, as the Apostle testifies, are so closely connected that if the priesthood is transferred, the law must necessarily be transferred also. Guided, therefore, by a natural instinct, men recognised that God is to be worshipped; and hence it follows that in every nation some, whose power might in a certain sense be called spiritual, were given the care of sacred things and of divine worship.

This power was also possessed by the Jews; but though it was superior in dignity to that with which priests were invested under the law of nature, yet it must be regarded as far inferior to the spiritual power that is found in the New Law. For the latter is heavenly, and surpasses all the power of Angels; it is derived not from the Mosaic priesthood, but from Christ our Lord who was a priest, not according to the order of Aaron, but according to the order of Melchisedech. For He it is who, Himself endowed with the supreme power of granting grace and remitting sins, left to His Church this power, although He limited it in extent and attached it to the Sacraments.

Names of this Sacrament

Hence to exercise this power certain ministers are appointed and solemnly consecrated, which consecration is called the Sacrament of Orders, or Sacred Ordination. The Fathers used this word, which in itself has a most extensive signification, to show the dignity and excellence of God's ministers.

In fact, order, when understood in its strict meaning and acceptation, is the arrangement of superior and inferior things so disposed as to stand in mutual relation towards each other. Now as in this ministry there are many grades and various functions, and as all these are disposed and arranged according to a definite plan, the name Order has been well and properly applied to it.

Holy Orders Is a Sacrament

That Sacred Ordination is to be numbered among the Sacraments of the Church, the Council of Trent has established by the same line of reasoning as we have already used several times. Since a Sacrament is a sign of a sacred thing, and since the outward action in this consecration denotes the grace and power bestowed on him who is consecrated, it becomes clearly evident that Order must be truly and properly regarded as a Sacrament. Thus the Bishop, handing to him who is being ordained a chalice with wine and water, and a paten with bread, says: Receive the power of offering sacrifice, etc. In these words, pronounced along with the application of the matter, the Church has always taught that the power of consecrating the Eucharist is conferred, and that a character is impressed on the soul which brings with it grace necessary for the due and proper discharge of that office, as the Apostle declares thus: I admonish thee that thou stir up the grace of God which is in thee, by the imposition of my hands; for God hath not given us the spirit of fear, but of power, and of love, and of sobriety.

Number of Orders

Now, to use the words of the holy Council: The ministry of so sublime a priesthood being a thing all divine, it is but befitting its worthier and more reverent exercise that in the Church's well-ordered disposition there should be several different orders of ministers destined to assist the priesthood by virtue of their office, -- orders arranged in such a way that those who have already received clerical tonsure should be raised, step by step, from the lower to the higher orders.

It should be taught, therefore, that these orders are seven in number, and that this has been the constant teaching of the Catholic Church. These orders are those of porter, lector, exorcist, acolyte, subdeacon, deacon and priest.

That the number of ministers was wisely established thus may be proved by considering the various offices that are necessary for the celebration of the Holy Sacrifice of the Mass and the consecration and administration of the Blessed Eucharist, this being the principal scope of their institution.

They are divided into major or sacred, and minor orders. The major or sacred orders are priesthood, deaconship and subdeaconship; while the minor orders are those of acolyte, exorcist, lector and porter, concerning each of which we shall now say a few words so that the pastor may be able to explain them to those especially whom he knows to be about to receive any of the orders in question.

Tonsure

In the beginning should be explained first tonsure, and it should be shown that this is a sort of preparation for the reception of orders. As men are prepared for Baptism by exorcisms and for Matrimony by engagement, so to those who dedicate themselves to God by tonsure the way is opened that leads to the Sacrament of Orders; for by the cutting off of hair is signified the character and disposition of him who desires to devote himself to the sacred ministry.

The Name "Cleric"

Regarding the name cleric, which is then given him for the first time, it is derived from the fact that he thereby begins to take the Lord for his lot and inheritance, just as those, who among the Jews were attached to the service of God, were forbidden by the Lord to have any part of the ground that would be distributed in the land of promise: , he said, am thy portion and inheritance. And although these words are true of all the faithful, yet it is certain that they apply in a special way to those who consecrate themselves to the service of God.

Origin And Meaning Of Tonsure

The hair of the head is cut off in the form of a crown. It should be always worn thus, and should be enlarged according as one is advanced to higher orders.

The Church teaches that this usage is derived from Apostolic origin, as mention is made of it by the most ancient and authoritative Fathers, such as St. Denis the Areopagite, St. Augustine and St. Jerome.

It is said that the Prince of the Apostles first introduced this usage in memory of the crown of thorns which was put upon our Saviour's head, so that the devices resorted to by the impious for the ignominy and torture of Christ might be used by His Apostles a sign of honour and glory, as well as to signify that the ministers of the Church should strive to resemble Christ our Lord and represent Him in all things.

Some, however, assert that by tonsure is denoted the royal dignity, that is, the portion reserved especially for those who are called to the inheritance of the Lord. It will readily be seen that what the Apostle Peter says of all the faithful: You are a chosen generation, a kingly priesthood, a holy nation, applies especially and with much greater reason to the ministers of the Church.

Still there are some who consider that by the circle, which is the most perfect of all figures, is signified the profession of a more perfect life undertaken by ecclesiastics; while in view of the fact that the hair of their heads, which is a kind of bodily superfluity, is cut off, others think that it denotes contempt for external things, and detachment of soul from all human cares.

The Minor Orders

Porter

After tonsure it is customary to advance to the first order, which is that of porter. The function (of porter) is to guard the keys and doors of the church, and to allow no one to enter there to whom access has been forbidden. Formerly the porter used to assist at the Holy Sacrifice of the Mass, to see that no one approached too near the altar, or disturbed the priest during the celebration of the divine mysteries. Other duties were also assigned to him, as may be seen from the ceremonies used at his ordination.

Thus the Bishop, taking the keys from the altar, hands them to him who is being made porter, and says: Let your conduct be that of one who has to render to God an account of those things that are kept under these keys.

How great was the dignity of this order in the ancient Church may be inferred from a usage which exists in the Church in these times. For the office of treasurer, which is still numbered among the more honourable functions of the Church, was entrusted to porters, and carried with it also the guardianship of the sacristy.

Reader

The second degree of orders is the office of reader, whose duty it is to read in the church in a clear and distinct voice the books of the Old and of the New Testament, and especially those which are read during the nocturnal psalmody. Formerly it was also his duty to teach the faithful the first rudiments of the Christian religion.

Hence it is that when ordaining him, the Bishop, in the presence of the people, handing him a book in which are set down all that regards this office, says: Take, and be you an announcer of the word of God; if you faithfully and profitably discharge your office, you shall have a part with those who from the be- ginning have well ministered the word of God.

Exorcist

The third order is that of exorcists, to whom is given the power to invoke the name of the Lord over those who are possessed by unclean spirits. Hence the Bishop when ordaining them presents to them a book in which the exorcisms are contained, and at the same time pronounces this form of words: Take, and commit to memory, and have the power of imposing hands over the possessed, whether baptised or catechumen.

Acolyte

The fourth degree is that of acolytes, and it is the last of the orders that are called minor and not sacred. Their duty is to attend and serve the ministers who are in major orders, that is, the deacon and subdeacon, in the Sacrifice of the altar. They also carry and attend to the lights during the celebration of the Sacrifice of the Mass, and especially during the reading of the Gospel, from which fact they are also called candle-bearers.

Therefore at the ordination of acolytes the Bishop observes the following rite: First of all he carefully warns them of the nature of their office; then hands to each of them a light, saying: Receive this candlestick and candle, and remember that henceforth you are given the charge of lighting the candles of the church, in the name of the Lord. Then he hands them empty cruets in which are presented the wine and water for the Sacrifice, saying: Receive these cruets to supply wine and water for t) c Eucharist of Christ's blood, in the name of the Lord.

The Major Orders

Subdeacon

From the minor orders, which are not sacred, and of which we have been speaking until now, one lawfully enters and ascends to major and Sacred Orders.

Now the subdiaconate is the first degree of (major orders). Its function, as the name itself indicates, is to serve the deacon at the altar. It is the subdeacon who should prepare the altar linen, the vessels and the bread and wine necessary for the celebration of the Holy Sacrifice. He also it is who presents water to the Bishop or priest when he washes his hands during the Sacrifice of the Mass. It is also the subdeacon who now reads the Epistle which in former times was read at Mass by the deacon. He assists as witness at the Holy Sacrifice, and guards the celebrant from being disturbed by anyone during the sacred ceremonies.

The various duties that pertain to the subdeacon are indicated by the solemn ceremonies used at his ordination. In the first place the Bishop warns him that the obligation of perpetual continence is attached to this order, and declares that no one is to be admitted among the subdeacons who is not ready and willing to accept the obligation in question. Then, after the solemn recitation of the Litanies, the Bishop enumerates and explains the duties and functions of the subdeacon. Thereupon each one of those who are being ordained receives the chalice and sacred paten from the Bishop; and, to show that he is to serve the deacon, the subdeacon receives from the archdeacon cruets filled with wine and water, together with a basin and towel with which to wash and dry the hands. At the same time the Bishop pronounces these words: See what sort of ministry is entrusted to you; I admonish you therefore, to show yourself worthy to please God. Other prayers follow, and finally, when the Bishop has clothed the subdeacon with the sacred vestments, for each of which there are special words and ceremonies, he gives kiln the book of the Epistles, saying: Receive the book of the Epistles with power to read them in the Holy Church of God, as well for the living as for the dead.

Deacon

The second degree of Sacred Orders is that of the deacons, whose functions are much more extensive and have always been regarded as more holy. His duty it is to be always at the side of the Bishop, guard him while he preaches, serve him and the priest during the celebration of the divine mysteries, as well as during the administration of the Sacraments, and to read the Gospel in the Sacrifice of the Mass. In former times he frequently warned the faithful to be attentive to the holy mysteries; he administered our Lord's blood in those churches in which the custom existed that the faithful should receive the Eucharist under both species; and to him was entrusted the distribution of the Church's goods, as well as the duty of providing for all that was necessary to each one's sustenance. To the deacon also, as the eye of the Bishop, it belongs to see who they are in the city a that lead a good and holy life, and who not; who are present at the Holy Sacrifice and sermons at appointed times, and who not; so that he may be able to give an account of all to the Bishop, and enable him to admonish and advise each one privately, or to rebuke and correct publicly, according as he may deem more profitable. He should also read out the list of the catechumens and present to the Bishop those who are to be admitted to orders. Finally in the absence of a Bishop or priest, he can explain the Gospel, but not from the pulpit, thus letting it be seen that this is not his proper office.

The Apostle shows the great care that should be taken that no one unworthy of the diaconate be promoted to this order, when in his Epistle to Timothy he sets forth a deacon's character, virtues and integrity. The same point is also gathered from the rites and solemn ceremonies which the Bishop employs when ordaining him. The Bishop uses more numerous and more solemn prayers at the ordination of a deacon than at that of a subdeacon, and he also adds other kinds of sacred vestments. Moreover, he imposes hands on him, just as we read the Apostles used to do when ordaining the first deacons. Finally, he hands him the book of the Gospels, with these words: Receive the power to read the Gospel in the Church of God both for the living and the dead in the name of the Lord.

Priest

The third and highest degree of all Sacred Orders is the priesthood. The Fathers of the first centuries usually designated those who had received this order by two names. At one time they called them presbyters -- a Greek word signifying elders, not only because of the ripe years very necessary for this order, but much more on account of their gravity, knowledge and prudence; for it is written: Venerable old age is not that of long time nor counted by the number of years; but the understanding of a man is grey hairs and an unspotted life is old age. At other times they call them priests, both because they are consecrated to God, and because to them it belongs to administer the Sacraments and take charge of things sacred and divine.

Twofold Priesthood

But as Sacred Scripture describes a twofold priesthood, one internal and the other external, it will be necessary to have a distinct idea of each to enable pastors to explain the nature of the priesthood now under discussion.

The Internal Priesthood

Regarding the internal priesthood, all the faithful are said to be priests, once they have been washed in the saving waters of Baptism. Especially is this name given to the just who have the Spirit of God, and who, by the help of divine grace, have been made living members of the great High-priest, Jesus Christ; for, enlightened by faith which is inflamed by charity, they offer tip spiritual sacrifices to God on the altar of their hearts. Among such sacrifices must be reckoned every good and virtuous action done for the glory of God.

Hence we read in the Apocalypse: Christ hath washed us front our sins. in his own blood and hath made us a kingdom, and priests to God and his Father. In like manner was it said by the Prince of the Apostles: Be you also as living stones built up, a spiritual house a holy priesthood offering up spiritual sacrifices acceptable to God by Jesus Christ; while the Apostle exhorts us to present our bodies a living sacrifice holy , pleasing unto God your reasonable service. And long before this David had said: A sacrifice to God is an afflicted spirit: a contrite and humble heart O God thou wilt not despise. All this clearly regards the internal priesthood.

The External Priesthood

The external priesthood, on the contrary, does not pertain to the faithful at large, but only to certain men who have been ordained and consecrated to God by the lawful imposition of hands and by the solemn ceremonies of holy Church, and who are thereby devoted to a particular sacred ministry.

This distinction of the priesthood can be seen even in the Old Law. That David spoke of the internal priesthood, we have just shown. On the other hand, everyone knows the many and various precepts given by the Lord to Moses and Aaron regarding the external priesthood. Along with this He appointed the whole tribe of Levi to the ministry of the Temple, and He forbade by law that anyone belonging to another tribe should dare to intrude himself into that function. Hence it was that King Ozias was afflicted with leprosy by the Lord for having usurped the sacerdotal ministry, and had to suffer grave chastisements for his arrogance and sacrilege.

Now as the same distinction (of a twofold) priesthood may be noted in the New Law, the faithful should be cautioned that what we are now about to say concerns that external priesthood which is conferred on certain special individuals. This alone belongs to the Sacrament of Holy Orders.

Functions of the Priesthood

The office of a priest, then, is to offer Sacrifice to God and to administer the Sacraments of the Church. This is proved by the very ceremonies used at his ordination. When-ordaining a priest, the Bishop first of all imposes hands on him, as do all the other priests who are present. Then he puts a stole on his shoulders and arranges it over his breast in the form of a cross, declaring thereby that the priest is clothed with power from on high, enabling him to carry the cross of Christ our Lord and the sweet yoke of God's law, and to inculcate this law not only by words, but also by the example of a most holy and virtuous life.

He next anoints his hands with holy oil, and then gives him the chalice with wine and the paten with a host, saying at the same time: Receive the power to offer Sacrifice to God and to celebrate Masses both for the living and for the dead. By these words and ceremonies the priest is constituted an interpreter and mediator between God and man, which indeed must be regarded as the principal function of the priesthood.

Lastly, placing his hands a second time on the head (of the person ordained the Bishop) says: Receive the Holy Ghost; whose sins you shall forgive they are forgiven them, and whose sins you shall retain they are retained, thus communicating to him that divine power of forgiving and retaining sin which was given by our Lord to His disciples. Such, then, are the special and principal functions of the sacerdotal order.

Degrees of the Priesthood

Priests

Now although (the sacerdotal order) is one alone, yet it has various degrees of dignity and power. The first degree is that of those who are simply called priests, and of whose functions we have hitherto been speaking.

Bishops

The second is that of Bishops, who are placed over the various dioceses to govern not only the other ministers of the Church, but the faithful also, and to promote their salvation with supreme vigilance and care. Hence it is that in Sacred Scripture they are often called pastors of the sheep. Their office and duty has been well described by St. Paul in his sermon to the Ephesians, as we read in the Acts of the Apostles; while St. Peter, the Prince of the Apostles, has also laid down a divine rule for the exercise of the episcopal office. And if Bishops strive to conform their actions according to this rule, there can be no doubt that they will be good pastors and will be also esteemed as such. Bishops are also called pontiffs. This name is derived from the pagans, who thus designated their chief priests.

Archbishops

The third degree is that of Archbishops, who preside over a number of Bishops and who are called Metropolitans, because they are Bishops of those cities which are regarded as the metropolis of their respective provinces. Hence they enjoy greater dignity and more extensive power than Bishops, although their Ordination is the same.

Patriarchs

In the fourth degree come Patriarchs, that is to say, the first and highest of the Fathers. Formerly, besides the Roman Pontiff, there were in the universal Church only four Patriarchs, who, however, were not of equal dignity. Thus Constantinople, though it reached the patriarchal honour only after all the others, yet it obtained a higher rank by reason of being the capital of the Empire. Next in rank came the Patriarch of Alexandria, which Church had been founded by St. Mark the Evangelist by order of the Prince of the Apostles. The third was that of Antioch, where Peter fixed his first See. Finally, that of Jerusalem, a See first governed by James, the brother of our Lord.

The Pope

Above all these, the Catholic Church has always placed the Supreme Pontiff of Rome, whom Cyril of Alexandria, in the Council of Ephesus, named the Chief Bishop, Father and Patriarch of the whole world. He sits in that chair of Peter in which beyond every shadow of doubt the Prince of the Apostles sat to the end of his days, and hence it is that in him the Church recognises the highest degree of dignity, and a universality of jurisdiction derived, not from the decrees of men or Councils, but from God Himself. Wherefore he is the Father and guide of all the faithful, of all the Bishops, and of all the prelates, no matter how high their power and office; and as successor of St. Peter, as true and lawful Vicar of Christ our Lord, he governs the universal Church.

From what has been said, therefore, pastors should teach what are the principal duties and functions of the various ecclesiastical orders and degrees, and also who is the minister of this Sacrament.

The Minister of Holy Orders

Beyond all doubt, it is to the Bishop that the administration (of orders) belongs, as is easily proved by the authority of Holy Scripture, by most certain tradition, by the testimony of all the Fathers, by the decrees of the Councils, and by the usage and practice of Holy Church.

It is true that permission has been granted to some abbots occasionally to administer those orders that are minor and not sacred; yet there is no doubt whatever that it is the proper office of the Bishop, and of the Bishop alone to confer the orders called holy or major.

To ordain subdeacons, deacons and priests, one Bishop suffices; but in accordance with an Apostolic tradition that has been always observed in the Church, Bishops are consecrated by three Bishops.

The Recipient of Holy Orders

We now come to indicate who are fit to receive this Sacrament, and especially the priestly order, and what are the principal dispositions required of them.

From (what we shall lay down concerning the dispositions requisite for the priesthood) it will be easy to determine what ought to be observed in conferring the other orders, due account being taken of the office and dignity of each. Now the extreme caution I hat should be used in conferring this Sacrament is gathered from the fact that, while all the other Sacraments impart grace to the recipient for his own use and sanctification, he, on the other hand, who receives Holy Orders is made partaker of heavenly grace precisely that by his ministry he may promote the welfare of the Church and therefore of all mankind.

Hence we readily understand why it is that ordinations take place only on special days, on which, moreover, in accordance with a very ancient practice of the Catholic Church, a solemn fast is appointed in order that by holy and fervent prayer the faithful may obtain from God ministers who will be well qualified to exercise properly and to the advantage of the Church the power of so great a ministry.

Qualifications for the Priesthood

Holiness Of Life

The chief and most necessary quality requisite in him who is to be ordained a priest is that he be recommended by integrity of life and morals: first because, by procuring or permitting his ordination while conscious of mortal sin, a man renders himself guilty of a new and enormous crime; and secondly, because the priest is bound to give to others the example of a holy and innocent life.

In this connection pastors should set forth the rules which the Apostle laid down to Titus and Timothy, and he should also explain that those bodily defects, which, by the Lord's command excluded from the service of the altar in the Old Law, should for the most part be understood of deformities of soul in the New Law. This is why the holy custom has been established in the Church that he who is about to be admitted to orders should first take great care to cleanse his conscience in the Sacrament of Penance.

Competent Knowledge

In the second place there is required of the priest not only that knowledge which concerns the use and administration of the Sacraments; but he should also be versed in the science of Sacred Scripture, so as to be able to instruct the people in the mysteries of the Christian faith and the precepts of the divine law, lead them to piety and virtue, and reclaim them from sin.

The priest's duties are twofold. The first is to consecrate and administer the Sacraments properly; the second is to instruct the people entrusted to him in all that they must know or do in order to be saved. Hence the words of the Prophet Malachias: The lips of the priest shall keep knowledge, and they shall seek the Law at his mouth; because he is the angel of the Lord of hosts.

Now to fulfil the first of these duties it is enough for him to be endowed with a moderate share of knowledge. As for the second, it is no mere ordinary, but very special knowledge that is required. At the same time, however, it should be remembered that a profound knowledge of abstruse questions is not demanded of all priests in an equal degree. It is enough that each one knows all that is necessary for the discharge of his office and ministry.

Canonical Fitness

This Sacrament should not be conferred on children, nor on the insane or mad, because they are devoid of the use of reason. Yet if it does happen to be administered to them, we must unhesitatingly believe that the sacramental character becomes impressed on their souls. As for the precise age requisite for the reception of the various orders, this will easily be found in the decrees of the Council of Trent.

Slaves also are excluded. He who is not his own master and who is in the power of another, should not be dedicated to the divine service.

Homicides and men of blood are also rejected, because they are excluded by a law of the Church and are declared irregular.

The same must be said of the illegitimate and of all those not born in lawful wedlock. It is only right that those who are dedicated to the divine service should have nothing in them which could expose them to the well-deserved derision or contempt of others.

Finally, those who are notably maimed or deformed should not be admitted. A defect or deformity of this kind cannot but offend the eye and stand in the way of the due administration of the Sacraments.

Effects of Holy Orders

This much being explained, it now remains for pastors to point out the effects of this Sacrament. It is evident that the Sacrament of Orders, while mainly concerned, as already explained, with the welfare and beauty of the Church, nevertheless also confers on the soul of him who is ordained the grace of sanctification, fitting and qualifying him for the proper discharge of his functions and for the administration of the Sacraments, in the same way as by the grace of Baptism each one is qualified to receive the other Sacraments.

Another grace is clearly conferred by this Sacrament; namely, a special power with reference to the most Blessed Sacrament of the Eucharist. This power is full and perfect in the priest, because he alone can consecrate the body and blood of our Lord; but it is greater or less in the inferior ministers in proportion as their ministry approaches the Sacrament of the Altar.

This power is also called a spiritual character, because those who have been ordained are distinguished from the rest of the faithful by a certain interior mark impressed on the soul, by which they are dedicated to the divine worship. It is this grace which the Apostle seems to have had in view when he said to Timothy: Neglect not the grace that is in thee, which was given thee by prophecy, with imposition of hands of the priesthood; and again: I admonish thee, that thou stir up the grace of God which is in thee by the imposition of my hands.

Admonition

This much will suffice for the Sacrament of Orders. We have aimed at presenting nothing more than the principal points that bear on the subject, so as to supply the pastor with sufficient matter for instructing the faithful, and directing them to Christian piety.

THE SACRAMENT OF MATRIMONY

Importance Of Instruction On This Sacrament

As it is the duty of the pastor to seek the holiness and perfection of the faithful, his earnest desires must be in full accordance with those expressed by the Apostle when writing to the Corinthians: I would that all men were even as myself, that is, that all should embrace the virtue of continence. No greater happiness can befall the faithful in this life than to have their souls distracted by no worldly cares, the unruly desires of the flesh tranquillised and restrained, and the mind fixed on the practice of piety and the contemplation of heavenly things.

But as, according to the same Apostle, every one hath his proper gift from God, one after this manner, and another after that; and as marriage is gifted with great and divine blessings, so much so as truly and properly to hold a place among the other Sacraments of the Catholic Church, and as its celebration was honoured by the presence of our Lord Himself, it is clear that this subject should be explained, particularly since we find that St. Paul and the Prince of the Apostles have in many places minutely described to us not only the dignity but also the duties of the married state. Filled with the Spirit of God (these Apostles) well understood the numerous and important advantages which must flow to Christian society from a knowledge, and an inviolable observance by the faithful of the sanctity of marriage; while they saw that from ignorance or disregard of (its holiness), many and serious calamities and losses must be brought upon the Church.

Nature and Meaning of Marriage

The nature and meaning of marriage are, therefore, to be first explained. Vice not infrequently assumes the semblance of virtue, and hence care must be taken that the faithful be not deceived by a false appearance of marriage, and thus stain their souls with turpitude and wicked lusts. To explain this subject, let us begin with the meaning of the word itself.

Names Of This Sacrament

The word matrimony is derived from the fact that the principal object which a female should propose to herself in marriage is to become a mother; or from the fact that to a mother it belongs to conceive, bring forth and train her offspring.

It is also called wedlock (conjugium) from joining together, because a lawful wife is united to her husband, as it were, by a common yoke.

It is called nuptials, because, as St. Ambrose observes, the bride veiled her face through modesty -- a custom which would also seem to imply that she was to be subject and obedient to her husband.

Definition Of Matrimony

Matrimony, according to the general opinion of theologians, is defined: The conjugal union of man and woman, contracted between two qualified persons, which obliges them to live together throughout life.

In order that the different parts of this definition may be better understood, it should be taught that, although a perfect marriage has all the following conditions, -- namely, internal consent, external compact expressed by words, the obligation and tie which arise from the contract, and the marriage debt by which it is consummated; yet the obligation and tie expressed by the word union alone have the force and nature of marriage.

The special character of this union is marked by the word conjugal. This word is added because other contracts, by which men and women bind themselves to help each other in consideration of money received or other reason, differ essentially from matrimony.

Next follow the words between qualified persons; for persons excluded by law cannot contract marriage, and if they do their marriage is invalid. Persons, for instance, within the fourth degree of kindred, a boy before his fourteenth year, and a female before her twelfth, the ages established by law, cannot contract marriage.

The words, which obliges them to live together throughout life, express the indissolubility of the tie which binds husband and wife.

Essence And Cause Of Marriage

Hence it is evident that marriage consists in the tie spoken of above. Some eminent theologians, it is true, say that it consists in the consent, as when they define it: The consent of the man and woman. But we are to understand them to mean that the consent is the efficient cause of marriage, which is the doctrine of the Fathers of the Council of Florence; because, without the consent and contract, the obligation and tie cannot possibly exist.

The Kind of Consent Required in Matrimony

It is most necessary that the consent be expressed in words denoting present time.

Mutual

Marriage is not a mere donation, but a mutual agreement; and therefore the consent of one of the parties is insufficient for marriage, the consent of both being essential.

External

To declare this consent words are obviously necessary. If the internal consent alone, without any external indication, were sufficient for marriage, it would then seem to follow as a necessary consequence, that were two persons, living in the most separate and distant countries, to consent to marry, they would contract a true and indissoluble marriage, even before they had mutually signified to each other their consent by letter or messenger -- a consequence as repugnant to reason as it is opposed to the decrees and established usage of holy Church.

Present

Rightly was it said that the consent must be expressed in words which have reference to present time; for words which signify a future time, promise, but do not actually unite in marriage. Besides, it is evident that what is to be done has no present existence, and what has no present existence can have little or no firmness or stability. Hence a man who has only promised to marry a certain woman acquires by the promise no marriage rights, since his promise has not yet been fulfilled. Such promises are, it is true, obligatory, and their violation involves the offending party in a breach of faith. But he who has once entered into the matrimonial alliance, regret it as he afterwards may, cannot possibly change, or invalidate, or undo what has been done.

As, then, the marriage contract is not a mere promise, but a transfer of right, by which the man actually yields the dominion of his body to the woman, the woman the dominion of her body to the man, it must therefore be made in words which designate the present time, the force of which words abides with undiminished efficacy from the moment of their utterance, and binds the husband and wife by a tie that cannot be broken.

Instead of words, however, it may be sufficient for marriage to substitute a nod or other unequivocal sign of internal consent. Even silence, when the result of female modesty, may be sufficient, provided the parents answer for their daughter.

The Essence of Marriage Constituted by the Consent

Hence pastors should teach the faithful that the nature and force of marriage consists in the tie and obligation; and that, without consummation, the consent of the parties, expressed in the manner already explained, is sufficient to constitute a true marriage. It is certain that our first parents before their fall, when, according to the holy Fathers, no consummation took place, were really united in marriage. Hence the Fathers say that marriage consists not in its use but in the consent. This doctrine is repeated by St. Ambrose in his book On Virgins.

Twofold Consideration of Marriage

When these matters have been explained, it should be taught that matrimony is to be considered from two points of view, either as a natural union, since it was not invented by man but instituted by nature; or as a Sacrament, the efficacy of which transcends the order of nature.

Marriage As A Natural Contract

As grace perfects nature, and as that was not first which is spiritual, but that which is natural; afterwards that which is spiritual, the order of our matter requires that we first treat of Matrimony as a natural contract, imposing natural duties, and next consider what pertains to it as a Sacrament.

Instituted By God

The faithful, therefore, are to be taught in the first place that marriage was instituted by God. We read in Genesis that God created them male and female, and blessed them, saying: "Increase and multiply"; and also: "It is not good for man to be alone: let us make him a help like unto himself.,' And a little further on: But for Adam there was not found a helper like himself. Then the Lord God cast a deep sleep upon Adam; and when he was fast asleep, he took one of his ribs, and filled up flesh for it. And the Lord God built a rib which he took from Adam. into a woman, and brought her to Adam; and Adam said: "This is now bone of my bones, and flesh of my flesh: she shall be called woman, because she was taken out of man: wherefore a man shall leave father and mother, and shall cleave to his wife; and they shall be two in one flesh," These words, according to the authority of our Lord Himself, as we read in St. Matthew, prove the divine institution. of Matrimony.

Marriage Is Indissoluble By Divine Law

Not only did God institute marriage; He also, as the Council of Trent declares, rendered it perpetual and indissoluble.' What God hath joined together, says our Lord, let not man separate.

Although it belongs to marriage as a natural contract to be indissoluble, yet its indissolubility arises principally from its nature as a Sacrament, as it is the sacramental character that, in all its natural relations, elevates marriage to the highest perfection. In any event, dissolubility is at once opposed to the proper education of children, and to the other advantages of marriage.

Marriage Not Obligatory On All

The words increase and multiply, which were uttered by the Lord, do not impose on every individual an obligation to marry, but only declare the purpose of the institution of marriage. Now that the human race is widely diffused, not only is there no law rendering marriage obligatory, but, on the contrary, virginity is highly exalted and strongly recommended in Scripture as superior to marriage, and as a state of greater perfection and holiness. For our Lord and Saviour taught as follows: He that can take it, let him take it; and the Apostle says: Concerning virgins I have no commandment from the Lord; but I give counsel as having obtained mercy from the Lord to be faithful.

The Motives And Ends Of Marriage

We have now to explain why man and woman should be joined in marriage. First of all, nature itself by an instinct implanted in both sexes impels them to such companionship, and this is further encouraged by the hope of mutual assistance in bearing more easily the discomforts of life and the infirmities of old age.

A second reason for marriage is the desire of family, not so much, however, with a view to leave after us heirs to inherit our property and fortune, as to bring up children in the true faith and in the service of God. That such was the principal object of the holy Patriarchs when they married is clear from Scripture. Hence the Angel, when informing Tobias of the means of repelling the violent assaults of the evil demon, says: I will show thee who they are over whom the devil can prevail; for they who in such manner receive matrimony as to shut out God from themselves and from their mind, and to give themselves to their lust, as the horse and mule which have not understanding, over them the devil hath power. He then adds: Thou shalt take the virgin with the fear of the Lord, moved rather for love of children than for lust, that in the seed of Abraham thou mayest obtain a blessing in children. It was also for this reason that God instituted marriage from the beginning; and therefore married persons who, to prevent conception or procure abortion, have recourse to medicine, are guilty of a most heinous crime -- nothing less than wicked conspiracy to commit murder.

A third reason has been added, as a consequence of the fall of our first parents. On account of the loss of original innocence the passions began to rise in rebellion against right reason; and man, conscious of his own frailty and unwilling to fight the battles of the flesh, is supplied by marriage with an antidote by which to avoid sins of lust. For fear of fornication, says the Apostle, let every man have his own wife, and let every woman have her own husband; and a little after, having recommended to married persons a temporary abstinence from the marriage debt, to give themselves to prayer, he adds: Return together again, lest Satan tempt you for your incontinency.

These are ends, some one of which, those who desire to contract marriage piously and religiously, as becomes the children of the Saints, should propose to themselves. If to these we add other causes which induce to contract marriage, and, in choosing a wife, to prefer one person to another, such as the desire of leaving an heir, wealth, beauty, illustrious descent, congeniality of disposition -- such motives, because not inconsistent with the holiness of marriage, are not to be condemned. We do not find that the Sacred Scriptures condemn the Patriarch Jacob for having chosen Rachel for her beauty, in preference to Lia.

So much should be explained regarding Matrimony as a natural contract.

Marriage Considered as a Sacrament

It will now be necessary to explain that Matrimony is far superior in its sacramental aspect and aims at an incomparably higher end. For as marriage, as a natural union, was instituted from the beginning to propagate the human race; so was the sacramental dignity subsequently conferred upon it in order that a people might be begotten and brought up for the service and worship of the true God and of Christ our Saviour.

Thus when Christ our Lord wished to give a sign of the intimate union that exists between Him and His Church and of His immense love for us, He chose especially the sacred union of man and wife. That this sign was a most appropriate one will readily appear from the fact that of all human relations there is none that binds so closely as the marriage-tie, and from the fact that husband and wife are bound to one another by the bonds of the greatest affection and love. Hence it is that Holy Writ so frequently represents to us the divine union of Christ and the Church under the figure of marriage.

Marriage Is A Sacrament

That Matrimony is a Sacrament the Church, following the authority of the Apostle, has always held to be certain and incontestable. In his Epistle to the Ephesians he writes: Men should love their wives as their own bodies. He that loveth his wife loveth himself. For no man ever hated his own flesh, but nourisheth it and cherisheth it, as also Christ doth the church; for we are members of his body, of his flesh, and of his bones. For this cause shall a man leave his father and mother, and shall adhere to his wife, and they shall be two in one flesh. This is a great sacrament; but I speak in Christ and in the church. Now his expression, this is a great sacrament, undoubtedly refers to Matrimony, and must be taken to mean that the union of man and wife, which has God for its Author, is a Sacrament, that is, a sacred sign of that most holy union that binds Christ our Lord to His Church.

That this is the true and proper meaning of the Apostle's words is shown by the ancient holy Fathers who have interpreted them, and by the explanation furnished by the Council of Trent. It is indubitable, therefore, that the Apostle compares the husband to Christ, and the wife to the Church; that the husband is head of the wife as Christ is the head of the Church; and that for this very reason the husband should love his wife and the wife love and respect her husband. For Christ loved his church, and gave himself for her; while as the same Apostle teaches, the church is subject to Christ.

That grace is also signified and conferred by this Sacrament, which are two properties that constitute the principal characteristics of each Sacrament, is declared by the Council as follows: By his passion Christ, the Author and Perfecter of the venerable

Sacraments, merited for us the grace that perfects the natural love (of husband and wife), confirms their indissoluble union, and sanctifies them. It should, therefore, be shown that by the grace of this Sacrament husband and wife are joined in the bonds of mutual love, cherish affection one towards the other, avoid illicit attachments and passions, and so keep their marriage honourable in all things, . . . and their bed undefiled.

Marriage before Christ

It Was Not A Sacrament

How much the Sacrament of Matrimony is superior to the marriages made both previous to and under the (Mosaic) Law may be judged from the fact that though the Gentiles themselves were convinced there was something divine in marriage, and for that reason regarded promiscuous intercourse as contrary to the law of nature, while they also considered fornication, adultery and other kinds of impurity to be punishable offences; yet their marriages never had any sacramental value.

Among the Jews the laws of marriage were observed far more religiously, and it cannot be doubted that their unions were endowed with more holiness. As they had received from God the promise that in the seed of Abraham all nations should be blessed," it was justly considered by them to be a very pious duty to bring forth children, and thus contribute to the propagation of the chosen people from whom Christ the Lord and Saviour was to derive His birth in His human nature. Still their unions also fell short of the real nature of a Sacrament.

Before Christ Marriage Had Fallen From Its Primitive Unity And Indissolubility

It should be added that if we consider the law of nature after the fall and the Law of Moses we shall easily see that-marriage had fallen from its original honour and purity. Thus under the law of nature we read of many of the ancient Patriarchs that they had several wives at the same time; while under the Law of Moses it was permissible, should cause exist, to repudiate one's wife by giving her a bill of divorce. Both these (concessions) have been suppressed by the law of the Gospel, and marriage has been restored to its original state.

Christ Restored to Marriage its Primitive Qualities

Unity Of Marriage

Though some of the ancient Patriarchs are not to be blamed for having married several wives, since they did not act thus without divine dispensation, yet Christ our Lord has clearly shown that polygamy is not in keeping with the nature of Matrimony. These are His words: For this cause shall a man leave father and mother, and shall cleave unto his wife, and they shall be two in one flesh; and He adds: wherefore they are no more two but one flesh. In these words He makes it clear that God instituted marriage to be the union of two, and only two persons. The same truth He has taught very distinctly in another passage, wherein He says: Whosoever shall put away his wife and marry another, committeth adultery against her; and if the wife shall put away her husband, and be married to another, she committeth adultery. For if it were lawful for a man to have several wives, there is no reason why he who takes to himself a second wife, along with the wife he already has, should be regarded as more guilty of adultery than if he had dismissed his first wife and taken a second.

Hence it is that when an infidel who, following the customs of his country has married several wives, happens to be converted to the true religion, the Church orders him to dismiss all but the first, and regard her alone as his true and lawful wife.

Indissolubility Of Marriage

The self-same testimony of Christ our Lord easily proves that the marriage-tie cannot be broken by any sort of divorce. For if by a bill of divorce a woman were freed from the law that binds her to her husband, she might marry another husband without being in the least guilty of adultery. Yet our Lord says clearly: Whosoever shall put away his wife and shall marry another committeth adultery. Hence it is plain that the bond of marriage can be dissolved by death alone, as is confirmed by the Apostle when he says: A woman is bound by the law as long as her husband liveth; but if her husband die she is at liberty; let her marry whom she will, only in the Lord; and again: To them that are married, not I but the Lord commandeth, that the wife depart not from her husband; and if she depart that she remain unmarried or be reconciled to her husband. To the wife, then, who for a just cause has left her husband, the Apostle offers this alternative: Let her either remain unmarried or be reconciled to her husband. Nor does holy Church permit husband and wife to separate without weighty reasons.

Advantages Of Indissolubility

Lest, however, the law of Matrimony should seem too severe on account of its absolute indissolubility, the advantages of this indissolubility should be pointed out.

The first (beneficial consequence) is that men are given to understand that in entering Matrimony virtue and congeniality of disposition are to be preferred to wealth or beauty -- a circumstance that cannot but prove of the very highest advantage to the interests of society at large.

In the second place, if marriage could be dissolved by divorce, married persons would hardly ever be without causes of disunion, which would be daily supplied by the old enemy of peace and purity; while, on the contrary, now that the faithful must remember that even though separated as to bed and board, they remain none the less bound by the bond of marriage with no hope of marrying another, they are by this very fact rendered less prone to strife and discord. And even if it sometimes happens that husband and wife become separated, and are unable to bear the want of their partnership any longer, they are easily reconciled by friends and return to their common life.

The pastor should not here omit the salutary admonition of St. Augustine who, to convince the faithful that they should not consider it a hardship to receive back the wife they have put away for adultery, provided she repents of her crime, observes: Why should not the Christian husband receive back his wife when the Church receives her? And why should not the wife pardon her adulterous but penitent husband when Christ has already pardoned him? True it is that Scripture calls him foolish who keepeth an adulteress ; but the meaning refers to her who refuses to repent of her crime and quit the disgraceful course she has entered on.

From all this it will be clear that Christian marriage is far superior in dignity and perfection to that of Gentiles and Jews.

The Three Blessings of Marriage

The faithful should also be shown that there are three blessings of marriage: children, fidelity and the Sacrament. These are blessings which to some degree compensate for the inconveniences referred to by the Apostle in the words: Such shall have tribulation of the flesh, and they lead to this other result that sexual intercourse, which is sinful outside of marriage, is rendered right and honourable.

Offspring

The first blessing, then, is a family, that is to say, children born of a true and lawful wife. So highly did the Apostle esteem this blessing that he says: The woman shall be saved by bearing children.' These words are to be understood not only of bearing children, but also of bringing them up and training them to the practice of piety; for the Apostle immediately subjoins: If she continue in faith. Scripture says: Hast thou children? Instruct them and bow down their necks from childhood. The same is taught by the Apostle; while Tobias, Job and other holy Patriarchs in Sacred Scripture furnish us with beautiful examples of such training. The duties of both parents and children will, however, be set forth in detail when we come to speak of the fourth Commandment.

Fidelity

The second advantage of marriage is faith, not indeed that virtue which we receive in Baptism; but the fidelity which binds wife to husband and husband to wife in such a way that they mutually deliver to each other power over their bodies, promising at the same time never to violate the holy bond of Matrimony. This is easily inferred from the words pronounced by Adam when taking Eve as his wife, and which were afterwards confirmed by Christ our Lord in the Gospel: Wherefore a man shall leave father and mother and shall cleave to his wife and they shall be two in one flesh. It is also inferred from the words of the Apostle: The wife hath not power of her own body, but the husband: and in like manner, the husband hath not power of his own body but the wife. Justly, then, did the Lord in the Old Law ordain the most severe penalties against adulterers who violated this conjugal fidelity.

Matrimonial fidelity also demands that they love one another with a special, holy and pure love; not as adulterers love one another but as Christ loves His Church. This is the rule laid down by the Apostle when he says: Husbands, love your wives as Christ also loved the church. And surely (Christ's) love for His Church was immense; it was a love inspired not by His own advantage, but only by the advantage of His spouse.

Sacrament

The third advantage is called the Sacrament, that is to say, the indissoluble bond of marriage. As the Apostle has it: The Lord commanded that the wife depart not from the husband, and if she depart that she remain unmarried or be reconciled to' her husband; and let not the husband put away his wife. And truly, if marriage as a Sacrament represents the union of Christ with His Church, it also necessarily follows that just as Christ never separates Himself from His Church, so in like manner the wife can never be separated from her husband in so far as regards the marriage-tie.

The Duties of Married People

The more easily to preserve the holy state (of marriage) from dissensions, the duties of husband and wife as inculcated by St. Paul and by the Prince of the Apostles must be explained.

Duties Of A Husband

It is the duty of the husband to treat his wife generously and honourably. It should not be forgotten that Eve was called by Adam his companion. The woman, he says, whom thou gavest me as a companion. Hence it was, according to the opinion of some of the holy Fathers, that she was formed not from the feet but from the side of man; as, on the other hand, she was not formed from his head, in order to give her to understand that it was not hers to command but to obey her husband.

The husband should also be constantly occupied in some honest pursuit with a view to provide necessaries for the support of his family and to avoid idleness, the root of almost every vice.

He is also to keep all his family in order, to correct their morals, and see that they faithfully discharge their duties.

Duties Of A Wife

On the other hand, the duties of a wife are thus summed up by the Prince of the Apostles: Let wives be subject to their husbands. that if any believe not the word, they may be won without the word by the conversation of the wives, considering your chaste conversation with fear. Let not their adorning be the outward plaiting of the hair, or the wearing of gold, or the putting on of apparel: but the hidden man of the heart in the incorruptibility of a quiet and meek spirit, which is rich in the sight of God. For after this manner heretofore the holy women also, who trusted in God, adorned themselves, being in subjection to their own husbands, as Sarah obeyed Abraham, calling hint lord.

To train their children in the practice of virtue and to pay particular attention to their domestic concerns should also be especial objects of their attention. The wife should love to remain at home, unless compelled by necessity to go out; and she should never presume to leave home without her husband's consent.

Again, and in this the conjugal union chiefly consists, let wives never forget that next to God they are to love their husbands, to esteem them above all others, yielding to them in all things not inconsistent with Christian piety, a willing and ready obedience.

The Law of the Church on Marriage

The Rite To Be Observed

Having explained these matters, pastors should next teach what rites are to be observed in contracting marriage. There is no need, however, that we dwell on these questions here. The Council of Trent has laid down fully and accurately what must be chiefly observed; and this decree will not be unknown to pastors. It will suffice, then, to admonish them-to study to make themselves acquainted, from the doctrine of the Council, with what regards this subject, and to explain it carefully to the faithful.

But above all, lest young persons, whose period of life is marked by extreme indiscretion, should be deceived by a merely nominal marriage and foolishly rush into sinful love-unions, the pastor cannot too frequently remind them that there can be no true and valid marriage unless it be contracted in the presence of the parish priest, or of some other priest commissioned by him, or by the Ordinary, and that of a certain number of witnesses.

The Impediments Of Marriage

The impediments of marriage are also to be explained, a subject so minutely and accurately treated by many grave and learned writers on the virtues and vices as to render it an easy task to draw upon their labours, particularly as the pastor has occasion to have such works continually in his hands. The instructions, therefore, which such books contain, and also the decrees of the Council with regard to the impediments arising from spiritual relationship, from public honesty, and from fornication, the pastor should peruse with attention and expound with care.

The Recipient of Matrimony

Dispositions With Which The Sacrament Is To Be Approached

From the above may be learned the dispositions with which the faithful should contract matrimony. They should consider that they are about to enter upon a work that is not human but divine. The example of the Fathers of the Old Law, who esteemed marriage as a most holy and religious rite, although it had not then been raised to the dignity of a Sacrament, shows the singular purity of soul and piety (with which Christians should approach marriage).

Consent Of Parents

Among other things, children should be exhorted earnestly that they owe as a tribute of respect to their parents, or to those under whose guardianship and authority they are placed, not to contract marriage without their knowledge, still less in defiance of their express wishes. It should be observed that in the Old Law children were always given in marriage by their fathers; and that the will of the parent is always to have very great influence on the choice of the child, is clear from these words of the Apostle He that giveth his virgin in marriage doth well; and he that giveth her not, doth better.

The Use Of Marriage

Finally, the use of marriage is a subject which pastors should so treat as to avoid any expression that may be unfit to meet the ears of the faithful, that may be calculated to offend the piety of some, or excite the laughter of. others. The words of the Lord are chaste words; and the teacher of a Christian people should make use of the same kind of language, one that is characterised by singular gravity and purity of soul. Two lessons of instruction to the faithful are, then, to be specially insisted upon.

The first is that marriage is not to be used for purposes of lust or sensuality, but that its use is to be restrained within those limits which, as we have already shown, have been fixed by the Lord. It should be remembered that the Apostle admonishes: They that have wives, let them be as though they had them not, and that St. Jerome says: The love which a wise man cherishes towards his wife is the result of judgment, not the impulse of passion; he governs the impetuosity of desire, and is not hurried into indulgence. There is nothing more shameful than that a husband should love his wife as an adulteress.

But as every blessing is to be obtained from God by holy prayer, the faithful are also to be taught sometimes to abstain from the marriage debt, in order to devote themselves to prayer. Let the faithful understand that (this religious continence), according to the proper and holy injunction of our predecessors, is particularly to be observed for at least three days before Communion, and oftener during the solemn fast of Lent.

Thus will they find the blessings of marriage to be daily increased by an abundance of divine grace; and living in the pursuit of piety, they will not only spend this life in peace and tranquillity, but will also repose in the true and firm hope, which confoundeth not, of arriving, through the divine goodness, at the possession of that life which is eternal.

PART III : THE DECALOGUE

Importance Of Instruction On The Commandments

St. Augustine in his writings remarks that the Decalogue is the summary and epitome of all laws: Although the Lord had spoken many things, He gave to Moses only two stone tablets, called "tables of testimony," to be placed in the Ark. For if carefully examined and well understood, whatever else is commanded by God will be found to depend on the Ten Commandments which were engraved on those two tables, just as these Ten Commandments, in turn, are reducible to two, the love of God and of our neighbour, on which "depend the whole law and the prophets."

Since, then, the Decalogue is a summary of the whole Law, the pastor should give his days and nights to its consideration, that he may be able not only to regulate his own life by its precepts, but also to instruct in the law of God the people committed to his care. The lips of the priest shall keep knowledge, and they shall seek the law at his mouth, because he is the angel of the Lord of hosts. To the priests of the New Law this injunction applies in a special manner; they are nearer to God, and should be transformed from glory to glory, as by the Spirit of the Lord. Since Christ our Lord has called them light, it is their special duty to be a light to them that are in darkness, the instructors of the foolish, the teachers of infants; and if a man be overtaken in any fault, they who are spiritual should instruct such a one.

In the tribunal of penance the priest holds the place of a judge, and pronounces sentence according to the nature and gravity of the offence. Unless, therefore, he is desirous that his ignorance should prove an injury to himself and to others, he must bring with him to the discharge of this duty the greatest vigilance and the most practiced acquaintance with the interpretation of the law, in order to be able to pronounce, according to this divine rule, on every act and omission; and, as the Apostle says, to teach sound doctrine, free from error, and heal the diseases of the soul, which are sins, in order that the people may be acceptable to God, pursuers of good works.

Motives for Observing the Commandments

In these instructions the pastor should propose to himself and to others motives for keeping the Commandments

God Is The Giver Of The Commandments

Now among all the motives which induce men to obey this law the strongest is that God is its author. True, it is said to have been delivered by angels, but no one can doubt that its author is God. This is most clear not only from the words of the Legislator Himself, which we shall shortly explain, but also from innumerable other passages of Scripture that will readily occur to pastors.

Who is not conscious that a law is inscribed on his heart by God, teaching him to distinguish good from evil, vice from virtue, justice from injustice? The force and import of this unwritten law do not conflict with that which is written. Who is there, then, who will dare to deny that God is the author of the written, as He is of the unwritten law ?

But, lest the people, aware of the abrogation of the Mosaic Law, may imagine that the precepts of the Decalogue are no longer obligatory, it should be taught that when God gave the Law to Moses, He did not so much establish a new code, as render more luminous that divine light b which the depraved morals and long-continued perversity of man had at that time almost obscured. It is most certain that we are not bound to obey the Commandments because they were delivered by Moses, but because they are implanted in the hearts of all, and have been explained and confirmed by Christ our Lord.

The reflection that God is the author of the law is highly useful, and exercises great influence in persuading (to its observance); for we cannot doubt His wisdom and justice, nor can we escape His infinite power and might. Hence, when by His Prophets He commands the law to be observed, He proclaims that He is the Lord God; and the Decalogue itself opens: I am the Lord thy God; and elsewhere (we read): If I am a master, where is my fear?

That God has deigned to make clear to us His holy will on which depends our eternal salvation (is a consideration) which, besides animating the faithful to the observance of His Commandments, must call forth their gratitude Hence Scripture, in more passages than one, recalling this great blessing, admonishes the people to recognise their own dignity and the bounty of the Lord Thus in Deuteronomy it is said: This is your wisdom and understanding in the sight of nations, that hearing all these precepts they may say: Behold a wise and understanding people, a great nation; again, in the Psalm (we read): He hath not done in like manner to every nation, and his judgments he hath not made manifest to them.

The Commandments Were Proclaimed With Great Solemnity

If the pastor explain the circumstances which accompanied the promulgation of the Law, as recorded in Scripture, the faithful will easily understand with what piety and humility they should receive and reverence the Law received from God.

All were commanded by God that for three days before the promulgation of the Law they should wash their garments and abstain from conjugal intercourse, in order that they might be more holy and better prepared to receive the Law, and that on the third day they should be in readiness When they had reached the mountain from which the Lord was to deliver the Law by Moses, Moses alone was commanded to ascend the mountain. Thither came God with great majesty, filling the place with thunder and lightning, with fire and dense clouds, and began to speak to Moses, and delivered to him the Commandments

In this the divine wisdom had solely for object to admonish us that the law of the Lord should be received with pure and humble minds, and that over the neglect of His commands impend the heaviest chastisements of the divine justice.

The Observance Of The Commandments Is Not Difficult

The pastor should also teach that the Commandments of God are not difficult, as these words of St Augustine are alone sufficient to show: How, I ask, is it said to be impossible for man to love -- to love, I say, a beneficent Creator, a most loving Father, and also, in the persons of his , brethren to love his own flesh? Yet, "he who loveth has fulfilled the law." Hence the Apostle St. John expressly says that the commandments of God are not heavy; for as St. Bernard observes, nothing more just could be exacted from man, nothing that could confer on him a more exalted dignity, nothing more advantageous. Hence St. Augustine, filled with admiration of God's infinite goodness, thus addresses God : What is man that Thou wouldst be loved by him ? And if he loves Thee not, Thou threatenest t him with heavy punishment. Is it not punishment enough that I love Thee not ?

But should anyone plead human infirmity to excuse himself for not loving God, it should be explained that He who demands our love pours into our hearts by the Holy Ghost the fervour of His love; and this good Spirit our heavenly Father gives to those that ask him with reason, therefore, did St. Augustine pray: Give what thou commandest and command what thou pleasest. As, then, God is ever ready to help us, especially since the death of Christ the Lord, by which the prince of this world was cast out, there is no reason why anyone should be disheartened by the difficulty of the undertaking. To him who loves, nothing is difficult.

The Observance Of The Commandments Is Necessary

Furthermore, it will contribute much to persuade (obedience to the law) if it is explained that such obedience is necessary, especially since in these our days there are not wanting those who, to their own serious injury, have the impious hardihood to assert that the observance of the law, whether easy or difficult, is by no means necessary to salvation.

This wicked and impious error the pastor should refute from Scripture, especially from the same Apostle by whose authority they attempt to defend their wickedness. What, then, are the words of the Apostle? Circumcision is nothing, and uncircumcision is nothing, but the keeping of the commandments of God. Again, inculcating the same doctrine, he says: , new creature, in Christ, alone avails. By a new creature in Christ he evidently means him who observes the Commandments of God; for, he who observes the Commandments of God loves God, as our Lord Himself testifies in St. John: If anyone love me, he will keep my word.

A man, it is true, may be justified, and from wicked may become righteous, before he has fulfilled, by external acts, each of the Commandments; but no one who has arrived at the use of reason can be justified, unless he is resolved to keep all of God's Commandments.

The Observance Of The Commandments Is Attended By Many Blessings

Finally, to leave nothing unsaid that may be calculated to induce the faithful to an observance of the law, the pastor should point out how abundant and sweet are its fruits. This he will easily accomplish by referring to the eighteenth Psalm, which celebrates the praises of the divine law. The highest eulogy of the law is that it proclaims the glory and the majesty of God more eloquently than even the heavenly bodies, whose beauty and order excite the admiration of all peoples, even the most uncivilised, and compel them to acknowledge the glory, wisdom and power of the Creator and Architect of the universe.

The law of the Lord also converts souls to God; for knowing the ways of God and His holy will through the medium of His law, we turn our steps into the ways of the Lord.

It also gives wisdom to little ones; for they alone who fear God are truly wise. Hence, the observers of the law of God are filled with pure delights, with knowledge of divine mysteries, and are blessed with plenteous joys and rewards both in this life and in the life to come.

In our observance of the law, however, we should not act so much for our own advantage as for the sake of God who, by means of the law, has revealed His will to man. If other creatures are obedient to God's will, how much more reasonable that man should follow it?

God's Goodness Invites Us To Keep His Commandments

Nor should it be omitted that God has preeminently displayed His clemency and the riches of His goodness in this, that while He might have forced us to serve His glory without a reward, He has, notwithstanding, deigned to identify His own glory with our advantage, thus rendering what tends to His honour, conducive to our interests.

This is a great and striking consideration; and the pastor, therefore, should teach in the concluding words of the Prophet that in keeping them there is a great reward. Not only are we promised those blessings which seem to have reference to earthly happiness, such, for example, as to be blessed in the city, and blessed in the field: but we are also promised a great reward in heaven, good measure, pressed down, shaken together and running over, which, aided by the divine mercy, we merit by our holy and pious actions.

The Promulgation of the Law

I am the Lord thy God who brought thee out of the land of Egypt, out of the house of bondage. Thou shalt not have strange gods before me. Thou shalt not make to thyself a graven thing. The Law, although delivered to the Jews by the Lord from the mountain, was long before written and impressed by nature on the heart of man, and was therefore rendered obligatory by God for all men and all times.

The People To Whom The Law Was Given

It will be very useful, however, to explain carefully the words in which it was proclaimed to the Hebrews by Moses, its minister and interpreter, and also the history of the Israelites, which is so full of mysteries.

Epitome Of Jewish History

(The pastor) should first tell that from among the nations of the earth God chose one which descended from Abraham; that it was the divine will that Abraham should be a stranger in the land of Canaan, the possession of which He had promised him; and that, although for more than four hundred years he and his posterity were wanderers before they dwelt in the promised land, God never withdrew from them, throughout their wanderings, His protecting care. They passed from nation to nation and from one kingdom to another people; He suffered no man to hurt them, and He even reproved kings for their sakes.

Before they went down into Egypt He sent before them one by whose prudence they and the Egyptians were rescued from famine. In Egypt such was His kindness towards them that although opposed by the power of Pharaoh who sought their destruction, they increased to an extraordinary degree; and when they were severely harassed and cruelly treated as slaves, God raised up Moses as a leader to lead them out in a strong hand. It is especially this deliverance that the Lord refers to in the opening words of the Law: I am the Lord thy God who brought thee out of the land of Egypt, out of the house of bondage.

Lessons To Be Drawn From Jewish History

From all this the pastor should especially note that out of all the nations God chose only one whom He called His people, and by whom He willed to be known and worshipped; not that they were superior to other nations in justice or in numbers, and of this God Himself reminds the Hebrews, but rather because He wished, by the multiplication and aggrandisement of an inconsiderable and impoverished nation, to display to mankind His power and goodness.

Such having been their condition, he was closely united to them, and loved them, and Lord of heaven and earth as He was, He disdained not to be called their God. He desired that the other nations might thus be excited to emulation and that mankind, seeing the happiness of the Israelites, might embrace the worship of the true God. In the same way St. Paul says that by discussing the happiness of the Gentiles and their knowledge of the true God, he provoked to emulation those who were his own flesh.

The faithful should next be taught that God suffered the Hebrew Patriarchs to wander for so long a time, and their posterity to be oppressed and harassed by a galling servitude, in order to teach us that none are friends of God except those who are enemies of the world and pilgrims on earth, and that an entire detachment from the world gives us an easier access to the friendship of God. Further He wished that, being brought to His service, we should understand how much happier are they who serve God, than they who serve the world. Of this Scripture itself admonishes us: Yet they shall serve him, that they may know the difference between my service and the service of the kingdom of the earth.

(The pastor) should also explain that God delayed the fulfilment of His promise until after the lapse of more than four hundred years, in order that His people might be sustained by faith and hope; for, as we shall show when we come to explain the first Commandment, God wishes His children to depend on Him at all times and to repose all their confidence in His goodness.

The Time And Place In Which The Law Was Promulgated

Finally, the time and place, in which the people of Israel received this Law from God should be noted. They received it after they had been delivered from Egypt and had come into the wilderness; in order that, impressed by the memory of a recent benefit and awed by the dreariness of the place in which they journeyed, they might be the better disposed to receive the Law. For man becomes closely attached to those whose bounty he has experienced, and when he has lost all hope of assistance from his fellow-man, he then seeks refuge in the protection of God.

From all this we learn that the more detached the faithful are from the allurements of the world and the pleasures of sense, the more disposed they are to accept heavenly doctrines. As the Prophet has written: Whom shall he teach knowledge, and whom shall he make to understand the hearing? Them that are weaned from the milk, that are drawn away from the breasts.

THE FIRST COMMANDMENT : "*I am the lord thy god, who brought thee out of the land of Egypt, out of the house of bondage. Thou shalt not have strange gods before me. Thou shalt not make to thyself a graven thing, nor the likeness of any thing that is in heaven above, or in the earth beneath, nor of those things that are in the waters under the earth. Thou shalt not adore them, nor serve them. I am the lord thy god, mighty, jealous, visiting the iniquity of the fathers upon the children, to the third and fourth generation of them that hate me, and showing mercy unto thousands of them that love me, and keep my commandments.*"

"I am the Lord thy God"

The pastor should use his best endeavours to induce the faithful to keep continually in view these words: I am the Lord thy God. From them they will learn that their Lawgiver is none other than their Creator, by whom they were made and are preserved, and that they may truly repeat: He is the Lord our God, and we are the people of his pasture and the sheep of his hand. The frequent and earnest inculcation of these words will also serve to induce the faithful more readily to observe the Law and avoid sin.

"Who Brought thee out of the Land of Egypt, out of the House of Bondage"

The next words, who brought thee out of the land of Egypt, out of the house of bondage, seem to relate solely to the Jews liberated from the bondage of Egypt. But if we consider the meaning of the salvation of the entire human race, those words are still more applicable to Christians, who are liberated by God not from the bondage of Egypt, but from the slavery of sin and the powers of darkness, and are translated into the kingdom of his beloved Son. Contemplating the greatness of this favour, Jeremias foretold: Behold the days come, saith the Lord, when it shall be said no more: The Lord liveth that brought forth. the children of Israel out of the land of Egypt; but: The Lord liveth that brought the children of Israel out of the land of the north and out of all the lands to which I cast them out; and I will bring them again into their land which gave to their fathers. Behold, I send many fishers, saith the Lord, and they shall fish them, etc. And, indeed, our most indulgent Father has gathered together, through His beloved Son, His children that were dispersed, that being made free from sin and made the servants of justice, we may serve before him in holiness and justice all our days.'

Against every temptation, therefore, the faithful should arm themselves with these words of the Apostle as with a shield: Shall we who are dead to sin live any longer therein? We are no longer our own, we are His who died and rose again for us. He is the Lord our God who has purchased us for Himself at the price of His blood. Shall we then be any longer capable of sinning against the Lord our God, and crucifying Him again? Being made truly free, and with that liberty wherewith Christ has made us free, let us, as we heretofore yielded our members to serve injustice, henceforward yield them to serve justice to sanctification.

"Thou shalt not have Strange Gods before Me"

The pastor should teach that the first part of the Decalogue contains our duties towards God; the second part, our duties towards our neighbour. The reason (for this order) is that the services we render our neighbour are rendered for the sake of God; for then only do we love our neighbour as God commands when we love him for God's sake. The Commandments which regard God are those which were inscribed on the first table of the Law.

The Above Words Contain A Command And A Prohibition

(The pastor) should next show that the words just quoted contain a twofold precept, the one mandatory, the other prohibitory. When it is said: Thou shalt not have strange gods before me, it is equivalent to saying: Thou shalt worship me the true God; thou shalt not worship strange gods.

What They Command

The (mandatory part) contains a precept of faith, hope and charity. For, acknowledging God to be immovable, immutable, always the same, we rightly confess that He is faithful and entirely just. Hence in assenting to His oracles, we necessarily yield to Him all belief and obedience. Again, who can contemplate His omnipotence, His clemency, His willing beneficence, and not repose in Him all his hopes? Finally, who can behold the riches of His goodness and love, which He lavishes on us, and not love Him? Hence the exordium and the conclusion used by God in Scripture when giving His commands: I, the Lord.

What They Forbid

The (negative) part of this Commandment is comprised in these words: Thou shalt not have strange gods before me. This the Lawgiver subjoins, not because it is not sufficiently expressed in the affirmative part of the precept, which means: Thou shalt worship me, the only God, for if He is God, He is the only God; but on account of the blindness of many who of old professed to worship the true God and yet adored a multitude of gods. Of these there were many even among the Hebrews, whom Elias reproached with having halted between two sides, and also among the Samaritans, who worshipped the God of Israel and the gods of the nations.

Importance Of This Commandment

After this it should be added that this is the first and principal Commandment, not only in order, but also in its nature, dignity and excellence. God is entitled to infinitely greater love and obedience from us than any lord or king. He created us, He governs us, He nurtured us even in the womb, brought us into the world, and still supplies us with all the necessaries of life and maintenance.

Sins Against This Commandment

Against this Commandment all those sin who have not faith. hope and charity. such sinners are very numerous, for they include all who fall into heresy, who reject what holy mother the Church proposes for our belief, who give credit to dreams. fortune-telling, and such illusions; those who, despairing of salvation, trust not in the goodness of God; and those who rely solely on wealth, or health and strength of body. But these matters are developed more at length in treatises on sins and vices.

Veneration And Invocation Of Angels And Saints Not Forbidden By This Commandment

In explanation of this Commandment it should be accurately taught that the veneration and invocation of holy Angels and of the blessed who now enjoy the glory of heaven, and likewise the honour which the Catholic Church has always paid even to the bodies and ashes of the Saints, are not forbidden by this Commandment. If a king ordered that no one else should set himself up as king, or accept the honours due to the royal person, who would be so foolish as to infer that the sovereign was unwilling that suitable honour and respect should be paid to his magistrates? Now although Christians follow the example set by the Saints of the Old Law, and are said to adore the Angels, yet they do not give to Angels that honour which is due to God alone.

And if we sometimes read that Angels refused to be worshipped by men, we are to know that they did so because the worship which they refused to accept was the honour due to God alone.

It Is Lawful To Honour And Invoke The Angels

The Holy Spirit who says: Honour and glory to God alone, commands us also to honour our parents and elders; and the holy men who adored one God only are also said in Scripture to have adored, that is, supplicated and venerated kings. If then kings, by whose agency God governs the world, are so highly honoured, shall it be deemed unlawful to honour those angelic spirits whom God has been pleased to constitute His ministers, whose services He makes use of not only in the government of His Church, but also of the universe, by whose aid, although we see them not, we are every day delivered from the greatest dangers of soul and body ? Are they not worthy of far greater honour, since their dignity so far surpasses that of kings?

Add to this their love towards us, which, as we easily see from Scripture, prompts them to pour out their prayers for those countries over which they are placed, as well as for us whose guardians they are, and whose prayers and tears they present before the throne of God Hence our Lord admonishes us in the Gospel not to offend the little ones because their angels in heaven always see the face of their Father who is in heaven.

Their Intercession, therefore, we ought to invoke, because they always see tile face of God, and are constituted by Him the willing advocates of our salvation. The Scriptures bear witness to such invocation. Jacob entreated the Angel with whom he wrestled to bless him; nay, he even compelled him, declaring that he would not let him go until he had blessed him. And not only did he invoke the blessing of the Angel whom he saw, but also of him whom he saw not. The angel, said he, who delivers me from all evils, bless these boys.

It Is Lawful To Honour And Invoke The Saints

From all this we may conclude that to honour the Saints who nave slept in the Lord, to invoke them, and to venerate their sacred relics and ashes, far from diminishing, tends considerably to increase the glory of God, in proportion as man's hope is thus animated and fortified, and he himself encouraged to imitate the Saints.

This is a practice which is also supported by the authority' of the second Council of Nice, the Councils of Gangra, and of Trent, and by the testimony of the Fathers. In order, however, that the pastor may be the better prepared to meet the objections of those who deny this doctrine, he should consult particularly St. Jerome against Vigilantius and St. Damascene. To the teaching of these Fathers should be added as a consideration of prime importance that the practice was received from the Apostles, and has always been retained and preserved in the Church of God.

But who can desire a stronger or more convincing proof than that which is supplied by the admirable praises given in Scripture to the Saints? For there are not wanting eulogies which God Himself pronounced on some of the Saints. If, then, Holy Writ celebrates their praises, why should not men show them singular honour ?

A stronger claim which the Saints have to be honoured and invoked is that they constantly pray for our salvation and obtain for us by their merits and influence many blessings from God. If there is joy in heaven over the conversion of one sinner, will not the citizens of heaven assist those who repent? When they are invoked, will they not obtain for us the pardon of sins, and the grace of God ?

Objections Answered

Should it be said, as some say, that the patronage of the Saints is unnecessary, because God hears our prayers without the intervention of a mediator, this impious assertion is easily met by the observation of St. Augustine: There are many things which God does not grant without a mediator and intercessor. This is confirmed by the well-known examples of Abimelech and the friends of Job who were pardoned only through the prayers of Abraham and of Job

Should it be alleged that to recur to the patronage and intercession of the Saints argues want or weakness of faith, what will (the objectors) answer regarding the centurion whose faith was highly eulogised by the Lord God Himself, despite the fact that he had sent to the Redeemer the ancients of the Jews, to intercede for his sick servant?

True, there is but one Mediator, Christ the Lord, who alone has reconciled us to the heavenly Father through His blood, and who, having obtained eternal redemption, and having entered once into the holies, ceases not to intercede for us. But it by no means follows that it is therefore unlawful to have recourse to the intercession of the Saints. If, because we have one Mediator Jesus Christ, it were unlawful to ask the intercession of the Saints, the Apostle would never have recommended himself with so much earnestness to the prayers of his brethren on earth. For the prayers of the living would lessen the glory and dignity of Christ's Mediatorship not less than the intercession of the Saints in heaven.

The Honour And Invocation Of Saints Is Approved By Miracles

But who would not be convinced of the honour due the Saints and of the help they give us by the wonders wrought at their tombs? Diseased eyes, hands, and other members are restored to health; the dead are raised to life, and demons are expelled from the bodies of men ! These are facts which St. Ambrose and St. Augustine, most unexceptionable witnesses, declare in their writings, not that they heard, as many did, nor that they read, as did man- very reliable men, but that they saw.

But why multiply proofs? If the clothes, the handkerchiefs, and even the very shadows of the Saints, while yet on earth, banished disease and restored health, who will have the hardihood to deny that God can still work the same wonders by the holy ashes, the bones and other relics of the Saints ? Of this we have a proof in the restoration to life of the dead body which was accidentally let down into the grave of Eliseus, and which, on touching the body (of the Prophet), was instantly restored to life.

"Thou shalt not make to thyself a graven thing, nor the likeness of any thing that is in heaven above, or in the earth beneath, nor of those things that are in the waters under the earth: thou shalt not adore them nor serve them"

Some, supposing these words which come next in order to constitute a distinct precept, reduce the ninth and tenth Commandments to one. St. Augustine, on the contrary, considering the last two to be distinct Commandments, makes the words just quoted a part of the first Commandment. His division is much approved in the Church, and hence we willingly adopt it. Furthermore, a very good reason for this arrangement at once suggests itself. It was fitting that to the first Commandment should be added the rewards or punishments entailed by each one of the Commandments.

The Above Words Do Not Forbid All Images

Let no one think that this Commandment entirely forbids the arts of painting, engraving or sculpture. The Scriptures inform us that God Himself commanded to be made images of Cherubim, and also the brazen serpent. The interpretation, therefore, at which we must arrive, is that images are prohibited only inasmuch as they are used as deities to receive adoration, and so to injure the true worship of God.

They Forbid Idols And Representations Of The Deity

As far as this Commandment is concerned, it is clear that there are two chief ways in which God's majesty can be seriously outraged. The first way is by worshipping idols and images as God, or believing that they possess any divinity or virtue entitling them to our worship, by praying to, or reposing confidence in them, as the Gentiles did, who placed their hopes in idols, and whose idolatry the Scriptures frequently condemn. The other way is by attempting to form a representation of the Deity, as if He were visible to mortal eyes, or could be reproduced by colours or figures. Who, says Damascene, can represent God, invisible, as He is, incorporeal, uncircumscribed by limits, and incapable of being reproduced under any shape. This subject is treated more at large in the second Council of Nice. Rightly, then, did the Apostles say (of the Gentiles): They changed the glory of the incorruptible God into a likeness of birds, and of four-footed beasts, and of creeping things; for they worshipped all these things as God, seeing that they made the images of these things to represent Him. Hence the Israelites, when they exclaimed before the image of the calf: These are thy gods, Israel, that have brought thee out of the land of Egypt, are denounced as idolaters, because they changed their glory into the likeness of a calf that eateth grass.

When, therefore, the Lord had forbidden the worship of strange gods, He also forbade the making of an image of the Deity from brass or other materials, in order thus utterly to do away with idolatry. It is this that Isaias declares when he asks: To whom then have you likened God, or what image will you make for hill? That this is the meaning of the prohibition contained in the Commandment is proved, not only from the writings of the holy Fathers, who, as may be seen in the seventh General Council, give to it this interpretation: but is also clearly declared in these words of Deuteronomy, by which Moses sought to withdraw the people from the worship of idols: You saw not, he says, any similitude in the day that the Lord spoke to you in Horeb, from the midst of the fire. These words this wisest of legislators spoke, lest through error of any sort, they should make an image of the Deity, and transfer to any thing created, the honour due to God.

They Do Not Forbid Representations Of The Divine Persons And Angels

To represent the Persons of the Holy Trinity by certain forms under which they appeared in the Old and New Testaments no one should deem contrary to religion or the law of God. For who can be so ignorant as to believe that such forms are representations of the Deity? -- forms, as the pastor should teach, which only express some attribute or action ascribed to God. Thus when from the description of Daniel God is painted as the Ancient of days, seated on a throne, with the books opened before hint, the eternity of God is represented and also the infinite wisdom, by which He sees and judges all the thoughts and actions of men.'

Angels, also, are represented under human form and with wings to give us to understand that they are actuated by benevolent feelings towards mankind, and are always prepared to execute the Lord's commands; for they are all ministering spirits, sent to minister for them who shall receive the inheritance of salvation.

What attributes of the Holy Ghost are represented under the forms of a dove, and of tongues of fire, in the Gospel and in the Acts of the Apostles, is a matter too well known to require lengthy explanation.

They Do Not Forbid Images Of Christ And The Saints

But to make and honour the images of Christ our Lord, of His holy and virginal Mother, and of the Saints, all of whom were clothed with human nature and appeared in human form, is not only not forbidden by this Commandment, but has always been deemed a holy practice and a most sure indication of gratitude. This position is confirmed by the monuments of the Apostolic age, the General Councils of the Church, and the writings of so many among the Fathers, eminent alike for sanctity and learning, all of whom are of one accord upon the subject.

Usefulness Of Sacred Images

But the pastor should not content himself with showing that it is lawful to have images in churches, and to pay them honour and respect, since this respect is referred to their prototypes. He should also show that the uninterrupted observance of this practice down to the present day has been attended with great advantage to the faithful, as may be seen in the work of Damascene on images, and in the seventh General Council, the second of Nice.

But as the enemy of mankind, by his wiles and deceits, seeks to pervert even the most holy institutions, should the faithful happen at all to offend in this particular, the pastor, in accordance with the decree of the Council of Trent's should use every exertion in his power to correct such an abuse, and, if necessary, explain the decree itself to the people.

He will also inform the unlettered and those who may be ignorant of the use of images, that they are intended to instruct in the history of the Old and New Testaments, and to revive from time to time their memory; that thus, moved by the contemplation of heavenly things, we may be the more ardently inflamed to adore and love God Himself. He should, also, point out that the images of the Saints are placed in churches, not only to be honoured, but also that they may admonish us by their examples to imitate their lives and virtues.

"I am the Lord thy God, mighty, jealous, visiting the iniquity of the fathers upon the children, to the third and fourth generation of them that hate me, and showing mercy unto thousands of them that love me, and keep my commandments."

In this concluding clause of this Commandment two things occur which demand careful exposition. The first is, that while, on account of the enormous guilt incurred by the violation of the first Commandment, and the propensity of man towards its violation, the punishment is properly indicated in this place, it is also attached to all the other Commandments.

Every law enforces its observance by rewards and punishments; and hence the frequent and numerous promises of God in Sacred Scripture. To omit those that we meet almost on every page of the Old Testament, it is written in the Gospel: If thou wilt enter into life, keep the commandments; and again: He that doth the will of my Father who is in heaven, he shall enter into the kingdom of heaven; and also: Every tree that doth not yield good fruit shall be cut down and cast into the fire; Whosoever is angry with his brother shall be guilty of the judgment; If you will not forgive men, neither will your Father forgive you your offences.

How The Sanction Contained In The Above Words Should Be Proposed

The other observation is that this concluding part (of the Commandment) is to be proposed in a very different manner to the spiritual and to the carnal Christian. To the spiritual who is animated by the Spirit of God, and who yields to Him a willing and cheerful obedience, it is, in some sort, glad tidings and a strong proof of the divine goodness towards him. In it he recognises the care of his most loving God, who, now by rewards, now by punishments, almost compels His creatures to adore and worship Him. The spiritual man acknowledges the infinite goodness of God towards himself in vouchsafing to issue His commands to him and to make use of his service to the glory of the divine name. And not only does he acknowledge the divine goodness, he also cherishes a strong hope that when God commands what He pleases, He will also give strength to fulfil hat He commands.

But to the carnal man, who is not yet freed from a servile spirit and who abstains from sin more through fear of punishment than love of virtue, (this sanction) of the divine law, which closes each of the Commandments, is burdensome and severe. Wherefore they should be encouraged by pious exhortation, and led by the hand, as it were, in the way of the law. The pastor, therefore, as often as he has occasion to explain any of the Commandments should keep this in view.

Mighty

But both the carnal and the spiritual should be spurred on, especially by two considerations which are contained in this concluding clause, and are highly calculated to enforce obedience to the divine law.

The one is that God is called the strong. That appellation needs to be fully expounded; because the flesh, unappalled by the terrors of the divine menaces, frequently indulges in the foolish expectation of escaping, in one way or another, God's wrath and threatened punishment. But when one is deeply impressed with the conviction that God is the strong, he will exclaim with the great David: Whither shall I go from thy spirit? or whither shall I pee from thy face?

The flesh, also, distrusting the promises of God, sometimes magnifies the power of the enemy to such an extent, as to believe itself unable to withstand his assaults; while, on the contrary, a firm and unshaken faith, which wavers not, but relies confidently on the strength and power of God, animates and confirms man. For it says: The Lord is my light and my salvation; whom shall I fear?

Jealous

The second spur is the jealousy of God. Man is sometimes tempted to think that God takes no interest in human affairs, and does not even care whether we observe or neglect His law. This error is the source of the great disorders of life. But when we believe that God is a jealous God, the thought easily keeps us within the limits of our duty.

The jealousy attributed to God does not, however, imply disturbance of mind; it is that divine love and charity by which God will suffer no human creature to be unfaithful to Him with impunity, and which destroys all those who are disloyal to Him. The jealousy of God, therefore, is the most tranquil and impartial justice, which repudiates as an adulteress the soul corrupted by. erroneous opinions and criminal passions.

This jealousy of God, since it shows His boundless and incomprehensible goodness towards us, we find most sweet and pleasant. Among men there is no love more ardent, no greater or more intimate tie, than that of those who are united by marriage. Hence when God frequently compares Himself to a spouse or husband and calls Himself a jealous God, He shows the excess of His love towards us.

Zeal In The Service Of God

The pastor, therefore, should here teach that men should be so warmly interested in promoting the worship and honour of God as to be said rather to be jealous of Him than to love Him, in imitation of Him who says of Himself: With zeal have I been zealous for the Lord God of hosts, or rather of Christ Himself, who says: The zeal of thy house hath eaten me up.

"Visiting The Iniquity," Etc.

Concerning the threat contained in this Commandment it should be explained that God will not suffer sinners to go unpunished, but will chastise them as a father, or punish them with the rigour and severity of a judge. This was elsewhere explained by Moses when he said: Thou shalt know that the Lord thy God is a strong and faithful God, keeping his covenant and mercy to them that love him, and to them that keep his commandments, unto a thousand generations; and repaying forthwith them that hate him. You will not, says Josue, be able to serve the Lord; for he is a holy God, and mighty and jealous, and will not forgive your wickedness and sins. If you leave the Lord and serve strange gods, he will turn and will afflict you, and will destroy you.

The faithful are also to be taught that the punishments here threatened await the third and fourth generation of the impious and wicked; not that the children are always chastised for the sins of their ancestors, but that while these and their children may go unpunished, their posterity shall not all escape the wrath and vengeance of the Almighty. This happened in the case of King Josias. God had spared him for his singular piety, and allowed him to be gathered to the tomb of his fathers in peace, that his eyes might not behold the evils of the times that were to befall Juda and Jerusalem, on account of the wickedness of his grandfather Manasses; yet, after his death the divine vengeance so overtook his posterity that even the children of Josias were not spared.

How the words of this Commandment are not at variance with the statement of the Prophet: The soul that sins shall die, is clearly shown by the authority of St. Gregory, supported by the testimony of all the ancient Fathers. Whoever, he says, follows the bad example of a wicked father is also bound by his sins; but he who does not follow the example of his father, shall not at all suffer for the sins of the father Hence it follows that a wicked son, who dreads not to add his own malice to the vices of his father, by which he knows the divine wrath to have been excited, pays the penalty not only of his own sins, but also of those of his father. It is just that he who dreads not to walk in the footsteps of a wicked father, in presence of a rigorous judge, should be compelled in the present life to expiate the crimes of his wicked parent.

"And Showing Mercy, Etc.

The pastor should next observe that the goodness and mercy of God far exceed His justice. He is angry to the third and fourth generation; but He bestows His mercy on thousands.

"Of Them That Hate Me"

The words of them that hate me display the grievousness of sin. What more wicked, what more detestable than to hate God, the supreme goodness and sovereign truth? This, however, is the crime of all sinners; for as he that hath God's commandments and keepeth them, loveth God, so he who despises His law and violates His Commandments, is justly said to hate God.

Of Them That Love Me

The concluding words: And to them that love me, point out the manner and motive of observing the law. Those who obey the law of God must needs be influenced in its observance by the same love and charity which they bear to God, a principle which should be brought to mind in the instructions on all the other Commandments.

THE SECOND COMMANDMENT : *"Thou shalt not take the name of the lord thy god in vain"*

Why This Commandment Is Distinct From The First

The second Commandment of the divine law is necessarily comprised in the first, which commands us to worship God in piety and holiness For he who requires that honour be paid him, also requires that he be spoken of with reverence, and must forbid the contrary, as is clearly shown by these words of the Lord in Malachy: The son honoureth the father and the servant his master if then I be a father, where is my honour?

However, on account of the importance of the obligation, God wished to make the law, which commands His own divine and most holy name to be honoured, a distinct Commandment, expressed in the clearest and simplest terms.

Importance Of Instruction On This Commandment

The above observation should strongly convince the pastor that on this point it is not enough to speak in general terms; that the importance of the subject is such as to require it to be dwelt upon at considerable length, and to be explained to the faithful in all its bearings with distinctness, clearness and accuracy.

This diligence cannot be deemed superfluous, since there are not wanting those who are so blinded by the darkness of error as not to dread to blaspheme His name, whom the Angels glorify Men are not deterred by the Commandment laid down from shamelessly and daringly outraging Him divine Majesty every day, or rather every hour and moment of the day Who is ignorant that every assertion is accompanied with an oath and teems with curses and imprecations? To such lengths has this impiety been carried, that there is scarcely anyone who buys, or sells, or transacts business of any sort, without having recourse to swearing, and who, even in matters the most unimportant and trivial, does not profane the most holy name of God thousands of times.

It therefore becomes more imperative on the pastor not to neglect, carefully and frequently, to admonish the faithful how grievous and detestable is this crime.

Positive Part of this Commandment

But in the exposition of this Commandment it should first be shown that besides a negative, it also contains a positive precept, commanding the performance of a duty To each of these a separate explanation should be given; and for the sake of easier exposition what the Commandment requires should be first set forth, and then what it forbids It commands us to honour the name of God, and to swear by it with reverence It prohibits us to contemn the divine name, to take it in vain, or swear by it falsely, unnecessarily or rashly.

In the part which commands us to honour the name of God, the command, as the pastor should show the faithful, is not directed to the letters or syllables of which that name is composed, or in any respect to the mere name; but to the meaning of a word used to express the Omnipotent and Eternal Majesty of the Godhead, Trinity in Unity Hence we easily infer the superstition of those among the Jews who, while they hesitated not to write, dared not to pronounce the name of God, as if the divine power consisted in the four letters, and not in the signification.

Although this Commandment uses the singular number, Thou shalt not take the name of God, this is not to be understood to refer to any one name, but to every name by which God is generally designated For He is called by many names, such as the Lord, the Almighty, the Lord of hosts, the King of kings, the Strong, and by others of similar nature, which we meet in Scripture and which are all entitled to the same and equal veneration

Various Ways Of Honouring God's Name

It should next be taught how due honour is to be given to the name of God Christians, whose tongues should constantly celebrate the divine praises, are not to be ignorant of a matter so important, indeed, most necessary to salvation The name of God may be honoured in a variety of ways; but all may be reduced to those that follow.

Public Profession Of Faith

In the first place, God's name is honoured when we publicly and confidently confess Him to be our Lord and our God; and when we acknowledge and also proclaim Christ to be the author of our salvation.

Respect For The Word Of God

(It is also honoured) when we pay a religious attention to the word of God, which announces to us His will; make it the subject of our constant meditation; and strive by reading or hearing it, according to our respective capacities and conditions of life, to become acquainted with it.

Praise And Thanksgiving

Again, we honour and venerate the name of God, when, from a sense of religious duty, we celebrate His praises, and under all circumstances, whether prosperous or adverse, return Him unbounded thanks Thus spoke the Prophet Bless the Lord, O my soul, and never forget all he hath done for thee. Among the Psalms of David there are many, in which, animated with singular piety towards God, he chants in sweetest strains the divine praises There is also the example of the admirable patience of Job, who, when visited with the heaviest and most appalling calamities, never ceased, with lofty and unconquered soul, to give praise to God When, therefore, we labour under affliction of mind or body, when oppressed by misery and misfortune, let us instantly direct all our thoughts, and all the powers of our souls, to the praises of God, saying with Job Blessed be the name of the Lord.

Prayer

The name of God is not less honoured when we confidently invoke His assistance, either to relieve us from our afflictions, or to give us constancy and strength to endure them with fortitude This is in accordance with the Lord's own wishes Call upon me, He says, in the day of trouble: I will deliver thee, and thou shalt glorify me. We have illustrious examples of such supplications in many passages of Scripture, and especially in the sixteenth, forty-third, and one hundred and eighteenth Psalms.

Oaths

Finally, we honour the name of God when we solemnly call upon Him to witness the truth of what we assert This mode of honouring God's name differs much from those already-enumerated Those means are in their own nature so good, so desirable, that our days and nights could not be more happily or more holily spent than in such practices of piety I will bless the Lord at all times, says David, his praise shall be always in my mouth. On the other hand, although oaths are in themselves good, their frequent use is by no means praiseworthy.

The reason of this difference is that oaths have been instituted only as remedies to human frailty, and a necessary means of establishing the truth of what we assert As it is inexpedient to have recourse to medicine unless, when it becomes necessary, and as its frequent use is harmful; so with regard to oaths, it is not profitable to have recourse to them, unless there is a weighty and just cause; and frequent recurrence to them, far from being advantageous, is on the contrary highly prejudicial Hence the excellent observation of St Chrysostom Oaths were introduced among men, not at the beginning of the world, but long after; when vice had spread far and wide over the earth; when all things were disturbed and universal confusion reigned out; when, to complete human depravity, almost all mankind debased the dignity of their nature by the degrading service of idols. Then at length it was that the custom of oaths was introduced. For the perfidy and wickedness of men was so great that it was with difficulty that anyone could be induced to credit the assertion of another, and they began to call on God as a witness.

Meaning Of An Oath

Since in explaining this part of the Commandment the chief object is to teach the faithful how to render an oath reverential and holy, it is first to be observed, that to swear, whatever the form of words may be, is nothing else than to call God to witness; thus to say, God is witness, and By God, mean one and the same thing.

To swear by creatures, such as the holy Gospels, the cross, the names or relics of the Saints, and so on, in order to prove our statements, is also to take an oath Of themselves, it is true, such objects give no weight or authority to an oath; it is God Himself who does this, whose divine majesty shines forth in them Hence to swear by the Gospel is to swear by God Himself, whose truth is contained and revealed in the Gospel (This holds equally true with regard to those who swear) by the Saints, who are the temples of God, who believed the truth of His Gospel, were faithful in its observance, and spread it far and wide among the nations and peoples.

This is also true of oaths uttered by way of execration, such as that of St Paul I call God to witness upon my soul. By this form of oath one submits himself to God's judgment, who is the avenger of falsehood We do not, however, deny that some of these forms may be used without constituting an oath; but even in such cases it will be found useful to observe what has been said with regard to an oath, and to conform exactly to the same rule and standard.

Oaths Are Affirmatory And Promissory

Oaths are of two kinds The first is an affirmatory oath, and is taken when we religiously affirm anything, past or present. Such was the affirmation of the Apostle in his Epistle to the Galatians: Behold, before God, I lie not. The second kind, to which comminations may be reduced, is called promissory It looks to the future, and is taken when we promise and affirm for certain that such or such a thing will be done Such was the oath of David, who, swearing by the Lord his God, promised to Bethsabee his wife that her son Solomon should be heir to his kingdom and successor to his throne.

Conditions Of A Lawful Oath

Although to constitute an oath it is sufficient to call God to witness, yet to constitute a holy and just oath many other conditions are required, which should be carefully explained These, as St Jerome observes, are briefly enumerated in the words of Jeremias Thou shalt swear: as the Lord liveth, in truth and in judgment and in justice, words which briefly sum up all the conditions that constitute the perfection of an oath, namely, truth, judgment, justice.

First Condition: Truth

Truth, then, holds the first place in an oath What is asserted must be true and he who swears must believe what he swears to be true, being influenced not by rash judgment or mere conjecture, but by solid reasons.

Truth is a condition not less necessary in a promissory than in an affirmatory oath He who promises must be disposed to perform and fulfil his promise at the appointed time As no conscientious man will promise to do what he considers opposed to the most holy Commandments and will of God; so, having promised and sworn to do what is lawful, he will never fail to adhere to his engagement, unless, perhaps by a change of circumstances it should happen that, if he wished to keep faith and observe his promises, he must incur the displeasure and enmity of God That truth is necessary to an oath David also declares in these words: He that sweareth to his neighbour, and deceiveth not.

Second Condition: Judgment

The second condition of an oath is judgment. An oath is not to be taken rashly and inconsiderately, but after deliberation and reflection. When about to take an oath, therefore, one should first consider whether he is obliged to take it, and should weigh well the whole case, reflecting whether it seems to call for an oath. Many other circumstances of time, place, etc., are also to be taken into consideration; and one should not be influenced by love or hatred, or any other passion, but by the nature and necessity of the case.

Unless this careful consideration and reflection precede, an oath must be rash and hasty; and of this character are the irreligious affirmations of those, who, on the most unimportant and trifling occasions, swear without thought or reason from the influence of bad habit alone. This we see practiced daily everywhere among buyers and sellers. The latter, to sell at the highest price, the former to purchase at the cheapest rate, make no scruple to strengthen with an oath their praise or dispraise of the goods on sale.

Since, therefore, judgment and prudence are necessary, and since children are not able, on account of their tender years, to understand and judge accurately, Pope St. Cornelius decreed that an oath should not be administered to children before puberty, that is, before their fourteenth year.

Third Condition: Justice

The last condition (of an oath) is justice, which is especially requisite in promissory oaths. Hence, if a person swear to do what is unjust or unlawful, he sins by taking the oath, and adds sin to sin by executing his promise. Of this the Gospel supplies an example. King Herod, bound by a rash oath, gave to a dancing girl the head of John the Baptist as a reward for her dancing. Such was also the oath taken by the Jews, who, as we read in the Acts of the Apostles, bound themselves by oath not to eat, until they had killed Paul.

Lawfulness Of Oaths

These explanations having been given, there can be no doubt that they who observe the above conditions and who guard their oaths with these qualities as with bulwarks, may swear with a safe conscience.

This is easily established by many proofs. For the law of God, which is pure and holy, commands: Thou shalt fear the Lord thy God, and shalt serve him only, and thou shalt swear by his name. All they, writes David, shall be praised that swear by him.

The Scriptures also inform us that the most holy Apostles, the lights of the Church, sometimes made use of oaths, as appears from the Epistles of the Apostle.

Even the Angels sometimes swear. The angel, writes St. John in the Apocalypse, swore by him who lives for ever.

Nay, God Himself, the Lord of Angels, swears, and, as we read in many passages of the Old Testament, has confirmed His. promises with an oath. This He did to Abraham and to David. Of the oath sworn by God David says: The Lord hath sworn, and he will not repent: thou art a priest for ever according to the order of Melchisedech.

In fact, if we consider the whole matter attentively, and examine the origin and purpose of an oath, it can be no difficult matter to explain the reasons why it is a laudable act.

An oath has its origin in faith, by which men believe God to be the author of all truth, who can never deceive others nor be deceived, to whose eyes all things are naked and open, who, in fine, superintends all human affairs with an admirable providence, and governs the world. Filled with this faith we appeal to God as a witness of the truth, as a witness whom it would be wicked and impious to distrust.

With regard to the end of an oath, its scope and intent is to establish the justice and innocence of man, and to terminate disputes and contests. This is the doctrine of the Apostle in his Epistle to the Hebrews.

An Objection Against Oaths

Nor does this doctrine at all clash with these words of the Redeemer, recorded in St. Matthew: You have heard that it was said to them of old: "Thou shalt not foreswear thyself, but thou shalt perform thy oaths to the Lord"; but I say to you not to swear at all; neither by heaven, for it is the throne of God; neither by the earth, for it is his footstool; nor by Jerusalem, for it is the city of the great king; neither shalt thou swear by thy head, because thou canst not make one hair white or black. But let your speech be "yea, yea"; "no, no"; and that which is over and above these is of evil.

It cannot be asserted that these words condemn oaths universally and under all circumstances, since we have already seen that the Apostles and our Lord Himself made frequent use of them. The object of our Lord was rather to reprove the perverse opinion of the Jews, who had persuaded themselves that the only thing to be avoided in an oath was a lie. Hence in matters the most trivial and unimportant they did not hesitate to make frequent use of oaths, and to exact them from others. This practice the Redeemer condemns and reprobates, and teaches that an oath is never to be taken unless necessity require it. For oaths have been instituted on account of human frailty. They are really the outcome of evil, being a sign either of the inconstancy of him who takes them, or of the obstinacy of him who refuses to believe without them. However, an oath can be justified by necessity.

When our Lord says: Let your speech be "yea, yea"; "no, no," He evidently forbids the habit of swearing in familiar conversation and on trivial matters. He therefore admonishes us particularly against being too ready and willing to swear; and this should be carefully explained and impressed on the minds of the faithful. That countless evils grow out of the unrestrained habit of swearing is proved by the evidence of Scripture, and the testimony of the most holy Fathers. Thus we read in Ecclesiasticus: Let not thy mouth be accustomed to swearing, for in it there are many falls; and again: A man that sweareth much shall be filled with iniquity, and a scourge shall not depart from his house. In the works of St. Basil and St. Augustine against lying, much more can be found on this subject.

Negative Part of this Commandment

So far we have considered what this Commandment requires. It now remains to speak of what it prohibits; namely, to take the name of God in vain. It is clear that he who swears rashly and without deliberation commits a grave sin. That this is a most serious sin is declared by the words: Thou shalt not take the name of thy God in vain, which seem to assign the reason why this crime is so wicked and heinous; namely, that it derogates from the majesty of Him whom we profess to recognise as our Lord and our God. This Commandment, therefore, forbids to swear falsely, because he who does not shrink from so great a crime as to appeal to God to witness falsehood, offers a grievous Injury to God, charging Him either with ignorance, as though the truth of any matter could be unknown to Him, or with malice and dishonesty, as though God could bear testimony to falsehood.

Various Ways In Which Cod's Name Is Dishonoured: False Oaths

Among false swearers are to be numbered not only those who affirm as true what they know to be false, but also those who swear to what is really true, believing it to be false. For since the essence of a lie consists in speaking contrary to one's belief and conviction, these persons are evidently guilty of a lie, and of perjury.

On the same principle, he who swears to that which he thinks to be true, but which is really false, also incurs the guilt of perjury, unless he has used proper care and diligence to arrive at a full knowledge of the matter. Although he-swears according to his belief, he nevertheless sins against this Commandment.

Again, he who binds himself by oath to the performance of anything, not intending to fulfil his promise, or, having had the intention, neglect its performance, guilty of the same sin. This equally applies to those who, having bound themselves to God by vow, neglect its fulfilment.

Unjust Oaths

This Commandment is also violated, if justice, which is one of the three conditions of an oath, be wanting. Hence he who swears to commit a mortal sin, for example, to perpetrate murder, violates this Commandment, even though he speak seriously and from his heart, and his oath possess what we before pointed out as the first condition of every oath, that is, truth.

To these are to be added oaths sworn through a sort of contempt, such as an oath not to observe the Evangelical counsels, such as celibacy and poverty. None, it is true, are obliged to embrace these divine counsels, but by swearing not to observe them, one contemns and despises them.

Rash Oaths

This Commandment is also sinned against, and judgment is violated when one swears to what is true and what he believes to be true if his motives are light conjectures and far-fetched reasons. For, notwithstanding its truth, such an oath is not unmixed with a sort of falsehood, seeing that he who swears with such indifference exposes himself to extreme danger of perjury.

Oaths By False Gods

To swear by false gods is likewise to swear falsely. What more opposed to truth than to appeal to lying and false deities as to the true God?

Irreverent Speech

Scripture when it prohibits perjury, says: Thou shalt not profane the name of thy God, thereby forbidding all irreverence towards all other things to which, in accordance with this Commandment, reverence is due. Of this nature is the Word of God, the majesty of which has been revered not only by the pious, but also sometimes by the impious, as is narrated in Judges of Eglon, King of the Moabites.

But he who, to support heresy and the teaching of the wicked. distorts the Sacred Scriptures from their genuine and true meaning, is guilty of the greatest injury to the Word of God; and against this crime we are warned by these words of the Prince of the Apostles: There are certain things hard to be understood. which the unlearned and unstable wrest, as they do also the other Scriptures, to their own destruction.

It is also a foul and shameful contamination of the Scripture, that wicked men pervert the words and sentences which it contains, and which should be honoured with all reverence, turning them to profane purposes, such as scurrility, fable, vanity, flattery, detraction, divination, satire and the like -- crimes which the Council of Trent commands to be severely punished.

Neglect Of Prayer

In the next place, as they honour God who, in their affliction implore His help, so they, who do not invoke His aid, deny Him due honour; and these David rebukes when he says: They have not called upon the Lord, they trembled for fear where there was no fear.

Blasphemy

Still more enormous is the guilt of those who, with impure and defiled lips, dare to curse or blaspheme the holy name of God-that name which is to be blessed and praised above measure by all creatures, or even the names of the Saints who reign with Him in glory.' So atrocious and horrible is this crime that the Sacred Scriptures, sometimes when speaking of blasphemy use the word blessing.

Sanction of this Commandment

As, however, the dread of punishment has often a powerful effect in checking the tendency to sin, the pastor, in order the more effectively to move the minds of men and the more easily to induce to an observance of this Commandment, should diligently explain the remaining words, which are, as it were, its appendix: For the Lord will not hold him guiltless that shall take the name of the Lord his God in vain.

In the first place (the pastor) should teach that with very good reason has God joined threats to this Commandment. From this is understood both the grievousness of sin and the goodness of God toward us, since far from rejoicing in man's destruction, He deters us by these salutary threats from incurring His anger, doubtless in order that we may experience His kindness rather than His wrath. The pastor should urge and insist on this consideration with greatest earnestness. in order that the faithful may be made sensible of the grievousness of the crime, may detest it still more, and may employ increased care and caution to avoid its commission.

He should also observe how prone men are to this sin, since it was not sufficient to give the command, but also necessary to accompany it with threats. The advantages to be derived from this thought are indeed incredible; for as nothing is more injurious than a listless security, so the knowledge of our own weakness is most profitable.

He should next show that God has appointed no particular punishment. The threat is general; it declares that whoever is guilty of this crime shall not escape unpunished. The various chastisements, therefore, with which we are every day visited, should warn us against this sin. It is easy to conjecture that men are afflicted with heavy calamities because they violate this Commandment; and if these things are called to their attention, it is likely that they will be more careful for the future.

Deterred, therefore, by a holy dread, the faithful should use every exertion to avoid this sin. If for every idle word that men shall speak, they shall render an account on the day of judgment, what shall we say of those heinous crimes which involve great contempt of the divine name?

THIRD COMMANDMENT : "*Remember that thou keep holy the sabbath day. Six days shalt thou labour, and do all thy works; but on the seventh day is the sabbath of the lord thy god; thou shalt do no work on it, neither thou nor thy son, nor thy daughter, nor thy man-servant, nor thy maid-servant, nor thy beast, nor the stranger that is within thy gates. For in six days the lord made heaven and earth, and the sea, and all things that are in them, and rested on the seventh day; wherefore the lord blessed the seventh day and sanctified it.*"

Reasons For This Commandment

This Commandment of the Law rightly and in due order prescribes the external worship which we owe to God; for it is, as it were, a consequence of the preceding Commandment. For if we sincerely and devoutly worship God, guided by the faith and hope we have in Him, we cannot but honour Him with external worship and thanksgiving. Now since we cannot easily discharge these duties while occupied in worldly affairs, a certain fixed time has been set aside so that it may be conveniently performed.

Importance Of Instruction On This Commandment

The observance of this Commandment is attended with wondrous fruit and advantage. Hence it is of the highest importance for the pastor to use the utmost diligence in its exposition. The word Remembers with which the Commandment commences, must animate him to zeal in this matter; for if the faithful are bound to remember this Commandment, it becomes the duty of the pastor to recall it frequently to their minds in exhortation and instruction.

The importance of its observance for the faithful may be inferred from the consideration that those who carefully comply with it are more easily induced to keep all the other Commandments. For among the other works which are necessary on holydays, the faithful are bound to assemble in the church to hear the Word of God. When they have thus learned the divine justifications, they will be disposed to observe, with their whole heart, the law of the Lord. Hence the sanctification and observance of the Sabbath is very often commanded in Scripture, as may be seen in Exodus, Leviticus, Deuteronomy, and in the prophecies of Isaias, Jeremias," and Ezechiel, all of which contain this precept on the observance of the Sabbath.

Rulers and magistrates should be admonished and exhorted to lend the sanction and support of their authority to the pastors of the Church, particularly in upholding and extending the worship of God, and in commanding obedience to the injunctions of the priests.

How The Third Differs From The Other Commandments

With regard to the exposition of this Commandment, the faithful are carefully to be taught how it agrees with, and how it differs from the others, in order that they may understand why we observe and keep holy not Saturday but Sunday.

The point of difference is evident. The other Commandments of the Decalogue are precepts of the natural law, obligatory at all times and unalterable. Hence, after the abrogation of the Law of Moses, all the Commandments contained in the two tables are observed by Christians, not indeed because their observance is commanded by Moses, but because they are in conformity with nature which dictates obedience to them.

This Commandment about the observance of the Sabbath, on the other hand, considered as to the time appointed for its fulfilment, is not fixed and unalterable, but susceptible of change, and belongs not to the moral, but the ceremonial law. Neither is it a principle of the natural law; we are not instructed by nature to give external worship to God on that day, rather than on any other. And in fact the Sabbath was kept holy only from the time of the liberation of the people of Israel from the bondage of Pharaoh. The observance of the Sabbath was to be abrogated at the same time as the other Hebrew rites and ceremonies, that is, at the death of Christ. Having been, as it were, images which foreshadowed the light and the truth, these ceremonies were to disappear at the coming of that light and truth, which is Jesus Christ. Hence St. Paul, in his Epistle to the Galatians, when reproving the observers of the Mosaic rites, says: You observe days and months and times and years; I am afraid of you lest perhaps I have laboured in vain amongst you. And he writes to the same effect to the Colossians.

So much regarding the difference (between this and the other Commandments) .

How The Third Is Like The Other Commandments

This Commandment is like the others, not in so far as it is a precept of the ceremonial law, but only as it is a natural and moral precept. The worship of God and the practice of religion, which it comprises, have the natural law for their basis. Nature prompts us to give some time to the worship of God. This is demonstrated by the fact that we find among all nations public festivals consecrated to the solemnities of religion and divine worship.

As nature requires some time to be given to necessary functions of the body, to sleep, repose and the like, so she also requires that some time be devoted to the mind, to refresh itself by the contemplation of God. Hence, since some time should be devoted to the worship of the Deity and to the practice of religion, this (Commandment) doubtless forms part of the moral law.

The Jewish Sabbath Changed To Sunday By The Apostles

The Apostles therefore resolved to consecrate the first day of the week to the divine worship, and called it the Lord's day. St. John in the Apocalypse makes mention of the Lord's day; and the Apostle commands collections to be made on the first day of the week, that is, according to the interpretation of St. Chrysostom, on the Lord's day. From all this we learn that even then the Lord's day was kept holy in the Church.

Four Parts Of This Commandment

In order that the faithful may know what they are to do and what to avoid on the Lord's day, it will not be foreign to his purpose, if the pastor, dividing the Commandment into its four natural parts, explain each word of it carefully.

First Part of this Commandment

In the first place, then, he should explain generally the meaning of these words: Remember that thou keep holy the sabbath day.

"Remember"

The word remember is appropriately made use of at the beginning of the Commandment to signify that the sanctification of that particular day belonged to the ceremonial law. Of this it would seem to have been necessary to remind the people; for, although the law of nature commands us to devote a certain portion of time to the external worship to God, it fixes no particular day for the performance of this duty.

They are also to be taught, that from these words we may learn how we should employ our time during the week; that we are to keep constantly in view the Lord's day, on which we are, as it were, to render an account to God for our occupations and conduct; and that therefore our works should be such as not to be unacceptable in the sight of God, or, as it is written, be to us an occasion of grief, and a scruple of heart.

Finally, we are taught, and the instruction demands our serious attention, that there will not be wanting occasions which may lead to a forgetfulness of this Commandment, such as the evil example of others who neglect its observance, and an inordinate love of amusements and sports, which frequently withdraw from the holy and religious observance of the Lord's day.

Sabbath

We now come to the meaning of the word sabbath. Sabbath is a Hebrew word which signifies cessation. To keep the Sabbath, therefore, means to cease from labor and to rest. In this sense the seventh day was called the Sabbath, because God, having finished the creation of the world, rested on that day from all the work which He had done. Thus it is called by the Lord in Exodus.

Later on, not only the seventh day, but, in honour of that day, the entire week was called by the same name; and in this meaning of the word, the Pharisee says in St. Luke: I fast twice in a sabbath. So much will suffice with regard to the signification of the word sabbath.

"Keep Holy"

In the Scriptures keeping holy the Sabbath means a cessation from bodily labor and from business, as is clear from the following words of the Commandment: Thou shalt do no work on it. But this is not all that it means; otherwise it would have been sufficient to say in Deuteronomy, Observe the day of the sabbath; but it is added, and sanctify it; and these additional words prove that the Sabbath is a day sacred to religion, set apart for works of piety and devotion.

We sanctify the Sabbath fully and perfectly, therefore, when we offer to God works of piety and religion. This is evidently the Sabbath, which Isaias calls delightful; for festivals are, as it were, the delight of God and of pious men. And if to this religious and holy observance of the Sabbath we add works of mercy, the rewards promised us in the same chapter are numerous and most important.

The true and proper meaning, therefore, of this Commandment tends to this, that we take special care to set apart some fixed time, when, disengaged from bodily labor and worldly affairs, we may devote our whole being, soul and body, to the religious veneration of God.

Second Part of this Commandment

The second part of the precept declares that the seventh day was consecrated by God to His worship; for it is written: Six days shalt thou labour, and do all thy works; but on the seventh day is the sabbath of the Lord thy God. From these words we learn that the Sabbath is consecrated to the Lord, that we are required on that day to render Him the duties of religion, and to know that the seventh day is a sign of the Lord's rest.

"The Seventh Day Is The Sabbath Of The Lord Thy God"

This particular day was fixed for the worship of God, because it would not have been well to leave to a rude people the choice of a time of worship, lest, perhaps, they might have imitated the festivals of the Egyptians.

The last day of the week was, therefore, chosen for the worship of God, and in this there is much that is symbolic. Hence in Exodus,' and in Ezechiel the Lord calls it a sign: See that you keep my sabbath because it is a sign between me and you in your generation, that you may know that I am the Lord who sanctify you.

It was a sign that man should dedicate and sanctify himself to God, since even the very day is devoted to Him. For the holiness of the day consists in this, that on it men are bound in a special manner to practice holiness and religion.

It was also a sign, and, as it were, a memorial of the stupendous work of the creation. Furthermore, to the Jews it was a traditional sign, reminding them that they had been delivered by the help of God from the galling yoke of Egyptian bondage. This the Lord Himself declares in these words: Remember that thou also didst serve in Egypt, and the Lord thy God brought thee out from thence with a strong hand and a stretched out arm. Therefore hath he commanded thee that thou shouldst observe the sabbath day.

It is also a sign of a spiritual and celestial sabbath. The spiritual sabbath consists in a holy and mystical rest, wherein the old man being buried with Christ, is renewed to life and carefully applies himself to act in accordance with the spirit of Christian piety. For those who were once darkness but are now light in the Lord, should walk as children of the light, in all goodness and justice and truth, having no fellowship with the unfruitful works of darkness.

The celestial sabbath, as St. Cyril observes on these words of the Apostle, There remaineth therefore a day of rest for the people of God, is that life in which, living with Christ, we shall enjoy all good, when sin shall be eradicated, according to the words: No lion shall be there, nor shall any mischievous beast go up by it, nor be found there; but a path shall be there, and it shall be called the holy way; for in the vision of God the souls of the Saints obtain every good. The pastor therefore should exhort and animate the faithful in the words: Let us hasten therefore to enter into that rest.

Other Festivals Observed By The Jews

Besides the seventh day, the Jews observed other festivals and holydays, instituted by the divine law to awaken the recollection of the principal favours (conferred on them by the Almighty).

The Sabbath, Why Changed To Sunday

But the Church of God has thought it well to transfer the celebration and observance of the Sabbath to Sunday.

For, as on that day light first shone on the world, so by the Resurrection of our Redeemer on the same day, by whom was thrown open to us the gate to eternal life, we were called out of darkness into light; and hence the Apostles would have it called the Lord's day.

We also learn from the Sacred Scriptures that the first day of the week was held sacred because on that day the work of creation commenced, and on that day the Holy Ghost was given to the Apostles.

Other Festivals Observed By The Church

From the very infancy of the Church and in the following centuries other days were also appointed by the Apostles and the holy Fathers, in order to commemorate the benefits bestowed by God. Among these days to be kept sacred the most solemn are those which were instituted to honour the mysteries of our redemption. In the next place are the days which are dedicated to the most Blessed Virgin Mother, to the Apostles, Martyrs and other Saints who reign with Christ. In the celebration of their victories the divine power and goodness are praised, due honour is paid to their memories, and the faithful are encouraged to imitate them.

"Six Days Shalt Thou Labour And Do All Thy Work"

And as the observance of the precept is very strongly assisted by these words: Six days shalt thou labour, but on the seventh day is the sabbath of God, the pastor should therefore carefully explain them to the people. For from these words it can be gathered that the faithful are to be exhorted not to spend their lives in indolence and sloth, but that each one, mindful of the words of the Apostle, should do his own business, and work with his own hands, as he had commanded them.

These words also enjoin as a duty commanded by God that in six days we do all our works, lest we defer to a festival what should have been done during the other days of the week, thereby distracting the attention from the things of God.

Third Part of this Commandment

The third part of the Commandment comes next to be explained. It points out, to a certain extent, the manner in which we are to keep holy the Sabbath day, and explains particularly what we are forbidden to do on that day.

Works Forbidden

Thou shalt do no work on it, says the Lord, thou, nor thy son, nor thy daughter, nor thy man-servant, nor thy maid-servant, nor thy beast, nor the stranger that is within thy gates.

These words teach us, in the first place, to avoid whatever may interfere with the worship of God. Hence it is not difficult to perceive that all servile works are forbidden, not because they are improper or evil in themselves, but because they withdraw the attention from the worship of God, which is the great end of the Commandment.

The faithful should be still more careful to avoid sin, which not only withdraws the mind from the contemplation of divine things, but entirely alienates us from the love of God.

Works Permitted

But whatever regards the celebration of divine worship, such as the decoration of the altar or church on occasion of some festival, and the like, although servile works, are not prohibited; and hence our Lord says: The priests in the temple break the sabbath, and are without blame.

Neither are we to suppose that this Commandment forbids attention to those things on a feast day, which, if neglected, will be lost; for this is expressly permitted by the sacred canons.

There are many other things which our Lord in the Gospel declares lawful on festivals and which may be seen by the pastor in St. Matthew and St. John.

Why Animals Are Not To Be Employed On The Sabbath

To omit nothing that may interfere with the sanctification of the Sabbath, the Commandment mentions beasts of burden, because their use will prevent its due observance. If beasts be employed on the Sabbath, human labor also becomes necessary to direct them; for they do not labor alone, but assist the labours of man. Now it is not lawful for man to work on that day. Hence it is not lawful for the animals to work which man uses.

But the Commandment has also another purpose. For. if God commands the exemption of cattle from labor on the Sabbath, still more imperative is the obligation to avoid all acts of inhumanity towards servants, or others whose labor and industry we employ.

Works Commanded Or Recommended

The pastor should also not omit carefully to teach what works and actions Christians should perform on festival days. These are: to go to church, and there, with heartfelt piety and devotion, to assist at the celebration of the Holy Sacrifice of the Mass; and to approach frequently the Sacraments of the Church, instituted for our salvation in order to obtain a remedy for the wounds of the soul.

Nothing can be more seasonable or salutary for Christians than frequent recourse to confession; and to this the pastor will be enabled to exhort the faithful by using the instructions and proofs which have been explained in their own place on the Sacrament of Penance.

But not only should he urge his people to have recourse to that Sacrament, he should also zealously exhort them again and again to approach frequently the Holy Sacrament of the Eucharist.

The faithful should also listen with attention and reverence to sermons. Nothing is more intolerable, nothing more unworthy than to despise the words of Christ, or hear them with indifference.

Likewise the faithful should give themselves to frequent prayer and the praises of God; and an object of their special attention should be to learn those things which pertain to a Christian life, and to practice with care the duties of piety, such as giving alms to the poor and needy, visiting the sick, and administering consolation to the sorrowful and afflicted. Religion clean and undefiled before God and the Father is this, says St. James, to visit the fatherless and widows in their tribulation.

From what has been said it is easy to perceive how this Commandment may be violated.

Motives for the Observance of this Commandment

It is also a duty of the pastor to have ready at hand certain main arguments by which he may especially persuade the people to observe this Commandment with all zeal and the greatest exactitude.

Reasonableness Of This Duty

To the attainment of this end it will materially conduce, if the people understand and clearly see how just and reasonable it is to devote certain days exclusively to the worship of God in order to acknowledge, adore, and venerate our Lord from whom we have received such innumerable and inestimable blessings.

Had He commanded us to offer Him every day the tribute of religious worship, would it not be our duty, in return for His inestimable and infinite benefits towards us, to endeavour to obey the command with promptitude and alacrity? But now that the days consecrated to His worship are but few, there is no excuse for neglecting or reluctantly performing this duty, which moreover obliges under grave sin.

The Observance Of This Commandment Brings Many Blessings

The pastor should next point out the excellence of this precept. Those who are faithful in its observance are admitted, as it were, into the divine presence to speak freely with God; for in prayer we contemplate the divine majesty, and commune with Him; in hearing religious instruction, we hear the voice of God, which reaches us through the agency of those who devoutly preach on divine things; and at the Holy Sacrifice of the Mass, we adore Christ the Lord, present on our altars. Such are the blessings which they preeminently enjoy who faithfully observe this Commandment.

Neglect Of This Commandment A Great Crime

But those who altogether neglect its fulfilment resist God and His Church; they heed not God's command, and are enemies of Him and His holy laws, of which the easiness of the command is itself a proof. We should, it is true, be prepared to undergo the severest labor for the sake of God; but in this Commandment He imposes on us no labor; He only commands us to rest and disengage ourselves from worldly cares on those days which are to be kept holy. To refuse obedience to this Commandment is, therefore, a proof of extreme boldness; and the punishments with which its infraction has been visited by God, as we learn from the Book of Numbers,' should be a warning to us.

In order, therefore, to avoid offending God in this way, we should frequently ponder this word: Remember, and should place before our minds the important advantages and blessings which, as we have already seen, flow from the religious observance of holydays, and also numerous other considerations of the same tendency, which the good and zealous pastor should develop at considerable length to his people as circumstances may require.

THE FOURTH COMMANDMENT : *"Honour thy father and thy mother, that thou mayest be long lived upon the land which the lord thy god will give thee."*

Relative Importance Of The Preceding And The Following Commandments

The preceding Commandments are supreme both in dignity and in importance; but those which follow rank next in order because of their necessity. For the first three tend directly to God; while the object of the others is the charity we owe to our neighbour, although even these are ultimately referred to God, since we love our neighbour on account of God, our last end. Hence Christ our Lord has declared that the two Commandments which inculcate the love of God and of our neighbour are like unto each other.

Importance Of Instruction On The Fourth Commandment

The advantages arising from the present subject can scarcely be expressed in words; for not only does it bring with it its own fruit, and that in the richest abundance and of superior excellence, but it also affords a test of our obedience to and observance of the first Commandment. He that loveth not his brother whom he seeth, says St. John, how can he love God whom he seeth not? In like manner, if we do not honour and reverence our parents whom we ought to love next to God and whom we continually see, how can we honour or reverence God, the supreme and best of parents, whom we see not? Hence we can easily perceive the similarity between these two Commandments.

The application of this Commandment is of very great extent. Besides our natural parents, there are many others whose power, rank, usefulness, exalted functions or office, entitle them to parental honour.

Furthermore.(this Commandment) lightens the labor of parents and superiors; for their chief care is that those under them should live according to virtue and the divine Law. Now the performance of this duty will be considerably facilitated, if it be known by all that highest honour to parents is an obligation, sanctioned and commanded by God.

The Two Tables Of The Law

To impress the mind with this truth it will be found useful to distinguish the Commandments of the first, from those of the second table. This distinction, therefore, the pastor should first explain.

Let him begin by showing that the divine precepts of the Decalogue were written on two tables, one of which, in the opinion of the holy Fathers, contained the three preceding, while the rest were given on the second table.

This order of the Commandments is especially appropriate, since the very collocation points out to us their difference in nature. For whatever is commanded or prohibited in Scripture by the divine law springs from one of two principles, the love of God or of our neighbour: one or the other of these is the basis of every duty required of us. The three preceding Commandments teach us the love which we owe to God; and the other seven, the duties which we owe to our neighbour and to public society. The arrangement, therefore, which assigns some of the Commandments to the first and others to the second table is not without good reason.

In the first three Commandments, which have been explained, God, the supreme good, is, as it were, the subject matter; in the others, it is the good of our neighbour. The former require the highest love, the latter the love next to the highest. The former have to do with our last end, the latter with those things that lead us to our end.

Again, the love of God terminates in God Himself, for God is to be loved above all things for His own sake; but the love of our neighbour originates in, and is to be regulated by, the love of God. If we love our parents, obey our masters, respect our superiors, our ruling principle in doing so should be that God is their Creator, and wishes to give pre-eminence to those by whose cooperation He governs and protects other men; and as He requires that we yield a dutiful respect to such persons, we should do so, because He deems them worthy of this honour. If, then, we honour our parents, the tribute is paid to God rather than to man. Accordingly we read in St. Matthew concerning duty to superiors: He that receiveth you, receiveth me; and the Apostle in his Epistle to the Ephesians, giving instruction to servants, says: Servants, be obedient to them that are your lords according to the flesh, with fear and trembling, in the simplicity of your heart, as to Christ: not serving to the eye, as it were pleasing men, but as the servants of Christ.

Moreover, no honour, no piety, no devotion can be rendered to God sufficiently worthy of Him, since love of Him admits of infinite increase. Hence our charity should become every day more fervent towards Him, who commands us to love Him with our whole heart, our whole soul, and with all our strength. The love of our neighbour, on the contrary, has its limits, for the Lord commands us to love our neighbour as ourselves.

To outstep these limits by loving our neighbour as we love God would be an enormous crime. If any man come to me, says the Lord and hate not his father and mother, and wife and children, and brethren and sisters, yea, and his own life also; he cannot be my disciple. In the same way, to one who would first attend the burial of his father, and then follow Christ, it was said: Let the dead bury their dead; and the same lesson is more clearly conveyed in St. Matthew: He that loveth father or mother more than me, is not worthy of me.

Parents, no doubt, are to be highly loved and respected; but religion requires that supreme honour and homage be given to Him alone, who is the Creator and Father of all, and that all our love for our earthly parents be referred to our eternal Father who is in heaven. Should, however, the injunctions of parents be at any time opposed to the Commandments of God, children are, o{ course, to prefer the will of God to the desires of their parents, always keeping in view the divine maxim: We ought to obey God rather than men.

Explanation of the Fourth Commandment: "Honour"

After these preliminaries the pastor should explain the words of the Commandment, beginning with honour. To honour is to think respectfully of anyone, and to hold in the highest esteem all that relates to him. It includes love, respect, obedience and reverence.

Very properly, then, is the word honour used here in preference to the word fear or love, although parents are also to be much loved and feared. Respect and reverence are not always the accompaniments of love; neither is love the inseparable companion of fear; but honour, when proceeding from the heart, combines both fear and love.

"Thy Father"

The pastor should next explain who they are, whom the Commandment designates as fathers; for although the law refers primarily to our natural fathers, yet the name belongs to others also, and these seem to be indicated in the Commandment, as we can easily gather from numerous passages of Scripture. Besides our natural fathers, then, there are others who in Scripture are called fathers, as was said above, and to each of these proper honour is due.

In the first place, the prelates of the Church, her pastors and priests are called fathers, as is evident from the Apostle, who, writing to the Corinthians, says: I write not these things to confound you; but I admonish you as my dearest children. For if you have ten thousand instructors in Christ, yet not many fathers. For in Christ Jesus by the gospel I have begotten you. It is also written in Ecclesiasticus: Let us praise men of renown, and our fathers in their generation.

Those who govern the State, to whom are entrusted power, magistracy, or command, are also called fathers; thus Naaman was called father by his servants.

The name father is also applied to those to whose care, fidelity, probity and wisdom others are committed, such as teachers, instructors masters and guardians; and hence the sons of the Prophets called Elias and Eliseus their father. Finally, aged men, advanced in years, we also call fathers.

Why Parents Should Be Honoured

In his instructions the pastor should chiefly emphasise the obligation of honouring all who are entitled to be called fathers, especially our natural fathers, of whom the divine Commandment particularly speaks. They are, so to say, images of the immortal God. In them we behold a picture of our own origin; from them we have received existence, them God made use of to infuse into us a soul and reason, by them we were led to the Sacraments, instructed in our religion, schooled in right conduct and holiness, and trained in civil and human knowledge.

"And Thy Mother"

The pastor should teach that the name mother is mentioned in this Commandment, in order to remind us of her benefits and claims in our regard, of the care and solicitude with which she bore us, and of the pain and labor with which she gave us birth and brought us up.

Manner Of Honouring Parents

The honour which children are commanded to pay to their parents should be the spontaneous offering of sincere and dutiful love. This is nothing more than their due, since for love of us, they shrink from no labor, no exertion, no danger. Their highest pleasure it is to fed that they are loved by their children, the dearest objects of their affection. Joseph, when he enjoyed in Egypt the highest station and the most ample power after the king himself, received with honour his father, who had come into Egypt. Solomon rose to meet his mother as she approached; and having paid her respect, placed her on a royal throne on his right hand.

We also owe to our parents other duties of respect, such as to supplicate God in their behalf, that they may lead prosperous and happy lives, beloved and esteemed by all who know them, and most pleasing in the sight of God and of the Saints in heaven.

We also honour them by submission to their wishes and inclinations. My son, says Solomon, hear the instruct-on of thy father, and forsake not the law of thy mother; that grace may be added to thy head, and a chain of gold to thy neck. Of the same kind are the exhortations of St. Paul. Children, he says, obey your parents in the Lord, for this is just; and also, children, obey your parents in all things, for this is well-pleasing to the Lord. (This doctrine) is confirmed by the example of the holiest men. Isaac, when bound for sacrifice by his father, meekly and uncomplainingly obeyed; and the Rechabites, not to depart from the counsel of their father, always abstained from wine.

We also honour our parents by the imitation of their good example; for, to seek to resemble closely anyone is the highest mark of esteem towards him. We also honour them when we not only ask, but follow their advice.

Again we honour our parents when we relieve their necessities, supplying them with necessary food and clothing according to these words of Christ, who, when reproving the impiety of the Pharisees, said: Why do you also transgress the commandments of God because of your traditions? For God said: "Honour thy father and thy mother," and "He that shall curse father or mother let him die the death." But you say: "Whosoever shall say to his father or mother, The gift whatsoever proceedeth from me, shall profit thee." And he shall not honour his father or his mother; and you have made void the commandment of God for your tradition.

But if at all times it is our duty to honour our parents, this duty becomes still more imperative when they are visited by severe illness. We should then see to it that they do not neglect confession and the other Sacraments which every Christian should receive at the approach of death. We should also see that pious and religious persons visit them frequently to strengthen their weakness, assist them by their counsel, and animate them to the hope of immortality, that having risen above the concerns of this world, they may fix their thoughts entirely on God. Thus blessed with the sublime virtues of faith, hope and charity, and fortified by the helps. of religion, they will not only look at death without fear, since it is necessary, but will even welcome it, as it hastens their entrance into eternity.

Finally, we honour our parents, even after their death, by attending their funerals, procuring for them suitable obsequies and burial, having due suffrages and anniversary Masses offered for them, and faithfully executing their last wills.

Manner Of Honouring Other Superiors

We are bound to honour not only our natural parents, but also others who are called fathers, such as Bishops and priests, kings, princes and magistrates, tutors, guardians and masters, teachers, aged persons and the like, all of whom are entitled, some in a greater, some in a less degree, to share our love, our obedience, and our assistance.

The Honour Due To Bishops And Priests

Of Bishops and other pastors it is written: Let the priests that rule well be esteemed worthy of double honour especially they who labour in the word and doctrine.

What wondrous proofs of love for the Apostle must the Galatians have shown ! For he bears this splendid testimony of their benevolence: I bear you witness that if it could be done, you would hove plucked out your own eyes, and would have given them to me.

The priest is also entitled to receive whatever is necessary for his support. Who, says the Apostle, serveth as a soldier at his own charges? Give honour to the priests, it is written in Ecclesiasticus, and purify thyself with thy arms; give them their portion, as it is commanded thee, of the first fruits and of purifications.

The Apostle also teaches that they are entitled to obedience: Obey your prelates, and be subject to them; for they watch as being to render an account of your souls. Nay, more. Christ the Lord commands obedience even to wicked pastors: Upon the chair of Moses have sitten the scribes and Pharisees: all things, therefore, whatsoever they shall say to you, observe and do; but according to their works do ye not, for they say and do not.

The Honour Due To Civil Rulers

The same is to be said of civil rulers, governors, magistrates and others to whose authority we are subject. The Apostle in his Epistle to the Romans, explains at length the honour, respect and obedience that should be shown them, and he also bids us to pray for them. St. Peter says: Be ye subject, therefore, to every human creature for God's sake; whether it be to the king as excelling, or to governors as sent by him.

For whatever honour we show them is given to God, since exalted human dignity deserves respect because it is an image of the divine power, and in it we revere the providence of God who has entrusted to men the care of public affairs and who uses them as the instruments of His power.

If we sometimes have wicked and unworthy officials it is not their faults that we revere, but the authority from God which they possess. Indeed, while it may seem strange, we are not excused from highly honouring them even when they show themselves hostile and implacable towards us. Thus David rendered great services to Saul even when the latter was his bitter foe, and to this he alludes when he says: With them that hated peace I was peaceable.

However, should their commands be wicked or unjust, they should not be obeyed, since in such a case they rule not according to their rightful authority, but according to injustice and perversity.

'That Thou Mayest be Long-lived,'' etc.

Having explained the above matters, the pastor should next consider the reward promised to the observance of this Commandment and its appropriateness. That reward is great, indeed, for it consists principally in length of days. They who always preserve the grateful remembrance of a benefit deserve to be blessed with its prolonged enjoyment. Children, therefore, who honour their parents, and gratefully acknowledge the blessing of life received from them are deservedly rewarded with the protracted enjoyment of that life to an advanced age.

Reward Promised For Observance Of This Commandment

The (nature of the) divine promise also demands distinct explanation. It includes not only the eternal life of the blessed, but also the life which we lead on earth, according to the interpretation of St. Paul: Piety is profitable to all things, having promise of the life that now is, and of that which is to come

Many very holy men, it is true, such as Job, David, Paul, desired to die, and a long life is burdensome to the afflicted and wretched: but the reward which is here promised is, notwithstanding, neither inconsiderable, nor to be despised.

The additional words, which the Lord thy God will give thee, promise not only length of days, but also repose, tranquillity, and security to live well; for in Deuteronomy it is not only said, that thou mayest live a long time, but it is also added, and that it may be well with thee, words afterwards quoted by the Apostle.

Why This Reward Is Not Always Conferred On Dutiful Children

These blessings, we say, are conferred on those whose piety God rewards; otherwise the divine promises would not be fulfilled, since the more dutiful child is sometimes the more short lived.

Now this happens sometimes because it is better for him to depart from this world before he has strayed from the path of virtue and of duty; for he was taken away lest wickedness should alter his understanding, or deceit beguile his soul. Or because destruction and general upheaval are impending, he is called away that he may escape the calamities of the times. The just man, says the Prophet, is taken away from before the face of evil, lest his virtue and salvation be endangered when God avenges the crimes of men. Or else, he is spared the bitter anguish of witnessing the calamities of his friends and relations in such evil days. The premature death of the good, therefore, gives special reason for fear.

Punishment For Violation Of This Commandment

But if God promises rewards and blessings to grateful children, He also reserves the heaviest chastisements to punish those who are wanting in filial piety; for it is written: He that curseth his father or mother shall die the death: He that afflicteth his father and chaseth away his mother, is infamous and unhappy." He that curseth his father and mother, his lamp shall be put out in the midst of darkness: The eye that mocketh at his father, and that despiseth the labour of his mother in bearing him, let the ravens of the brooks pick it out, and the young eagles eat it. There are on record many instances of undutiful children, who were made the signal objects of the divine vengeance. The disobedience of Absalom to his father David did not go unpunished. On account of his sin he perished miserably, transfixed by three lances.

Of those who resist the priest it is written: He that will be proud, and refuse to obey the commandment of the priest, who ministereth at that time to the Lord thy God, by the decree of the judge, that man shall die.

Duties of Parents Towards their Children

As the law of God commands children to honour, obey, and respect their parents so are there reciprocal duties which parents owe to their children. Parents are obliged to bring up their children in the knowledge and practice of religion, and to give them the best rules for the regulation of their lives; so that, instructed and trained in religion, they may serve God holily and constantly. It was thus, as we read, that the parents of Susanna acted.

The priest, therefore, should admonish parents to be to their children guides in the virtues of justice, chastity, modesty and holiness.

Three Things To Be Avoided By Parents

He should also admonish them to guard particularly against three things, in which they but too often transgress.

In the first place, they are not by words or actions to exercise too much harshness towards their children. This is the instruction of St. Paul in his Epistle to the Colossians: Fathers, he says, provoke not your children to anger, lest they be discouraged. For there is danger that the spirit of the child may be broken, and he become abject and fearful of everything. Hence (the pastor) should require parents to avoid too much severity and to choose rather to correct their children than to revenge themselves upon them.

Should a fault be committed which requires reproof and chastisement, the parent should not, on the other hand, by undue indulgence, overlook its correction. Children are often spoiled by too much lenity and indulgence on the part of their parents. The pastor, therefore, should deter from such excessive mildness by the warning example of Heli, the high-priest, who, on account of over-indulgence to his sons, was visited with the heaviest chastisements.

Finally, to avoid what is most shameful in the instruction and education of children, let them not propose to themselves aims that are unworthy. Many there are whose sole concern is to leave their children wealth, riches and an ample and splendid fortune; who encourage them not to piety and religion, or to honourable employment, but to avarice, and an increase of wealth, and who, provided their children are rich and wealthy, are regardless of their good name and eternal salvation. Can anything more shameful be thought or expressed? Of such parents it is true to say, that instead of bequeathing wealth to their children, they leave them rather their own wickedness and crimes for an inheritance; and instead of conducting them to heaven, lead them to the eternal torments of hell.

The priest, therefore, should impress on the minds of parents salutary principles and should exhort them to imitate the virtuous example of Tobias, that having properly trained up their children to the service of God and to holiness of life, they may, in turn, experience at their hands abundant fruit of filial affection, respect and obedience.

THE FIFTH COMMANDMENT : *"Thou shalt not kill"*

Importance Of Instruction On This Commandment

The great happiness proposed to the peacemakers, of being called the children of God, should prove a powerful incentive to the pastor to explain to the faithful with care and accuracy the obligations imposed by this Commandment. No means more efficacious can be adopted to promote peace among mankind, than the proper explanation of this Commandment and its holy and due observance by all. Then might we hope that men, united in the strictest bonds of union, would live in perfect peace and concord.

The necessity of explaining this Commandment is proved from the following. Immediately after the earth was overwhelmed in universal deluge, this was the first prohibition made by God to man. I will require the blood of your lives, He said, at the hand of every beast and at the hand of man. In the next place, among the precepts of the Old Law expounded by our Lord, this Commandment was mentioned first by Him; concerning which it is written in the Gospel of St. Matthew: It has been said thou shalt not kill, etc.

The faithful, on their part, should hear with willing attention the explanation of this Commandment, since its purpose is to protect the life of each one. These words, Thou shalt not kill, emphatically forbid homicide; and they should be heard by all with the same pleasure as if God, expressly naming each individual, were to prohibit injury to be offered him under a threat of the divine anger and the heaviest chastisements. As, then, the announcement of this Commandment must be heard with pleasure, so also should the avoidance of the sin which it forbids give pleasure.

Two Parts Of This Commandment

In the explanation of this Commandment the Lord points out its twofold obligation. The one is prohibitory and forbids us to kill; the other is mandatory and commands us to cherish sentiments of charity, concord and friendship towards our enemies, to have peace with all men, and finally, to endure with patience every inconvenience.

The Prohibitory Part of this Commandment

Exceptions: The Killing Of Animals

With regard to the prohibitory part, it should first be taught what kinds of killing are not forbidden by this Commandment. It is not prohibited to kill animals; for if God permits man to eat them, it is also lawful to kill them. When, says St. Augustine, we hear the words, "Thou shalt not kill," we do not understand this of the fruits of the earth, which are insensible, nor of irrational animals, which form no part of human society.

Execution Of Criminals

Another kind of lawful slaying belongs to the civil authorities, to whom is entrusted power of life and death, by the legal and judicious exercise of which they punish the guilty and protect the innocent. The just use of this power, far from involving the crime of murder, is an act of paramount obedience to this Commandment which prohibits murder. The end of the Commandment- is the preservation and security of human life.

Now the punishments inflicted by the civil authority, which is the legitimate avenger of crime, naturally tend to this end, since they give security to life by repressing outrage and violence. Hence these words of David: In the morning I put to death all the wicked of the land, that I might cut off all the workers of iniquity from the city of the Lord.

Killing In A Just War

In like manner, the soldier is guiltless who, actuated not by motives of ambition or cruelty, but by a pure desire of serving the interests of his country, takes away the life of an enemy in a just war.

Furthermore, there are on record instances of carnage executed by the special command of God. The sons of Levi, who put to death so many thousands in one day, were guilty of no sin; when the slaughter had ceased, they were addressed by Moses in these words: You have consecrated your hands this day to the Lord.

Killing By Accident

Again, death caused, not by intent or design, but by accident, is not murder. He that killeth his neighbour ignorantly, says the book of Deuteronomy, and who is proved to have had no hatred against him yesterday and the day before, but to have gone with him to the wood to hew wood, and in cutting down the tree the axe slipt out of his hand, and the iron slipping from the handle struck his friend and killed him, shall live. Such accidental deaths, because inflicted without intent or design, involve no guilt whatever, and this is confirmed by the words of St. Augustine: God forbid that what we do for a good and lawful end shall be imputed to us, if, contrary to our intention, evil thereby befall any one.

There are, however, two cases in which guilt attaches (to accidental death). The first case is when death results from an unlawful act; when, for instance, a person kicks or strikes a woman in a state of pregnancy, and abortion follows. The consequence, it is true, may not have been intended, but this does not exculpate the offender, because the act of striking a pregnant woman is in itself unlawful. The other case is when death is caused by negligence, carelessness or want of due precaution.

Killing In Self-Defence

If a man kill another in self-defence, having used every means consistent with his own safety to avoid the infliction of death, he evidently does not violate this Commandment.

Negative Part Of This Commandment Forbids Murder And Suicide

The above are the cases in which life may be taken without violating this Commandment; and with these exceptions all other killing is forbidden, whether we consider the person who kills, the person killed, or the means used to kill.

As to the person who kills, the Commandment recognises no exception whatever, be he rich or powerful, master or parent. All, without exception or distinction, are forbidden to kill.

With regard to the person killed, the law extends to all. There is no individual, however humble or lowly his condition, whose life is not shielded by this law.

It also forbids suicide. No man possesses such power over his own life as to be at liberty to put himself to death. Hence we find that the Commandment does not say: Thou shalt not kill another, but simply: Thou shalt not kill.

Finally, if we consider the numerous means by which murder may be committed, the law admits of no exception. Not only does it forbid to take away the life of another by laying violent hands on him, by means of a sword, a stone, a stick, a halter, or by administering poison; but also strictly prohibits the accomplishment of the death of another by counsel, assistance, help or any other means whatever.

Sinful Anger Is Also Forbidden By The Fifth Commandment

The Jews, with singular dullness of apprehension, thought that to abstain from taking life with their own hands was enough to satisfy the obligation imposed by this Commandment. But the Christian, instructed in the interpretation of Christ, has learned that the precept is spiritual, and that it commands us not only to keep our hands unstained, but our hearts pure and undefiled; hence what the Jews regarded as quite sufficient, is not sufficient at all. For the Gospel has taught that it is unlawful even to be angry with anyone: But I say to you that whosoever is angry with his brother, shall be in danger of the judgment. And whosoever shall say to his brother, "Raca," shall be in danger of the council. And whosoever shall say, "Thou fool," shall be in danger of hell fire. From these words it clearly follows that he who is angry with his brother is not free from sin, even though he conceals his resentment; that he who gives indication of his wrath sins grievously; and that he who does not hesitate to treat another with harshness, and to utter contumelious reproaches against him, sins still more grievously.

This, however, is to be understood of cases in which no just cause of anger exists. God and His laws permit us to be angry when we chastise the faults of those who are subject to us. For the anger of a Christian should spring from the Holy Spirit and not from carnal impulse, seeing that we should be temples of the Holy Ghost, in which Jesus Christ may dwell.

Our Lord has left us many other lessons of instruction with regard to the perfect observance of this law, such as Not to resist evil; but if one strike thee on thy right cheek, turn to him also the other. And if a man will contend with thee in judgment, and take away thy coat, let go thy cloak also unto him; and whosoever will force thee one mile, go with him two.

Remedies Against The Violation Of This Commandment

From what has been said, it is easy to see how inclined man is to those sins which are prohibited by this Commandment, and how many are guilty of murder, if not in fact, at least in desire. As, then, the Sacred Scriptures prescribe remedies for so dangerous a disease, the pastor should spare no pains in making them known to the faithful.

Of these remedies the most efficacious is to form a just conception of the wickedness of murder. The enormity of this sin is manifest from many and weighty passages of Holy Scripture. So much does God abominate homicide that He declares in Holy Writ that of the very beast of the field He will exact vengeance for the life of man, commanding the beast that injures man to be put to death. And if (the Almighty) commanded man to have a horror of blood,' He did so for no other reason than to impress on his mind the obligation of entirely refraining, both in act and desire, from the enormity of homicide.

The murderer is the worst enemy of his species, and consequently of nature. To the utmost of his power he destroys the universal work of God by the destruction of man, since God declares that He created all things for man's sake. Nay, as it is forbidden in Genesis to take human life, because God created man to his own image and likeness, he who makes away with God's image offers great injury to God, and almost seems to lay violent hands on God Himself!

David, thinking of this with a mind divinely illumined, complained bitterly of the bloodthirsty in these words: Their feet are swift to shed blood. He does not simply say, they kill, but, they shed blood, words which serve to mark the enormity of that execrable crime and to denote the barbarous cruelty of the murderer. With a view also to describe in particular how the murderer is precipitated by the impulse of the devil into the commission of such a crime, he says: Their feet are swift.

Positive Part of this commandment

Love Of Neighbour Inculcated

The mandatory part of this Commandment, as Christ our Lord enjoins, requires that we have peace with all men. Interpreting the Commandment He says: If therefore thou offer thy gift at the altar, and there thou remember that thy brother hath anything against thee; leave there thy offering before the altar, and go first to be reconciled to thy brother, and then coming thou shalt offer thy gift, etc.

Charity To All Commanded

In explaining this admonition, the pastor should show that it inculcates the duty of charity towards all without exception. In his instruction on the precept he should exhort the faithful as much as possible to the practice of this virtue, since it is especially included in this precept. For since hatred is clearly forbidden by this Commandment, as whosoever hateth his brother is a murderer, it follows, as an evident consequence, that the Commandment also inculcates charity and love.

Patience, Beneficence And Mildness Commanded

And since the Commandment inculcates charity and love, it must also enjoin all those duties and good offices which follow in their train. Charity is patient, says St. Paul. We are therefore commanded patience, in which, as the Redeemer teaches, we shall possess our souls. Charity is kind; beneficence is, therefore, the friend and companion of charity. The virtue of beneficence and kindness has a great range. Its principal offices are to relieve the wants of the poor, to feed the hungry, to give drink to the thirsty, to clothe the naked; and in all these acts of beneficence we should proportion our liberality to the wants and necessities of those we help.

These works of beneficence and goodness, in themselves exalted, become still more illustrious when done towards an enemy; for our Saviour says: Love your enemies, do good to them that hate you, which also the Apostle enjoins in these words: If thine enemy be hungry, give him to eat: if he thirst, give hint to drink. For, doing this, thou shalt heap coals of fire on his head. Be not overcome by evil, but overcome evil by good.

Finally, if we consider the law of charity, which is kind, we shall be convinced that to practice the good offices of mildness, clemency, and other kindred virtues, is a duty prescribed by that law.

Forgiveness Of Injuries Commanded

But the most important duty of all, and that which is the fullest expression of charity, and to the practice of which we should most habituate ourselves, is to pardon and forgive from the heart the injuries which we may have received from others. The Sacred Scriptures, as we have already observed, frequently admonish and exhort us to a full compliance with this duty. Not only do they pronounce blessed those who do this, but they also declare that God grants pardon to those who really fulfil this duty, while He refuses pardon to those who neglect it, or refuse to obey it.

How to Persuade Men to Forgive Injuries

As the desire of revenge is almost natural to man, it becomes necessary for the pastor to exert his utmost diligence not only to instruct, but also earnestly to persuade the faithful, that a Christian should forgive and forget injuries; and as this is a duty frequently inculcated by sacred writers, he should consult them on the subject, in order to be able to subdue the pertinacity of those whose minds are obstinately bent on revenge, and he should have ready the forcible and appropriate arguments which those Fathers piously employed. The three following considerations, however, demand particular exposition.

All We Have To Endure Comes From God

First, he who thinks himself injured ought above all to be persuaded that the man on whom he desires to be revenged was not the principal cause of the loss or injury. Thus that admirable man, Job, when violently injured by the Sabeans, the Chaldeans, and by Satan, took no account of these, but as a righteous and very holy man exclaimed with no less truth than piety: The Lord gave, the Lord hath taken away. The words and the example of that man of patience should, therefore, convince Christians, and the conviction is most just, that whatever chastisements we endure in this life come from the hand of God, the Father and Author of all justice and mercy. He chastises us not as enemies, but, in His infinite goodness, corrects us as children. To view the matter in its true light, men, in these cases, are nothing more than the ministers and agents of God. One man, it is true, may cherish the worst feelings towards another, he may harbour the most malignant hatred against him; but, without the permission of God, he can do him no injury. This is why Joseph was able patiently to endure the wicked counsels of his brethren, and David, the injuries inflicted on him by Semei.

Here also applies an argument which St. Chrysostom has ably and learnedly handled. It is that no man is injured but by himself. Let the man, who considers himself injured by another, consider the matter in the right way and he will certainly find that he has received no injury or loss from others. For although he may have experienced injury from external causes, he is himself his greatest enemy by wickedly staining his soul with hatred, malevolence and envy.

Advantages Of Forgiveness

The second consideration is that there are two advantages, which are the special rewards of those, who, influenced by a holy desire to please God, freely forgive injuries. In the first place, God has promised that he who forgives, shall himself obtain forgiveness of sins, a promise which clearly shows how acceptable to God is this duty of piety. In the next place, the forgiveness of injuries ennobles and perfects our nature; for by it man is in some degree made like to God, Who maketh his sun to shine on the good and the bad, and raineth upon the just and the unjust.

Disadvantages Of Revenge

Finally, the disadvantages which arise from the refusal to pardon others are to be explained. The pastor, therefore, should place before the eyes of the unforgiving man that hatred is not only a grievous sin, but also that the longer it is indulged the more deeply rooted it becomes. The man, of whose heart this passion has once taken possession, thirsts for the blood of his enemy. Filled with the hope of revenge, he will spend his days and nights brooding over some evil design, so that his mind seems never to rest from malignant projects, or even from thoughts of blood. Thus it follows that never, or at least not without extreme difficulty, can he be induced generously to pardon an offence, or even to mitigate his hostility. Justly, therefore, is hatred compared to a wound in which the weapon remains firmly embedded.

Moreover, there are many evil consequences and sins which are linked together with this one sin of hatred. Hence these words of St. John: He that hateth his brother, is in darkness, and walketh in darkness, and knoweth not whither he goeth; because the darkness hath blinded his eyes. He must, therefore, frequently fall; for how can anyone view in a favourable light the words or actions of him whom he hates? Hence arise rash and unjust judgments, anger, envy, detractions, and other evils of the same sort, in which are often involved those who are connected by ties of friendship or blood; and thus does it frequently happen that this one sin is the prolific source of many.

Not without good reason is hatred called the sin of the devil. The devil was a murderer from the beginning; and hence our Lord Jesus Christ, the Son of God, when the Pharisees sought His life, said that they were begotten of their father the devil.

Remedies Against Hatred

Besides the reasons already adduced, which afford good grounds for detesting this sin, other and most suitable remedies are prescribed in the pages of Holy Writ.

Of these remedies the first and greatest is the example of the Redeemer, which we should set before our eyes as a model for imitation. For He, in whom even suspicion of fault could not be found, when scourged with rods, crowned with thorns, and finally nailed to a cross, uttered that most charitable prayer: Father, forgive them, for they know not what they do. And as the Apostle testifies: The sprinkling of his blood speaketh better than Abel.

Another remedy, prescribed by Ecclesiasticus, is to call to mind death and judgment: Remember thy last end, and. thou shalt never sin." As if he had said: Reflect frequently and again and again that you must soon die, and since at death there will be nothing you desire or need more than great mercy from God, that now you should keep that mercy always before your mind. Thus the cruel desire for revenge will be extinguished; for you can discover no means better adapted, none more efficacious to obtain the mercy of God than the forgiveness of injuries and love towards those who in word or deed may have injured you or yours.

THE SIXTH COMMANDMENT : "*Thou shalt not commit adultery*"

The Position Of This Commandment In The Decalogue Is Most Suitable

The bond between man and wife is one of the closest, and nothing can be more gratifying to both than to know that they are objects of mutual and special affection. On the other hand, nothing inflicts deeper anguish than to feel that the legitimate love which one owes the other has been transferred elsewhere. Rightly, then, and in its natural order, is the Commandment which protects human life against the hand of the murderer, followed by that which forbids adultery and which aims to prevent anyone from injuring or destroying by such a crime the holy and honourable union of marriage -- a union which is generally the source of ardent affection and love.

Importance Of Careful Instruction On This Commandment

In the explanation of this Commandment, however, the pastor has need of great caution and prudence, and should treat with great delicacy a subject which requires brevity rather than copiousness of exposition. For it is to be feared that if he explained in too great detail or at length the ways in which this Commandment is violated, he might unintentionally speak of subjects which, instead of extinguishing, usually serve rather to inflame corrupt passion.

As, however, the precept contains many things which cannot be passed over in silence, the pastor should explain them in their proper order and place.

Two Parts Of This Commandment

This Commandment, then, resolves itself into two heads; the one expressed, which prohibits adultery; the other implied, which inculcates purity of mind and body.

What this Commandment Prohibits

Adultery Forbidden

To begin with the prohibitory part (of the Commandment), adultery is the defilement of the marriage bed, whether it be one's own or another's. If a married man have intercourse with an unmarried woman, he violates the integrity of his marriage bed; and if an unmarried man have intercourse with a married woman, he defiles the sanctity of the marriage bed of another.

Other Sins Against Chastity Are Forbidden

But that every species of immodesty and impurity are included in this prohibition of adultery, is proved by the testimonies of St. Augustine and St. Ambrose; and that such is the meaning of the Commandment is borne out by the Old, as well as the New Testament. In the writings of Moses, besides adultery, other sins against chastity are said to have been punished. Thus the book of Genesis records the judgment of Judah against his daughter-in-law. In Deuteronomy is found the excellent law of Moses, that there should be no harlot amongst the daughters of Israel. Take heed to keep thyself, my son, from all fornication, is the exhortation of

Tobias to his son; and in Ecclesiasticus we read: Be ashamed of looking upon a harlot.

In the Gospel, too, Christ the Lord says: From the heart come forth adulteries and fornications, which defile a man. The Apostle Paul expresses his detestation of this crime frequently, and in the strongest terms: This is the will of God, your sanctification, that you should abstain from fornication; Fly fornication; Keep not company with fornicators; Fornication, and an uncleanness and covetousness, let it not so much as be named among you; " Neither fornicators nor adulterers, nor the effeminate nor sodomites shall possess the kingdom of God.

Why Adultery Is Expressly Mentioned

But the reason why adultery is expressly forbidden is- because in addition to the turpitude which it shares with other kinds of incontinence, it adds the sin of injustice, not only against our neighbour, but also against civil society.

Again it is certain that he who abstains not from other sins against chastity, will easily fall into the crime of adultery. By the prohibition of adultery, therefore, we at once see that every sort of immodesty and impurity by which the body is defiled is prohibited. Nay, that every inward thought against chastity is forbidden by this Commandment is clear, as well from the very force of the law, which is evidently spiritual, as also from these words of Christ the Lord: You have heard that it was said to them of old: "Thou shalt not commit adultery." But I say to you, that whosoever shall look on a woman to lust after her, hath already committed adultery with her in his heart.

These are the points which we have deemed proper matter for public instruction of the faithful. The pastor, however, should add the decrees of the Council of Trent against adulterers, and those who keep harlots and concubines, omitting many other species of immodesty and lust, of which each individual is to be admonished privately, as circumstances of time and person may require.

What this Commandment Prescribes

Purity Enjoined

We now come to explain the positive part of the precept. The faithful are to be taught and earnestly exhorted to cultivate continence and chastity with all care, to cleanse themselves from all defilement of the flesh and of the spirit, perfecting sanctification in the fear of God.

First of all they should be taught that although the virtue of chastity shines with a brighter lustre in those who make the holy and religious vow of virginity, nevertheless it is a virtue which belongs also to those who lead a life of celibacy; or who, in the married state, preserve themselves pure and undefiled from unlawful desire.

Reflections which Help one to Practice Purity

The holy Fathers have taught us many means whereby to subdue the passions and to restrain sinful pleasure. The pastor, therefore, should make it his study to explain these accurately to the faithful, and should use the utmost diligence in their exposition. Of these means some are reflections, others are active measures.

Impurity Excludes From Heaven

The first kind consists chiefly in our forming a just conception of the filthiness and evil of this sin; for such knowledge will lead one more easily to detest it. Now the evil of this crime we may learn from the fact that, on account of it, man is banished and excluded from the kingdom of God, which is the greatest of all evils.

Impurity Is A Filthy Sin

The above-mentioned calamity is indeed common to every mortal sin. But what is peculiar to this sin is that fornicators are said to sin against their own bodies, according to the words of the Apostle: Fly fornication. Every-sin that a man doth is without the body; but he that committeth fornication, sinneth against his own body. The reason is that such a one does an injury to his own body violating its sanctity. Hence St. Paul, writing to the Thessalonians, says: This is the will of God, your sanctification; that you should abstain from fornication, that every one of you should know how to possess his vessel in sanctification and honour; not in the passion of lust, like the Gentiles that know not God.

Furthermore, what is still more criminal, the Christian who shamefully sins with a harlot makes the members of Christ the members of an harlot, according to these words of St. Paul: Know you not that your bodies are the members of Christ? Shall I then take the members of Christ and make them the members of a harlot? God forbid. Or know you not, that he who is joined to a harlot is made one body? Moreover, a Christian, as St. Paul testifies is the temple of the Holy Ghost ; and to violate this temple is nothing else than to expel the Holy Ghost.

Adultery Is A Grave Injustice

But the crime of adultery involves that of grievous injustice. If, as the Apostle says, they who are joined in wedlock are so subject to each other that neither has power or right over his or her body, but both are bound, as it were, by a mutual bond of subjection, the husband to accommodate himself to the will of the wife, the wife to the will of the husband; most certainly if either dissociate his or her person, which is the right of the other, from him or her to whom it is bound, the offender is guilty of an act of great injustice and wickedness.

Adultery Is Disgraceful

As dread of disgrace strongly stimulates to the performance of duty and deters from the commission of crime, the pastor should also teach that adultery brands its guilty perpetrators with an unusual stigma. He that is an adulterer, says Scripture, for the folly of his heart shall destroy his own soul: he gathereth to himself shame and dishonour, and his reproach shall not be blotted out.

Impurity Severely Punished

The grievousness of the sin of adultery may be easily inferred from the severity of its punishment. According to the law promulgated by God in the Old Testament, the adulterer was stoned to death. Nay more, because of the criminal passion of one man, not only the perpetrator of the crime, but a whole city was destroyed, as we read with regard to the Sichemites. The Sacred Scriptures abound with examples of the divine vengeance, such as the destruction of Sodom and of the neighbouring cities,' the punishment of the Israelites who committed fornication in the wilderness with the daughters of Moab, and the slaughter of the Benjamites. These examples the pastor can easily make use of to deter men from shameful lust.

Impurity Blinds The Mind And Hardens The Heart

But even though the adulterer may escape the punishment of death, he does not escape the great pains and torments that often overtake such sins as his. He becomes afflicted with blindness of mind a most severe punishment; he is lost to all regard for God, for reputation, for honour, for family, and even for life; and thus, utterly abandoned and worthless, he is undeserving of confidence in any matter of moment, and becomes unfitted to discharge any kind of duty.

Of this we find examples in the persons of David and of Solomon. David had no sooner fallen into the crime of adultery than he degenerated into a character the very reverse of what he had been before; from the mildest of men he became so cruel as to consign to death Urias, one of his most deserving subjects. Solomon, having abandoned himself to the lust of women, gave up the true religion to follow strange gods. This sin, therefore, as Osee observes, takes away man's heart and often blinds his understanding.

means of practicing purity

Avoidance Of Idleness

We now come to the remedies which consist in action. The first is studiously to avoid idleness; for, according to Ezechiel, it was by yielding to the enervating influence of idleness that the Sodomites plunged into the most shameful crime of criminal lust.

Temperance

In the next place, intemperance is carefully to be avoided. I fed them to the full, says the Prophet, and they committed adultery. An overloaded stomach begets impurity. This our Lord intimates in these words: Take heed to yourselves, lest perhaps your hearts be overcharged with surfeiting and drunkenness. Be not drunk with wine, says the Apostle, wherein is luxury.

Custody Of The Eyes

But the eyes, in particular, are the inlets to criminal passion, and to this refer these words of our Lord: If thine eye scandalise thee, pluck it out, and cast it from thee. The Prophets, also, frequently speak to the same effect. I made a covenant with mine eyes, says Job, that I would not so much as think upon a virgin. Finally, there are on record innumerable examples of the evils which have their origin in the indulgence of the eyes. It was thus that David sinned, thus that the king of Sichem fell, and thus also that the elders sinned who calumniated Susanna.

Avoidance Of Immodest Dress

Too much display in dress, which especially attracts the eye, is but too frequently an occasion of sin. Hence the admonition of Ecclesiasticus: Turn away thy face from a woman dressed up. As women are given to excessive fondness for dress, it will not be unseasonable in the pastor to give some attention to the subject, and sometimes to admonish and reprove them in the impressive words of the Apostle Peter: Whose adorning let it not be the outward plaiting of the hair, or the wearing of gold, or the putting on of apparel. St. Paul likewise says: Not with plaited hair, or gold, or pearls, or costly attire. Many women adorned with gold and precious stones, have lost the only true ornament of their soul and body.

Avoidance Of Impure Conversation, Reading, Pictures

Next to the sexual excitement, usually provoked by too studied an elegance of dress, follows another, which is indecent and obscene conversation. Obscene language is a torch which lights up the worst passions of the young mind; and the Apostle has said, that evil communications corrupt good manners. Immodest and passionate songs and dances are most productive of this same effect and are, therefore, cautiously to be avoided.

In the same class are to be numbered soft and obscene books which must be avoided no less than indecent pictures. All such things possess a fatal influence in exciting to unlawful attractions, and in inflaming the mind of youth. In these matters the pastor should take special pains to see that the faithful most carefully observe the pious and prudent regulations of the Council of Trent.

Frequentation Of The Sacraments

If the occasions of sin which we have just enumerated be carefully avoided, almost every excitement to lust will be removed. But the most efficacious means for subduing its violence are frequent use of confession and Communion, as also unceasing and devout prayer to God, accompanied by fasting and almsdeeds. Chastity is a gift of God. To those who ask it aright He does not deny it; nor does He suffer us to be tempted beyond our strength.

Mortification

But the body is to be mortified and the sensual appetites to be repressed not only by fasting, and particularly, by the fasts instituted by the Church, but also by watching, pious pilgrimages, and other works of austerity. By these and similar observances is the virtue of temperance chiefly manifested. In connection with this subject, St. Paul, writing to the Corinthians, says: Every one that striveth for the mastery, refraineth himself from all things; and they indeed that they may receive a corruptible crown, but we an incorruptible one. A little after he says: I chastise my body and bring it into subjection, lest, perhaps, when I have preached to others, I myself should become a castaway. And in another place he says: Make not provision for the flesh in its concupiscence.

THE SEVENTH COMMANDMENT : *"Thou shalt not steal"*

Importance Of Instruction On This Commandment

In the early ages of the Church, it was customary to impress on the minds of hearers the nature and force of this Commandment. This we learn from the reproof uttered by the Apostle against some who were most earnest in deterring others from vices, in which they themselves were found freely to indulge: Thou, therefore, that teachest another, teachest not thyself: thou that preachest that men should not steal, stealest. The salutary effect of such instructions was not only to correct a vice then very prevalent, but also to repress quarrels, litigation and other evils which generally grow out of theft. Since in these our days men are unhappily addicted to the same vices, with their consequent misfortunes and evils, the pastor, following the example of the holy Fathers and Doctors, should strongly insist on this point and explain with diligent care the force and meaning of this Commandment.

This Commandment A Proof Of The Love Of God Towards Us And A Claim On Our Gratitude

In the first place the pastor should exercise care and industry in declaring the infinite love of God for man. Not satisfied with having fenced round, so to say, our lives, our persons and our reputation, by means of the two Commandments, Thou shalt not kill, Thou shalt not commit adultery, God defends and places a guard over our property and possessions, by adding the prohibition, Thou shalt not steal. These words can have no other meaning than that which we indicated above when speaking of the other Commandments. They declare that God forbids our worldly goods, which are placed under His protection, to be taken away or injured by anyone.

Our gratitude to God, the author of this law, should be in proportion to the greatness of the benefit the law confers upon us. Now since the truest test of gratitude and the best means of returning thanks, consists not only in lending a willing ear to His precepts, but also in obeying them, the faithful are to be animated and encouraged to an observance of this Commandment.

Two Parts Of This Commandment

Like the preceding Commandments, this one also is divided into two parts. The first, which prohibits theft, is mentioned expressly; while the spirit and force of the second, which en- forces kindliness and liberality towards our neighbour, are implied in the first part.

Negative Part of this Commandment

Stealing Forbidden

We shall begin with the prohibitory part of the Commandment, Thou shalt not steal. It is to be observed, that by the word steal is understood not only the taking away of anything from its rightful owner, privately and without his consent, but also the possession of that which belongs to another, contrary to the will, although not without the knowledge, of the true owner; else we are prepared to say that He who prohibits theft does not also prohibit robbery, which is accomplished by violence and injustice, whereas, according to St. Paul, extortioners shall not possess the kingdom of

God, and their very company and ways should be shunned, as the same Apostle writes.

Theft And Robbery Forbidden

But though robbery is a greater sin than theft, inasmuch as it not only deprives another of his property, but also offers violence and insult to him; yet it cannot be a matter of surprise that the divine prohibition is expressed under the milder word, steal, instead of rob. There was good reason for this, since theft is more general and of wider extent than robbery, a crime which only they can commit who are superior to their neighbour in brute force and power. Furthermore, it is obvious that when lesser crimes are forbidden, greater enormities of the same sort are also prohibited.

Various Names Given To Stealing

The unjust possession and use of what belongs to another are expressed by different names, according to the diversity of the objects taken without the consent and knowledge of the owners To take any private property from a private individual is called theft; from the public, peculation. To enslave a freeman, or appropriate the slave of another is called man-stealing. To steal anything sacred is called sacrilege -- a crime most enormous and sinful, yet so common in our days that what piety and wisdom had set aside for the necessary expenses of divine worship, for the support of the ministers of religion, and the use of the poor is employed in satisfying individual avarice and the worst passions.

Desire Of Stealing Forbidden

But, besides actual theft, that is, the outward commission, the will and desire are also forbidden by the law of God. The law is spiritual and concerns the soul, the source of our thoughts and designs. From the heart, says our Lord in St. Matthew, come forth evil thoughts, murders, adulteries, fornications, thefts, false testimonies.

Gravity Of The Sin Of Stealing

The grievousness of the sin of theft is sufficiently seen by the light of natural reason alone, for it is a violation of justice which gives to every man his own. The distribution and allotment of property, fixed from the beginning by the law of nations and confirmed by human and divine laws, must be considered as inviolable, and each one must be allowed secure possession of what justly belongs to him, unless we wish the overthrow of human society. Hence these words of the Apostle: Neither thieves, nor covetous, nor drunkards, nor railers, nor extortioners, shall possess the kingdom of God.

The long train of evils which this sin entails are a proof at once of its mischievousness and enormity. It gives rise to hasty and rash judgments, engenders hatred, originates enmities, and sometimes subjects the innocent to cruel condemnation.

What shall we say of the necessity imposed by God on all of satisfying for the injury done? Without restitution, says St. Augustine, the sin is not forgiven. The difficulty of making such restitution, on the part of those who have been in the habit of enriching themselves with their neighbour's property, we may learn not only from personal observation and reflection, but also from the testimony of the Prophet Habacuc: Woe to him that heapeth together what is not his own. How long also doth he load himself with thick clay? The possession of other men's property he calls thick clay, because it is difficult to emerge and extricate one's self from (ill-gotten goods).

The Chief Kinds Of Stealing

There are so many kinds of stealing that it is most difficult to enumerate them all; but since the others can be reduced to theft and robbery, it will be sufficient to speak of these two. To inspire the faithful with a detestation of such grievous crimes and to deter them from their commission, the pastor should use all care and diligence. Now let us consider these two kinds of stealing.

Various Forms Of Theft

They are guilty of theft who buy stolen goods, or retain the property of others, whether found, seized, or pilfered. If you have found, and not restored, says St. Augustine, you have stolen. If the true owner cannot, however, be discovered, whatever is found should go to the poor. If the finder refuse to make restitution, he gives evident proof that, were it in his power, he would make no scruple of stealing all that he could lay his hands on.

Those who, in buying or selling, have recourse to fraud and lying, involve themselves in the same guilt. The Lord will avenge their trickery. Those who sell bad and adulterated goods as real and genuine, or who defraud the purchasers by weight, measure, number, or rule, are guilty of a species of theft still more criminal and unjust. It is written in Deuteronomy: Thou shalt not have divers weights in thy bag. Do not any unjust thing, says Leviticus, in judgment, in rule, in weight or in measure. Let the balance be just, and the weights equal, the bushel just, and the sextary equal.

And elsewhere it is written: Divers weights are an abomination before the Lord; a deceitful balance is not good.

It is, also, a downright theft, when labourers and artisans exact full wages from those to whom they have not given just and due labor. Again, dishonest servants and agents are no better than thieves, nay they are more detestable than other thieves; against these everything may be locked, while against a pilfering servant nothing in a house can be secure by bolt or lock.

They, also, who obtain money under pretence of poverty, or by deceitful words, may be said to steal, and their guilt is aggravated since they add falsehood to theft.

Persons charged with offices of public or private trust, who altogether neglect, or but indifferently perform their duties, while they enjoy the salary and emoluments of such offices, are also to be reckoned in the number of thieves.

To enumerate the various other modes of theft, invented by the ingenuity of avarice, which is versed in all the arts of making money, would be a tedious and, as already said, a most difficult task.

Various Forms Of Robbery

The pastor, therefore, should next come to treat of robbery, which is the second general division of these crimes. First, he should admonish the Christian people to bear in mind the teaching of the Apostle: They that will become rich fall into temptation, and the snare of the devil; and never to forget the rule: All things whatsoever you will that men do to you, do you also to them; and always to bear in mind the words of Tobias: See thou never do to another what thou wouldst hate to have done to thee by another.

Robbery is more comprehensive than theft. Those who pay not the labourer his hire are guilty of robbery, and are exhorted to repentance by St. James in these words: Go to now, ye rich men, weep and howl for your miseries, which shall come upon you. He adds the reason for their repentance: Behold the hire of the labourers, who have reaped down your fields, which by fraud has been kept back by you, crieth: and the cry of them hath entered into the ears of the Lord of sabaoth. This sort of robbery is strongly condemned in Leviticus, Deuteronomy, Malachy, and Tobias.

Among those who are guilty of robbery are also included persons who do not pay, or who turn to other uses or appropriate to themselves, customs, taxes, tithes and such revenues, which are owed to the Church or civil authorities.

To this class also belong usurers, the most cruel and relentless of extortioners, who by their exorbitant rates of interest, plunder and destroy the poor. Whatever is received above the capital and principal, be it money, or anything else that may be purchased or estimated by money, is usury; for it is written in Ezechiel: He hath not lent upon usury, nor taken an increase; and in Luke our Lord says: Lend, hoping for nothing thereby. Even among the pagans usury was always considered a most grievous and odious crime. Hence the question, "What is usury ?" was answered: "What is murder?" And, indeed, he who lends at usury sells the same thing twice, or sells that which has no real existence.

Corrupt judges, whose decisions are venal, and who, bought over by money or other bribes, decide against the just claims of the poor and needy, also commit robbery.

Those who defraud their creditors, who deny their just debts, and also those who purchase goods on their own, or on another's credit, with a promise to pay for them at a certain time, and do not keep their word, are guilty of the same crime of robbery. And it is an aggravation of their guilt that, in consequence of their want of punctuality and their fraud, prices are raised to the great injury of the public. To such persons seem to apply the words of David: The sinner shall borrow, and not pay again.

But what shall we say of those rich men who exact with rigour what they lend to the poor, even though the latter are not able to pay them, and who, disregarding God's law, take as security even the necessary clothing of the unfortunate debtors ? For God says: If thou take of thy neighbour a garment in pledge, thou shalt give it him again before sunset, for that same is the only thing wherewith he is covered, the clothing of his body, neither hath he any other to sleep in: if he cry to me I will hear him, because I am compassionate. Their rigorous exaction is justly termed rapacity, and therefore robbery.

Among those whom the holy Fathers pronounced guilty of robbery are persons who, in times of scarcity, hoard up their corn, thus culpably rendering supplies scarcer and dearer. This holds good with regard to all necessaries of life and sustenance. These are they against whom Solomon utters this execration: He that hideth up corn, shall be cursed among the people. Such persons the pastor should warn of their guilt, and should reprove with more than ordinary freedom; he should explain to them at length the punishments which await such sins.

So much for what the seventh Commandment forbids.

Positive Part of this Commandment

Restitution Enjoined

We now come to the positive part of this Commandment, in which the first thing to be considered is satisfaction or restitution; for without restitution the sin is not forgiven.

Who Are Held To Restitution

But as the law of making restitution to the injured party is binding not only on the person who commits theft, but also on all who cooperate in the sin, it is necessary to explain who are indispensably bound to this satisfaction or restitution. There are several classes (who are thus bound).

The first consists of those who order others to steal, and who are not only the authors and accomplices of theft, but also the most criminal among thieves.

Another class embraces those, who, when they cannot command others to commit theft persuade and encourage it. These, since they are like the first class in intention, though unlike them in power, are equally guilty of theft.

A third class is composed of those who consent to the theft committed by others.

The fourth class is that of those who are accomplices in, and derive gain from theft; if that can be called gain, which, unless they repent, consigns them to everlasting torments. Of them David says: If thou didst see a thief, thou didst run with him.

The fifth class of thieves are those who, having it in their power to prohibit theft, so far from opposing or preventing it, fully and freely suffer and sanction its commission.

The sixth class is constituted of those who are well aware that the theft was committed, and when it was committed; and yet, far from mentioning it, pretend they know nothing about it.

The last class comprises all who assist in the accomplishment of theft, who guard, defend, receive or harbour thieves.

All these are bound to make restitution to those from whom anything has been stolen, and are to be earnestly exhorted to the discharge of so necessary a duty.

Neither are those who approve and commend thefts entirely innocent of this crime. Children also who steal from their parents, and wives who steal from their husbands are not guiltless of theft.

Almsdeeds Enjoined

This Commandment also implies an obligation to sympathise with the poor and needy, and to relieve their difficulties and distresses by our means and good offices. Concerning this subject, which cannot be insisted on too often or too strongly, the pastor will find abundant matter to enrich his discourses in the works of St. Cyprian, St. John Chrysostom, St. Gregory Nazianzen, and other eminent writers on almsdeeds.

Inducements To Practice Almsgiving

The pastor, therefore, should encourage the faithful to be willing and anxious to assist those who have to depend on charity, and should make them realise the great necessity of giving alms and of being really and practically liberal to the poor, by reminding them that on the last day God will condemn and consign to eternal fires those who have omitted and neglected the duty of almsgiving, while on the contrary He will praise and introduce into His heavenly country those who have exercised mercy towards the poor. These two sentences have been already pronounced by the lips of Christ the Lord: Come, ye blessed of my Father, possess the kingdom prepared for you; and: Depart front me, ye cursed, into everlasting fire.

Priests should also cite those texts which are calculated to persuade (to the performance of this important duty): Give and it shall be given to you. They should dwell on the promise of God, the richest and most abundant that can be conceived: There is no man who hath left house, or brethren, etc., that shall not receive an hundred times as much now in this time and in the world to come life everlasting; and he should add these words of our Lord: Make unto yourselves friends of the mammon of iniquity, that when you shall fail, they may receive you into everlasting dwellings.

Ways Of Giving Alms

They should also explain the parts of this necessary duty, so that whoever is unable to give may at least lend to the poor what they need to sustain life, according to the command of Christ our Lord: Lend, hoping for nothing thereby. The happiness of doing this is thus expressed by holy David: Acceptable is the man that showeth mercy and lendeth.

But if we are not able to give to those who must depend on the charity of others for their sustenance, it is an act of Christian piety, as well as a means of avoiding idleness, to procure by our labor and industry what is necessary for the relief of the poor. To this the Apostle exhorts all by his own example. For yourselves, he says to the Thessalonians, know how you ought to imitate us; and again, writing to the same people: Use your endeavour to be quiet, and that you do your own business, and work with your own, hands, as we commanded you; and to the Ephesians: He that stole, let him steal no more; but rather let him labour working with his hands the thing which is good, that he may have something to give to him that suffereth need.'

Frugality Is Enjoined

We should also practice frugality and draw sparingly on the kindness of others, that we may not be burden or a trouble to them. The exercise of considerateness is conspicuous in all the Apostles, but preeminently so in St. Paul. Writing to the Thessalonians he says: You remember, brethren, our labour and toil; working night and day lest we should be chargeable to any of you, we preached amongst you the gospel of God. And in another place the same Apostle says: In labour and in toil, we worked night and day, lest we should be burdensome to any of you.

Sanction Of This Commandment

The Punishment Of Its Violation

To inspire the faithful with an abhorrence of all infamous sins against this Commandment, the pastor should have recourse to the

Prophets and the other inspired writers, to show the detestation in which God holds the crimes of theft and robbery, and the awful threats which He denounces against their perpetrators. Hear this, exclaims the Prophet Amos, you that crush the poor, and make the needy of the land to fail, saying: "When will the month be over, and we shall sell our wares, and the sabbath, and we shall open the corn; that we may lessen the measure, and increase the sickle, and may convey in deceitful balances? Many passages of the same kind may be found in Jeremias, Proverbs,' and Ecclesiasticus. Indeed it cannot be doubted that such crimes are the seeds from which have sprung in great part the evils which in our times oppress society.

The Reward Of Observing This Commandment

That Christians may accustom themselves to those acts of generosity and kindness towards the poor and the needy which are inculcated by the second part of this Commandment, the pastor should place before them those ample rewards which God promises in this life and in the next to the beneficent and the bountiful.

Excuses for Stealing Refuted

As there are not wanting those who would even excuse their thefts, these are to be admonished that God will accept no excuse for sin; and that their excuses, far from extenuating, serve only greatly to aggravate their guilt.

The Plea Of Rank And Position

How insufferable the vanity of those men of exalted rank who excuse themselves by alleging that they act not from cupidity or avarice, but stoop to take what belongs to others only from a desire to maintain the grandeur of their families and of their ancestors, whose repute and dignity must fall, if not upheld by the possession of another man's property. Of this harmful error they are to be disabused; and they are to be convinced that the only means to preserve and augment their wealth and to enhance the glory of their ancestors is to obey the will of God and observe His Commandments. Once His will and Commandments are contemned, the stability of property, no matter how securely settled, is overturned; kings are dethroned, and hurled from the highest stations of honour; while the humblest individuals, men too, towards whom they cherished the most implacable hatred, are sometimes called by God to occupy their place.

It is incredible to what degree the divine wrath is kindled against such offenders, and this we know from the testimony of Isaias, who records these words of God: Thy princes are faithless, companions of thieves; they all love bribes, they run after rewards. Therefore, saith the Lord, the God of Hosts, the mighty one of Israel: Ah! I will comfort myself over my adversaries; and I will be revenged of my enemies; and I will turn my hand to thee, and I will clean purge away thy dross.

The Plea Of Greater Ease And Elegance

Some there are, who plead in justification of such conduct, not the ambition of maintaining splendour and glory, but a desire of acquiring the means of living in greater ease and elegance. These are to be refuted, and should be shown how impious are the words and conduct of those who prefer their own ease to the will and the glory of God whom, by neglecting His Commandments, we offend extremely. And yet what real advantage can there be in theft? Of how many very serious evils is it not the source? Confusion and repentance, says Ecclesiasticus, is upon a thief. But even though no disadvantage overtake the thief, he offers an insult to the divine name, opposes the most holy will of God, and contemns His salutary precepts. From hence result all error, all dishonesty, all impiety.

The Plea Of The Other's Wealth

But do we not sometimes hear the thief contend that he is not guilty of sin, because he steals from the rich and the wealthy, who, in his mind, not only suffer no injury, but do not even feel the loss? Such an excuse is as wretched as it is baneful.

The Plea Of Force Of Habit

Others imagine that they should be excused, because they have contracted such a habit of stealing as not to be able easily to refrain from such desires and practices. If such persons listen not to the admonition of the Apostle: He that stole, let him now steal no more, let them recollect that one day, whether they like it or not, they will become accustomed to an eternity of torments.

The Plea Of Favourable Opportunity

Some excuse themselves by saying that the opportunity presented itself. The proverb is well known: Those who are not thieves are made so by opportunity. Such persons are to be disabused of their wicked idea by reminding them that it is our duty to resist every evil propensity. If we yield instant obedience to every inordinate impulse, what measure, what limits will there be to crime and disorder? Such an excuse, therefore,- is of the lowest character, or rather is an avowal of a complete want of restraint and justice. To say that you do not commit sin, because you have no opportunity of sinning, is almost to acknowledge that you are always prepared to sin when opportunity offers.

The Plea Of Revenge

There are some who say that they steal in order to gratify revenge, having themselves suffered the same injury from others. To such offenders it should be answered first of all that no one is allowed to return injury for injury; next that no person can be a judge in his own cause; and finally that still less can it be lawful to punish one man for the wrong done you by another.

The Plea Of Financial Embarrassment

Finally, some find a sufficient justification of theft in their own embarrassments, alleging that they are overwhelmed with debt, which they cannot pay off otherwise than by theft. Such persons should be given to understand that no debt presses more heavily upon all men than that which we mention each day in these words of the Lord's Prayer: Forgive us our debts. Hence it is the height of folly to be willing to increase our debt to God by new sin, in order to be able to pay our debts to men. It is much better to be consigned to prison than to be cast into the eternal torments of hell; it is by far a greater evil to be condemned by the judgment of God, than by that of man. Hence it becomes our duty to have recourse to the assistance and mercy of God from whom we can obtain whatever we need.

There are also other excuses, which, however, the judicious and zealous pastor will not find it difficult to meet, so that thus he may one day be blessed with a people who are followers of good works.

THE EIGHTH COMMANDMENT : *"Thou shalt not bear false witness against thy neighbour"*

Importance Of Instruction On This Commandment

The great utility, nay the necessity, of carefully explaining this Commandment, and of emphasising its obligation, we learn from these words of St. James: If any man offend not in word, the same is a perfect man; and again, The tongue is indeed a little member, and boasteth great things. Behold how small a fire, what a great wood it kindleth; and so on, to the same effect.

From these words we learn two truths. The first is that sins of the tongue are very prevalent, which is confirmed by these words of the Prophet: Every man is a liar, so that it would almost seem as if this were the only sin which extends to all mankind. The other truth is that the tongue is the source of innumerable evils. Through the fault of the evil-speaker are often lost the property, the reputation, the life, and the salvation of the Injured person, or of him who inflicts the injury. The injured person, unable to bear patiently the contumely, avenges it without restraint. The offender, on the other hand, deterred by a perverse shame and a false idea of what is called honour, cannot be induced to make reparation to him whom he has offended.

This Commandment Should Call Forth Our Gratitude

Hence the faithful are to be exhorted to thank God as much as they can for having given this salutary Commandment, not to bear false witness, which not only forbids us to injure others, but which also, if duly observed, prevents others from injuring us.

Two Parts Of This Commandment

In its explanation we shall proceed as we have done with regard to the others, pointing out that in it are contained two laws. The first forbids us to bear false witness. The other commands us to lay aside all dissimulation and deceit, and to measure our words and actions by the standard of truth, a duty of which the Apostle admonishes the Ephesians in these words: Doing the truth in charity, let us grow up in all things in him.

Negative Part Of This Commandment

With regard to the prohibitory part of this Commandment, although by false testimony is understood whatever is positively but falsely affirmed of anyone, be it for or against him, be it in a public court or elsewhere; yet the Commandment specially prohibits that species of false testimony which is given on oath in a court of justice. For a witness swears by the Deity, because the words of a man thus giving evidence and using the divine name, have very great weight and possess the strongest claim to credit. Such testimony, therefore, because it is dangerous, is specially prohibited; for even the judge himself cannot reject the testimony of sworn witnesses, unless they be excluded by exceptions made in the law, or unless their dishonesty and malice are notorious. This is especially true since it is commanded by divine authority that in the mouth of two or three every word shall stand.

"Against Thy Neighbour"

In order that the faithful may have a clear comprehension of this Commandment it should be explained who is our neighbour, against whom it is unlawful to bear false witness. According to the interpretation of Christ the Lord, our neighbour is he who needs our assistance, whether bound to us by ties of kindred or not, whether a fellow-citizen or a stranger, a friend or an enemy.' It is wrong to think that one may give false evidence against an enemy, since by the command of God and of our Lord we are bound to love him.

Moreover, as every man is bound to love himself, and is thus, in some sense, his own neighbour, it is unlawful for anyone to bear false witness against himself. He who does so brands himself with infamy and disgrace, and injures both himself and the Church of which he is a member, much as the suicide, by his act, does a wrong to the state. This is the doctrine of St. Augustine, who says: To those who do not understand (the precept) properly, it might seem lawful to give false testimony against one's self, because the words "against thy neighbour" are subjoined in the Commandment. But let no one who bears false testimony against himself think that he has not violated this Commandment, for the standard of loving our neighbour is the love which we cherish towards ourselves.

False Testimony In Favour Of A Neighbour Is Also Forbidden

But if we are forbidden to injure our neighbour by false testimony, let it not be inferred that the contrary is lawful, and that we may help by perjury those who are bound to us by ties of kinship or religion. It is never allowed to have recourse to lies or deception, much less to perjury. Hence St. Augustine in his book to Crescentius On Lying teaches from the words of the Apostle that a lie, although uttered in false praise of anyone, is to be numbered among false testimonies. Treating of that passage, Yea, and we are found false witnesses of God, because we have given testimony against God, that he hath raised up Christ whom he hath not raised, if the dead rise not again, he says: The Apostle calls it false testimony to utter a lie with regard to Christ, even though it should seem to redound to His praise.

It also not infrequently happens, that by favouring one party we injure the other. False testimony is certainly the occasion of misleading the judge, who, yielding to such evidence, is sometimes obliged to decide against justice, to the injury of the innocent.

Sometimes, too, it happens that the successful party, who by means of perjured witnesses, has gained his case and escaped with impunity, exulting in his iniquitous victory, soon becomes accustomed to the work of corrupting and suborning false witnesses, by whose aid he hopes to obtain whatever he wishes.

To the witness himself it must be most grievous that his falsehood and perjury are known to him whom he has aided and abetted by his perjury; whilst encouraged by the success that follows his crime, he becomes every day more accustomed to wickedness and audacity.

"Thou Shalt Not Bear False Witness"

All Falsehoods In Lawsuits Are Forbidden

This precept then prohibits deceit, lying and perjury on the part of witnesses. The same prohibition extends also to plaintiffs, defendants, promoters, representatives, procurators and advocates; in a word, to all who take any part in lawsuits.

False Testimony Out Of Court Is Forbidden

Finally, God prohibits all testimony which may inflict injury or injustice, whether it be a matter of legal evidence or not. In the passage of Leviticus where the Commandments are repeated, we read: Thou shalt not steal; thou shalt not lie; neither shall any man deceive his neighbour.' To none, therefore can it be a matter of doubt, that this Commandment condemns lies of every sort, as these words of David explicitly declare: Thou wilt destroy all that speak a lie.

This Commandment Forbids Detraction

This Commandment forbids not only false testimony, but also the detestable vice and practice of detraction, -- a pestilence, which is the source of innumerable and calamitous evils. This vicious habit of secretly reviling and calumniating character is frequently reprobated in the Sacred Scriptures. With him, says David, I would not eat; and St. James: Detract not one another, my brethren.

Holy Writ abounds not only with precepts on the subject, but also with examples which reveal the enormity of the crime. Aman, by a crime of his own invention, had so incensed Assuerus against the Jews that he ordered the destruction of the entire race. Sacred history contains many other examples of the same kind, which priests should recall in order to deter the people from such iniquity.

Various Kinds Of Detraction

But, to understand well the nature of this sin of detraction, we must know that reputation is injured not only by calumniating the character, but also by exaggerating the faults of others. He who gives publicity to the secret sin of any man, in an unnecessary place or time, or before persons who have no right to know, is also rightly regarded as a detractor and evil-speaker, if his revelation seriously injures the other's reputation.

But of all sorts of calumnies the worst is that which is directed against Catholic doctrine and its teachers. Persons who extol the propagators of error and of unsound doctrine are guilty of a like crime.

Nor are those to be dissociated from the ranks of evil-speakers, or from their guilt, who, instead of reproving, lend a willing ear and a cheerful assent to the calumniator and reviler. As we read in St. Jerome and St. Bernard, it is not so easy to decide which is more guilty, the detractor, or the listener; for if there were no listeners, there would be no detractors.

To the same category belong those who cunningly foment divisions and excite quarrels; who feel a malignant pleasure in sowing discord, dissevering by fiction and falsehood the closest friendships and the dearest social ties, impelling to endless hatred and deadly combat the fondest friends. Of such pestilent characters the Lord expresses His detestation in these words: Thou shalt not be a detractor nor a whisperer among the people. Of this description were many of the advisers of Saul, who strove to alienate the king's affection from David and to arouse his enmity against him.

This Commandment Forbids Flattery

Among the transgressors of this Commandment are to be numbered those fawners and sycophants who, by flattery and insincere praise, gain the hearing and good will of those whose favour, money, and honours they seek, calling good evil, and evil good, as the Prophet says. Such characters David admonishes us to repel and banish from our society. The just man, he says, shall correct me in mercy, and shall reprove me; but let not the oil of the sinner fatten my head. This class of persons do not, it is true, speak ill of their neighbour; but they greatly injure him, since by praising his sins they cause him to continue in vice to the end of his life.

Of this species of flattery the most pernicious is that which proposes to itself for object the injury and the ruin of others. Thus Saul, when he sought to expose David to the sword and fury of the Philistines, in order to bring about his death, ad dressed him in these soothing words: Behold my eldest daughter Merob, her will I give thee to wife: only be a valiant man and fight the battles of the Lord. In the same way the Jews thus insidiously addressed our Lord: Master, we know that thou art a true speaker, and teachest the way of God in truth.

Still more pernicious is the language addressed sometimes by friends and relations to a person suffering with a mortal disease, and on the point of death, when they assure him that there is no danger of dying, telling him to be of good spirits, dissuading him from confession, as though the very thought should fill him with melancholy, and finally withdrawing his attention from all care and thought of the dangers which beset him in the last perilous hour.

This Commandment Forbids Lies Of All Kinds

In a word, lies of every sort are prohibited, especially those that cause grave injury to anyone, while most impious of all is a lie uttered against or regarding religion.

God is also grievously offended by those attacks and slanders which are termed lampoons, and other defamatory publications of this kind.

To deceive by a jocose or officious lie, even though it helps or harms no one, is, notwithstanding, altogether unworthy; for thus the Apostle admonishes us: Putting away lying, speak ye the truth. This practice begets a strong tendency to frequent and serious lying, and from jocose lying men contract the habit of lying, lose all reputation for truth, and ultimately find it necessary, in order to gain belief, to have recourse to continual swearing.

This Commandment Forbids Hypocrisy

Finally, the first part of this Commandment prohibits dissimulation. It is sinful not only to speak, but to act deceitfully. Actions, as well as words, are signs of what is in our mind; and hence our Lord, rebuking the Pharisees, frequently calls them hypocrites. So, far with regard to the negative, which is the first part of this Commandment.

Positive Part of this Commandment

Judges Must Pass Sentence According To Law And Justice

We now come to explain what the Lord commands in the second part. Its nature and purpose require that trials be conducted on principles of strict justice and according to law. It requires that no one usurp judicial powers or authority, for, as the Apostle writes, it were unjust to judge another man's servant.

Again it requires that no one pass sentence without a sufficient knowledge of the case. This was the sin of the priests and scribes who passed judgment on St. Stephen. The magistrates of Philippi furnish another example. They have beaten us publicly, says the Apostle, uncondemned, men that are Romans, and have cast us into prison; and now do they thrust us out privately.

This Commandment also requires that the innocent be not condemned, nor the guilty acquitted; and that (the decision) be not influenced by money, or favour, hatred or love. For so Moses admonished the elders whom he had constituted judges of the people: Judge that which is just, whether he be one of your country or a stranger. There shall be no difference of persons, you shall hear the little as well as the great; neither shall you respect any man's person, because it is the judgment of God.

Witnesses Must Give Testimony Truthfully

With regard to an accused person who is conscious of his own guilt, God commands him to confess the truth, if he is interrogated judicially. By that confession he, in some sort, bears witness to, and proclaims the praise and glory of God; and of this we have a proof in these words of Josue, when exhorting Achan to confess the truth: My son, give glory to the Lord the God of Israel.

But as this Commandment chiefly concerns witnesses, the pastor should give them special attention. The spirit of the precept not only prohibits false testimony, but also commands the truth to be told. In human affairs, to bear testimony to the truth is a matter of the highest importance, because there are innumerable things of which we must be ignorant unless we arrive at a knowledge of them on the faith of witnesses. In matters with which we are not personally acquainted and which we need to know, there is nothing so important as true evidence. Hence the words of St. Augustine: He who conceals the truth and he who utters falsehood are both guilty; the one, because he is unwilling to render a service; the other, because he has the will to do an injury.

We are not, however, at all times, obliged to disclose the truth; but when, in a court of justice, a witness is legally interrogated by the judge, he is emphatically bound to tell the whole truth. Here, however, witnesses should be most circumspect, lest, trusting too much to memory, they affirm for certain what they have not fully ascertained.

Lawyers And Plaintiffs Must Be Guided By Love Of Justice

Attorneys and counsel, plaintiffs and prosecutors, remain still to be treated of. The two former should not refuse to contribute their services and legal assistance, when the necessities of others call for their aid. They should deal generously with the poor. They should not defend an unjust cause, prolong lawsuits by trickery, nor encourage them for the sake of gain. As to remuneration for their services and labours, let them be guided by the principles of justice and of equity.

Plaintiffs and prosecutors, on their side, are to be warned not to be led by the influence of love, or hatred, or any other undue motive into exposing anyone to danger through unjust charges:

All Must Speak Truthfully And With Charity

To all conscientious persons is addressed the divine command that in all their intercourse with society, in every conversation, they should speak the truth at all times from the sincerity of their hearts; that they should utter nothing injurious to the reputation of another, not even of those by whom they know they have been injured and persecuted. For they should always remember that between them and others there exists such a close social bond that they are all members of the same body.

Inducements To Truthfulness

In order that the faithful may be more disposed to avoid the vice of lying, the pastor should place before them the extreme lowness and disgrace of this sin. In the Sacred Scriptures the devil is called the father of lies; for as, he stood not in the truth, he is a liar and the father thereof.

To banish so great a sin, (the pastor) should add the mischievous consequences of lying; but since they are innumerable, he must be content with pointing out the chief kinds of these evils and calamities.

In the first place, he should show how grievously lies and deceit offend God and how deeply they are hated by God. This he should prove from the words of Solomon: Six things there are which the Lord hateth, and the seventh his soul detesteth: haughty eyes, a lying tongue, hands that shed innocent blood, a heart that deviseth wicked plots, feet that are swift to run into mischief, a deceitful witness that uttereth lies, etc. Who, then, can protect or save from severest chastisements the man who is thus the object of God's special hate?

Again, what more wicked, what more base than, as St. James says, with the same tongue, by which we bless God and the Father, to curse men, who are made after the image and likeness of God, so that out of the same fountain flows sweet and bitter water. The tongue, which was before employed in giving praise and glory to God, afterwards, as far as it is able, by lying treats Him with ignominy and dishonour. Hence liars are excluded from a participation in the bliss of heaven. To David asking, Lord! who shall dwell in thy tabernacle? the Holy Spirit answers: He that speaketh truth in his heart, who hath not used deceit in his tongue.

Lying is also attended with this very great evil that it is an almost incurable disease. For since the guilt of the calumniator cannot be pardoned, unless satisfaction be made to the calumniated person, and since, as we have already observed, this duty is difficult for those who are deterred from its performance by false shame and a foolish idea of dignity, we cannot doubt that he who continues in this sin is destined to the unending punishments of hell. Let no one indulge the hope of obtaining the pardon of his calumnies or detractions, until he has repaired the injury which they have inflicted on the honour or fame of another, whether this was done in a court of justice, or in private and familiar conversation.

But the evil consequences of lying are widespread and extend to society at large. By duplicity and lying, good faith and truth, which form the closest links of human society, are dissolved, confusion ensues, and men seem to differ in nothing from demons.

How To Avoid Lying

The pastor should also teach that loquacity is to be avoided. By avoiding loquacity other evils will be obviated, and a great preventive opposed to lying, from which loquacious persons can scarcely abstain.

Excuses for Lying Refuted

The Plea Of Prudence

There are those who seek to justify their duplicity either by the unimportance of what they say, or by the example of the worldly wise who, they claim, lie at the proper time. The pastor should correct such erroneous ideas by answering what is most true, namely, that the wisdom of the flesh is death. He should exhort his listeners in all their difficulties and dangers to trust in God, not in the artifice of lying; for those who have recourse to subterfuge, plainly show that they trust more to their own prudence than to the providence of God.

The Plea Of Revenge

Those who lay the blame of their own falsehood on others, who first deceived them by lies, are to be taught the unlawfulness of avenging their own wrongs, and that evil is not to be rendered for evil, but rather that evil is to be overcome by good. Even if it were lawful to return evil for evil, it would not be to- our interest to harm ourselves in order to get revenge. The man who seeks revenge by uttering falsehood inflicts very serious injury on himself.

The Pleas Of Frailty, Habit, And Bad. Example

Those who plead human frailty are to be taught that it is a duty of religion to implore the divine assistance, and not to yield to human infirmity.

Those who excuse themselves by habit are to be admonished to endeavour to acquire the contrary habit of speaking the truth; particularly as those who sin habitually are more guilty than others.

There are some who adduce in their own justification the example of others, who, they contend, constantly indulge in falsehood and perjury. Such persons should be undeceived by reminding them that bad men are not to be imitated, but reproved and corrected; and that, when we ourselves are addicted to the same vice, our admonitions have less influence in reprehending and correcting it in others.

The Pleas Of Convenience, Amusement, And Advantage

With regard to those who defend their conduct by saying that to speak the truth is often attended with inconvenience, priests should answer that (such an excuse) is an accusation, not a defence, since it is the duty of a Christian to suffer any inconvenience rather than utter a falsehood.

There remain two other classes of persons who seek to justify lying: those who say that they tell lies for the sake of amusement, and those who plead motives of interest, claiming that without recourse to lies, they can neither buy nor sell to advantage. The pastor should endeavour to reform both these kinds of liars. He should correct the former by showing how strong a habit of sinning is contracted by their practice, and by strongly impressing upon them the truth that for every idle word they shall render an account. As for the second class, he should upbraid them with greater severity, because their very excuse is a most serious accusation against themselves, since they show thereby that they yield no faith or confidence to these words of God: Seek first the kingdom of God and his justice, and all these things shall be added unto you.

THE NINTH AND TENTH COMMANDMENTS : *"Thou shalt not covet thy neighbour's house: neither shalt thou desire his wife, nor his servant, nor his hand-maid, nor his ox, nor his ass, nor anything that is his."*

Importance Of Instruction On These Two Commandments

It is to be observed, in the first place, that these two precepts, which were delivered last in order, furnish a general principle for the observance of all the rest. What is commanded in these two amounts to this, that if we wish to observe the preceding precepts of the law, we must be particularly careful not to covet. For he who does not covet, being content with what he has, will not desire what belongs to others, but will rejoice in their prosperity, will give glory to the immortal God, will render Him boundless thanks, and will observe the Sabbath, that is, will enjoy perpetual repose, and will respect his superiors. In fine, he will injure no man in word or deed or otherwise; for the root of all evil is concupiscence, which hurries its unhappy victims into every species of crime and wickedness. Keeping these considerations in mind, the pastor should be more diligent in explaining this Commandment, and the faithful more ready to hear (his instruction).

Why These Two Commandments Are Explained Here Together

We have united these two Commandments because, since their subject-matter is similar, they may be treated together. However, the pastor may explain them either together or separately, according as he may deem it more effective for his exhortations and admonitions. If, however, he has undertaken the exposition of the Decalogue, he should point out in what these two Commandments are dissimilar; how one covetousness differs from another -- a difference noticed by St. Augustine, in his book of

Questions on Exodus. The one covetousness looks only to utility and interest, the other to unlawful desire and criminal pleasure. He, for instance, who covets a field or house, pursues profit rather than pleasure, while he who covets another man's wife yields to a desire of pleasure, not of profit.

Necessity Of Promulgating These Two Commandments

The promulgation of these two Commandments was necessary for two reasons. The first is to explain the sixth and seventh Commandments. Reason alone shows that to prohibit adultery is also to prohibit the desire of another man's wife, because, were the desire lawful, its indulgence must be so too; nevertheless, many of the Jews, blinded by sin, could not be induced to believe that such desires were prohibited by God. Nay, even after the Law had been promulgated and become known, many who professed themselves its interpreters, continued in the same error, as we learn from these words of our Lord recorded in St. Matthew: You have heard that it was said to them of old: "Thou shalt not commit adultery," but I say to you, etc.

The second reason (for the promulgation) of these two Commandments is that they distinctly and in express terms prohibit some things of which the sixth and seventh Commandments do not contain an explicit prohibition. The seventh Commandment, for instance, forbids an unjust desire or endeavour to take what belongs to another; but this Commandment further prohibits even to covet it in any way, even though it could be acquired justly and lawfully, if we foresee that by such acquisition our neighbour would suffer some loss.

These Two Commandments Teach God's Love For Us And Our Need Of Him

But before we come to the exposition of the Commandments, the faithful are first to be informed that by this law we are taught not only to restrain our inordinate desires, but also to know the boundless love of God towards us.

By the preceding Commandments God had, as it were, fenced us round with safeguards, securing us and ours against injury of every sort; but by the addition of these two Commandments, He intended chiefly to provide against the injuries which we might inflict on ourselves by the indulgence of inordinate desires, as would easily happen were we at liberty to covet all things indiscriminately. By this law then, which forbids to covet, God has blunted in some degree the keenness of desire, which excites to every kind of evil, so that by reason of His command these desires are to some extent diminished, and we ourselves, freed from the annoying importunity of the passions, are enabled to devote more time to the performance of the numerous and important duties of piety and religion which we owe to God.

Nor is this the only lesson of instruction which we derive from these Commandments. They also teach us that the divine law is to be observed not only by the external performance of duties, but also by the internal concurrence of the heart. Between divine and human laws, then, there is this difference, that human laws are fulfilled by an external compliance alone, whereas the laws of God, since He reads the heart, require purity of heart, sincere and undefiled integrity of soul.

The law of God, therefore, is a sort of mirror, in which we behold the corruption of our own nature; and hence these words of the Apostle: I had not known concupiscence, if the law did not say: "Thou shalt not covet." ' Concupiscence, which is the fuel of sin, and which originated in sin, is always inherent in our fallen nature;

from it we know that we are born in sin, and, therefore, do we humbly fly for assistance to Him, who alone can efface the stains of sin.

Two Parts Of These Commandments

In common with the other Commandments, however, these two are partly mandatory, partly prohibitory.

Negative Part

"Thou Shalt Not Covet"

With regard to the prohibitory part, the pastor should explain what sort of concupiscence is prohibited by this law, lest some may think that which is not sinful to be sinful.

What Sort Of Concupiscence Is Not Forbidden

Such is the concupiscence of the spirit against the flesh; Or that which David so earnestly desired, namely, to long after the justifications of God at all times.

Concupiscence, then, is a certain commotion and impulse of the soul, urging men to the desire of pleasures, which they do not actually enjoy. As the other propensities of the soul are not always sinful, neither is the impulse of concupiscence always vicious. It is not, for instance, sinful to desire food and drink; when cold, to wish for warmth; when warm, to wish to become cool. This lawful species of concupiscence was implanted in us by the Author of nature; but in consequence of the sin of our first parents it passed the limits prescribed by nature and became so depraved that it frequently excites to the desire of those things which conflict with the spirit and reason.

However, if well regulated, and kept within proper bounds, it is often still the source of no slight advantage. In the first place, it leads us to supplicate God continually, and humbly to beg of Him those things which we most earnestly desire. Prayer is the interpreter of our wishes; and if this lawful concupiscence did not exist within us, prayer would be far less frequent in the Church of God. It also makes us esteem the gifts of God more highly; for the more eagerly we desire anything, the dearer and more pleasing will be its possession to us. Finally, the gratification which we receive from the acquisition of the desired object increases the devotion of our gratitude to God.

If then it is sometimes lawful to covet, it must be conceded that not every species of concupiscence is forbidden. St. Paul, it is true, says that concupiscence is sin; but his words are to be understood in the same sense as those of Moses, whom he cites, as the Apostle himself declares when, in his Epistle to the Galatians he calls it the concupiscence of the flesh for he says: Walk in the -spirit, and you shall not fulfil the lusts of the flesh.

Hence that natural, well-regulated concupiscence which does not go beyond its proper limits, is not prohibited; still less do these Commandments forbid that spiritual desire of the virtuous mind, which prompts us to long for those things that war against the flesh, for the Sacred Scriptures themselves exhort us to such a desire: Covet ye my words, Come over to me all ye that desire me.

What Sort Of Concupiscence Is Here Prohibited

It is not, then, the mere power of desire, which can move either to a good or a bad object that is prohibited by these Commandments; it is the indulgence of evil desire, which is called the concupiscence of the flesh, and the fuel of sin, and which when accompanied by the consent of the will, is always sinful. Therefore only that covetousness is forbidden which the Apostle calls the concupiscence of the flesh, that is to say, those motions of desire which are contrary to the dictates of reason and outstep the limits prescribed by God.

Two Kinds Of Sinful Concupiscence

This kind of covetousness is condemned, either because it desires what is evil, such as adultery, drunkenness, murder, and such heinous crimes, of which the Apostle says: Let us not covet evil things, as they also coveted; or because, although the objects may not be bad in themselves, yet there is some other reason which makes it wrong to desire them, as when, for instance, God or His Church prohibit their possession; for it is not permitted us to desire these things which it is altogether unlawful to possess. Such were, in the Old Law, the gold and silver from which idols were made, and which the Lord in Deuteronomy forbade anyone to covet

Another reason why this sort of vicious desire is condemned is that it has for its object that which belongs to another, such as a house, maid-servant, field, wife, ox, ass and many other things, all of which the law of God forbids us to covet, simply because they belong to another. The desire of such things, when consented to, is criminal, and is numbered among the most grievous sins. For sin is committed the moment the soul, yielding to the impulse of corrupt desires, is pleased with evil things, and either consents to, or does not resist them, as St. James, pointing out the beginning and progress of sin, teaches when he says: Every man is tempted by his own concupiscence, being drawn away and allured; then, when concupiscence hath conceived, it bringeth forth sin; but sin, when it is completed, begetteth death.

When, therefore, the Law says: Thou shalt not covet, it means that we are not to desire those things which belong to others. A thirst for what belongs to others is intense and insatiable; for it is written: A covetous man shall not be satisfied with money; and of such a one Isaias says: Woe to you that join house to house, and lay field to field.

The Various Objects We Are Forbidden To Covet

But a distinct explanation of each of the words (in which this Commandment is expressed) will make it easier to understand the deformity and grievousness of this sin.

Thy Neighbour's House

The pastor, therefore, should teach that by the word house is to be understood not only the habitation in which we dwell, but all our property, as we know from the usage and custom of the sacred writers. Thus when it is said in Exodus that the Lord built houses for the midwives, the meaning is that He improved their condition and means.

From this interpretation, therefore, we perceive, that we are forbidden to indulge an eager desire of riches, or to envy others their wealth, or power, or rank; but, on the contrary, we are directed to be content with our own condition, whether it be high or low. Furthermore, it is forbidden to desire the glory of others since glory also is comprised under the word house.

"Nor His Ox, Nor His Ass'

The words that follow, nor his ox, nor his ass, teach us that not only is it unlawful to desire things of greater value, such as a house, rank, glory, because they belong to others; but also things of little value, whatever they may be, animate or inanimate.

"Nor His Servant

The words, nor his servant, come next, and include captives as well as other slaves whom it is no more lawful to covet than the other property of our neighbour. With regard to the free who serve voluntarily either for wages, or out of affection or respect, it is unlawful, by words, or hopes, or promises, or rewards to bribe or solicit them, under any pretext whatever, to leave those to whose service they have freely engaged themselves; nay more, if, before the period of their contract has expired, they leave their employers, they are to be admonished, on the authority of this Commandment, to return to them by all means.

"Thy Neighbour's"

The word neighbour is mentioned in this Commandment to mark the wickedness of those who habitually covet the lands, houses and the like, which lie in their immediate vicinity; for neighbourhood, which should make for friendship, is transformed by covetousness from a source of love into a cause of hatred.

Goods For Sale Not Included Under This Prohibition

But this Commandment is by no means transgressed by those who desire to purchase or have actually purchased, at a fair price, from a neighbour, the goods which he has for sale. Instead of doing him an injury, they, on the contrary, very much assist their neighbour, because to him the money will be much more convenient and useful than the goods he sells.

"His Wife"

The Commandment which forbids us to covet the goods of our neighbour, is followed by another, which forbids us to covet our neighbour's wife -- a law that prohibits not only the adulterer's criminal desire of his neighbour's wife, but even the wish to marry her. For of old when a bill of divorce was permitted, it might easily happen, that she who was put away by one husband might be married to another. But the Lord forbade the desire of another's wife lest husbands might be induced to abandon their wives, or wives conduct themselves with such bad temper towards their husbands as to make it necessary to send them away.

But now this sin is more grievous because the wife, although separated from her husband, cannot be taken in marriage by another until the husband's death. He, therefore, who covets another man's wife will easily fall from this into another desire, for he will wish either the death of the husband or the commission of adultery.

The same principle holds good with regard to women who have been betrothed to another. To covet them is also unlawful; and whoever strives to break their engagement violates one of the most holy of promises.

And if to covet the wedded wife of another is entirely unlawful, it is on no account right to desire in- marriage the virgin who is consecrated to religion and to the service of God. But should anyone desire in marriage a married woman whom he thinks to be single, and whom he would not wish to marry if he knew she had a husband living, certainly he does not violate this Commandment. Pharaoh and Abimelech, as the Scripture informs us, were betrayed into this error; they wished to marry Sarah, supposing her to be unmarried, and to be the sister, not the wife of Abraham.

Positive Part

Detachment From Riches Enjoined

In order to make known the remedies calculated to overcome the vice of covetousness, the pastor should explain the positive part of the Commandment, which consists in this, that if riches abound, we set not our hearts upon them, that we be prepared to sacrifice them for the sake of piety and religion, that we contribute cheerfully towards the relief of the poor, and that, if we ourselves are poor, we bear our poverty with patience and joy. And, indeed, if we are generous with our own goods, we shall extinguish (in our own hearts) the desire of what belongs to another.

Concerning the praises of poverty and the contempt of riches, the pastor will find little difficulty in collecting abundant matter for the instruction of the faithful from the Sacred Scriptures and the works of the Fathers.

The Desire Of Heavenly And Spiritual Things Enjoined

Likewise this Commandment requires us to desire, with all the ardour and all the earnestness of our souls, the consummation, not of our own wishes, but of the holy will of God, as it is expressed in the Lord's Prayer. Now it is His will that we be made eminent in holiness; that we preserve our souls pure and undefiled; that we practice those duties of mind and spirit which are opposed to sensuality; that we subdue our unruly appetites, and enter, under the guidance of reason and of the spirit, upon a virtuous course of life; and finally that we hold under restraint those senses in particular which supply matter to the passions.

Thoughts which Help one to Keep these Commandments

In order to extinguish the fire of passion, it will be found most efficacious to place before our eyes the evil consequences of its indulgence.

Among those evils the first is that by obedience to the impulse of passion, sin gains uncontrolled sway over the soul; hence the Apostle warns us: Let not sin, therefore, reign in your mortal body, so as to obey the lusts thereof. Just as resistance to the passions destroys the power of sin, so indulgence of the passions expels God from His kingdom and introduces sin in His place.

Again, concupiscence, as St. James teaches, is the source from which flows very sin. Likewise St. John says: All that is in the world is the concupiscence of the mesh, the concupiscence of the eyes, and the pride of life.

A third evil of sensuality is that it darkens the understanding. Blinded by passion man comes to regard whatever he desires as lawful and even laudable.

Finally, concupiscence stifles the seed of the divine word, sown in our souls by God, the great husband man. Some, it is written in St. Mark, are sown among thorns; these are they who hear the word, and the cares of the world, and the deceitfulness of riches, and the lust after other things, entering in, choke the word, and it is made fruitless.

Chief Ways in which These two Commandments are Violated

They who, more than others, are the slaves of concupiscence, the pastor should exhort with greater earnestness to observe this Commandment. Such are the following: those who are addicted to improper amusements, or who are immoderately given to recreation; merchants, who wish for scarcity, and who cannot bear that other buyers or sellers hinder them from selling at a higher or buying at a lower rate; those who wish to see their neighbour reduced to want in order that they themselves may profit in buying or selling; soldiers who thirst for war, in order to enrich themselves with plunder; physicians, who wish for the spread of disease; lawyers, who are anxious for a great number of-cases and litigations; and artisans who, through greed for gain, wish for a scarcity of the necessaries of life in order that they may increase their profits.

They too, sin gravely against this Commandment, who, because they are envious of the praise and glory won by others, strive to tarnish in some degree their fame, particularly if they themselves are idle and worthless characters; for fame and glory are the reward of virtue and industry, not of indolence and laziness.

PART IV : THE LORD'S PRAYER

PRAYER

Importance Of Instruction On Prayer

One of the duties of the pastoral office, which is of the highest importance to the spiritual interests of the faithful, is to instruct them on Christian prayer; the nature and efficacy of which must remain unknown to many, if not taught by the pious and faithful diligence of the pastor. To this, therefore, should the care of the pastor be directed in a special manner, that his devout hearers may understand how and for what they are to ask God.

Whatever is necessary to the performance of the duty of prayer is comprised in that divine formula which Christ the Lord deigned to make known to His Apostles, and through them and their successors to all Christians. Its thoughts and words should be so deeply impressed on the mind and memory as to be ever in readiness. To assist pastors, however, in teaching the faithful concerning this prayer, we have set down from those writers who are conspicuous for learning and fullness in this matter, whatever appeared to us most suitable, leaving it to pastors to draw upon the same sources for further information, should they deem it necessary.

Necessity of Prayer

In the first place the necessity of prayer should be insisted upon. Prayer is a duty not only recommended by way of counsel, but also commanded by obligatory precept. Christ the Lord declared this when He said: We should pray always. This necessity of prayer the Church points out in the prelude, if we may so call it, which she prefixes to the Lord's Prayer: Admonished by salutary precepts, and taught by divine instruction, we presume to say, etc.

Therefore, since prayer is necessary to the Christian, the Son of God, yielding to the request of the disciples, Lord, teach us to pray, gave them a prescribed form of prayer, and encouraged them to hope that the objects of their petitions would be granted. He Himself was to them a model of prayer; He not only prayed assiduously, but watched whole nights in prayer.

The Apostles, also, did not omit to recommend this duty to those who had been converted to the faith of Jesus Christ. St. Peter and St. John are most diligent in their admonitions to the devout; and the Apostle, mindful of its nature, frequently admonishes Christians of the salutary necessity of prayer.

Besides, so various are our temporal and spiritual necessities, that we must have recourse to prayer as the best means for communicating our wants and receiving whatever we need. For since God owes nothing to anyone, we must ask of Him in prayer those things we need, seeing that He has constituted prayer as a necessary means for the accomplishment of our desires, particularly since it is clear that there are blessings which we cannot hope to obtain otherwise than through prayer. Thus devout prayer has such efficacy that it is a most powerful means of casting out demons; for there is a certain kind of demon which is not cast out but by prayer and fasting.

Those, therefore, who do not practice assiduous and regular prayer deprive themselves of a powerful means of obtaining gifts of singular value. To succeed in obtaining the object of your desires, it is not enough that you ask that which is good; your entreaties must also be assiduous. Every one that asketh, says St. Jerome, receiveth, as it is written. If, therefore, it is not given you, this is because you do not ask. Ask, therefore, and you shall receive.

The Fruits of Prayer

Moreover, this necessity of prayer is also productive of the greatest delight and usefulness, since it bears most abundant fruits. When it is necessary to instruct the faithful concerning these fruits, pastors will find ample matter in sacred writers. We have made from these sources a selection which appeared to us to suit the present purpose.

Prayer Honours God

The first fruit which we receive is that by praying we honour God, since prayer is a certain act of religion, which is compared in Scripture to a sweet perfume. Let my prayer, says the Prophet, be directed as incense in thy sight. By prayer we confess our subjection to God; we acknowledge and proclaim Him to be the author of all good, in whom alone we center all our hopes, who alone is our refuge, in all dangers and the bulwark of our salvation. Of this fruit we are admonished also in these words: Call upon me in the day of trouble; I -will deliver thee, and thou shalt glorify me.

Prayer Obtains What We Request

Another most pleasing and invaluable fruit of prayer is that it is heard by God. Prayer is the key of heaven, says St. Augustine; prayer ascends, and the mercy of God descends. High as are the heavens, and low as is the earth, God hears the voice of man. Such is the utility, such the efficacy of prayer, that through it we obtain a plenitude of heavenly gifts. Thus by prayer we secure the guidance and aid of the Holy Spirit, the security and preservation of the faith, deliverance from punishment, divine protection under temptation, victory over the devil. In a word, there is in prayer an accumulation of spiritual joy; and hence our Lord said: Ask, and you shall receive, that your joy may be full.

Proof

Nor can we, for a moment, doubt that God in His goodness awaits and is at all times ready to hear our petitions -- a truth to which the Sacred Scriptures bear ample testimony. Since, however, the texts are easy of access, we shall content ourselves with citing as an example the words of Isaias: Then shalt thou call, and the Lord will hear: thou shalt cry, and he will say, "Here I am"; and again, It shall come to pass, that before they call, I will hear: as they are yet speaking, I will hear. With regard to instances of persons, who have obtained from God the objects of their prayers, they are almost innumerable, and too well known to require special mention.

Unwise And Indevout Prayers Unheard

Sometimes, indeed, it happens that what we ask of God we do not obtain. But it is then especially that God looks to our welfare, either because He bestows on us other gifts of higher value and in greater abundance, or because what we ask, far from being necessary or useful, would prove superfluous and injurious. God, says St. Augustine, denies some things in His mercy which He grants in His wrath.

Sometimes, also, such is the remissness and negligence with which we pray, that we ourselves do not attend to what we say. Since prayer is an elevation of the soul to God, if, while we pray, the mind, instead of being fixed upon God, is distracted, and the tongue slurs over the words at random, without attention, without devotion, with what propriety can we give to such empty sounds the name of Christian prayer?

We should not, therefore, be at all surprised, if God does not comply with our requests; either because by our negligence and indifference we almost show that we do not really desire what we ask, or because we ask those things, which, if granted, would be prejudicial to our interests.

To Devout Prayer And Dispositions God Grants More Than Is Asked

On the other hand, to those who pray with devout attention, God grants more than they ask. This the Apostle declares in his Epistle to the Ephesians, and the same truth is unfolded ill the parable of the prodigal son, who would have deemed it a kindness to be admitted into the number of his father's servants.

Nay, God heaps His favours not only on those who seek them, but also on those who are rightly disposed; and this, not only with abundance, but also with readiness. This is shown by the words of Scripture: The Lord hath heard the desire of the poor. For God hastens to grant the inner and hidden desires of the needy without awaiting their utterance.

Prayer Exercises And Increases Faith

Another fruit of prayer is, that it exercises and augments the virtues of the soul, particularly the virtue of faith. As they who have not faith in God, cannot pray as they ought, for how can they call on him, whom they have not believed ? so the faithful, in proportion to the fervour of their prayers, possess a stronger and a more assured faith in the protecting providence of God, which requires principally that in all needs we have recourse to Him.

Prayer Strengthens Our Hope In God

God, it is true, might bestow on us all things abundantly, although we did not ask them or even think of them, just as He bestows on the irrational creation all things necessary for the support of life. But our most bountiful Father wishes to be invoked by His children; He wishes that, praying as we ought each day of our lives, we may pray with increased confidence. He wishes that in obtaining our requests we may more and more bear witness to and declare His goodness towards us.

Prayer Increases Charity

Our charity is also augmented. In recognising God as the author of every blessing and of every good, we are led to cling to Him with the most devoted love. And as those who cherish a mutual affection become more ardently attached by frequent interviews and conversations, so the oftener the soul prays devoutly and implores the divine mercy, thus holding converse with God, the more exquisite is the sense of delight which she experiences in each prayer, and the more ardently is she inflamed to love and adore Him.

Prayer Disposes The Soul For Divine Blessings

Furthermore, God wishes us to make use of prayer, in order that burning with the desire of asking what we are anxious to obtain, we may thus by our perseverance and zeal make such advances in spiritual life, as to be worthy to obtain those blessings which the soul could not obtain before because of its dryness and lack of devotion.

Prayer Makes Us Realise Our Own Needfulness

Moreover, God wishes us to realise, and always keep in mind, that, unassisted by His heavenly grace, we can of ourselves do nothing, and should therefore apply ourselves to prayer with all the powers of our souls.

Prayer Is A Protection Against The Devil

The weapons which prayer supplies are most powerful against our bitterest foes. With the cries of our prayers, says St. Hilary, we must fight against the devil and his armed hosts.

Prayer Promotes A Virtuous Life

From prayer we also derive this important advantage that though we are inclined to evil and to the indulgence of various passions, as a consequence of our natural frailty, God permits us to raise our hearts to Him, in order that while we address Him in prayer, and endeavour to deserve His gifts, we may be inspired with a love of innocence, and, by effacing our sins, be purified from every stain of guilt.

Prayer Disarms The Divine Vengeance

Finally, as St. Jerome observes, prayer disarms the anger of God. Hence, these words of God addressed to Moses: Let me alone, when Moses sought by his prayer to stay the punishments God was about to inflict on His people. Nothing is so efficacious in appeasing God, when His wrath is kindled; nothing so effectually delays or averts the punishments prepared for the wicked as the prayers of men.

The Parts Of Prayer

The necessity and advantages of Christian prayer being explained, the faithful should also know how many, and what are the parts of which it is composed; for that this pertains to the perfect discharge of this duty, we learn from the Apostle. In his Epistle to Timothy, exhorting to pious and holy prayer, he carefully enumerates the parts of which it consists: I desire therefore first of all that supplications, prayers, intercessions, and thanksgivings be made for all men. Although the shades of distinction between these different parts of prayer are delicate, yet the pastor, should he deem the explanation useful to his people, should consult, among others, St. Hilary and St. Augustine.

The Two Chief Parts Of Prayer Petition And Thanksgiving

There are two principal parts of prayer, petition and thanksgiving, and since these are the sources, as it were, from which all the others spring, they appear to us to be of too much importance to be omitted. For we approach God and offer Him the tribute of our worship, either to obtain some favour, or to return Him thanks for those with which His bounty every day enriches and adorns us.

God Himself indicated both these most necessary parts of prayer when He declared by the mouth of David: Call upon me in the day of trouble: I will deliver thee, and thou shalt glorify me.

Who does not perceive how much we stand in need of the goodness and beneficence of God, if he but consider the extreme destitution and misery of man?

On the other hand, all that have eyes and understanding know God's loving kindness toward man and the liberal bounty He exercises in our behalf. Wherever we cast our eyes, wherever we turn our thoughts, the admirable light of the divine goodness and beneficence beams upon us. What have we that is not the gift of His bounty? If, then, all things are the gifts and favours bestowed on us by His goodness, why should not everyone, as much as possible, celebrate the praises of God, and thank Him for His boundless beneficence.

Degrees Of Petition And Thanksgiving

Of these duties of petition and thanksgiving each contains many subordinate degrees. In order, therefore, that the faithful may not only pray, but also pray in the best manner, the pastor should propose to them the most perfect mode of praying, and should exhort them to use it to the best of their ability.

The Highest Degree Of Prayer: The Prayer Of The Just

What, then, is the best manner and the most exalted degree of prayer? It is that which is made use of by the pious and the just. Resting on the solid foundation of the true faith, they rise successively from one degree of prayer and virtue to another, until, at length, they reach that height of perfection, whence they can contemplate the infinite power, goodness, and wisdom of God; where, too, they are animated with the assured hope of obtaining not only those blessings which they desire in this life, but also those unutterable rewards which God has pledged Himself to grant to him who piously and religiously implores His assistance.

Soaring, as it were, to heaven, on these two wings, the soul approaches, in fervent desire, the Divinity; adores with supreme praise and thanksgiving Him from whom she has received such inestimable blessings; and, like an only child, animated with singular piety and profound veneration, trustfully tells her most beloved Father all her wants.

This sort of prayer the Sacred Scriptures express by the words pouring out. In his sight, says the Prophet, I pour out my prayer, but before him I declare my trouble. This means that he who comes to pray should conceal or omit nothing, but pour out all, flying with confidence into the bosom of God, his most loving Father. To this the Sacred Scriptures exhort us in these words: Pour out thy heart before him, cast thy care upon the Lord. This is that degree of prayer to which St. Augustine alludes when he says in that book entitled Enchiridion: What faith believes, that hope and charity implore.

The Second Degree Of Prayer: The Prayer Of Sinners

Another degree of prayer is that of those who are weighed down by the guilt of mortal sin, but who strive, with what is called dead faith, to raise themselves from their condition and to ascend to God. But, in consequence of their languid state and the extreme weakness of their faith, they cannot raise themselves from the earth. Recognising their crimes and stung with remorse of conscience, they bow themselves down with humility, and, far as they are removed from God, implore of Him with penitential sorrow, the pardon of their sins and the peace of reconciliation.

The prayers of such persons are not rejected by God, but are heard by Him. Nay, in His mercy, He generously invites such as these to have recourse to Him, saying: Come to me, all you that labour, and are heavily laden, and I will refresh you, of this class was the publican, who, though he did not dare to raise his eyes towards heaven, left the Temple, as (our Lord) declares, more justified than the Pharisee.

The Third Degree Of Prayer: The Prayer Of Unbelievers

A third degree of prayer is that which is offered by those who have not as yet been illumined with the light of faith; but who, when the divine goodness illumines in their souls the feeble natural light, are strongly moved to the desire and pursuit of truth and most earnestly pray for a knowledge of it.

If they persevere in such dispositions, God, in His mercy, will not neglect their earnest endeavours, as we see verified by the example of Cornelius the centurion. The doors of the divine mercy are closed against none who sincerely ask for mercy.

The Lowest Degree Of Prayer: The Prayer Of The Impenitent

The last degree is that of those who not only do not repent of their sins and enormities, but, adding crime to crime, dare frequently to ask pardon of God for those sins, in which they are resolved to continue. With such dispositions they would not presume to ask pardon from their fellow-man.

The prayer of such sinners is not heard by God. It is recorded of Antiochus: Then this wicked man prayed to the Lord, of whom he was not to obtain mercy. Whoever lives in this deplorable condition should be vehemently exhorted to wean himself from all affection to sin, and to return to God in good earnest and from the heart.

What We Should Pray For

Under the head of each Petition we shall point out in its proper place, what is, and what is not a proper object of prayer. Hence it will suffice here to remind the faithful in a general way that they ought to ask of God such things as are just and good, lest, praying for what is not suitable, they may be repelled in these words: You know not what you ask. Whatever it is lawful to desire, it is lawful to pray for, as is proved by the Lord's ample promise: You shall ask whatever you will, and it shall be done unto you, words in which He promises to grant all things.

Spiritual Goods

In the first place, then, the standard which should regulate all our wishes is that we desire above all else God, the supreme Good. After God we should most desire those things which unite us most closely to Him; while those which would separate us from Him, or occasion that separation, should have no share whatever in our affections.

External Goods And Goods Of Body

Taking, then, as our standard the supreme and perfect Good, we can easily infer how we are to desire and ask from God our Father those other things which are called goods. Goods which are called bodily, such as health, strength, beauty and those which are external, such as riches, honours, glory, often supply the means and give occasion for sin; and, therefore, it is not always either pious or salutary to ask for them. We should pray for these goods of life only in so far as we need them, thus referring all to God. It cannot be deemed unlawful to pray for those things for which Jacob and Solomon prayed. If, says Jacob, he shall give me bread to eat and raiment to put on, the Lord shall be my God. Give me, says Solomon, only the necessaries of life.

But when we are supplied by the bounty of God with necessaries and comforts, we should not forget the admonition of the Apostle: Let them that buy, be as if they possessed not, and those that use this world, as if they used it not; for the figure of this world passeth away; and again, If riches abound, set not your heart upon them. God Himself teaches us that only the use and fruit of these things belong to us and that we are obliged to share them with others. If we are blessed with health, if we abound in other external and corporal goods, we should recollect that they are given to us in order to enable us to serve God with greater fidelity, and as the means of lending assistance to others.

Goods Of The Mind

It is also lawful to pray for the goods and adornments of the mind, such as a knowledge of the arts and sciences, provided our prayers are accompanied with this condition, that they serve to promote the glory of God and our own salvation.

The only thing which can be absolutely and unconditionally the object of our wishes, our desires and our prayers, is, as we have already observed, the glory of God, and, next to it, whatever can serve to unite us to that supreme Good, such as faith and the fear and love of God, of which we shall treat at length when we come to explain the Petitions.

For Whom We Ought to Pray

The objects of prayer being known, the faithful are next to be taught for whom they are to pray. Prayer comprehends petition and thanksgiving. We shall first treat of petition.

The Prayer Of Petition Should Be Offered For All

We are to pray for all mankind, without exception of enemies, nation or religion; for every man, be he enemy, stranger or infidel, is our neighbour, whom God commands us to love, and for whom, therefore, we should discharge a duty of love, which is prayer. To the discharge of this duty the Apostle exhort: when he says: I desire that prayer be made for all men. In such prayers we should first ask for those things that concern spiritual interests, and next for what pertains to temporal welfare.

Those For Whom We Should Especially Offer Our Petitions: Pastors

Before all others the pastors of our souls have a right to our prayers, as we learn from the example of the Apostle in his Epistle to the Colossians, in which he asks them to pray for him, that God may open unto him a door of speech, a request which he also makes in his Epistle to the Thessalonians. In the Acts of the Apostles we also read that prayers were offered in the Church without intermission for Peter. St. Basil, in his work On Morals, urges to a faithful compliance with this obligation. We must, he says, pray for those who are charged with preaching the word of truth.

Rulers Of Our Country

In the next place, as the same Apostle teaches, we should pray for our rulers.

Who does not know what a singular blessing a people enjoy in public officials who are just and upright? We should, therefore, beseech God to make them such as they ought to be, fit persons to govern others.

The Just

To offer up our prayers also for the good and pious is a practice taught by the example of holy men. Even the good and the pious need the prayers of others. Providence has wisely ordained it so, in order that the just, realising the necessity they are under of being aided by the prayers of those who are inferior to them, may not be inflated with pride.

Enemies And Those Outside The Church

The Lord has also commanded us, to pray for those that persecute and calumniate us. The practice of praying for those who are not within the pale of the Church, is, as we know on the authority of St. Augustine, of Apostolic origin. We pray that the faith may be made known to infidels; that idolaters may be rescued from the error of their impiety; that the Jews, emerging from the darkness with which they are encompassed, may arrive at the light of truth; that heretics, returning to soundness of mind, may be instructed in the Catholic faith; and that schismatics may be united in the bond of true charity and may return to the communion of their holy mother, the Church, from which they have separated.

Many examples prove that prayers for such as these are very efficacious when offered from the heart. Instances occur every day in which God rescues individuals of every condition of life from the powers of darkness, and transfers them into the kingdom of His Beloved Son, from vessels of wrath making them vessels of mercy. That the prayers of the pious have very great influence in bringing about this result no one can reasonably doubt.

The Dead

Prayers for the dead, that they may be liberated from the fire of purgatory, are derived from Apostolic teaching. But on this subject we have said enough when explaining the Holy Sacrifice of the Mass.

Sinners

Those who are said to sin unto death derive little advantage from prayers and supplications. It is, however, the part of Christian charity to offer up our prayers and tears for them, in order, if possible, to obtain their reconciliation with God.

With regard to the execrations uttered by holy men against the wicked, it is certain, from the teaching of the Fathers, that they are either prophecies of the evils which are to befall sinners or denunciations of the crimes of which they are guilty, that the sinner may be saved, but sin destroyed.

The Prayer Of Thanksgiving Should Be Offered For All

In the second part of prayer we render most grateful thanks to God for the divine and immortal blessings which He has always bestowed, and still continues to bestow every day on the human race.

Our Thanksgiving Should Especially Be Offered: For The Saints

This duty we discharge especially when we give singular praises to God for the victory and triumph which all the Saints, aided by His goodness, have achieved over their domestic and external enemies.

For The Blessed Virgin Mary

To this sort of prayer belongs the first part of the Angelic Salutation, when used by us as a prayer: Hail Mary, full of grace, the Lord is with thee, blessed art thou among women. For in these words we render to God the highest praise and return Him most gracious thanks, because He has bestowed all His heavenly gifts on the most holy Virgin; and at the same time we congratulate the Virgin herself on her singular privileges.

To this form of thanksgiving the Church of God has wisely added prayers and an invocation addressed to the most holy Mother of God, by which we piously and humbly fly to her patronage, in order that, by her intercession, she may reconcile God to us sinners and may obtain for us those blessings which we stand in need of in this life and in the life to come. We, therefore, exiled children of Eve, who dwell in this vale of tears, should constantly beseech the Mother of mercy, the advocate of the faithful, to pray for us sinners. In this prayer we should earnestly implore her help and assistance; for that she possesses exalted merits with God, and that she is most desirous to assist us by her prayers, no one can doubt without impiety and wickedness.

To Whom We Should Pray

To God

That God is to be prayed to and His name invoked is the language of the law of nature, inscribed upon the human heart. It is also the doctrine of Holy Scripture, in which we hear God commanding: Call upon me in the day of trouble. By the word God, we mean the three Persons (of the adorable Trinity).

To The Saints

We must also have recourse to the intercession of the Saints who are in glory. That the Saints are to be prayed to is a truth so firmly established in the Church of God, that no pious person can experience a shadow of doubt on the subject. But as this point was explained in its proper place, under a separate head, we refer the pastor and others to that place.

God And The Saints Addressed Differently

To remove, however, the possibility of error on the part of the unlearned it will be found useful to explain to the faithful the difference between these two kinds of invocation.

We do not address God and the Saints in the same manner, for we implore God to grant us blessings or to deliver us from evils; while we ask the Saints, since they are the friends of God, to take us under their patronage and to obtain for us from God whatever we need. Hence we make use of two different forms of prayer. To God, we properly say: Have mercy on us, Hear us; but to the Saints, Pray for us. Still we may also ask the Saints, though in a different sense, that they have mercy on us, for they are most merciful. Thus we may beseech them that, touched with the misery of our condition, they would interpose in our behalf their influence and intercession before God.

In the performance of this duty, it is strictly incumbent on all not to transfer to any creature the right which belongs exclusively to God. For instance, when we say the Our Father before the image of a Saint we should bear in mind that we beg of the Saint to pray with us and to obtain for us those favours which we ask of God, in the Petitions of the Lord's Prayer, -- in a word, that he become our interpreter and intercessor with God. That this is an office which the Saints discharge, St. John the Apostle teaches in the Apocalypse.

Preparation for Prayer

In Scripture we read: Before prayer, prepare thy soul, and be not as a man that tempteth God. He tempts God who prays well but acts badly, and while he converses with God allows his mind to wander.

Since, then, the dispositions with which we pray are of such vital importance, the pastor should teach his pious hearers how to pray.

Humility

The first preparation, then, for prayer is an unfeigned humility of soul, an acknowledgment of our sinfulness, and a conviction that, when we approach God in prayer, our sins render us undeserving, not only of receiving a propitious hearing from Him, but even of appearing in His presence.

This preparation is frequently mentioned in the Scriptures: He hath had regard to the prayer of the humble, and he hath not despised their petitions; the prayer of him that humbleth himself shall pierce the clouds. Many other passages of the same kind will suggest themselves to learned pastors. Hence we abstain from citing more here.

Two examples, however, at which we have already glanced in another place, and which are apposite to our purpose, we shall not pass over in silence. The publican, who, standing afar off, would not so much as lift up his eyes toward heaven, and the woman, a sinner, who, moved with sorrow, washed the feet of Christ the Lord, with her tears, illustrate the great efficacy which Christian humility imparts to prayer.

Sorrow For Sin

The next (preparation) is a feeling of sorrow, arising from the recollection of our past sins, or, at least, some sense of regret, that we do not experience that sorrow. If the sinner bring not with him to prayer both, or, at least one of these dispositions, he cannot hope to obtain pardon.

Freedom From Violence, Anger, Hatred And Inhumanity

There are some crimes, such as violence and murder, which are in a special way obstacles to the efficacy of our prayers, and we must, therefore, preserve our hands unstained by outrage and cruelty. Of such crimes the Lord says by the mouth of Isaias: When you stretch forth your hands, I will turn away my eyes from you; and when you multiply prayer, I will not hear, for your hands are full of blood

Anger and strife we should also avoid, for they have great influence in preventing our prayers from being heard. Concerning them the Apostle says: 1 will that men pray in every place lifting up pure hands, without anger and contention.

Implacable hatred of any person on account of injuries received we must guard against; for while we are under the influence of such feelings,- it is impossible that we should obtain from God the pardon of our sins. When you shall stand to pray, He says, forgive, if you have aught against any man; and, if you will not forgive men, neither will your heavenly Father forgive you your offences.

Hardness and inhumanity to the poor we should also avoid. For concerning men of this kind it was said He that stoppeth his ear against the cry of the poor, shall also cry himself, and shall not be heard.

Freedom From Pride And Contempt Of God's Word

What shall we say of pride? How much it offends God, we learn from these words: God resisteth the proud, and giveth grace to the humble. What of the contempt of the divine oracles? He that turneth away his ears, says Solomon, from hearing the law, his prayer shall be an abomination.

Here, however, we are not to understand that we are forbidden to pray for the forgiveness of the injuries we have done, of murder, anger, insensibility to the wants of the poor, of pride, contempt of God's word, in fine, of any other sin.

Faith And Confidence

Faith is another necessary quality for this preparation of soul. Without faith, we can have no knowledge of the omnipotence or mercy of the supreme Father, which are the sources of our confidence in prayer, as Christ the Lord Himself has taught: All things whatsoever you shall ask in prayer, believing, you shall receive. St. Augustine, speaking of this faith, thus comments on the Lord's words: Without faith prayer is useless.

The chief requisite, therefore, of a good prayer is, as we have already said, a firm and unwavering faith. This the Apostle shows by an antithesis: How shall they call on him whom they have not believed? Believe, then, we must, both in order to pray, and that we be not wanting in that faith which renders prayer fruitful. For it is faith that leads to prayer, and it is prayer that, by removing all doubts, gives strength and firmness to faith. This is the meaning of the exhortation of St. Ignatius to those who would approach God in prayer: Be not of doubtful mind in prayer; blessed is he who hath not doubted. Wherefore, to obtain from God what we ask, faith and an assured confidence, are of first importance, according to the admonition of St. James: Let him ask in faith, nothing wavering.

Motives Of Confidence In Prayer

There is much to inspire us with confidence in prayer. Among these are to be numbered the beneficence and bounty of God, displayed towards us, when He commands us to call Him Father, thus giving us to understand that we are His children. Again there are the numberless instances of those whose prayers have been heard.

Further we have as our chief advocate, Christ the Lord, who is ever ready to assist us, as we read in St. John: If any man sin we have an advocate with the Father, Jesus Christ, the just; and he is the propitiation for our sins.' In like manner Paul the Apostle says: Christ Jesus, that died, yea, that is risen also again, who is at the right hand of God, who also maketh intercession for us. To Timothy he writes: For there is one God, and one mediator of God and men, the man Christ Jesus; and to the Hebrews he writes: Wherefore, it behoved him in all things to be made like unto his brethren, that he might become a merciful and faithful high-priest before God. Unworthy, then, as we are, of obtaining our requests, yet considering and resting our claims upon the dignity of our great Mediator and Intercessor, Jesus Christ, we should hope and trust most confidently, that, through His merits, God will grant us all that we ask in the proper way.

Finally, the Holy Ghost is the author of our prayers; and under His guiding influence, we cannot fail to be heard. We have received the spirit of adoption of sons, whereby we cry, "Abba, (Father)." This spirit succours our infirmity and enlightens our ignorance in the discharge of the duty of prayer; nay, even, as the Apostle says, He asketh for us with unspeakable groanings.

Should we, then, at any time waver, not being sufficiently strong in faith, let us say with the Apostles: Lord, increase our faith; and, with the father (of the demoniac): Help my unbelief.

Correspondence With God's Will

But what most ensures the accomplishment of our desires is the union of faith and hope with that conformity of all our thoughts, actions, and prayers to God's law and pleasure. If, He says, you abide in me, and my words abide in you, you shall ask whatever you will, and it shall be done unto you.

Fraternal Charity

In order, however, that our prayers may have this power of obtaining all things from God, we must, as was previously served, forget injuries, cherish sentiments of good will, and practice kindness towards our neighbour.

How to Pray Well

The manner of praying is also a matter of the highest moment. Though prayer in itself is good and salutary, yet if not performed in a proper manner it is unavailing. Often we do not obtain what we ask, because, in the words of St. James, we ask amiss. Pastors, therefore, should instruct the faithful in the best manner of asking well and of making private and public prayer. The rules of Christian prayer have been formed on the teaching of Christ the Lord.

We Must Pray In Spirit And In Truth

We must, then pray in spirit and in truth; for the heavenly Father seeks those who adore Him in spirit and in truth. He prays in this manner whose prayer proceeds from an interior and intense ardour of soul.

Mental Prayer

This spiritual manner of praying does not exclude the use of vocal prayer. Nevertheless, that prayer which is the vehement outpouring of the soul, deservedly holds the first place; and although not uttered with the lips, it is heard by God to whom the secrets of hearts are open. He heard the silent prayer of Anna, the mother of Samuel, of whom we read, that she prayed, shedding many tears and only moving her lips. Such was also the prayer of David, for he says: My heart hath said to thee, my f ace hath sought thee. In reading the Bible one will meet many similar examples.

Vocal Prayer

But vocal prayer has also its advantages and necessity. It quickens the attention of the mind, and kindles the fervour of him who prays. We sometimes, says St. Augustine, in his letter to Proba, animate ourselves to intensify our holy desire by having recourse to words and other signs; filled with vehement ardour and piety, we find it impossible at times not to express our feelings in words; for while the soul exults with joy, the tongue should also give utterance to that exultation. And surely it becomes us to make to God this complete sacrifice of soul and body, a kind of prayer which the Apostles were accustomed to use, as we learn from many passages of the Acts and of the Apostle.

Private And Public Prayer

There are two sorts of prayer, private and public. Private prayer is employed in order to assist interior attention and devotion; whereas in public prayer, which has been instituted to excite the piety of the faithful, and has been prescribed for certain fixed times, the use of words is indispensably required.

Those Who Do Nor Pray In Spirit

This practice of praying in spirit is peculiar to Christians, and is not at all used by infidels. Of these Christ the Lord has said: When you pray, speak not much, as the heathens; for they think that in their much speaking they may be heard. Be not ye, therefore, like to them, for your Father knoweth what is needful for you before you ask him.

But though (our Lord) prohibits loquacity, He is so far from forbidding continuance in prayer which proceeds from the eager and prolonged devotion of the soul that by His own example He exhorts us to such prayer. Not only did He spend whole nights in prayer, but also prayed the third time, saying the self-same words. The inference, therefore, to be drawn from the prohibition is that prayers consisting of mere empty sounds are not to be addressed to God.

Those Who Do Not Pray In Truth

Neither do the prayers of the hypocrite proceed from the heart; and against the imitation of their example, Christ the Lord warns us in these words: When ye pray, ye shall not be as the hypocrites that love to stand and pray in the synagogues, and corners of the streets, that they may be seen by men. Amen I say, to you they have received their reward. But thou, when thou shalt pray, enter into thy chamber, and having shut the door, pray to thy Father in secret; and thy Father who seeth in secret will repay thee. Here the word chamber may be understood to mean the human heart, which we should not only enter, but should also close against every distraction from without that could deprive our prayer of its perfection. For then will our heavenly Father, who sees perfectly our hearts and secret thoughts, grant our petitions.

We Must Pray With Perseverance

Another necessary condition of prayer is constancy. The great efficacy of perseverance, the Son of God exemplifies by the conduct of the judge, who, while he feared not God, nor regarded man, yet, overcome by the persistence and importunity of the widow, yielded to her entreaties." In our prayers to God we should, therefore, be persevering.

We must not imitate the example of those who become tired of praying, if, after having prayed once or twice, they succeed not in obtaining the object of their prayers. We should never be weary of the duty of prayer, as we are taught by the authority of Christ the Lord and of the Apostle. And should the will at any time fail us, we should beg of God by prayer the strength to persevere.

We Must Pray In The Name Of Jesus Christ

The Son of God would also have us present our prayers to the Father in His name; for, by His merits and the influence of His mediation, our prayers acquire such weight that they are heard by our heavenly Father. For He Himself says in St. John: Amen, Amen, I say unto you, if you ask the Father any thing in my name, he will give it you. Hitherto you have not asked any thing in my name: ask and you shall receive, that your joy may be full; and again: Whatsoever you shall ask the Father in my name, that will I do.

We Must Pray With Fervour, Uniting Petition To Thanksgiving

Let us imitate the fervour of the Saints in prayer; and to petition let us unite thanksgiving, imitating the example of the Apostles, who, as may be seen in the Epistles of St. Paul, always observed this salutary practice.

Fasting And Almsdeeds Should Be Joined To Prayer

To prayer let us unite fasting and almsdeeds. Fasting is most intimately connected with prayer. For the mind of one who is filled with food and drink is so borne down as not to be able to raise itself to the contemplation of God, or even to understand what prayer means.

Almsdeeds have also an intimate connection with prayer. For what claim has he to the virtue of charity, who, possessing the means of affording relief to those who depend on the assistance of others, refuses help to his neighbour and brother ? How can he, whose heart is devoid of charity, demand assistance from God unless, while imploring the pardon of his sins, he at the same time humbly beg of God to grant him the virtue of charity ?

This triple remedy was, therefore, appointed by God to aid man in the attainment of salvation. For by sin we offend God, wrong our neighbour, or injure ourselves. The wrath of God we appease by pious prayer; our offences against man we redeem by almsdeeds; the stains of our own lives we wash away by fasting. Each of these remedies, it is true, is applicable to every sort of sin; they are, however, peculiarly adapted to those three which we have specially mentioned.

OPENING WORDS OF THE LORD'S PRAYER

"Our Father who art in heaven"

Importance Of Instruction On These Words

The form of Christian prayer given us by Jesus Christ is so composed and arranged that before coming to requests and petitions certain words must be used as a sort of preface calculated to increase our confidence in God when we are about to address Him devoutly in prayer; and this being so it will be the pastor's duty to explain each of these words separately and with precision, so that the faithful may have recourse to prayer more readily because of the knowledge that they are going to commune and converse with a God who is also their Father. Regarding this preface, if we merely consider the number of words of which it is composed, it is brief indeed; but if we regard the ideas, it is of the greatest importance and replete with mysteries.

"Father"

The first word, which, by the order and institution of God we employ in this prayer, is Father. Our Saviour could, indeed, have commenced this divine prayer with some other word, conveying more the idea of majesty, such, for instance, as Lord or Creator. Yet He omitted all such expressions because they might rather inspire fear, and instead of them He has chosen a term inspiring confidence and love in those who pray and ask anything of God; for what is sweeter than the name Father, conveying, as it does, the idea of indulgence and tenderness ? The reasons why this name Father is applicable to God, can be easily explained to the faithful by speaking to them on the subjects of creation, providence, and redemption.

God Is Called Father Because He Created Us

Thus having created man to His own image -- a favour He accorded to no other living creature -- it is with good reason that, in view of this unique privilege with which He has honoured man, Sacred Scripture calls God the Father of all men; not only of the faithful, but also of the unbelieving.

God Is Called Father Because He Provides For Us

From His providence also may be drawn an argument. By a special superintending care and providence over our interests God displays a paternal love for us.

God's Care For Us Is Seen In The Appointment Of Guardian Angels

But in order to comprehend more clearly the fatherly care of God for men, it will be well in the explanation of this particular point to say something regarding the guardian Angels under whose protection men are placed.

By God's providence Angels have been entrusted with the office of guarding the human race and of accompanying every human being so as to preserve him from any serious dangers. Just as parents, whose children are about to travel a dangerous and infested road, appoint guardians and helpers for them, so also in the journey we are making towards our heavenly country our heavenly Father has placed over each of us an Angel under whose protection and vigilance we may be enabled to escape the snares secretly prepared by our enemy, repel the dreadful attacks he makes on us, and under his guiding hand keep the right road, and thus be secure against all false steps which the wiles of the evil one might cause us to make in order to draw us aside from the path that leads to heaven.

How We Are Helped By The Angels

And the immense advantage springing from the special care and providence of God with regard to men, the execution of which is entrusted to Angels, who by nature hold an intermediate place between God and man, will be clear from a multitude of examples with which Sacred Scripture supplies us in abundance, and which show that in God's goodness it has often happened that Angels have wrought wondrous works under the very eyes of men. This gives us to understand that many and equally important services, which do not fall under our sight, are wrought by our Angels, the guardians of our salvation, in our interest and for our advantage.

The Angel Raphael, the divinely appointed companion and guide of Tobias, conducted him and brought him back safe and sound; saved him from being devoured by an enormous fish; made known to him the extremely useful properties possessed by the liver, gall and heart of the monster; expelled the demon; repressed and fettered his power and prevented him from injuring Tobias; taught the young man the true and legitimate notion and use of matrimony; and finally restored to the elder Tobias the use of his sight.

In the same way the Angel who liberated the Prince of the Apostles, will supply copious material for the instruction of the pious flock regarding the striking fruits of the vigilance and protection of the Angels. The pastor need do no more than depict the Angel lighting up the darkness of the prison, touching Peter's side and awakening him from his sleep, loosing his chains, breaking his bonds, ordering him to rise, to take up his sandals and to follow; and then the pastor will point out how Peter was led forth out of prison by the same Angel, how he was enabled to pass without let or hindrance through the midst of the guard, how the doors were thrown open, and finally how he was placed in safety.

The historical part of Sacred Scripture, as we have already remarked, is full of such examples, all of which go to show the extent of the benefits bestowed by God on man through the ministry and intervention of Angels whom He deputes not only on particular and private occasions, but also appoints to take care of us from our very births. He furthermore appoints them to watch over the salvation of each one of the human race.

This teaching, if carefully explained, will have the effect of interesting and compelling the minds of the faithful to acknowledge and venerate more and more the paternal care and providence of God towards them.

God's Care For Us Seen In The Love He Has Ever Shown To Man

And here the pastor should especially praise and proclaim the treasures of God's goodness towards the human race. Though from the time of our first parents and from the moment of our first sin down to this very day we have offended Him by countless sins and crimes, yet He still retains His love for us and never renounces His singular solicitude for our welfare.

To imagine that He has forgotten us would be an act of folly and nothing short of a most outrageous insult. God was angry with the Israelites because of the blasphemy they had been guilty of in imagining that they had been abandoned by providence. Thus do we read in Exodus: They tempted the Lord, saying: "Is the Lord amongst us or not?" and in Ezechiel the divine anger is inflamed against the same people for having said: The Lord seeth us not: the

Lord hath forsaken the earth. These examples should suffice to deter the faithful from entertaining the criminal notion that God can ever possibly forget mankind. To the same effect we may read in Isaias the complaint uttered by the Israelite. against God; and, on the other hand, the kindly similitude with which God refutes their folly: Sion said: "The Lord hath forsaken me, and the Lord hath forgotten me." To which God answers: Can a woman forget her infant, so as not to have pity on the son of her womb? And if she should forget, yet will not I forget thee. Behold, I have engraven thee in my hands.

Although these passages clearly establish the point under discussion, yet thoroughly to convince the faithful that never for a moment can God forget man or cease to lavish on him tokens of His paternal tenderness, the pastor should still further confirm this by the striking example of our first parents. They had ignored and violated God's command. When you hear them sharply accused and that dreadful sentence of condemnation pronounced against them: Cursed is the earth in thy work, with labour and toil shalt thou eat thereof all the days of thy life; thorns and thistles shall it bring forth to thee; and thou shalt eat the herbs of the earth; " when you see them driven out of Paradise; when you read that to preclude all hope of their return a cherub was stationed at the entrance of Paradise, brandishing a flaming sword turning every way; and finally, when you know that, to avenge the injury done Him, God had afflicted them with punishments, internal and external, would you- not be inclined to think that man's case was hopeless? Would you not consider that not only was he bereft of all divine help, but was even abandoned to every misfortune? Yet, surrounded as he then was by so many evidences of divine wrath and vengeance, a gleam of the goodness of God towards him is seen to shine forth. For the Lord God, says Sacred Scripture, made for Adam and his wife garments of skins and clothed them, which was a very clear proof that at no time would God abandon man.

This truth, that the love of God can be exhausted by no human iniquity, was indicated by David in these words: Will God in his anger shut up his mercies? It was set forth by Habacuc when, addressing God, he said: When thou art angry thou wilt remember mercy; and by Micheas, who thus expresses it: Who is a God like to thee who takest away iniquity and passest by the sin of the remnant of thy inheritance? He will send his fury in no more, because he delighteth in mercy.

And thus precisely does it happen. At the very moment when we imagine ourselves to be utterly lost and altogether bereft of His protection, then it is that God in His infinite goodness seeks us out in a special way and takes care of us. Even in His anger He stays the sword of His justice, and ceases not to pour out the inexhaustible treasures of His mercy.

God Is Called Father Because He Has Granted Us Redemption

The creation of the world and God's providence are, then, of great weight in bringing into relief the singular love of God for the human race and the special care He takes of man. But far above these two shines the work of redemption, so much so indeed that our most bountiful God and Father has crowned His infinite goodness towards us by granting us this third favour.

Accordingly the pastor should instruct his spiritual children and constantly recall to their minds the surpassing love of God for us, so that they may be fully alive to the fact that having been redeemed in a wonderful manner they are thereby made the sons of God. To them, says St. John, He gave power to be made the sons of God . . . and they are born of God.

This is why Baptism, the first pledge and token of our redemption, is called the Sacrament of regeneration; for it is by Baptism that we are born children of God: That which is born of the Spirit, says our Lord, is spirit; and: You must be born again. In the same way we have the words of St. Peter: Being born again, not of corruptible seed, but incorruptible, by the word of God who liveth.

By reason of this redemption we have received the Holy Ghost and have been made worthy of the grace of God. As a consequence of this gift we are the adopted sons of God, as the Apostle Paul wrote to the Romans when he said: Ye have not received the spirit of bondage again in fear, but you have received the spirit of adoption of sons, whereby we cry: "Abba, Father." The force and efficacy of this adoption are thus set forth by St. John: Behold what manner of charity the Father hath bestowed upon us, that we should be called, and should be the sons of God.

Duties We Owe Our Heavenly Father

These points having been explained, the faithful should be reminded of all they owe in return to God, their most loving Father, so that they may be aware of the extent of the love, piety, obedience and respect they are bound to render to Him who has created them, who watches over them, and who has redeemed them; and with what hope and trust they should invoke Him.

But to enlighten the ignorant and to correct the false ideas of such as imagine prosperity and success in life to be the only test that God preserves and maintains His love towards us, and that the adversities and trials which come from His hand are a sign that He is not well disposed towards us and that He entertains hostile dispositions towards us, it will be necessary to point out that even if the hand of the Lord sometimes presses heavily upon us, it is by no means because He is hostile to us, but that by striking us He heals us, and that the wounds coming from God are remedies.

He chastises sinners so as to improve them by this lesson, and inflicts temporal punishments in order to deliver them from eternal torments. For though He visits our iniquities with a rod and our sins with stripes, yet his mercy he will not take away from us.

The faithful, therefore, should be recommended to recognise in such chastisements the fatherly love of God, and ever to have in their hearts and on their lips the saying of Job, the most patient of men: He woundeth and cureth; he striketh and his hands shall heal; as well as to repeat frequently the words written by Jeremias in the name of the people of Israel: Thou hast chastised me and I was instructed, as a young bullock unaccustomed to the yoke: convert me and I shall be converted; for thou art the Lord my God; and to keep before their eyes the example of Tobias who, recognising in the loss of his sight the paternal hand of God raised against him, cried out: I bless thee, O Lord God of Israel, because thou hast chastised me and thou hast saved me.

In this connection the faithful should be particularly on their guard against believing that any calamity or affliction that befalls them can take place without the knowledge of God; for we have His own words: A hair of your heads shall not perish. Let them rather find consolation in that divine oracle read in the Apocalypse: Those whom I love I rebuke and chastise; and let them find comfort in the exhortation addressed by St. Paul to the Hebrews: My son, neglect not the discipline of the Lord; neither be thou weaned whilst thou art rebuked by him: for whom the Lord loveth he chastiseth, and he scourgeth every son whom he receiveth.... But if you be without chastisement, ... then are you bastards and not sons.... Moreover if we have had the fathers of our flesh for instructors, and we reverenced them, shall we not much more obey the Father of spirits and live?

"Our"

When we invoke the Father and when each one of us calls Him our Father, we are to understand thereby that from the privilege and gift of divine adoption it necessarily follows that all the faithful are brethren and should love each other as such: You are all brethren for one is your Father who is in heaven." This is why the Apostles in their Epistles address all the faithful as brethren.

Another necessary consequence of this adoption is that not only are the faithful thereby united in the bonds of brotherhood, but that, the Son of God being truly man, we are called and really are his brethren also. Thus, in his Epistle to the Hebrews the Apostle, speaking of the Son of God, wrote as follows: He is not ashamed to call them brethren, saying: "I will declare thy name to my brethren. And long before this, David had foretold this of Christ the Lord; while Christ Himself thus addresses the women in the Gospel: Go, tell my brethren that they go into Galilee; there they shall see me. These words, as we know, He pronounced only after His Resurrection and when He had already put on immortality, thus showing that no one is at liberty to imagine that the bonds of brotherhood with us have been severed by His Resurrection and Ascension into heaven. Not only has the Resurrection of Christ not dissolved this union and love, but we know that one day, when from His throne of glory and majesty He shall judge mankind of all ages, He will call even the very least of the faithful by the name of brethren.

Indeed, how can we be other than brethren of Christ, seeing that we are called His co-heirs? Doubtless He is the first begotten, the appointed heir of all things; but we are begotten in the second place after Him, and are His co-heirs according to the measure of heavenly gifts we receive and according to the extent of the charity by which we show ourselves servants and cooperators of the Holy Ghost. He it is who by His inspirations moves and inflames us to virtue and good works, in order that we may be strengthened by His grace valiantly to undertake the combat that must be waged to secure salvation. And if we wisely and firmly carry on this combat we shall at the close of our earthly career be rewarded by our heavenly Father with the just recompense of that crown promised and held out to all those who run the same course. God, says the Apostle, is not unjust that He should forget your work and love.

Dispositions That Should Accompany The Words, "Our Father": Fraternal Regard

How sincere should be the manner in which we ought to utter the word our, we learn from St. Chrysostom. God, he says, listens willingly to the Christian who prays not only for himself but for others; because to pray for ourselves is an inspiration of nature; but to pray for others is an inspiration of grace; necessity compels us to pray for ourselves, whereas fraternal charity calls on us to pray for others. And he adds: That prayer which is inspired by fraternal charity is more agreeable to God than that which is dictated by necessity.

In connection with the important subject of salutary prayer, the pastor should be careful to remind and exhort all the faithful of every age, condition and rank, never to forget the bonds of universal brotherhood that bind them, and consequently ever to treat each other as friends and brothers, and never to seek arrogantly to raise themselves above their neighbours.

Though there are in the Church of God various gradations of office, yet this diversity of dignity and position in no way destroys the bond of fraternal union; just as in the human body the various uses and different functions of our organs in no way cause this or that part of the body to lose the name or office of an organ of the body.

Take, for instance, one who wields kingly power. If he is a Christian, is he not the brother of all those united in the communion of the Christian faith? Yes, beyond all doubt; and why? Because there is not one God giving existence to the rich and noble, and another giving existence to the poor and to subjects.

There is but one God, the Father and Lord of all; and consequently we have all the same nobility of spiritual birth, all the same dignity, all the same glory of race; for all have been regenerated by the same Spirit through the same Sacrament of faith, and have been made children of God and co-heirs to the same inheritance. The wealthy and great have not one Christ for their God; the poor and lowly, another; they are not initiated by different Sacraments; nor can they expect a different inheritance in the kingdom of heaven. We are all brethren and, as the Apostle says in his Epistle to the Ephesians: We are members of Christ's body, of his flesh and of his bones. This is a truth which the same Apostle thus expresses in his Epistle to the Galatians: You are the children of God, by faith in Jesus Christ; for as many of you as have been baptised in Christ, have put on Christ. There is neither Greek nor Jew, neither bond nor free, neither male nor female; for you are all one in Christ Jesus.

Now this is a point which calls for accuracy on the part of the pastor of souls, and one on which he should purposely dwell at considerable length; for it is a subject that is calculated both to strengthen and animate the poor and lowly, and to restrain and repress the arrogance of the rich and powerful. Indeed it was to remedy this latter evil that the Apostle insisted on brotherly charity and so often impressed it on the ears of his hearers.

Filial Confidence And Piety

Do not, then, forget, oh Christian, that when about to address this prayer to God, you ought to approach Him as a son to his Father; and hence in beginning your prayers and in pronouncing the words Our Father you should consider the rank to which God in His goodness has raised you when He commands you to fly to Him, not as a timid and fearful servant to his master, but willingly and confidently, like a child to its father.

In this remembrance and in this thought, consider with what fervour and piety you should pray. Endeavour to act as becomes a child of God; that is to say, see that your prayers and actions are never unworthy of that divine origin with which He has been pleased in His infinite bounty to ennoble you. It is to the discharge of this duty that the Apostle exhorts us when he says: Be ye therefore imitators of God as most dear children, so that what the Apostle wrote to the Thessalonians may be truly said of us: You are all the children of light, and the children of the day.

"Who art in Heaven"

Meaning Of These Words

All who have a correct idea of God will grant that He is where and in all places. This is not to be taken in the sense that He is distributed into parts and that He occupies and governs one place with one part and another place with another part. God is a Spirit, and therefore utterly incapable of division into parts. Who will dare to assign to any particular place or circumscribe within any limits that God who says of Himself: Do I not fill heaven and earth? On the contrary, these words must be taken in this sense, that by His power and virtue He embraces heaven and earth and all things contained therein; but that He Himself is not contained in any place. God is present to all things, either creating them, or preserving them after He has created them; but He is confined to no place, is limited by no bounds, nor in any way hindered from being everywhere present by His substance and power, as is indicated by holy David in the words: If I ascend into heaven thou art there.

But though God is present in all places and in all things, without being bound by any limits, as has been already said, yet in Sacred

Scripture it is frequently said that He has His dwelling in heaven. And the reason is because the heavens which we see above our heads are the noblest part of the world, remain ever Incorruptible, surpass all other bodies in power, grandeur and beauty, and are endowed with fixed and regular motion.

God, then, in order to lift up the minds of men to contemplate His infinite power and majesty, which are so preeminently visible in the work of the heavens, declares in Sacred Scripture that heaven is His dwelling-place. Yet at the same time He often affirms, what indeed is most true, that there is no part of the universe to which He is not present intimately by His nature and His power.

Lessons Taught By The Words, "Who Art In Heaven"

In connection with this consideration, however, let the faithful keep before their minds not only the image of the common Father of all, but also of a God reigning in heaven; and hence when about to pray, let them remember that they should raise heart and soul to heaven, and that the more the name of Father inspires them with hope and trust, the more should the sublime nature and divine majesty of our Father who is in heaven inspire them with sentiments of Christian humility and respect.

These words, furthermore, determine what we ought to ask of God in prayer; for every demand regarding the needs and wants of this life, if it have not some reference to the goods of heaven and if it be not directed to that end, is vain and unworthy of a Christian.

Let the pastor, therefore, instruct his pious hearers regarding this particular element of prayer, confirming his own words by the authority of the Apostle: If you be risen with Christ, seek the things that are above, where Christ is sitting at the right hand of God. Mind the things that are above, not the things that are upon the earth.

THE FIRST PETITION OF THE LORD'S PRAYER :
"HALLOWED BE THY NAME"

Why This Petition Is Placed First

What we are to ask of God and in what order, the Master and Lord of all has Himself taught and commanded. For prayer is the ambassador and interpreter of our thoughts and desires; and consequently we pray well and properly when the order of our petitions follows the order in which the things sought are desirable.

Now, genuine charity tells us to direct our whole soul and all our affections to God, for He alone being the one supreme Good, it is but reasonable that we love Him with superior and singular love. On the other hand, God cannot be loved from the heart and above all things else, unless we prefer His honour and glory to all things created. For all the good that we or others possess, all that in any way bears the name of good, comes from Him, and is therefore inferior to Him, the sovereign Good.

Hence, that our prayers may be made with due order, our Saviour has placed this Petition regarding the sovereign Good at the head of all the other Petitions of the Lord's Prayer, thus showing us that before asking the things necessary for ourselves or for others, we ought to ask those that appertain to God's honour, and to manifest and make known to Him the affections and desires of our hearts in this regard. Acting thus, we shall be faithful to the claims and rules of charity, which teaches us to love God more than ourselves and to ask, in the first place, those things we desire on His account, and next, those things we desire on our own.

Object Of The First Three Petitions

But as our desires and petitions concern such things only as are needed, and as nothing can be added to God; that is to say. to the Divine Nature, nor can His Divine Substance, which is ineffably rich in all perfection, be in any way increased, we must remember that the things we ask of God on God's own account are extrinsic and concern His exterior glory.

Thus we desire and beg that His name may be more and better known in the world, that His kingdom may be extended, and that each day new servants may come to obey His holy will. These three things, His name, His kingdom, and obedience (to His will), do not appertain to the intrinsic nature and perfection of God, but are extrinsic thereto.

To enable the faithful to understand still more clearly the force and bearing of these Petitions, the pastor should take care to point out to them that the words, On earth as it is in heaven, may be understood of each of the first three Petitions, as follows: Hallowed be thy name on earth as it is in heaven; Thy kingdom come on earth as it is in heaven; and, Thy will be done on earth as it is in heaven.

Hallowed Be Thy Name

In praying that the name of God may be hallowed, our meaning is that the sanctity and glory of the divine name may be increased.

On Earth As It Is In Heaven"

But in this connection the pastor should observe and should point out to his pious hearers that our Saviour does not in this expression say that the name of God is to be sanctified on earth in the same manner as it is in heaven; that is, that its earthly sanctification is to be equal in magnificence to its heavenly, a thing which is absolutely impossible, but only that such sanctification proceed from love and from the inmost affections of the soul. True, indeed, the divine name has in itself no need to be sanctified, since it is terrible and -holy,' as God Himself in His very Nature is holy, nor can any holiness be attributed Him which He has not possessed from all eternity; yet seeing that here below an honour far inferior to that which He deserves is rendered to Him, and that sometimes even He is dishonoured by cursing and blasphemy, we therefore desire and beg that His name may be exalted here on earth with praise, honour, and glory, after the example of that praise, honour and glory which are given Him in heaven.

What Sanctification of God's Name we should Pray For

That The Faithful May Glorify Him

In other words we pray that our minds, our souls and our lips may be so devoted to the honour and worship of God as to glorify Him. with all veneration both interior and exterior, and, after the model of the heavenly citizens, to celebrate with all our might the greatness, the glory and the holiness of the name of God.

That Unbelievers May Be Converted

Thus, then, as the heavenly spirits with perfect unanimity exalt and glorify God, so do we pray that the same be done over all the earth; that all nations may come to know, worship, and reverence God; that all without a single exception may embrace the Christian religion, may devote themselves wholly to the service of God, and may be convinced that in Him is the source of all sanctity and that there is nothing pure, nothing holy, that does not proceed from the sanctity of His divine name. According to the testimony of the Apostle, The church is cleansed by the laver of water in the word of life. and the word of life signifies the name of the Father and of the Son and of the Holy Ghost in which we are baptised and sanctified.

And since there is no expiation, no purity, no integrity, in him over whom the divine name has not been invoked, we desire and pray that all mankind may abandon the darkness of their impious infidelity, and, enlightened by the rays of divine light, may come to recognise the power of this name and look to it alone for true sanctity, and that thus receiving the Sacrament of Baptism in the name of the holy and undivided Trinity, they may receive the plenitude of sanctity from the right hand of God Himself.

That Sinners May Be Converted

Moreover, our desires and our supplications extend equally to those, who, stained with sin and wickedness, have lost the purity of their Baptism and their robe of innocence, thus permitting the unclean spirit to take up his abode once more in their unhappy souls. We therefore desire and pray God that in these also His name may be sanctified; that they may reenter into themselves and, returning to a right frame of mind, may recover their former holiness through the Sacrament of Penance, and become once more the pure and holy temple and dwelling-place of God.

That God May Be Thanked For His Favours

Finally, we pray that God may make His light to shine on the minds of all, so as to enable them to see that every best gift and e very perfect gift coming from the Father of lights, is conferred on us by Him, and consequently that temperance, justice, life, health, in a word, all goods of soul, body and possessions, all goods both natural and supernatural, must be recognised as gifts given by Him from whom, as the Church proclaims, proceed all blessings. If the sun by its light, if the stars by their motion and revolutions, are of any advantage to man; if the air with which we are surrounded serves to sustain us; if the earth with its abundance of produce and its fruits furnishes the means of subsistence to all men; if our rulers by their vigilance enable us to enjoy peace and tranquillity, it is to the infinite goodness of God that we owe these and innumerable blessings of a similar kind,-nay, those very causes which philosophers call secondary, we should regard as so many hands of God, wonderfully fashioned and fitted for our use, by means of which He distributes His blessings and diffuses them everywhere in profusion.

That The Church May Be Recognised By All

But what we most particularly ask in this Petition is that all may acknowledge and revere the spouse of Jesus Christ, our most holy mother the Church, in which alone is to be found the copious and inexhaustible fountain that cleanses and effaces all the stains of sin, and from which are drawn all the Sacraments of salvation and sanctification, those Sacraments through which, like so many sacred channels, is diffused over us by the hand of God the dew, of sanctity. To that Church alone and to those whom she embraces in her bosom and holds in her arms, appertains the invocation of that divine name, outside of which there is no other name under heaven given to men whereby we must be saved.

What Sanctification Of God's Name We Should Practice

The pastor should be careful to insist particularly on the fact that it is the duty of a good son not only to pray to God his Father in words, but also to endeavour by his conduct and actions to promote the sanctification of the divine name. And would to God there were none who, though continually praying for the sanctification of God's name, yet, as far as in them lies, violate and profane it by their deeds, and by whose fault God Himself is sometimes blasphemed. It was of such as these that the Apostle said: The name of God through you is blasphemed among the Gentiles; and in Ezechiel we read: They entered among the nations whither they went, and profaned my holy name, when it was said of them: "This is the people of the Lord, and they are come forth out of his land"; for according to the sort of life and conduct led by those professing a particular religion, so precisely in the eyes of the unlettered multitude will be the opinion held of that religion and of its author.

Those, therefore, who live according to the dictates of the Christian religion which they have embraced, and who regulate their prayers and actions by its precepts, furnish others with a powerful motive for greatly praising, honouring and glorifying the name of our heavenly Father. As for us, it is a duty which the Lord has imposed on us, to lead others by shining deeds of virtue to praise and glorify the name of God. This is how He addresses us in the Gospel: Let your light so shine before men, that they may see your good works and glorify your Father who is in heaven; and the Prince of the Apostles says: Having your conversation good among the Gentiles, that they may, by the good works which they shall behold in you, glorify God.

THE SECOND PETITION OF THE LORD'S PRAYER :
"THY KINGDOM COME"

Importance Of Instruction On This Petition

The kingdom of heaven which we pray for in this second Petition is the great end to which is referred, and in which terminates all the preaching of the Gospel; for from it St. John the Baptist commenced his exhortation to penance: Do penance, for the kingdom of heaven is at hand. With it also the Saviour of the world opened His preaching. In that admirable discourse on the mount in which He points out to His disciples the way to happiness, having proposed, as it were, the subject-matter of His discourse, our Lord commences with the kingdom of heaven: Blessed are the poor in spirit, for theirs is the kingdom of heaven. Again, to those who would detain Him with them, He assigns as the necessary cause of His departure: To other cities, also, I must preach the kingdom of God; therefore am I sent. This kingdom He afterwards commanded the Apostles to preach. And to him who expressed a wish to go and bury his father, He replied: Go thou, and preach the kingdom of God. And after He had risen from the dead, during those forty days in which He appeared to the Apostles, He spoke of the kingdom of God.

This second Petition, therefore, the pastor should treat with the greatest attention, in order to impress on the minds of his faithful hearers its great importance and necessity.

Greatness Of This Petition

In the first place pastors will be greatly assisted towards an accurate and careful explanation of this Petition by the thought that (the

Redeemer Himself) commanded this Petition, although united to the others, to be also offered separately, in order that we may seek with the greatest earnestness that for which we pray; for He says: Seek first the kingdom of God and his justice, and all these things shall be added unto you.

So great and so abundant are the heavenly gifts contained in this Petition, that it includes all things necessary for the security of soul and body. The king who pays no attention to those things on which depends the safety of his kingdom we should deem unworthy of the name. If a man is so anxious for the welfare of his kingdom, what must be the solicitude, what the providential care, with which the King of kings guards the life and safety of man?

We compress, therefore, within the small compass of this Petition for God's kingdom all that we stand in need of in our present pilgrimage, or rather exile, and all this God graciously promises to grant us; for He immediately subjoins: All these things shall be added unto you. Thus does he declare that He is that king who with bountiful hand bestows upon man an abundance of all things, whose infinite goodness enraptured David when he sang: The Lord ruleth me, and I shall want nothing.

Necessity Of Rightly Making This Petition

It is not enough, however, that we utter an earnest petition for the kingdom of God; we must also add to our prayer the use of all those means by which that kingdom is sought and found.- The five foolish virgins uttered earnestly the same petition in these words: Lord, Lord, open to us; but they used not the means necessary to secure its attainment, and were therefore rightly excluded. For God Himself has said: Not every one that saith to me, Lord, Lord, shall enter into the kingdom of heaven.

Motives For Adopting The Necessary Means

The priest, therefore, who is charged with the care of souls, should draw from the exhaustless fountain of the divine Scriptures those powerful motives which are calculated to move the faithful to the desire and pursuit of the kingdom of heaven, which portray in vivid coloring our deplorable condition, and which should make so sensible an impression upon them that, entering into themselves, they may call to mind that supreme happiness and those unutterable goods with which the eternal abode of God our Father abounds.

Here below we are exiles, inhabitants of a land in which dwell those demons whose hatred for us cannot be softened, who are the determined and implacable foes of mankind. What shall we say of those intestine conflicts and domestic battles in which the soul and the body, the flesh and the spirit, are continually engaged against each other, in which we have always to fear defeat, nay, in which instant defeat becomes inevitable, unless we be defended by the protecting hand of God? Feeling this weight of misery the Apostle exclaims: Unhappy man that I am, who shall deliver me from the body of this death?

The misery of our condition, it is true, strikes us at once of itself; but if contrasted with that of other creatures, it strikes us still more forcibly. Although irrational and even inanimate, the lower creatures are seldom seen so to depart from the acts, the instincts and the movements imparted to them by nature, as to fail of obtaining their appointed and determined end. This is so obvious in the case of beasts, fishes and birds that there is no need to dwell on it. But if we look to the heavens, do we not behold the verification of these words of David? For ever, O Lord, thy word standeth firm in the heavens. Constant in their motions, uninterrupted in their revolutions, they never depart in the least from the laws divinely prescribed. The earth, too, and universal nature, as we at once perceive, adhere strictly to, or at least depart but very little from the laws of their being.

But unhappy man is guilty of frequent falls. Seldom does he carry out his good resolutions; often he abandons and despises what he has well commenced; his best purposes which pleased for a time, are often suddenly abandoned, and he plunges into designs as degrading as they are pernicious.

What then is the cause of this misery and inconstancy? Manifestly a contempt of the divine inspirations. We close our ears to the admonitions of God, our eyes to the divine lights which shine before us; nor do we hearken to those salutary commands which are delivered by our heavenly Father.

To paint to the eyes of the faithful the misery-of man's condition, to detail its various causes, and to point out the efficacious remedies are, therefore, among the objects which should employ the zealous exertions of the pastor. In the discharge of this duty, his labor will be not a little lightened if he consults what has been said on the subject by those holy men, John Chrysostom and Augustine, and still more if he refers to our exposition of the Creed. For with a knowledge of these truths, who will be so obstinate in sin as not to endeavour, with the help of God's preventing grace, to rise, like the prodigal son spoken of in the Gospel, to stand erect, and hasten into the presence of his heavenly Father and king ?

"Thy Kingdom"

Having pointed out the advantages to be derived by the faithful from this Petition, the pastor should next explain the favours which it seeks. This becomes the more necessary as the words, kingdom of God, have a variety of significations, the exposition of each of which will not be found without its advantages in elucidating other passages of Scripture, and is necessary to a knowledge of the present subject.

The Kingdom Of Nature

In their ordinary sense, which is frequently employed by Scripture, the words, kingdom of God, signify not only that power which God possesses over all men and over the entire universe, but, also, His providence which rules and governs all things. In his hands, says the Prophet, are all the ends of the earth. The word ends includes those things also which lie buried in the depths of the earth, and are concealed in the most hidden recesses of creation. In this sense Mardochaeus exclaims: O Lord, Lord, almighty king, for all things are in thy power, and there is none that can resist thy will: thou art God of all, and there is none that can resist thy majesty.

The Kingdom Of Grace

By the kingdom of God is also understood that special and singular providence by which God protects and watches over pious and holy men. It is of this peculiar and admirable care that David speaks when he says: The Lord rules me, I shall want nothing, and Isaias: The Lord our king he will save us.

But although, even in this life, the pious and holy are placed, in a special manner, under this kingly power of God; yet our Lord Himself informed Pilate that His kingdom was not of this world, that is to say, had not its origin in this world, which was created and is doomed to perish. In this perishable way power is exercised by kings, emperors, commonwealths, rulers, and all whose titles to the government of states and provinces is founded upon the desire or election of men, or who have intruded themselves, by violent and unjust usurpation, into sovereign power.

Not so Christ the Lord, who, as the Prophet declares, is appointed king by God, and whose kingdom, as the Apostle says, is justice: The kingdom of God's justice and peace, and joy in the Holy Ghost. Christ our Lord reigns in us by the interior virtues of faith, hope and charity. By these virtues we are made a portion, as it were, of His kingdom, become subject in a special manner to God, and are consecrated to His worship and veneration; so that, as the Apostle could say: I live, yet not I, but Christ liveth in me, we too are able to say: I reign, yet not , but Christ reigneth in me.

This kingdom is called justice, because it has for its basis the justice of Christ the Lord. Of it our Lord says in St. Luke: The kingdom of God is within you. For although Jesus Christ reigns by faith in all who are within the bosom of our holy mother, the Church; yet in a special manner He reigns over those who are endowed with a superior faith, hope and charity, and have yielded themselves pure and living members to God. It is in these that the kingdom of God's grace is said to consist.

The Kingdom Of Glory

By the words kingdom of God is also meant that kingdom of His glory, of which Christ our Lord says in St. Matthew: Come ye blessed of my Father, possess the kingdom which was prepared for you from the beginning of the world. This kingdom the thief, when he had admirably acknowledged his crimes, begged of Christ in the words related by St. Luke: Lord, remember me, when thou comest into thy kingdom. Of this kingdom St. John speaks when he says: Unless a man be born again of water and the Spirit, he cannot enter into the kingdom of God; and of it the Apostle says to the Ephesians: No fornicator, or unclean, or covetous person (which is a serving of idols) hath inheritance in the kingdom of Christ and of God. To it also refer some of the parables made use of by Christ the Lord when speaking of the kingdom of heaven.

But the kingdom of grace must precede that of glory; for God's glory cannot reign in anyone in whom His grace does not already reign. Grace, according to the Redeemer, is a fountain of water springing up to eternal life; while as regards glory, what can we call it except a certain perfect and absolute grace? As long as we are clothed with this frail mortal flesh, as long as we wander in this gloomy pilgrimage and exile, weak and far away from God, we often stumble and fall, because we rejected the aid of the kingdom of grace, by which we were supported. But when the light of the kingdom of glory, which is perfect, shall have shone upon us, we shall stand forever firm and secure. Then shall all that is defective and unsuitable be utterly removed; then shall every infirmity be strengthened and invigorated; in a word, God Himself will then reign in our souls and bodies. But on this subject we have dealt already at greater length in the exposition of the Creed, when speaking of the resurrection of the flesh.

"Come"

Having thus explained the ordinary acceptation of the words, kingdom of God, we now come to point out the particular objects contemplated by this Petition.

We Pray For The Propagation Of The Church

In this Petition we ask God that the kingdom of Christ, that is, His Church, may be enlarged; that Jews and infidels may embrace the faith of Christ and the knowledge of the true God; that schismatics and heretics may return to soundness of mind, and to the communion of the Church of God which they have deserted; and that thus may be fulfilled and realised the words of the Lord, spoken by the mouth of Isaias: Enlarge the place of thy tent, and stretch out the skins of thy tabernacles; lengthen thy cords, and strengthen thy stakes, for thou shalt pass on to the right hand and to the left, for he that made thee shall rule over thee. And again: The Gentiles shall walk in thy light, and kings in the brightness of thy rising; lift up thy eyes round about and see; all these are gathered together, they are come to thee; thy sons shall come from afar, and thy daughters shall rise up at thy side.

For The Conversion Of Sinners

But in the Church there are to be found those who profess they know God, but in their works deny Him; whose conduct shows that they have only a deformed faith; who, by sinning, become the dwelling-place of the devil, where the demon exercises uncontrolled dominion. Therefore do we pray that the kingdom of God may also come to them so that the darkness of sin being dispelled from around them, and their minds being illumined by the rays of the divine light, they may be restored to their lost dignity of children of God; that heresy and schism being removed, and all offences and causes of sins being eradicated from His kingdom, our heavenly Father may cleanse the floor of His Church; and that, worshipping God in piety and holiness, she may enjoy undisturbed peace and tranquillity.

That Christ May Reign Over All

Finally, we pray that God alone may live, alone may reign within us; that death may no longer exist, but may be absorbed in the victory achieved by Christ our Lord, who, having broken and scattered the power of all His enemies, may, in His might, subject all things to His dominion.

Dispositions That Should Accompany This Petition

The pastor should also be mindful to teach the faithful, as the nature of this Petition demands, the thoughts and reflections with which their minds should be impressed in order to offer this prayer devoutly to God.

We Should Prize God's Kingdom Above All Things

He should exhort them, in the first place, to consider the force and import of that similitude of the Redeemer: The kingdom of heaven is like a treasure hidden in a field: which when a man hath found he hideth, and for joy thereof goeth and selleth all that he hath, and buyeth that field. He who knows the riches of Christ the Lord will despise all things when compared to them; to him wealth, riches, power, will appear as dross. Nothing can be compared to, or stand in competition with that inestimable treasure. Whoever, then, is blessed with this knowledge will say with the Apostle: I esteem all things to be but loss, and count them but as dung, that I may gain Christ. This is that precious jewel of the Gospel, and he who sells all his earthly goods to purchase it shall enjoy an eternity of bliss.

Happy we, should Jesus Christ shed so much light on us, as to enable us to discover this jewel of divine grace, by which He reigns in the hearts of those that are His. Then should we be prepared to sell all that we have on earth, even ourselves, to purchase and secure its possession; then might we say with confidence: Who shall separate us from the love of Christ?

But would we know the incomparable excellence of the kingdom of God's glory, let us hear the words and teaching of the Apostle: Eye hath not seen, nor ear heard, neither hath it entered into the heart of man, what things God hath prepared for them that love him.

We Must Realise That We Are Exiles

To obtain the object of our prayers it will be found most helpful to reflect within ourselves who we are, -- namely, children of Adam, exiled from Paradise by a just sentence of banishment, and deserving, by our unworthiness and perversity, to become the objects of God's supreme hatred, and to be doomed to eternal punishment.

This consideration should excite in us humility and lowliness. Thus our prayers will be full of Christian humility; and wholly distrusting ourselves, like the publican, we will fly to the mercy of God. Attributing all to His bounty we will render immortal thanks to Him who has imparted to us that Holy Spirit, relying on whom we are emboldened to say: Abba (Father).

We Must Labor To Obtain God's Kingdom

We should also be careful to consider what is to be done, what avoided, in order to arrive at the kingdom of heaven. For we are not called by God to lead lives of ease and indolence. On the contrary, He declares that the kingdom of God suffereth violence, and the violent bear it away; and, If thou wilt enter into life, keep the commandments. It is not enough, therefore, that we pray for the kingdom of God; we must also use our best exertions. It is a duty incumbent on US to cooperate with the grace of God, to use it in pursuing the path that leads to heaven. God never abandons us; He has promised to be with us at all times. We have therefore only this to see to, that we forsake not God, or abandon ourselves.

In this kingdom of the Church, God has provided all those succours by which He defends the life of man, and accomplishes his eternal salvation; whether they are invisible to us, such as the hosts of angelic spirits, or visible, such as the Sacraments, those unfailing sources of heavenly grace. Defended by these divine safeguards, not only may we securely defy the assaults of our most determined enemies, but may even lay prostrate, and trample under foot, the tyrant himself with all his nefarious legions.

Recapitulation

To conclude, let us then earnestly implore the Spirit of God that He may command us to do all things in accordance with His holy will; that He may so overthrow the empire of Satan that it shall have no power over us on the great accounting day; that Christ may be victorious and triumphant; that the divine influence of His law may be spread throughout the world; that His ordinances may be observed; that there be found no traitor, no deserter; and that all may so conduct themselves, as to come with joy into the presence of God their King, and may reach the possession of the celestial kingdom, prepared for them from all eternity, in the fruition of endless bliss with Christ Jesus.

THE THIRD PETITION OF THE LORD'S PRAYER :
"THY WILL BE DONE"

The Relation Of This Petition To The Previous One

Whoever desires to enter into the kingdom of heaven should ask of God that His will may be done. For Christ the Lord has said: Not every one that says to me, Lord, Lord, shall enter into the kingdom of heaven; but he that doth the will of my Father who is in heaven, he shall enter into the kingdom of heaven. Consequently this Petition follows immediately after the one which prays for the kingdom of heaven.

Necessity Of This Petition

In order that the faithful may know the necessity of this Petition and the numerous and salutary gifts which we obtain through it, the pastor should direct their attention to the misery and wretchedness in which the sin of Adam has involved mankind.

Man's Proneness To Act Against God's Will

From the beginning God implanted in all creatures an inborn desire of pursuing their own happiness that, by a sort of natural impulse, they may seek and desire their own end, from which they never deviate, unless impeded by some external obstacle.- This impulse of seeking God, the author and father of his happiness, was in the beginning all the more noble and exalted in man because of the fact that he was endowed with reason and judgment. But, while irrational creatures, which, at their creation were by nature Food, continued, and still continue in that original state and-condition, unhappy man went astray, and lost not only original justice, with which he had been supernaturally gifted and adorned by God, but also obscured that singular inclination toward virtue which had been implanted in his soul. All, He says, have gone aside, they are become unprofitable together; there is none that doth good, no, not one. For the imagination and thought of man's heart are prone to evil from his youth. Hence it is not difficult to perceive that of himself no man is wise unto salvation; that all are prone to evil; and that man has innumerable corrupt propensities, since he tends downwards and is carried with ardent precipitancy to anger, hatred, pride. ambition, and to almost every species of evil.

Man's Blindness Concerning God's Will

Although man is continually beset by these evils, yet his greatest misery is that many of these appear to him not to be evils at all. It is a proof of the most calamitous condition of man, that he is so blinded by passion and cupidity as not to see that what he deems salutary generally contains a deadly poison, that he rushes headlong after those pernicious evils as if they were good and desirable, while those things which are really good and virtuous are shunned as the contrary. Of this false estimate and corrupt judgment of man God thus expresses His detestation: Woe to you that call evil good, and good evil; that put darkness for light and light for darkness; that put bitter for sweet, and sweet for bitter.

In order, therefore, to delineate in vivid coloring the misery of our condition, the Sacred Scripture compares us to those who have lost their sense of taste and who, in consequence, loathe wholesome food, and prefer that which is unwholesome.

Man's Weakness In Fulfilling God's Will

It also compares us to sick persons who, as long as their malady lasts, are incapable of fulfilling the duties and offices proper to persons of sound and vigorous health. In the same way neither can we, without the assistance of divine grace, undertake actions such as are acceptable to God. Even should we, while in this condition, succeed in doing anything good, it will be of little or no avail towards attaining the bliss of heaven. But to love and serve God as we ought is something too noble and too sublime for us to accomplish by human powers in our present lowly and feeble condition, unless we are assisted by the grace of God.

Another very apt comparison to denote the miserable condition of mankind is that wherein we are likened to children who, if left to go their own way, are thoughtlessly attracted by everything that presents itself. Truly we are children, thoughtless children, wholly devoted to vain conversations and frivolous actions, once we become destitute of divine assistance; and hence the reproof which divine wisdom directs against us: O children, how long will you love childishness, and fools covet those things which are hurtful to themselves? while the Apostle thus exhorts us: Do not become children in sense.

Not only this, but our folly and blindness are even greater than those of children; for they are merely destitute of human prudence which they can of themselves acquire in course of time; whereas, if not assisted by God's help and grace, we can never aspire to that divine prudence which is so necessary to salvation. And if God's assistance should fail us, we at once cast aside those things that are truly good and rush headlong to voluntary ruin.

Remedy For These Evils

But should this darkness of spirit be removed with God's help; should we but perceive these our miseries; and, shaking off our insensibility, should we take account of the presence of the law of the members and recognise the struggle of the senses against the law of the spirit; and were we aware of every inclination of our nature to evil; how in that event could we fail to seek with earnest endeavour a suitable remedy for the great evils with which our nature is oppressed, and how fail to sigh for that salutary rule in accordance with which every Christian's life should be modelled and guided?

Now this is what we ask when we address to God these words: Thy will be done. We fell into this state of misery by disobeying and despising the divine will. God vouchsafes to propose to us, as the sole corrective of such great evils, a conformity to His will, which by sinning we despised; He commands us to regulate all our thoughts and actions by this standard. Now it is precisely His help to accomplish this that we ask when we suppliantly address to God the prayer, Thy will be done.

Man's Passions Rebel Against God's Will

The same should also be the fervent prayer of those in whose souls God-already reigns; who have been already illumined with the divine light, which enables them to obey the will of God. Although thus prepared, they have still to struggle against their own passions on account of the tendency to evil implanted in man's sensual appetite. Hence even though we are of the number of the just, we are still exposed to great danger from our own frailty, and should always fear lest, drawn aside and allured by our concupiscences, which war in our members, we should again stray from the path of salvation. Of this danger Christ the Lord admonishes us in these words: Watch ye and pray that ye enter not into temptation; the spirit indeed is willing but the flesh is weak.

It is not in the power of man, not even of him who has been justified by the grace of God, to reduce the irregular desires of the flesh to such a state of utter subjection that they may never afterwards rebel. By justifying grace God no doubt heals the wounds of the soul; but not those also of the flesh concerning which the Apostle wrote: J know that there dwelleth not in me, that is to say, in my flesh, that which is good.

The moment the first man forfeited original justice, which enabled him to bridle the passions, reason was no longer able to restrain them within the bounds of duty, or to repress those inordinate desires which are repugnant to reason. This is why the Apostle tells us that sin, that is to say, the incentive to sin, dwells in the flesh, thus giving us to understand that it does not make a mere temporary stay within us as a passing guest, but that as long as we live it maintains its abode in our members as a permanent inhabitant of the body.

Continually beset as we are by our domestic and interior enemies, it is easy for us to understand that we must fly to God's help and beg of Him that His will may be done in us.

"Thy Will"

Though the faithful are not to be left in ignorance of the import of this Petition, yet in this connection many questions concerning the will of God may be passed over which are discussed at great length and with much utility by scholastic doctors. Accordingly we shall content ourselves with saying that by the will of God is here meant that will which is commonly called the will of sign; that is to say, whatever God has commanded or counselled us to do or to avoid.

Hence, under the word will are here comprised all things that have been proposed to us as a means of securing the happiness of heaven, whether they regard faith or whether they regard morals, all, in a word, that Christ the Lord has commanded or forbidden either directly or through His Church. It is of this will that the Apostle thus writes: Become not unwise, but understand what is the will of God.

"Be Done"

We Ask That We May Fulfil What God Desires Of Us

When, therefore, we pray, Thy will be done, we first of all ask our heavenly Father to give us the strength to obey His Commandments, and to serve Him in holiness and justice all our days; to do all things according to His will and pleasure; to discharge all the duties prescribed for us in Sacred Scripture; under His guidance and assistance to perform all that becomes those who are born, not of the will of the flesh but of God, thus following the example of Christ the Lord who was made obedient unto death, even unto the death of the cross; finally, to be ready to bear all things rather than depart from His holy will in even the slightest degree.

Assuredly there is no one who burns with a more ardent desire and anxiety to obtain (the effect of this Petition) than he who has been so blessed as to be able to understand the sublime dignity attaching to those who obey God. For such a one thoroughly understands how true it is to say that to serve God and obey Him is to reign. Whoever, says the Lord, shall do the will of my Father who is in heaven, he is my brother and sister and mother that is to say, to him am I attached by the closest bonds of good will and love.

The Saints, with scarcely a single exception, failed not to make the principal gift contemplated by this Petition the object of their fervent prayers to God. All, indeed, have in substance made use of this admirable prayer, but not unfrequently in different words. David, whose strains breathe such wondrous sweetness, pours out the same prayer in various aspirations: O ! that my ways may be directed to keep thy justifications; Lead me into the path of thy commandments; Direct my steps according to thy word, and let no iniquity have dominion over me. In the same spirit he says: Give me understanding, and I will learn thy commandments; Teach me thy judgments; Give me understanding that I may know thy testimonies. He often expresses and repeats the same sentiment in other words. These passages should be carefully noticed and explained to the faithful, that all may know and comprehend the greatness and profusion of salutary gifts which are comprehended in the first part of this Petition.

We Ask That We May Not Yield To Our Own Inordinate Desires

In the second place, when we say, Thy will be done, we express our detestation of the works of the flesh, of which the Apostle writes: The works of the flesh are manifest, which are fornication, uncleanness immodesty, lust, etc.; if you live according to the flesh you shall die. We also beg of God not to suffer us to yield to the suggestions of sensual appetite, of our lusts, of our infirmities, but to govern our will by His will.

The sensualist, whose every thought and care is absorbed in the transient things of this world, is estranged from the will of God. Borne along by the tide of passion, he indulges his licentious appetites. In this gratification he places all his happiness, and considers that man happy who obtains whatever he desires. We, the contrary, beseech God in the language of the Apostle that we make not provision for the flesh in its concupiscence, but that His will be done.

We are not easily induced to entreat God not to satisfy our inordinate desires. This disposition of soul is difficult of attainment, and by offering such a prayer we seem in some sort to hate ourselves. To those who are slaves to the flesh such conduct appears folly; but be it ours cheerfully to incur the imputation of folly for the sake of Christ who has said: If any man will come after me, let him deny himself. This is especially so since we know that it is much better to desire what is right and just, than to obtain what is opposed to reason and religion and to the laws of God. Unquestionably the condition of the man who attains the gratification of his rash and inordinate desires is less enviable than that of him who does not obtain the object of his pious prayers.

We Ask That Our Mistaken Requests Be Not Granted

Our prayers, however, have not solely for object that God should deny us what accords with our desires, when it is clear that they are depraved; but also that He would not grant us those things for which, under the persuasion and impulse of the devil, who transforms himself into an Angel of light, we sometimes pray, believing them to be good.

The desire of the Prince of the Apostles to dissuade the Lord from His determination to meet death, appeared not less reasonable than religious; yet the Lord severely rebuked him, because he was led, not by supernatural motives, but by natural feeling.

What stronger proof of love towards the Lord than that shown by the request of St. James and St. John, who, filled with indignation against the Samaritans for refusing to entertain their Master, besought Him to command fire to descend from heaven and consume those hard-hearted and inhuman men? Yet they were reproved by Christ the Lord in these words: You know not of what spirit you are; the son of man came not to destroy souls but to save them.

We Ask That Even Our Good Requests Be Granted Only When They Are According To God's Will

We should beseech God that His will be done, not only when our desires are wrong, or have the appearance of wrong. We should ask this even when the object of our desire is not really evil, as when the will, obeying its instinctive impulse, desires what is necessary for our preservation, and rejects what seems to be opposed thereto. When about to pray for such things we should say from our hearts, Thy will be done, in imitation of the example of Him from whom we receive salvation and the science of salvation, who, when agitated by a natural dread of torments and of a cruel death, bowed in that horror of supreme sorrow with meek submission to the will of His heavenly Father: Not my will but thine be done.

We Ask That God May Perfect In Us What His Grace Has Begun

But, such is the degeneracy of our nature that, even when we have done violence to our passions and subjected them to the will of God, we cannot avoid sin without His assistance, by which we are protected from evil and directed in the pursuit of good. To this Petition, therefore, we must have recourse, beseeching God to perfect in us those things which He has begun; to repress the turbulent emotions of passion; to subject our sensual appetites to reason; in a word, to render us entirely conformable to His holy will.

We Ask That All May Know God's Will

We pray that the whole world may receive the knowledge of God's will, that the mystery of God, hidden from all ages and generations, may be made known to all.

"On Earth as it is in Heaven"

We also pray for the standard and model of this obedience, that our conformity to the will of God be regulated according to the rule observed in heaven by the blessed Angels and choirs of heavenly spirits, that, as they willingly and with supreme joy obey God, we too may yield a cheerful obedience to His will in the manner most acceptable to Him.

God requires that in serving Him we be actuated by the greatest love and by the most exalted charity; that although we devote ourselves entirely to Him with the hope of receiving heaven as reward, yet the reason we look forward to that reward should be that the Divine Majesty has commanded us to cherish that hope. Let all our hopes, therefore, be based on the love of God, who promises to reward our love with eternal happiness.

There are some who serve another with love, but who do so solely with a view to some recompense, which is the end and aim of their love; while others, influenced by love and loyalty alone, look to nothing else in the services which they render than the goodness and worth of him whom they serve, and, knowing and admiring his qualities consider themselves happy in being able to render him these services. This is the meaning of the clause On earth as it is in heaven appended (to the Petition).

It is then, our duty to endeavour to the best of our ability to be obedient to God, as we have said the blessed spirits are, whose profound obedience is praised by David in the Psalm in which he sings: Bless the Lord, all ye hosts; ye ministers of his that do his will.

Should anyone, adopting the interpretation of St. Cyprian, understand the words in heaven, to mean in the good and the pious, and the words on earth, in the wicked and the impious, we do not disapprove of the interpretation, by the word heaven understanding the spirit, and by the word earth, the flesh, that every person and every creature may in all things obey the will of God.

This Petition Contains an Act of Thanksgiving

This Petition also includes thanksgiving. We revere the most holy will of God, and in transports of joy celebrate all His works with the highest praise and acknowledgment, being assured that He has done all things well. It is certain that God is omnipotent; and the consequence necessarily forces itself on the mind that all things were created at His command. We also confess the truth that He is the supreme Good. We must, therefore, confess that all His works are good, for to all He imparted His own goodness. But if we cannot fathom in everything the divine plan, let us in all things banish every doubt and hesitation from the mind, and with the Apostle declare that his ways are unsearchable.

But the most powerful incentive to revere the will of God is that He has deigned to illumine by His heavenly light; for, He hath delivered us from the power of darkness, and hath translated us into the kingdom of the Son of his love.

The Dispositions that should Accompany this Petition

A Sense Of Our Own Weakness Of Will

To close our exposition of this Petition we must revert to a subject at which we glanced in the beginning. It is that the faithful in uttering this Petition should be humble and lowly in spirit: keeping in view the violence of their inborn passions which revolt against the will of God; recollecting that in this duty (of obedience) man is excelled by all other creatures, of whom it is written: All things serve thee; and reflecting, that he who is unable without divine help to undertake, not to say, perform, anything acceptable to God, must be very weak indeed.

Appreciation Of The Dignity Of Doing God's Will

But as there is nothing greater, nothing more exalted, as we have already said, than to serve God and live in obedience to His law and Commandments, what more desirable to a Christian than to walk in the ways of the Lord, to think nothing, to undertake nothing, at variance with His will? In order that the faithful may adopt this rule of life, and adhere to it with greater fidelity, (the pastor) should borrow from Scripture examples of individuals, who, by not referring their views to the will of God, have failed in all their undertakings.

Resignation To God's Will

Finally, the faithful are to be admonished to acquiesce in the simple and absolute will of God. Let him, who thinks that he occupies a place in society inferior to his deserts, bear his lot with patient resignation; let him not abandon his proper sphere, but abide in the vocation to which he has been called. Let him subject his own judgment to the will of God, who provides better for our interests than we can even desire ourselves. If troubled by poverty, by sickness, by persecution, or afflictions and anxieties of any sort, let us be convinced that none of these things can happen to us without the permission of God, who is the supreme Arbiter of all things. We should, therefore, not suffer our minds to be too much disturbed by them, but bear up against them with fortitude, having always on our lips the words: The will of the Lord be done; and also those of holy Job, As it hath pleased the Lord, so it is done: blessed be the name of the Lord.

THE FOURTH PETITION OF THE LORD'S PRAYER :
"GIVE US THIS DAY OUR DAILY BREAD"

The Relation Of The Following Petitions To Those That Preceded

The fourth and following Petitions, in which we particularly and expressly pray for the needs of soul and body, are subordinate to those which preceded. According to the order of the Lord's Prayer we ask for what regards the body and the preservation of life after we have prayed for the things which pertain to God. For since man has God as his last end, the goods of human life should be subordinated to those that are divine. These goods should be desired and prayed for, either because the divine order so requires, or because we need them to obtain divine blessings, that being assisted by these (temporal things) we may reach our destined end, the kingdom and glory of our heavenly Father, and the reverential observance of those commands which we know to emanate from His holy will. In this Petition, therefore, we should refer all to God and His glory.

How To Pray For Temporal Blessings

In the discharge of his duty towards the faithful the pastor, therefore, should endeavour to make them understand that, in praying for the use and enjoyment of temporal blessings, our minds and our desires are to be directed in conformity with the law of God, from which we are not to swerve in the least. By praying for the transient things of this world, we especially transgress; for, as the Apostle says, We know not what we should pray for as we ought. These things, therefore, we should pray for as we ought, lest, praying for anything as we ought not, we receive from God for answer, You know not what you ask.

Means Of Ascertaining Purity Of Intention In Offering This Petition

A sure standard for judging what petition is good, and what bad, is the purpose and intention of the petitioner. Thus if a person prays for temporal blessings under the impression that they constitute the sovereign good, and rests in them as the ultimate end of his desires, wishing nothing else, he unquestionably does not pray as he ought. As St. Augustine observes, we ask not these temporal things as our goods, but as our necessaries. The Apostle also in his Epistle to the Corinthians teaches that whatever regards the necessary purposes of life is to be referred to the glory of God: Whether you eat or drink, or whatever else you do, do all to the glory of God.

Necessity of the Fourth Petition

In order that the faithful may see the importance of this Petition, the pastor should remind them how much we stand in need of external things, in order to support and maintain life; and this they will the more easily understand, if he compares the wants of our first parent with those of his posterity.

Man Needs Many Things For His Bodily Life

It is true that in that exalted state of innocence, from which he himself, and, through his transgression, all his posterity fell, he had need of food to recruit his strength; yet there is a great difference between his wants and those to which we are subject. He stood not in need of clothes to cover him, of a house to shelter him, of weapons to defend him, of medicine to restore health, nor of many other things which are necessary to us for the protection and preservation of our weak and frail bodies. To enjoy immortality, it would have been sufficient for him to eat of the fruit which the blessed tree of life yielded without any labor from him or his posterity.

Nevertheless, since he was placed in that habitation of pleasure in order to be occupied, he was not, in the midst of these delights, to lead a life of indolence. But to him no employment would have been troublesome, no duty unpleasant. From the cultivation of those beautiful gardens he would always have derived fruits the most delicious, and his labours and hopes would never have been frustrated.

To Supply His Bodily Wants Man Must Labor

His posterity, on the contrary, are not only deprived of the fruit of the tree of life, but also condemned to this dreadful sentence: Cursed is the earth in thy work; with labour and toil shalt thou eat thereof all the days of thy life; thorns and thistles shall it bring forth to thee, and thou shalt eat the herbs of the earth. In the sweat of thy face shalt thou eat bread, till thou return to the earth, out of which thou wast taken; for dust thou art, and into dust thou shalt return.

Without God's Help Man's Labor Is Vain

Our condition, therefore, is entirely different from what his and that of his posterity would have been, had Adam listened to the voice of God. All things have been thrown into disorder, and have changed sadly for the worse. Of the resultant evils, this is not the least, that the heaviest cost, and labor, and toil, are frequently expended in vain; either because the crops are unproductive, or because the fruits of the earth are smothered by noxious weeds that spring up about them, or perish when stricken and prostrated by heavy rains, storms, hail, blight or blast. Thus is the entire labor of the year quickly reduced to nothing by some calamity of air or soil, inflicted in punishment of our crimes, which provoke the wrath of God and prevent Him from blessing our efforts. The dreadful sentence pronounced against us in the beginning remains.

Pastors, therefore, should apply themselves earnestly to the treatment of this subject, in order that the faithful may know that men fall into these perplexities and miseries through their own fault; that they may understand that while they must sweat and toil to procure the necessaries of life, unless God bless their labours, their hope must prove fallacious, and all their exertions unavailing. For neither he that planteth is anything, nor he that watereth but God who giveth the increase; unless the Lord build the house, they labour in vain that build it.

Inducements to Use this Petition

Parish priests, therefore, should point out that the things necessary to human existence, or, at least, to its comfort, are almost innumerable; for by this knowledge of our wants and weaknesses, Christians will be compelled to have recourse to their heavenly Father, and humbly to ask of Him both earthly and spiritual blessings.

They will imitate the prodigal son, who, when he began to suffer want in a far distant country, and could find no one to give him even husks in his hunger, at length entering into himself, perceived that from the evils by which he was oppressed, he could expect relief from no one but from his father.

Here the faithful will also have recourse more confidently to prayer, if, in reflecting on the goodness of God, they recollect that His paternal ears are ever open to the cries of His children. When He exhorts us to ask for bread, He promises to bestow it on us abundantly, if we ask it as we ought; for, by teaching us how to ask, He exhorts; by exhorting, He urges; by urging, He promises; by promising, He puts us in hope of most certainly obtaining our request.

"Bread"

When, therefore, the faithful are thus animated and encouraged, (the pastor) should next proceed to declare the objects of this Petition; and first, what that bread is which we ask.

It should then be known that, in the Sacred Scriptures, by the word bread, are signified many things, but especially two: first, whatever we use for food and for other corporal wants; secondly, whatever the divine bounty has bestowed on us for the life and salvation of the soul.

We Ask For Temporal Blessings

In this Petition, then, according to the interpretation and authority of the holy Fathers, we ask those helps of which we stand in need in this life on earth.

It Is Lawful To Pray For Temporal Blessings

Those, therefore, who say that it is unlawful for Christians to ask from God the earthly goods of this life, are by no means to be listened to; for not only the unanimous teaching of the Fathers, but also very many examples, both in the Old and New Testaments, are opposed to this error.

Thus Jacob, making a vow, prayed as follows: If God shall be with me, and shall keep me in the way, by which I walk, and shall give me bread to eat, and raiment to put on, and I shall return prosperously to my father's house, the Lord shall be my God, and this stone, which I have set up for a title, shall be called the house of God; and of all things thou shalt give to me, I will offer up tithes to thee. Solomon also asked a certain means of subsistence in this life, when he prayed: Give me neither beggary nor riches: give me only the necessaries of life.

Nay, the Saviour of mankind Himself commands us to pray for those things which no one will dare deny appertain to the benefit of the body. Pray, He says, that your flight be not in the winter, or on the sabbath. St. James also says: Is any one of you sad? Let him pray. Is he cheerful in mind? Let him, sing. And the Apostle thus addressed himself to the Romans: I beseech you, brethren, through our Lord Jesus Christ, and by the charity of the Holy Ghost, that you assist me in your prayers for me to God, that l may be delivered front the unbelievers that are in Judea. As, then, the faithful are divinely permitted to ask these temporal succours, and as this perfect form of prayer was given us by Christ the Lord, there remains no doubt that such a request constitutes one of the seven Petitions.

The Wants, Not The Luxuries Of This Life Are Meant By The Word "Bread"

We also ask our daily bread; that is, the things necessary for sustenance, understanding by the word bread, what is sufficient for raiment and for food, whether that food be bread,- or flesh, or fish, or anything else. In this sense we find Eliseus to have used the word when admonishing the king to provide bread for the Assyrian soldiers, to whom was then given a large quantity of various kinds of food. We also know that of Christ the Lord it is written, that He went into the house of a certain prince of the Pharisees on the sabbath day to eat bread, by which words we see are signified the things that constitute food and drink.

To comprehend the full signification of this Petition, it is, moreover, to be observed that by this word bread ought not to be understood an abundant and exquisite profusion of food and clothing, but what is necessary and simple, as the Apostle has written: Having food and wherewith to he covered, with these we are content; and Solomon, as said above: Give me only the necessaries of life.

"Our"

Of this frugality and moderation we are admonished in the next word; for when we say our, we ask for bread sufficient to satisfy our necessities, not to gratify luxury.

We do not say our in the sense that we are able of ourselves, and independently of God, to procure bread; for we read in David: All expect of thee that thou give them food in season: when thou givest to them they shall gather up: when thou openest thy hand they shall all be filled with good; and in another place, The eyes of all hope in thee, O Lord, and thou givest them meat in due season. (We say our bread, then), because it is necessary for us and is given to us by God, the Father of all, who, by His providence, feeds all living creatures.

It is-also called our bread for this reason, that it is to be acquired by us lawfully, not by injustice, fraud or theft. What we procure in evil ways is not our own, but the property of another. Its acquisition or possession, or, at least, its loss, is generally calamitous; while, on the contrary, there is in the honest and laborious gains of good men peace and great happiness, according to these words of the Prophet: For thou shalt eat the labours of thy hands: blessed art thou, and it shall be well with thee. Indeed to those who seek subsistence by honest labor, God promises the fruit of His kindness in the following passage: The Lord will send forth a blessing upon thy storehouses, and upon all the works of thy hands, and will bless thee.

Not only do we beg of God to grant us to use, with the aid of His goodness, the fruit of our virtuous toil -- and that is truly called ours -- but we also pray for a good mind, that we may be able well and prudently to use what we have honestly acquired.

"Daily"

By the word (daily) also is suggested the idea of frugality and moderation, to which we referred a short time ago; for we pray not for variety or delicacy of food, but for that which may satisfy the wants of nature. This should bring the blush of shame to those who, disdaining ordinary food and drink, look for the rarest viands and wines.

Nor by this word daily are they less censured to whom Isaias holds out those awful threats: Woe to you that join house to house, and lay field to field, even to the end of the place: shall you alone dwell in the midst of the earth? Indeed the cupidity of such men is insatiable, and it is of them that Solomon has written: A covetous man shall-not be satisfied with money. To them also applies that saying of the Apostle: They who would become rich fall into temptation, and into the snare of the devil.

We also call it our daily bread, because we use it to recruit the vital power that is daily consumed by the natural heat of the system.

Finally, another reason for the use of the word daily is the necessity of continually praying to God, in order that we may be kept in the practice of loving and serving Him, and that we may be thoroughly convinced of the fact that on Him depend our life and salvation.

"Give"

With regard to the two words give us, what ample matter they supply for exhorting the faithful piously and holily to worship and revere the infinite power of God, in whose hands are all things, and to detest that abominable boast of Satan: To me all things are delivered, and to whom I will I give them, must be obvious to everyone. For it is by the sovereign will of God alone that all things are dispensed, and preserved, and increased.

But what necessity, some one may say, is there imposed on the rich to pray for their daily bread, seeing that they abound in all things? They are under the necessity of praying thus, not that those things be given them which by the goodness of God they have in abundance, but that they may not lose their possessions. Hence the Apostle writes that the rich should learn from this not to be highminded, nor to trust in uncertain riches, but in the living God, who giveth us abundantly all things to enjoy.

St. Chrysostom adduces as a reason for the necessity of this Petition, not only that we may be supplied with food, but that we be supplied with it by the hand of the Lord, which imparts to our daily bread so wholesome and salutary an influence as to render the food profitable to the body, and the body subject to the soul.

"us"

But why say give us, in the plural number, and not give me? Because it is the duty of Christian charity that each individual be not solicitous for himself alone, but that he be also active in the cause of his neighbour; and that, while he attends to his own interests, he forget not the interests of others.

Moreover, the gifts which are bestowed by God on anyone are given, not that he alone should possess them, or that he should live luxuriously in their enjoyment, but that he should impart his superfluities to others. For, as St. Basil and St. Ambrose say, It is the bread of the hungry that you withhold; it is the clothes of the naked that you lock up; that money you bury under ground is the redemption, the freedom of the wretched.

"This Day"

The words this day remind us of our common infirmity. For who is there that, although he does not expect to be able by his own individual exertions to provide for his maintenance during a considerable time does not feel confident of having it in his power to procure necessary food for the day? Yet even this confidence God will not permit us to entertain, but has commanded us to ask Him for the food even of each successive day; and the necessary reason is, that as we all stand in need of daily bread, each should also make daily use of the Lord's Prayer.

So far we have spoken of the bread which we eat and which nourishes and supports the body; which is common to believers and unbelievers, to pious and impious, and is bestowed on all by the admirable bounty of God, Who maketh his sun to rise on the good and the bad, and raineth upon the just and the unjust.

The Spiritual Bread Asked for in this Petition

It remains to speak of the spiritual bread which we also ask in this Petition, by which are meant all things whatever that are required in this life for the health and safety of the spirit and soul. For as the food by which the body is nourished and supported is of various sorts, so is the food which preserves the life of the spirit and soul not of one kind.

The Word Of God Is Our Spiritual Bread

The Word of God is the food of the soul, as Wisdom says: Come, eat my bread, and drink the wine which I have mingled for you. And when God deprives men of the means of hearing His Word, which He is wont to do when grievously provoked by our crimes, He is said to visit the human race with famine; for we thus read in Amos: I will send forth a famine into the land, not a famine of bread, or a thirst of water, but of hearing the word of the Lord.

And as an incapability of taking food, or of retaining it when taken, is a sure sign of approaching death, so is it a strong argument for their hopelessness of salvation, when men either seek not the Word of God, or, having it, endure it not, but utter against God the impious cry, Depart from us, We desire not the knowledge of thy ways. This is the spiritual folly and mental blindness of those who, disregarding their lawful pastors, the Catholic Bishops and priests, and, abandoning the Holy Roman Church, have transferred themselves to the direction of heretics that corrupt the Word of God.

Christ Is Our Spiritual Bread, Especially In The Holy Eucharist

Now Christ the Lord is that bread which is the food of the soul. I am, He says of Himself, the living bread which came down from heaven. It is incredible with what pleasure and delight this bread fills devout souls, even when they must contend with earthly troubles and disasters. Of this we have an example in the Apostles, of whom it is written: They, indeed, went into the presence of the council rejoicing. The lives of the Saints are full of similar examples; and of these inward joys of the good, God thus speaks: To him that overcometh, I will give the hidden manna.

But Christ the Lord is especially our bread in the Sacrament of the Eucharist, in which He is substantially contained. This ineffable pledge of His love He gave us when about to return to the Father, and of it He said: He that eateth my flesh, and drinketh my blood, abideth in me, and I in him, Take ye and eat: this is my body. For matter useful to the faithful on this subject the pastor should consult what we have already said on the nature and efficacy of this Sacrament.

The Eucharist is called our bread, because it is the food of the faithful only, that is to say, of those who, uniting charity to faith, wash away the defilement of their sins in the Sacrament of Penance, and mindful that they are the children of God, receive and adore this divine Sacrament with all possible holiness and veneration.

Why The Holy Eucharist Is Called Our "Daily" Bread

The Eucharist is called daily (bread) for two reasons. The first is that it is daily offered to God in the sacred mysteries of the Christian Church and is given to those who seek it piously and holily. The second is that it should be received daily, or, at least, that we should so live as to be worthy, as far as possible, to receive it daily. Let those who hold the contrary, and who say that we should not partake of this salutary banquet of the soul but at distant intervals, hear what St. Ambrose says: If it is daily bread, why do you receive it yearly?

Exhortations

In the explanation of this Petition the faithful are emphatically to be exhorted that when they have honestly used their best judgment and industry to procure the necessary means of subsistence, they leave the issue to God and submit their own wish to the will of Him who shall not suffer the just to waver for ever. For God will either grant what is asked, and thus they will obtain their wishes; or He will not grant it, and that will be a most certain proof that what is denied the good by Him is not conducive either to their interest or their salvation, since He is more desirous of their eternal welfare than they themselves. This topic the pastor will be able to amplify, by explaining the reasons admirably collected by St. Augustine in his letter to Proba.

In concluding his explanation of this Petition the pastor should exhort the rich to remember that they are to look upon their wealth and riches as gifts of God, and to reflect that those goods are bestowed on them in order that they may share them with the indigent. With this truth the words of the Apostle, in his First Epistle to Timothy,' will be found to accord, and will supply parish priests with an abundance of matter wherewith to elucidate this subject in a useful and profitable manner.

THE FIFTH PETITION OF THE LORD'S PRAYER :
"AND FORGIVE US OUR DEBTS, AS WE FORGIVE OUR DEBTORS"

The Importance Of Explaining This Petition

So many are the things which display at once God's infinite power and His equally infinite wisdom and goodness, that wheresoever we turn our eyes or direct our thoughts, we meet with the most certain signs of omnipotence and benignity. And yet there is truly nothing that more eloquently proclaims His supreme love and admirable charity towards us, than the inexplicable mystery of the Passion of Jesus Christ, whence springs that never-failing fountain to wash away the defilements of sin. (It is this fountain) in which, under the guidance and bounty of God, we desire to be merged and purified, when we beg of Him to forgive us our debts.

This Petition contains a sort of summary of those benefits with which the human race has been enriched through Jesus Christ. This Isaias taught when he said: The iniquity of the house of Jacob shall be forgiven; and this is all the fruit, that the sin thereof should be taken away. David also shows this, proclaiming those blessed who could partake of that salutary fruit: Blessed are they whose iniquities are forgiven.

The pastor, therefore, should study and explain accurately and diligently the meaning of this Petition, which, we perceive, is so important to the attainment of salvation.

Difference Between This And The Preceding Petitions

In this Petition we enter on a new manner of praying. For hitherto we asked of God not only eternal and spiritual goods, but also transient and temporal advantages; whereas, we now ask to be freed from the evils of the soul and of the body, of this life and of the life to come.

Dispositions with which this petition should be Offered

Since, however, to obtain what we ask we must pray in a becoming manner, it appears expedient to explain the disposition with which this prayer should be offered to God.

Acknowledgment Of Sin

The pastor, then, should admonish the faithful, that he who comes to offer this Petition must first acknowledge, and next feel sorrow and compunction for his sins. He must also be firmly convinced that to sinners, thus disposed and prepared, God is willing to grant pardon. This confidence is necessary to sinners, lest perhaps the bitter remembrance and acknowledgment of their sins should be followed by that despair of pardon, which of old seized the mind of Cain and of Judas, both of whom looked on God solely as an avenger and punisher, forgetting that He is also mild and merciful.

In this Petition, therefore, we ought to be so disposed, that, acknowledging our sins in the bitterness of our souls, we may fly to God as to a Father, not as to a Judge, imploring Him to deal with us not according to His justice, but according to His mercy.

We shall be easily induced to acknowledge our sins if we listen to God Himself admonishing us through the Sacred Scriptures in this regard. Thus we read in David: They are all gone aside; they are become unprofitable together; there is none that doeth good, no not one. Solomon speaks to the same purpose: There is no just man upon earth, that doth good, and sinneth not. To this subject apply also these words: Who can say: "my heart is clean, I am pure from sin?" The very same has been written by St. John to deter men from arrogance: If we say that we have no sin, we deceive ourselves, and the truth is not in us. Jeremias also says: Thou hast said: "I am without sin, and am innocent"; and therefore, let thy anger be turned away from me. Behold, I will contend with thee in judgment, because thou hast said: "I have not sinned."

Christ the Lord, who spoke by the mouth of all these, confirms their teaching by this Petition in which He commands us to confess our sins. The Council of Milevi forbids us to interpret it otherwise. It hath pleased the Council, that whosoever will have it that these words of the Lord's prayer, "forgive us our debts," are said by holy men in humility, not in truth, let him be anathema. For who can endure a person praying, and lying not to men, but to the Lord Himself, saying with the lips that he desires to be forgiven, but with the heart, that he has no debts to be forgiven ?

Sorrow For Sin

In making this necessary acknowledgment of our sins, it is Dot enough to call them to mind lightly; for it is necessary that the recollection of them be bitter, that it touch the heart, pierce the soul, and imprint sorrow. Wherefore, the pastor should treat this point diligently, that his pious hearers may not only recollect their sins, and iniquities, but recollect them with pain and sorrow; so that with true interior contrition they may betake themselves to God their Father, humbly imploring Him to pluck from the soul the piercing stings of sin.

Motives For Sorrow Over Sin: The Baseness Of Sin

The pastor, however, should not be content with placing before the eyes of the faithful the turpitude of sin. He should also depict the unworthiness and baseness of men, who, though nothing but rottenness and corruption, dare to outrage in a manner beyond all belief the incomprehensible majesty and ineffable excellence of God, particularly after having been created, redeemed and enriched by Him with countless and invaluable benefits.

The Consequences Of Sin

And for what? Only for this, that separating ourselves from God our Father, who is the supreme Good, and lured by the most base rewards of sin, we may devote ourselves to the devil, to become his most wretched slaves. Language is inadequate to depict the cruel tyranny which the devil exercises over those who, having shaken off the sweet yoke of God, and broken the most lovely bond of charity by which our spirit is bound to God our Father, have gone over to their relentless enemy, who is therefore called in Scripture, the prince and ruler of the world, the prince of darkness, and king over all the children of pride. Truly to those who are oppressed by the tyranny of the devil apply these words of Isaias: O Lord our God, other lords besides thee have had dominion over us.

If these broken covenants of love do not move us, let at least the calamities into which we fall by sin move us. The sanctity of the soul is violated, which we know to have been wedded to Christ. That temple of the Lord is profaned, against the contaminators of which the Apostle utters this denunciation: If any man violate the temple of God, him shall God destroy.

Innumerable are the evils brought upon man by sin, that almost infinite pest of which David says: There is no health in my flesh, because of thy wrath; there is no peace for my bones, because of my sins. In these words he marks the violence of the plague, confessing that it left no part of him uninfected by pestiferous sin; for the poison had penetrated into his bones, that is, it infected his understanding and will, which are the two most intimate faculties of the soul. This widespread pestilence the Sacred Scriptures point out, when they designate sinners as the lame, the deaf, the dumb, the blind, the paralysed.

But,- besides the anguish which he felt on account of the enormity of his sins, David was afflicted yet more by the knowledge that he had provoked the wrath of God against him by his sin. For the wicked are at war with God, who is offended beyond belief at their crimes; hence the Apostle says: Wrath and indignation, tribulation and anguish upon every soul of man that worketh evil. Although the sinful act is transient, yet the sin by its guilt and stain remains; and the imminent wrath of God pursues it, as the shadow does the body.

When, therefore, David was pierced by these tormenting thoughts, he was moved to seek the pardon of his sins. That the faithful, imitating the Prophet, may learn to grieve, that is, to become truly penitent, and cherish the hope of pardon, the pastor should call to their attention the example of David's penitential sorrow, and the lessons of instruction drawn from his fiftieth Psalm.

How great is the utility of this sort of instruction, which teaches us to grieve for our sins, God Himself declares by the mouth of Jeremias, who, when exhorting the Israelites to repentance, admonished them to awake to a sense of the evils that follow upon sin. See, he says, that it is an evil and a bitter thing for thee, to have left the Lord thy God, and that my fear is not with thee, saith the Lord, the God of hosts. They who lack this necessary sense of acknowledgment and grief, are said by the Prophets Isaias, Ezechiel and Zachary to have a hard heart, a stony heart, a heart of adamant, for, like stone, they are softened by no sorrow, having no sense of life, that is, of the salutary recognition (of their sinfulness).

Confidence In God's Mercy

But lest the faithful, terrified by the grievousness of their sins, despair of being able to obtain pardon, the pastor ought to encourage them to hope by the following considerations.

As is declared in an Article of the Creed, Christ the Lord has given power to the Church to remit sins.

Furthermore, in this Petition, our Lord has taught how great is the goodness and bounty of God towards mankind; for if God were not ready and prepared to pardon penitents their sins, never would He have prescribed this formula of prayer: Forgive us our trespass. Wherefore we ought to be firmly convinced, that since He commands us in this Petition to implore His paternal mercy, He will not fail to bestow it on us. For this Petition assuredly implies that God is so disposed towards us, as willingly to pardon those who are truly penitent.

God it is against whom, having cast off obedience, we sin; the order of whose wisdom we disturb, as far as in us lies; whom we offend; whom we outrage by words and deeds. But it is also God, our most beneficent Father, who, having it in His power to pardon all transgressions, has not only declared His willingness to do so, but has also obliged men to ask Him for pardon, and has taught in what words they are to do so. To no one, therefore, can it be a matter of doubt, that under His guidance it is in our power to be reconciled to God. And as this declaration of the divine willingness to pardon increases faith, nurtures hope and inflames charity, it will be worth while to amplify this subject, by citing some Scriptural authorities and some examples of penitents to whom God granted pardon of the most grievous crimes. Since, however, in the introduction to the Lord's Prayer and in that portion of the Creed which teaches the forgiveness of sins, we were as diffuse on the subject as circumstances allowed, the pastor will borrow from those places whatever may seem pertinent for instruction on this point, for the rest drawing on the fountains of the Sacred Scriptures.

"Debts"

The pastor should also follow the same plan which we thought should be used in the other Petitions. Let him explain, then, what the word debts here signifies, lest perhaps the faithful, deceived by its ambiguity, pray for something different from what should be prayed for.

First, then, we are to know, that we by no means ask for exemption from the debt we owe to God on so many accounts, the payment of which is essential to salvation, namely, that of loving Him with our whole heart, our whole soul, and our whole mind; neither do we ask to be in future exempt from the duties of obedience, worship, veneration, or any other similar obligation, comprised also under the word debts.

What we do ask is that He may deliver us from sins. This is the interpretation of St. Luke, who, instead of debts, makes use of the word sins, because by their commission we become guilty before God and incur a debt of punishment, which we must pay either by satisfaction or by suffering. It was of this debt that Christ the Lord spoke by the mouth of His Prophet: Then did I pay that which I took not away. From these words of God we may understand that we are not only debtors, but also unequal to the payment of our debt, the sinner being of himself utterly incapable of making satisfaction.

Wherefore we must fly to the mercy of God; and as justice, of which God is most tenacious, is an equal and corresponding attribute to mercy, we must make use of prayer, and the intercession of the Passion of our Lord Jesus Christ, without which no one ever obtained the pardon of his sins, and from which, as from its source, have flown all the efficacy and virtue of satisfaction. For of such value is that price paid by Christ the Lord on the cross, and communicated to us through the Sacraments, received either actually or in purpose and desire, that it obtains and accomplishes for us the pardon of our sins, which is the object of our prayer in this Petition.

Here we ask pardon not only for our venial offences, for which pardon may most easily be obtained, but also for grievous and mortal sins. With regard to grave sins, however, this Petition cannot procure forgiveness unless it derive that efficacy from the Sacrament of Penance, received, as we have already said, either actually or at least in desire.'

"Our"

The words our debts are used here in a sense entirely different from that in which we said our bread. That bread is ours, because it is given us by the munificence of God; whereas sins are ours, because with us rests their guilt. They are our voluntary acts, otherwise they would not have the character of sin.

Admitting, therefore, and confessing the guilt of our sins, we implore the clemency of God, which is necessary for their expiation. In this we make use of no palliation whatever, nor do we transfer the blame to others, as did our first parents Adam and Eve. We judge ourselves, employing, if we are wise, the prayer of the Prophet: Incline not my heart to evil words, to make excuses in sins.

"Forgive Us"

Nor do we say, forgive me, but forgive us; because the fraternal relationship and charity which subsist between all men, demand of each of us that, being solicitous for the salvation of all our neighbours, we pray also for them while offering prayers for ourselves.

This manner of praying, taught by Christ the Lord, and subsequently received and always retained by the Church of God, the Apostles most strictly observed themselves and taught others to observe.

Of this ardent zeal and earnestness in praying for the salvation of our neighbours, we have the splendid example of Moses in the Old, and of St. Paul in the New Testament. The former besought God thus: Either forgive them this trespass; or, if thou dost not, strike me out of the book that thou hast written; ' while the latter prayed after this manner: I wished myself to be anathema from Christ for my brethren.

"As we Forgive our Debtors"

The word as may be understood in two senses. It may be taken as having the force of a comparison, meaning that we beg of God to pardon us our sins, just as we pardon the wrongs and contumelies which we receive from those by whom we have been injured. It may also be understood as denoting a condition, and in this sense Christ the Lord interprets that formula. If, He says, you forgive men their offences, your heavenly Father will also forgive you your offences; but if you will not forgive men, neither will your Father forgive you your sins.

Either sense, however, equally contains the necessity of forgiveness, intimating, as it does that, if we desire that God should grant us the pardon of our offences, we ourselves must pardon those from whom we have received injury; for so rigorously does God exact from us forgetfulness of injuries and mutual affection and love, that He rejects and despises the gifts and sacrifices of those who are not reconciled to one another.

Necessity Of Forgiveness

Even the law of nature requires that we conduct ourselves towards others as we would have them conduct themselves towards us; hence he would be most impudent who would ask of God the pardon of his own offences while he continued to cherish enmity against his neighbour.

Those, therefore, on whom injuries have been inflicted, should be ready and willing to pardon, urged to it as they are by this form of prayer, and by the command of God in St. Luke: If thy brother sin against thee, reprove him; and if he repent, forgive him; and if he sin against thee seven times in a day, and seven times in a day turn again to thee, saying, "I repent," forgive him. In the Gospel of St. Matthew we read: Love your enemies; and the Apostle, and before him Solomon wrote: If thy enemy be hungry, give him to eat; if he thirst, give him to drink; and finally we read in the Gospel of St. Mark: When you shall stand to pray, forgive if you have anything against any man; that your Father also who is in heaven may forgive you your sins.

Reasons For Forgiveness

But since, on account of the corruption of nature, there is nothing to which man brings himself more reluctantly than to the pardon of injuries, let pastors exert all the powers and resources of their minds to change and bend the dispositions of the faithful to this mildness and mercy so necessary to a Christian. Let them dwell on those passages of Scripture in which we hear God commanding to pardon enemies.

Let them also insist on this certain truth, that one of the surest signs that men are children of God is their willingness-to forgive injuries and sincerely love their enemies; for in loving our enemies there shines forth in us some likeness to God our Father, who, by the death of His Son, ransomed from everlasting perdition and reconciled to Himself the human race, which before was most unfriendly and hostile to Him.

Let the close of this exhortation and injunction be the command of Christ the Lord, which, without utter disgrace and ruin, we cannot refuse to obey: Pray for them that persecute and calumniate you; that you may be the children of your Father who is in heaven.

This Petition Should Not be Neglected

But in this matter no ordinary prudence is required on the part of the pastor, lest, knowing the difficulty and necessity of this precept, anyone despair of salvation.

Those Unable To Forget Injuries

There are those who, aware that they ought to bury injuries in voluntary oblivion and ought to love those that injure them, desire to do so, and do so as far as they are able, but feel that they cannot efface from their mind all recollection of injuries. For there lurk in the mind some remains of private grudge, in consequence of which such persons are disturbed by misgivings of conscience, fearing that they have not in simplicity and frankness laid aside their enmities and consequently do not obey the command of God.

Here, therefore, the pastor should explain the contrary desires of the flesh and of the spirit; that the former is prone to revenge, the latter ready to pardon; that hence a continual struggle and conflict goes on between them. Wherefore he should point out that although the appetites of corrupt nature are ever opposing and rebelling against reason, we are not on this account to be uneasy regarding salvation, provided the spirit persevere in the duty and disposition of forgiving injuries and of loving our neighbour.

Those Who Do Not Love Their Enemies

There may be some who, because they have not yet been able to bring themselves to forget injuries and to love their enemies, are consequently deterred by the condition contained in this Petition from making use of the Lord's Prayer. To remove from their minds this pernicious error, the pastor should adduce the two following considerations.

(In the first place), whoever belongs to the number of the faithful, offers this prayer in the name of the entire Church, in which there must necessarily be some pious persons who have forgiven their debtors the debts here mentioned.

Secondly, when we ask this favour from God, we also ask for whatever cooperation with the Petition is necessary on our part in order to obtain the object of our prayer. Thus we ask the pardon of our sins and the gift of true repentance; we pray for the grace of inward sorrow; we beg that we may be able to abhor our sins, and confess them truly and piously to the priest. Since, then, it is necessary for us to forgive those who have inflicted on us any loss or injury, when we ask pardon of God we beg of Him at the same time to grant us grace to be reconciled to those against whom we harbour hatred.

Those, therefore, who are troubled by that groundless and perverse fear, that by this prayer they provoke still more the wrath of God, should be undeceived and should be exhorted to make frequent use of a prayer in which they beseech God our Father to grant them the disposition to forgive those who have injured them and to love their enemies.

How to Make this Petition Fruitful

Penitential Dispositions

But that this Petition may be really fruitful we should first seriously reflect that we are suppliants before God, soliciting from Him pardon, which is not granted but to the penitent; and that we should, therefore, be animated by that charity and piety which are fitting in penitents, whom it eminently becomes to keep before their eyes, as it were, their own crimes and enormities and to expiate them with tears.

Avoidance Of Dangers Of Sin

To this thought should be joined caution in guarding for the future against every occasion of sin, and against whatever I nay expose us to the danger of offending God our Father. With this solicitude the mind of David was occupied when he said: My sin is always before me; and: Every night I will wash my bed; I will water my couch with my tears.

Imitation Of Fervent Penitents

Let each one also call to mind the ardent love of prayer of those who obtained from God through their entreaties the pardon of their sins. Such was the publican, who, standing afar off through shame and grief, and with eyes fixed on the ground, only smote his breast, crying: O God, be merciful to me, a sinner. Such was also the woman, a sinner, who, standing behind Christ the Lord, washed His feet, wiped them with her hair, and kissed them. Lastly, there is the example of Peter, the Prince of the Apostles, who going forth wept bitterly.

Frequent Use Of The Sacraments

They should next consider that the weaker men are, and the more liable to diseases of the soul, which are sins, the more numerous and frequent are the remedies they need. Now the remedies of a sick soul are Penance and the Eucharist; these, therefore, the faithful should frequently make use of.

Almsdeeds

Next almsdeeds, as the Sacred Scriptures declare, are a medicine suited to heal the wounds of the soul. Wherefore, let those who desire to make pious use of this prayer act kindly to the poor according to their means. Of the great efficacy of alms in effacing the stains of sin, the Angel of the Lord in Tobias, holy Raphael, is a witness, who says: Alms deliver from death, and the same is that which purgeth away sins, and maketh to find mercy and life everlasting. Daniel is another witness, who thus admonished King Nabuchodonosor: Redeem thou thy sins with alms, and thy iniquities with works of mercy to the poor.

The Spirit Of Forgiveness

The best alms and the most excellent act of mercy is forgetfulness of injuries, and good will towards those who have injured us or ours, in person, in property, or in character. Whoever, therefore, desires to experience in a special manner the mercy of God, should make an offering to God Himself of all his enmities, remit every offence, and pray for his enemies with the greatest good will, seizing every opportunity of doing them good. But as this subject was explained when we treated of murder, we refer the pastor to that place.

The pastor ought to conclude his explanation of this Petition with this final reflection, that nothing is, or can be conceived, more unjust than that he who is so rigorous towards men as to extend indulgence to no one, should himself demand that God be mild and kind towards him.

THE SIXTH PETITION OF THE LORD'S PRAYER :
"AND LEAD US NOT INTO TEMPTATION."

Importance Of Instruction On This Petition

When the children of God, having obtained the pardon of their sins, are inflamed with the desire of giving to God worship and veneration; when they long for the kingdom of heaven; when they engage in the performance of all the duties of piety towards the Deity, relying entirely on His paternal will and providence, -- then it is that the enemy of mankind employs the more actively all his artifices, and prepares all his resources to attack them so violently as to justify the fear that, wavering and altered in their sentiments, they may relapse into sin, and thus become far worse than they had been before. To such as these may justly be applied the saying of the Prince of the Apostles: It had been better for them not to have known the way of justice, than, after they have known it, to turn back from that holy commandment which was delivered to them.

Hence Christ the Lord has commanded us to offer this Petition so that we may commend ourselves daily to God, and implore His paternal care and assistance, being assured that, if we be deserted by the divine protection, we shall soon fall into the snares of our most crafty enemy.

Nor is it in the Lord's Prayer alone that He has commanded us to beg of God not to suffer us to be led into temptation. In His address to the holy Apostles also, on the very eve of His death, after He had declared them clean, He admonished them of this duty in these words: Pray that ye enter not into temptation.

This admonition, reiterated by Christ the Lord, imposes on the pastor the weighty obligation of exciting the faithful to a frequent use of this prayer, so that, beset as men constantly are by the great dangers which the devil prepares, they may ever ad dress to God, who alone can repel those dangers, the prayer, Lead us not into temptation.'

Necessity of the Sixth Petition

Human Frailty

The faithful will understand how very much they stand in need of this divine assistance, if they remember their own weakness and ignorance, if they recollect this saying of Christ the Lord: The spirit indeed is willing, but the flesh is weak; if they call to mind how grievous and destructive are the misfortunes of men brought on through the instigation of the devil, unless they be upheld and assisted by the right hand of the Most High.

What more striking example can there be of human infirmity, than the holy band of the Apostles, who, though they had just before felt very courageous, at the first sight of danger, abandoned the Saviour and fled. A still more conspicuous example is the conduct of the Prince of the Apostles. He who a short time before loudly protested his courage and special loyalty to Christ the Lord, he who had been so confident in himself as to say, Though I should die with thee, I will not deny thee, became so affrighted at the voice of a poor maid-servant that he declared at once with an oath that he knew not the Lord. Doubtless his courage was not equal to his good-will. But if, by the frailty of human nature in which they confided, even the Saints have sinned grievously, what have not others to fear, who are so far below them in holiness?

The Assaults Of The Flesh

Wherefore, let the pastor remind the faithful of the conflicts and dangers in which we are continually engaged, as long as the soul is in this mortal body, assailed as we are on all sides by the world, the flesh and the devil.

How few are there who are not compelled to experience at their great cost what anger, what concupiscence can do in us? Who is not annoyed by these stings? who does not feel these goads? who does not burn with these smouldering fires? And, indeed, so various are these assaults, so diversified these attacks, that it is extremely difficult not to receive some grievous wound.

The Temptations Of The Devil

And besides these enemies that dwell and live with us, there are, moreover, those most bitter foes, of whom it is written: Our wrestling is not against, flesh and blood; but against principalities and powers, against the rulers of the world' of this darkness, against the spirits of wickedness in the high places. For to our inward conflicts are added the external assaults and attacks of the demons, who both assail us openly, and also insinuate themselves by stratagem into our souls, so much so that it is only with great difficulty that we can escape them.

The Apostle entitles the demons princes, on account of the excellence of their nature, since by nature they are superior to man, and to all other visible creatures. He also calls them powers, because they excel not only by their nature, but also by their power. He designates them rulers of the world of darkness, because they rule not the world of light and glory, that is to say, the good and the pious, but the world of gloom and darkness, namely, those who, blinded by the defilement and darkness of a wicked life, are satisfied to have for their leader the devil, the prince of darkness. He also terms the demons the spirits of wickedness, because there is a wickedness of the spirit, as well as of the flesh. What is called the wickedness of the flesh inflames the appetite to lusts and pleasures, which are perceived by the senses; while the wickedness of the spirit are evil purposes and depraved desires, which belong to the superior part of the soul, and which are so much worse than the wickedness of the flesh as mind itself and reason are higher and more excellent (than the senses). The wickedness of Satan the Apostle spoke of as in the high places, because the chief aim of the evil one is to deprive us of our heavenly inheritance.

Audacity Of The Demons

From all this we may understand that the power of these enemies is great, their courage undaunted, their hatred of us enormous and unmeasured; that they also wage against us a perpetual war, so that with them there can be no peace, no truce.

How great is their audacity is evidenced by the words of Satan, recorded by the Prophet: I will ascend into heaven. He attacked our first parents in Paradise; he assailed the Prophets; he beset the Apostles in order, as the Lord says in the Gospel, that he might sift them as wheat.' Nor was he abashed even by the presence of Christ the Lord Himself. His insatiable desire and unwearied diligence St. Peter therefore expressed when he said: Your adversary, the devil, as a roaring lion goeth about, seeking whom he may devour.

Number Of The Demons

But it is not Satan alone that tempts men, for sometimes a host of demons combine to attack an individual. This that evil spirit confessed, who, having been asked his name by Christ the Lord, replied, My name is legion; that is to say, a multitude of demons, tormented their unhappy victim. And of another demon it is written: He taketh with him seven other spirits more wicked than himself, and they enter in and dwell there.

Malignity And Power Of The Demons

There are many who, because they do not feel the assaults of demons against them, imagine that the whole matter is fictitious; nor is it surprising that such persons are not attacked by demons, to whom they have voluntarily surrendered themselves. They possess neither piety nor charity, nor any virtue worthy of a Christian; hence they are entirely in the power of the devil, and there is no need of any temptation to overcome them, since their souls have already become his willing abode.

But those who have dedicated themselves to God, leading a heavenly life upon earth, are the chief objects of the assaults of Satan. Against them he harbours bitterest hatred, laying snares for them each moment. Sacred Scripture is full of examples of holy men who, in spite of their firmness and resolution, were perverted by his violence or fraud. Adam, David, Solomon and others, whom it would be tedious to enumerate, experienced the violent and crafty cunning of demons, which neither human prudence nor human strength can overcome.

Prayer Protects Man's Weakness Against The Enemies Of His Soul

Who, then, can deem himself sufficiently secure in his own resources? Hence the necessity of offering to God pure and pious prayer, that He suffer us not to be tempted above our strength, but make issue with temptation, that we may be able to bear it.

But should any of the faithful, through weakness or ignorance, feel terrified at the power of the demons, they are to be encouraged, when tossed by the waves of temptation, to take refuge in this harbour of prayer. For however great the power and pertinacity of Satan, he cannot, in his deadly hatred of our race, tempt or torment us as much, or as long as he pleases; but all his power is governed by the control and permission of God. The example of Job is very well known. Satan could have touched nothing belonging to him, if God had not said to the devil: Behold, all that he hath is in thy hand; while on the other hand, had not the Lord added: Only put not forth thy hand upon his person, Job with his children and possessions, would have been at once destroyed by the devil. So restricted is the power of demons, that without the permission of God, they could not even enter into the swine mentioned by the Evangelists.

"Temptation"

To understand the meaning of this Petition, it is necessary to say what temptation signifies here, and also what it is to be led into temptation.

To tempt is to sound a person in order that by eliciting from him what we desire, we may extract the truth. This mode of tempting does not apply to God; for what is there that God does not know? All things are naked and open to his eyes.

Another kind of tempting implies more than this? inasmuch as it may have either a good or a bad purpose. Temptation has a good purpose, when someone's worth is tried, in order that when it has been tested and proved he may be rewarded and honoured, his example proposed to others for imitation, and all may be incited thereby to the praises of God. This is the only kind of tempting that can be found in God. Of it there is an example in

Deuteronomy: The Lord your God tries you, that it may appear whether you love him or not.

In this manner God is also said to tempt His own, when He visits them with want, disease and other sorts of calamities. This He does to try their patience, and to make them an example of Christian virtue. Thus we read that Abraham was tempted to immolate his son, by which fact he became a singular example of obedience and patience to all succeeding times. Thus also is it written of Tobias: Because thou wast acceptable to God, it was necessary that temptation should prove thee.

Men are tempted for a bad purpose, when they are impelled to sin or destruction. To do this is the work of the devil, for he tempts men with a view to deceive and precipitate them into ruin, and he is therefore called in Scripture, the tempter At one time, stimulating us from within, he employs the agency of the affections and passions of the soul. At another time, assailing us from without, he makes use of external things, as of prosperity, to puff us up with pride, or of adversity, to break our spirits. Sometimes he has for his emissaries and assistants abandoned men, particularly heretics, who, sitting in the chair of pestilence, scatter the deadly seeds of bad doctrines, thus unsettling and precipitating headlong those persons who draw no line of distinction between vice and virtue and are of themselves prone to evil.

"Lead us not into Temptation"

We are said to be led into temptation when we yield to temptations. Now this happens in two ways. First, we are led into temptation when, yielding to suggestion, we rush into that evil to which some one tempts us. No one is thus led into temptation by God; for to no one is God the author of sin, nay, He hates all who work iniquity; and accordingly we also read in St. James: Let no man, when he is tempted, say that he is tempted of God; for God is not a tempter of evils.

Secondly, we are said to be led into temptation by him who, although he himself does not tempt us nor cooperate in tempting us, yet is said to tempt because he does not prevent us from being tempted or from being overcome by temptations when he is able to prevent these things. In this manner God, indeed, suffers the good and the pious to be tempted, but does not leave them unsupported by His grace. Sometimes, however, we fall, being left to ourselves by the just and secret judgment of God, in punishment of our sins.

God is also said to lead us into temptation when we abuse, to our destruction, His blessings, which He has given us as a means of salvation; when, like the prodigal son, we squander our Father's substance, living riotously and yielding to our evil desires. In such a case we can say what the Apostle has said of the law: The commandment that was ordained to life, the same was found to be unto death to me.

Of this an opportune example is Jerusalem, as we learn from Ezechiel. God had so enriched that city with every sort of embellishment, that He said of it by the mouth of the Prophet: Thou wast perfect through my beauty, which I had put upon thee. Yet Jerusalem, favoured with such an abundance of divine gifts, was so far from showing gratitude to God, from whom she had received and was still receiving so many favours, was so far from making use of those heavenly gifts for the attainment of her own happiness, the end for which she had received them, that having cast away the hope and idea of deriving spiritual profit from them, she, most ungrateful to God her Father, was content to enjoy her present abundance with a luxury and riotousness which Ezechiel describes at considerable length in the same chapter. Wherefore those whom God permits to convert into instruments of vice the abundant opportunities of virtuous deeds which He has afforded them, are equally ungrateful to Him.

But we ought carefully to notice a certain usage of Sacred Scripture, which sometimes denotes the permission of God in words which, if taken literally, would imply a positive act on the part of God. Thus in Exodus we read: I will harden the heart of Pharoah; and in Isaias: Blind the heart of this people; and the Apostle to the Romans writes: God delivered them up to shameful affections, and to a reprobate sense. In these and other similar passages we are to understand, not at all any positive act on the part of God, but His permission only.

Objects of the Sixth Petition

What We Do Not Pray For

These observations having been premised, it will not be difficult to understand the object for which we pray in this Petition.

We do not ask to be totally exempt from temptation, for human life is one continued temptation. This, however, is useful and advantageous to man. Temptation teaches us to know ourselves, that is, our own weakness, and to humble ourselves under the powerful hand of God; and by fighting manfully, we expect to receive a never-fading crown of glory. For he that striveth for the mastery is not crowned, except he strive lawfully. Blessed is the man, says St. James, that endureth temptation; for when he hath been proved, he shall receive the crown of life, which God hath promised to them that love him. If we are sometimes hard pressed by the temptation of the enemy, it will also cheer us to reflect, that we have a high priest to help us, who can have compassion on our infirmities, having been tempted himself in all things.

What We Pray For In This Petition

What, then, do we pray for in this Petition ? We pray that the divine assistance may not forsake us, lest having been deceived, or worsted, we should yield to temptation; and that the grace of God may be at hand to succour us when our strength fails, to refresh and invigorate us in our trials.

We should, therefore, implore the divine assistance, in general, against all temptations, and especially when assailed by any particular temptation. This we find to have been the conduct of David, under almost every species of temptation. Against lying, he prays in these words: Take not thou the word of truth utterly out of my mouth; against covetousness: Incline my heart unto thy testimonies, and not to covetousness; and against the vanities of this life and the allurements of concupiscence, he prays thus: Turn away my eyes, that they may not behold vanity.

We pray, therefore, that we yield not to evil desires, and be not wearied in enduring temptation; that we deviate not from the way of the Lord; that in adversity, as in prosperity, we preserve equanimity and fortitude; and that God may never deprive us of His protection. Finally, we pray that God may crush Satan beneath our feet.

Dispositions which should Accompany this Petition

The pastor ought next to admonish the faithful concerning the chief thoughts and reflections that should accompany this prayer

Distrust Of Self And Confidence In God

It will, then, be found most efficacious, when offering this Petition that, remembering our weakness, we distrust our own strength; and that, placing all our hopes of safety in the divine goodness and relying on the divine protection, we encounter the greatest dangers with undaunted courage, calling to mind particularly the many persons, animated with such hope and resolution, who were delivered by God from the very jaws of Satan.

When Joseph was assailed by the criminal solicitations of a wicked woman, did not God rescue him from the imminent danger, and exalt him to the highest degree of glory? Did He not preserve Susanna, when beset by the ministers of Satan, and on the point of being made the victim of an iniquitous sentence? Nor is this surprising; for her heart, says the Scripture, trusted in the Lord. How exalted the praise, how great the glory of Job, who triumphed over the world, the flesh and the devil ! There are on record many similar examples to which the pastor should refer, in order to exhort with earnestness his pious hearers to this hope and confidence.

Remembrance Of The Victory Of Christ And His Saints

The faithful should also reflect who is their leader against the temptations of the enemy; namely, Christ the Lord, who was victorious in the same combat. He overcame the devil; He is that stronger man who, coming upon the strong armed man, overcame him, deprived him of his arms, and stripped him of his spoils. Of Christ's victory over the world, we read in St. John: Have confidence: I have overcome the world; and in the Apocalypse, He is called the conquering lion; and it is. said of Him that He went forth conquering that He might conquer, because by His victory He has given power to others to conquer.'

The Epistle of St. Paul to the Hebrews abounds with the victories of holy men, who by faith conquered kingdoms, stopped the mouths of lions, etc. While we read of such achievements, we should also take into account the victories which are every day won by men eminent for faith, hope and charity, in their interior and exterior conflicts with the demons, -- victories so numerous and so signal, that, were we spectators of them, we should deem no event of more frequent occurrence, none of more glorious issue. It was with reference to such defeats of the enemies that St. John wrote: I write unto you, young men, because you are strong, and the word of God abideth in you, and you have overcome the wicked one.'

Watchfulness

Satan, however, is overcome not by indolence, sleep, wine, revelling, or lust; but by prayer, labor, watching, fasting, continence and chastity. Watch ye and pray, that ye enter not into temptation, as we have already said, is the admonition of our Lord. They who make use of these weapons in the conflict put the enemy to flight; for the devil flees from those who resist him.

The Author of victory over Temptation

But from the consideration of these victories achieved by holy men which we have mentioned, let no one indulge feelings of self-complacency, nor flatter himself that, by his own single unassisted exertions, he is able to withstand the temptations and hostile assaults of the demons. This is not within the power of human nature, nor within the capacity of human frailty.

The strength by which we lay prostrate the satellites of Satan comes from God, who maketh our arms as a bow of brass; by whose aid the bow of the mighty is overcome, and the weak are girt with strength; who giveth us the protection of salvation, whose right hand upholdeth us: who teacheth our hands to war, and our fingers to battle. Hence to God alone must thanks be given for victory, since it is only through His guidance and help that we are able to conquer. This the Apostle did; for he said: Thanks to God, who hath given us the victory, through our Lord Jesus Christ. The voice from heaven, mentioned in the Apocalypse, also proclaims God to be the author of our victories: Now is come salvation, and strength, and the kingdom of our God, and the power of his Christ; because the accuser of our brethren is cast forth; and they overcame him by the blood of the Lamb." The same book declares that the victory obtained over the world and the flesh belongs to Christ the Lord, when it says: They shall fight with the Lamb, and the Lamb shall overcome them. But enough has now been said on the cause and the manner of conquering (temptation).

The Rewards of Victories over temptation

When these things have been explained, the pastor should instruct the faithful concerning the crowns prepared by God, and the eternal and superabundant rewards reserved for those who conquer. He should quote from the Apocalypse the following divine promises: He that shall overcome shall not be hurt by the second death; and in another place: He that shall overcome, shall thus be clothed in white garments, and I will not blot out his name out of the book of life, and I will confess his name before my Father, and before his angels. A little after, our divine Lord Himself thus addresses John: He that shall overcome, I will make him a pillar in the temple of my God: and he shall go out no more: and again: To him that shall overcome, I win give to sit with me in my throne; as I also have overcome, and am set down with my Father in his throne. Finally, having unveiled the glory of the Saints, and the never ending bliss which they shall enjoy in heaven, He adds, He that shall overcome shall possess these things.

THE SEVENTH PETITION OF THE LORD'S PRAYER :
"BUT DELIVER US FROM EVIL"

The Importance Of Instruction On This Petition

This Petition with which the Son of God concludes this divine prayer embodies the substance of all the other Petitions. To show its force and importance our Lord made use of this Petition when, on the eve of His Passion, He prayed to God His Father for the salvation of mankind. I pray, He said, that thou keep them from evil. In this Petition, then, which He not only commanded us to use, but made use of Himself, He has epitomised, as it were, the meaning and spirit of all the other Petitions. For if we obtain what this Petition asks, that is, the protection of God against evil, which enables us to stand secure and safe against the machinations of the world and the devil, then, as St. Cyprian remarks, nothing more remains to be asked.

Such, then, being the importance of this Petition, the diligence of the pastor in its exposition should be great. The difference between this and the preceding Petition consists in this, that in the one we beg to avoid sin, in the other, to escape punishment.

Necessity Of This Petition

It cannot be necessary to remind the faithful of the numerous evils and calamities to which we are exposed, and how much we stand in need of the divine assistance. The many and serious miseries of human life have been fully described by sacred and profane writers, and there is hardly any one who has not observed them either in his own life or in that of others.

We are all convinced of the truth of these words of Job, that model of patience: Man, born of woman, and living for a short time, is filled with many miseries. He cometh forth like a flower, and is destroyed, and fleeth as a shadow, and never continueth in the same state. That no day passes without its own trouble or annoyance is proved by these words of Christ the Lord: Sufficient for the day is the evil thereof. Indeed, the condition of human life is pointed out by the Lord Himself, when He admonishes us that we are to take up our cross daily and follow Him.

Since, therefore, everyone must realise the trials and dangers inseparable from this life, it will not be difficult to convince the faithful that they ought to implore of God deliverance from evil, since no inducement to prayer exercises a more powerful influence over men than a desire and hope of deliverance from those evils which oppress or threaten them. There is in the heart of everyone a natural inclination to have instant recourse to God in the face of danger, as it is written: Fill their faces with shame, and they shall seek thy name, Lord.

How this Petition should be Made

If, then, in calamities and dangers the unbidden impulse of nature prompts men to call on God, it surely becomes the duty of those to whose fidelity and prudence their salvation is entrusted to instruct them carefully in the proper performance of this duty.

WE SHOULD SEEK FIRST THE GLORY OF GOD

For there are some who, contrary to the command of Christ, reverse the order of this prayer. He who commands us to have recourse to Him in the day of tribulation, has also prescribed to us the order in which we should pray. It is His will that, before we pray to be delivered from evil, we ask that the name of God be sanctified, that His kingdom come, and so on through the other

Petitions, which are, as it were, so many steps by which we reach this last Petition.

Yet there are those who, if their head, their side, or their foot, ache; if they suffer loss of property; if menaces or dangers from an enemy alarm them; if famine, war or pestilence afflict them, omit all the other Petitions of the Lord's Prayer and ask only to be delivered from these evils. This practice is at variance with the command of Christ the Lord: Seek first the kingdom of God.

To pray, therefore, as we ought, we should have in view the greater glory of God, even when we ask deliverance from calamities, trials and dangers. Thus, when David offered this prayer: Lord, rebuke me not in thine anger, he subjoined a reason by which he showed that he was most desirous of God's glory, saying: For there is no one in death that is mindful of thee, and who shall confess to thee in hell. And again, having implored God to have mercy on him, he added: I will teach the unjust thy ways; and the wicked shall be converted to thee.

Our Chief Hope Of Deliverance Should Be In God

The faithful should be encouraged to use this salutary manner of praying and to imitate the example of the Prophet. And at the same time their attention should be called to the marked difference that exists between the prayers of the infidel and those of the Christian.

The infidel, too, begs of God to cure his diseases and to heal his wounds, to deliver him from approaching or impending evils; but he places his principal hope of deliverance in the remedies provided by nature, or prepared by man. He makes no scruple of using medicine no matter by whom prepared, no matter if accompanied by charms, spells or other diabolical arts, provided he can promise himself some hope of recovery.

Not so the Christian. When visited by sickness, or other adversity, he flies to God as his supreme refuge and defence. Acknowledging and revering God alone as the author of all his good and his deliverer he ascribes to Him whatever healing virtue resides in medicines, convinced that they help the sick only in so far as God wills it. For it is God who has given medicines to man to heal his corporal infirmities; and hence these words of Ecclesiasticus: The most High hath created medicines out of the earth, and a wise man will not abhor them. He, therefore, who has pledged his fidelity to Jesus Christ, does not place his principal hope of recovery in such remedies; he places it in God, the author of these medicines.

Hence the Sacred Scriptures condemn the conduct of those who, confiding in the power of medicine, seek no assistance from God. Nay more, those who regulate their lives by the laws of God, abstain from the use of all medicines which are not evidently intended by God to be medicinal; and, were there even a certain hope of recovery by using any other, they abstain from them as so many charms and diabolical artifices.

We Must Confidently Expect His Help

The faithful, then, are to be exhorted to place their confidence in God. Our most bountiful Father has commanded us to beg of Him our deliverance from evil, in order that His command should inspire us with the hope of obtaining the object of our prayers. Of this truth the Sacred Scriptures afford many illustrations, so that they whom reason does not inspire with confidence may be persuaded to hope by a multitude of examples. Abraham, Jacob, Lot, Joseph and David are to all unexceptional witnesses of the divine goodness; and the instances recorded in the New Testament of persons rescued from the greatest dangers, by the efficacy of devout prayer, are so numerous as to make it unnecessary to mention special cases. Therefore we shall content ourselves with one text from the Prophet, which is sufficient to confirm even the weakest: The just cried, and the Lord heard them; and delivered them out of all their troubles.

"From Evil"

We now come to explain the meaning and nature of the Petition. Let the faithful understand that in it we by no means ask deliverance from every evil.

What We Do Not Pray For

There are some things which are commonly considered evils, and which, notwithstanding, are of advantage to those who endure them. Such was the sting of the flesh to which the Apostle was subjected in order that, by the aid of divine grace, power might be perfected in infirmity. When the pious man learns the salutary influence of such things, far from praying for their removal, he rejoices in them exceedingly. We pray, therefore, against those evils only, which do not conduce to our spiritual interests; not against such as are profitable to our salvation.

What We Do Pray For

The full meaning of this Petition, therefore, is, that having been freed from sin and from the danger of temptation, we may be delivered from internal and external evils; that we may be protected from floods, fire and lightning; that the fruits of the earth be not destroyed by hail; that we be not visited by famine, sedition or war. We ask that God may banish disease, pestilence and disaster from us; that He may keep us from slavery, imprisonment, exile, betrayals, treachery, and from all other evils which fill mankind with terror and misery. Finally, we pray that God would remove all occasions of sin and iniquity.

We do not, however, pray to be delivered only from those things which all look upon as evils, but also from those things which almost all consider to be good, such as riches, honours, health, strength and even life itself; that is, we ask that these things be not detrimental or ruinous to our soul's welfare.

We also beg of God that we be not cut off by a sudden death; that we provoke not His anger against us; that we be not condemned to suffer the punishments reserved for the wicked; that we be not sentenced to endure the fire of purgatory, from which we piously and devoutly implore that others may be liberated.

This is the explanation of this Petition given by the Church in the Mass and Litanies, where we pray to be delivered from evil past, present and to come.

"Deliver Us"

The goodness of God delivers us from evil in a variety of ways. He prevents impending evils, as we read with regard to the Patriarch Jacob, whom He delivered from the enemies that were stirred up against him on account of the slaughter of the Sichimites. For we read: The terror of God fell upon all the cities round about, and they durst not pursue after them as they went away.

The blessed who reign with Christ the Lord in heaven have been delivered by the divine assistance from all evil; but, as for us, although the Almighty delivers us from some evils, it is not His will that, while journeying in this, our mortal pilgrimage, we should be entirely exempt from all. The consolations with which God sometimes refreshes those who labor under adversity are, however, equivalent to an exemption from all evil; and with these the

Prophet consoled himself when he said: According to the multitude of my sorrows in my heart, thy consolations have rejoiced my soul.

God, moreover, delivers men from evil when he preserves them unhurt in the midst of extreme danger, as He did in the case of the children thrown into the fiery furnace, whom the fire did not burn; and of Daniel, whom the lions did not injure.

Deliverance From Satan Especially Asked For

According to the interpretation of St. Basil the Great, St. Chrysostom and St. Augustine, the devil is specially called the evil one, because he was the author of man's transgression, that is, of his sin and iniquity, and also because God makes use of him as an instrument to chastise sinful and impious men. For the evils which mankind endures in punishment of sin are appointed by God; and this is the meaning of these words of Holy Writ: Shall there be evil in a city which the Lard hath not done? and: I am the Lord and there is none else: I form the light and create darkness: I make peace and create evil.

The devil is also called evil, because, although we have never injured him, he wages perpetual war against us, and pursues us with mortal hatred. If we put on the armour of faith and the shield of innocence, he can have no power to hurt us; nevertheless he unceasingly tempts us by external evils and every other means of annoyance within his reach. Wherefore we beseech God to deliver us from the evil one.

We say from evil, not from evils, because the evils which we experience from others we ascribe to the arch enemy as their author and instigator. Hence instead of cherishing resentment against our neighbour, we should turn our hatred and anger against Satan himself, by whom men are instigated to harm us.

Therefore if your neighbour has injured you in any respect, when you pray to God your Father, beg of Him not only to deliver you from evil, that is, from the injuries which your neighbour inflicts; but also to rescue your neighbour from the power of the devil, whose wicked suggestions impel men to wrong.

Patience and Joy under Continued Affliction

Next we must remember that if by prayers and supplications we are not delivered from evil, we should endure our afflictions with patience, convinced that it is the will of God that we should so endure them. If, therefore, God hear not our prayers, we are not to yield to feelings of peevishness or discontent; we must submit in all things to the divine will and pleasure, regarding as useful and salutary to us that which happens in accordance with the will of God, not that which is agreeable to our own wishes.

Finally, the pious hearers should be admonished that during our mortal career we should be prepared to meet every kind of affliction and calamity, not only with patience, but even with joy. For it is written: All that will live godly in Christ Jesus shall suffer persecution; and again: Through many tribulations we must enter into the kingdom of God; and further: Ought not Christ to have suffered these things, and so enter into his glory? A servant should not be greater than his master; and as St. Bernard says: Delicate members do not become a head crowned with thorns. The glorious example of Urias challenges our imitation. When urged by David to remain at home, he replied: The ark of God, and Israel, and Juda, dwell in tents; and shall I go into my house?

If to prayer we bring with us these reflections and these dispositions, although surrounded by menaces and encompassed by evils on every side, we shall, like the three children who passed unhurt amidst the flames, be preserved uninjured; or at least, like the Machabees, we shall bear up against adverse fortune with firmness and fortitude.

In the midst of contumelies and tortures we should imitate the blessed Apostles, who, after they had been scourged, rejoiced exceedingly that they were accounted worthy to suffer reproach for Christ Jesus. Filled with such sentiments, we shall sing in transports of joy: Princes have persecuted me without cause; and my heart hath been in awe of thy words; I will rejoice at thy words, as one that hath found great spoil.

THE SEAL OF THE LORD'S PRAYER

"Amen"

Necessity Of Explaining The Conclusion Of The Lord's Prayer

St. Jerome in his commentary on St. Matthew rightly calls this word what it really is, the seal of the Lord's Prayer. As then we have already admonished the faithful with regard to the preparation to be made before this holy prayer, so we deem it necessary that they should also know why we close our prayers with this word, and what it signifies; for devotion in concluding our prayers is not less important than attention in beginning them.

Fruits that Come at the Conclusion of Prayer

Assurance That We Have Been Heard

The faithful, then, should be taught that the fruits, which we gather from the conclusion of the Lord's Prayer are numerous and abundant, the greatest and most joyful of them being the attainment of what we ask. On this point enough has already been said.

Fervour And Illumination

By this concluding word, not only do we obtain a propitious hearing from God, but also receive other blessings of a higher order still, the excellence of which surpasses all powers of description.

For since, as St. Cyprian remarks, by prayer man converses with God, it happens in a wonderful manner that the divine Majesty is brought nearer to those who are engaged in prayer than to others, and enriches them with singular gifts. Those, therefore, who pray devoutly, may not be inaptly compared to persons who approach a glowing fire; if cold, they derive warmth; if warm, they derive heat. Thus, also, those who approach God (in prayer) depart with a warmth proportioned to their faith and fervour; the heart is inflamed with zeal for the glory of God, the mind is illumined after an admirable manner, and they are enriched exceedingly with divine gifts, as it is written: Thou hast prevented him with blessings of sweetness.

An example for all is that great man Moses. By intercourse and converse with God he so shone with the reflected splendours of the Divinity, that the Israelites could not look upon his eyes or countenance.

Sweetness

Those who pray with such vehement fervour enjoy in a wonderful manner the goodness and majesty of God. In the morning, says the Prophet, I will stand before thee, and will see; because thou art not a God that willest iniquity.

The more familiar these truths are to the mind, the more piously do we venerate, and the more fervently do we worship God, and the more delightfully do we taste how sweet is the Lord, and how truly blessed are all who hope in Him.

Confidence And Gratitude

Encircled by the most clear light from above we also discover our own lowliness and how exalted is the majesty of God, according to the saying of St. Augustine: Give me to know Thee: give me to know myself. Distrusting our own strength, we thus throw ourselves unreservedly upon the goodness of God, not doubting that He, who cherishes us in the bosom of His paternal wondrous love, will afford us in abundance whatever is necessary for life and salvation. Thus we shall turn to God with the warmest gratitude our hearts can conceive and our lips express. This we read that holy David did, who commenced by praying: Save me from all them that persecute me, and concluded with these words, I will give glory to the Lord according to his justice, and will sing to the name of the Lord the most High.'

Illustrations From The Psalms

There are innumerable prayers of the Saints of the same kind, whose beginnings are full of fear, but which end with hope and joy. This spirit, however, is eminently conspicuous in the prayers of David.

When agitated by fear he began his prayer thus: Many are they who rise up against me: many say to my soul, There is no salvation for him in his God; but at length, armed with fortitude and holy joy, he adds: I will not fear thousands of the people surrounding me.

In another Psalm, after he had lamented his misery, we see him towards the end, reposing confidence in God and rejoicing exceedingly in the hope of salvation: In peace in the self-same, I will sleep, and I will rest.

Again, with what fear and trembling must the Prophet not have been agitated when he exclaimed: O Lord, rebuke me not in thy indignation, nor chastise me in thy wrath! Yet, on the other hand, what confidence and joy must not have been his when he added: Depart from me, all ye workers of iniquity; for the Lord hath heard the voice of my weeping!

When filled with dread of the wrath and fury of Saul, with what lowliness and humility does he not implore the divine assistance: Save me, O Lord, by thy name, and Judge me in thy strength! and yet, in the same Psalm he adds these words of joy and confidence: Behold, God is my help; and the Lord is the helper of my soul.

Let him, therefore, who has recourse to holy prayer approach God his Father, fortified by faith and animated by hope, not doubting that he will obtain those blessings of which he stands in need.

Meaning of the Word "Amen"

First Explanation

The word amen, with which the Lord's Prayer concludes, contains, as it were, the germs of many of these thoughts and reflections which we nave just considered. Indeed, so frequent was this Hebrew word in the mouth of the Saviour, that it pleased the Holy Ghost to have it retained in the Church of God. Its meaning may be said to be: Know that thy prayers are heard. It has the force of a response, as if God answers the suppliant, and graciously dismisses him, after having favourably heard his prayers.

This-interpretation has been approved by the constant usage of the Church of God. In the Sacrifice of the Mass, when the Lord's Prayer is said she does not assign the word amen to the server who answers: But deliver us front evil. She reserves it as appropriate to the priest himself, who, as mediator between God and man, answers Amen, thus intimating that God has heard the prayers of His people.

This practice, however, is not common to all the prayers, but is peculiar to the Lord's Prayer. To the other prayers the server answers Amen, because in every other this word only expresses assent and desire. In the Lord's Prayer it is an answer, intimating that God has heard the petition of His suppliant.

Other Explanations Of The Word "Amen"

By many, the word amen is differently interpreted. The Septuagint interprets it, So be it; others translate it, Verily: Aquila renders it, Faithfully. Which of these versions we adopt, is a matter of little importance, provided we understand the word to have the sense already mentioned, namely, that when the priest (pronounces Amen), it signifies the concession of what hag been prayed for. This interpretation is supported by St- Paul in his Epistle to the Corinthians, where he says: All the promises of God are in him, "it is"; therefore also by him, amen to God, unto our glory.

Advantages of Terminating our Prayer with this Word

To us also this word is very appropriate, containing, as it does, some confirmation of the Petitions which we have already offered up. It also fixes our attention when we are engaged in holy prayer; for it frequently happens that in prayer a variety of distracting thoughts divert the mind to other objects.

Nay, more, by this word we most earnestly beg of God that all our preceding Petitions may be granted; or rather, understanding that they have been all granted, and feeling the divine assistance powerfully present with us, we cry out together with the Prophet: Behold God is my helper; and the Lord is the protector of my soul.

Nor can anyone doubt that God is moved by the name of His Son, and by a word so often uttered by Him who, as the Apostle says, was always heard for his reverence.

The Catechism of the Council of Trent for Parish Priests

Made in the USA
Las Vegas, NV
10 January 2025

16183758R00390